LONGMAN LINGUISTICS LIBRARY

A LINGUISTIC HISTORY OF ITALIAN

LONGMAN LINGUISTICS LIBRARY

For Series List see pp. xii and xiii

A Linguistic History of Italian

Martin Maiden

LONGMAN
LONDON AND NEW YORK

Longman Group Limited,
Longman House, Burnt Mill,
Harlow, Essex CM20 2JE, England
and Associated Companies throughout the world

Published in the United States of America
by Longman Publishing, New York

First published 1995

ISBN 0 582 059291 CSD
ISBN 0 582 059283 PPR

British Library Cataloguing-in-Publication Data

A catalogue record for this book is
available from the British Library

Library of Congress Cataloging-in-Publication Data

Maiden, Martin, 1957–
A linguistic history of Italian / Martin Maiden.
p. cm. — (Longman linguistics library)
Includes bibliographical references and index.
ISBN 0–582–05929–1. — ISBN 0–582–05928–3 (pbk.)
1. Italian language—History. I. Title. II. Series.
PC1075.M35 1994 93–46832
450′.9—dc20 CIP

Set by 8M in 10/11 pt Times
Produced by Longman Singapore Publishers (Pte) Ltd.
Printed in Singapore

Contents

LONGMAN LINGUISTICS LIBRARY: SERIES LIST

General editors
R. H. Robins, *University of London,*
Martin Harris, *University of Manchester*
Geoffrey Horrocks, *University of Cambridge*

A Short History of Linguistics
Third Edition
R. H. ROBINS

Text and Context
Explorations in the Semantics and Pragmatics of Discourse
TEUN A. VAN DIJK

Introduction to Text Linguistics
ROBERT DE BEAUGRANDE AND WOLFGANG ULRICH DRESSLER

Psycholinguistics
Language, Mind, and World
DANNY D. STEINBERG

Principles of Pragmatics
GEOFFREY LEECH

Generative Grammar
GEOFFREY HORROCKS

The English Verb
Second Edition
F. R. PALMER

A History of American English
J. L. DILLARD

English Historical Syntax
Verbal Constructions
DAVID DENISON

Pidgin and Creole Languages
SUZANNE ROMAINE

A History of English Phonology
CHARLES JONES

Generative and Non-linear Phonology
JACQUES DURAND

Modality and the English Modals
Second Edition
F. R. PALMER

Semiotics and Linguistics
YISHAI TOBIN

Multilingualism in the British Isles I: The Older Mother Tongues and Europe
EDITED BY SAFDER ALLADINA AND VIV EDWARDS

Multilingualism in the British Isles II: Africa, The Middle East and Asia
EDITED BY SAFDER ALLANDINA AND VIV EDWARDS

Dialects of English
Studies in Grammatical Variation
EDITED BY PETER TRUDGILL AND J. K. CHAMBERS

Introduction to Bilingualism
CHARLOTTE HOFFMANN

Verb and Noun Number in English: *A Functional Explanation*
WALLIS REID

English in Africa
JOSEF SCHMIED

Linguistic Theory
The Discourse of Fundamental Works
ROBERT DE BEAUGRANDE

General Linguistics
An Introductory Survey
Fourth Edition
R. H. ROBINS

Historical Linguistics
Problems and Perspectives
EDITED BY C. JONES

A History of Linguistics Vol. I
The Eastern Traditions of Linguistics
EDITED BY GIULIO LEPSCHY

A History of Linguistics Vol. II
Classical and Medieval Linguistics
EDITED BY GIULIO LEPSCHY

Aspect in the English Verb
Process and Result in Language
YISHAI TOBIN

The Meaning of Syntax
A Study of the Adjectives of English
CONNOR FERRIS

Latin American Spanish
JOHN M. LIPSKI

A Linguistic History of Italian
MARTIN MAIDEN

Modern Arabic
CLIVE HOLES

Preface

It is a curious observation that structural histories of Italian of the kind offered in this book have generally been executed by non-Italians. We find, for example, a German (Rohlfs), a Swiss (Meyer-Lübke), a Pole (Manćzak), a Hungarian (Fogarasi) and a Croatian (Tekavčić). Perhaps it is the case that such histories are best essayed by outsiders, who are less acutely sensitive to (but not necessarily any less aware of) the complex social and cultural milieux in which the language lives and from which the linguistic facts have to be brutally extirpated. At any rate, this book is another 'outsider's' view of what he perceives as the major elements in the structural evolution of the Italian language, and it aims to be accessible to those who know the modern language and seek the historical rationale behind some of its more idiosyncratic features, and to those who know something of the history of other Romance languages, and would like a detailed account of the place of Italian in the wider Romance picture.

I do not anticipate that all readers will pick up this book and read it straight through from cover to cover. An 'internal' structural history of a language such as this one does not easily lend itself, unlike 'external' histories, to presentation in the form of a chronologically linear narrative. But this volume is more than a work of reference. It aims to present a complex array of factual data, closely interconnected and, I hope, illuminated, by cross-referencing (so that readers may easily use the book for reference purposes). Into this framework is woven a series of extended discussions of topics which are particularly problematic or controversial (such as diphthongization, or auxiliary selection). I have attempted to be as comprehensive as possible within the space available, but there remain, no doubt, lacunae, and I have not hesitated to give particularly extensive treatment to certain topics (in morphology and phonology) on which I have conducted research myself.

A large number of people have helped me in a wide variety of ways in the preparation of this book. I wish to express particular gratitude to Thomas Cravens, Joseph Cremona, Giulio Lepschy, Peter Matthews, John Charles Smith and Nigel Vincent for the stimulating and truly invaluable comments they have made on the text at various stages of its emergence. If, on some occasions, I have waywardly failed to follow their sound counsel as closely as I might have, it will be entirely on my head. I thank, also, the editors of the Longman Linguistics Library series for their advice.

Downing College
Cambridge
June 1994

Abbreviations and symbols

*	Indicates a form which is unattested but is assumed to exist or to have existed.
**	Indicates a hypothetical form whose existence is denied.
*(?)	Indicates a form which is unattested but whose existence is considered unproven yet possible.
1Sg./2Pl. etc.	First person singular / second person plural, etc.
Acc.	Accusative
Cast.	Castilian
CL	Classical Latin
Conj.	Conjugation
Dec.	Declension
DO	Direct objcct
F.	Feminine
Fr.	French
Fut.	Future
Gen.	Genitive
Ind.	Indicative
Inf.	Infinitive
IO	Indirect Object
It.	Italian
Lit.	Literally
M.	Masculine
N.	Neuter
Nom.	Nominative
O	Old
Pers.	Person
Pl.	Plural
PP	Past participle

PPr.	Passato prossimo (perfect)
PR	Passato remoto (past historic)
Pres.	Present tense
Ptg.	Portuguese
RS	*Rafforzamento sintattico*
Sg.	Singular
SOSD	Stressed open syllable diphthongization
Subj.	Subjunctive
TR	Trapassato remoto

Chapter 1

Introduction

1 Perspectives and aims

The history of a language may be explored from two complementary perspectives, the 'internal' and the 'external'. An external history examines that language within the wider context of the social and cultural history of the people who use it, and in relation to other languages and dialects with which these users come into contact. An internal history is concerned with the detailed study of the evolution of the grammatical (and phonological) system of the language.[1] The two perspectives are not only complementary, they are usually inextricably interlinked – and this is most certainly true of Italian. This book bears the title *A Linguistic History of Italian* – rather than *A History of the Italian Language* – precisely because it takes the perspective of the 'linguist' in the narrow, but widely used, sense of one who is interested in the internal, grammatical and phonological, structure of languages. We focus primarily, and in close detail, on the internal history of Italian, without neglecting the crucial role played in many structural changes by 'external', cultural and social, factors. The 'external' history of the Italian language impinges profoundly on its structural development,[2] and we have given particular attention to the influence upon Italian of other Romance dialects with which it has been in contact, the linguistic effects of the emergence of Italian as a *literary*, rather than a *spoken* language, and of structural variation within Italian, present already in the fifteenth century, yet especially prominent in the modern language as a result of the acquisition of Italian by a predominantly dialect-speaking population in the nineteenth and twentieth centuries. No attempt has been made to explore in depth the external history of the language, but there exist some excellent general histories of Italian in which external history is treated in detail.[3]

It is hoped that what follows will be accessible, and of interest, not only to those with a specialist knowledge of Italian, but also to those concerned with the historical evolution of Romance and other languages. We have been at pains to make comparison with developments in other Romance varieties wherever these help to throw light on the history of Italian – or vice versa.

The 'linguistic' perspective, in our sense, has a distinguished pedigree in studies of the history of Italian. Among these, Rohlfs' encyclopaedic *Grammatica storica della lingua italiana e dei suoi dialetti* remains unsurpassed as a compendium of historical data. It is a reflection of the sheer vastness and complexity of the field that the three volumes of this work (around 1400 pages) in some respects only scratch the surface of the subject, yet still make forbidding reading for the novice. The other major linguistic history, that by Tekavčić (1980 – also in three volumes), is less detailed than Rohlfs', but offers a more transparent presentation of the facts, set in a broadly structuralist framework. The present *Linguistic History of Italian* aims to be complementary to such studies, and references to Rohlfs' work, in particular, abound. While we cannot match the breadth of these earlier histories, particularly where dialectological references are concerned, a wide range of phenomena brought to light or re-evaluated by more recent scholarship have been included here.

This book takes no particular theoretical stance, but frequently introduces, with due explanation, insights from various branches of general linguistic theory, when these help illuminate the nature and causes of changes in the history of Italian grammar. In particular, we try to provide some answers to the question 'Why is Italian grammar the way it is?', by laying bare the historical structural principles which account for many of the apparent idiosyncrasies of modern grammar. The historical perspective can also help to reveal patterns and structures which are present in the modern language, but are not always apparent to those who know only modern Italian. For example, the root alternation (cf. Ch.2: 4.6.3 and 5.2) between *muoio* 'I die' and *muori* 'you die', that between the agentive suffix *-aio* (e.g., *sellaio* 'saddlemaker') and the locational suffix *-eria* ('place where some activity is carried out' – e.g., *selleria* 'saddlemaker's shop'), and that between the infinitive stem and the future stem of first conjugation verbs (*parlare* 'to speak' vs. *parlerò* 'I shall speak') may appear superficially unrelated; but we shall see later that they reflect the effects of two sound changes which are characteristic of the dialect of Florence (and clearly proclaim the Florentine origins of Italian). The exceptional occurrence of the reflexive pronoun to the right of the verb in a few expressions such as *vendesi* 'for sale' (rather than *si vende*) seems arbitrary in modern Italian, but reflects a once general principle – still abundantly represented in classical Italian literature, but now largely abandoned – governing the syntax of unstressed pronouns. The riddle of the use of the auxiliary verbs *essere* and *avere* with intransitive verbs (why *è andato* 'he has gone' but *ha viaggiato* 'he has travelled'?) will become a little less opaque when we take into account a superficially quite disparate phenomenon, namely the rules governing the use of the pronoun *ne*. We should stress that 'historical' principles are not necessarily 'extinct' principles. Often (as in the last example), the relevant factors may still be at work in the grammar.

A number of technical terms of linguistic analysis are used in this book. As an aid to readers for whom these may be unfamiliar, we give a brief account of some of them later in this chapter. In general, we have sought to give as clear a definition as possible of the relevant notions when they are first introduced in the text. These references are marked in bold in the index.

2 The emergence of Italian

2.1 The dialectal background

There is much in the structural history of Italian that can be properly understood only within the wider context of the evolution of the Italian dialects, and extensive reference to dialectal developments is made throughout this book. A structural outline of the dialects will be offered in Chapter 5, but it is important at the outset to understand the nature of the relationship between Italian and the 'Italian dialects'. The Italian dialects are not 'dialects of Italian'. And they are not 'daughters' of Italian, in the sense of being regional variants of Italian historically descended from the Italian language. Rather, Italian has its roots in one of the speech varieties that emerged from Latin in the Italy of the first millennium A.D., namely that of Tuscany, and more precisely the kind of Tuscan spoken in Florence. Historically, then, the Italian language is simply a 'sister' of the other dialects of Italy. Indeed, the Florentine of the Middle Ages might be said to have been merely 'one of the crowd'. This linguistic 'crowd' is 'Romance', a group of speech varieties related by their common descent from spoken Latin, and spoken over large areas of the former Roman Empire (Iberia – modern Portugal and Spain; Gaul – modern France; Italy; Switzerland (the Cantons of Grisons and Ticino); Romania. The now extinct Dalmatian dialects were once spoken along the Dalmatian coast of Croatia. European colonial expansions led to the extensive introduction of Romance (Spanish, Portuguese and French – but not Italian) into the Americas.

We should stress that, from a structural perspective, there is really no difference between 'a dialect' and 'a language'. What is normally meant by 'a dialect' in the parlance of Italian dialectology is the characteristic speech of the natives of a particular town or region (although it could also be applied to the speech of a particular social group), as contrasted with the characteristic speech of other places, where all the speech varieties concerned are 'cognate' (descended from a common linguistic source, namely Latin). The label 'language' is usually attached to those Romance dialects which have acquired political and/or cultural prestige, are recognized as superordinate, within some territory (often, but not necessarily, a nation-state), to other related speech varieties, are imitated by those seeking to speak or write 'correctly' and, usually, are set down in prescriptive grammars. We cannot here explore further the issues involved in defining the notion of 'a language' (and the intimately related one of 'standard' language). Readers are referred particularly to the work of Muljačić (e.g., 1985), for Romance languages, and Joseph (1987), for illuminating accounts of the relevant conceptual problems. Among the Romance varieties usually recognized as 'languages' are the national idioms of nation-states, such as Portuguese, Spanish, French, Italian and Romanian. Italy and Romania are latecomers, in this respect, having become nation-states only in the nineteenth century. Others, such as Catalan, Sardinian, Dalmatian, and Rhaeto-Romance in Switzerland, are also traditionally recognized as languages, because of their cultural importance, because they have also been accorded official recognition by the state in which they are used, because of their sharp distinctness from other Romance varieties, or through any combination of these factors.

The subgroup of Romance to which Florentine belongs is often labelled 'Italo-Romance'. This term is primarily geographical, and refers to the Romance dialects of Italy, usually excluding certain Romance varieties spoken principally outside Italy (such as the Franco-Provençal of Val d'Aosta, and parts of north-western Piedmont, and the Occitan of south-western Piedmont, both classified as Gallo-Romance dialects, the Rhaeto-Romance Ladin spoken in parts of Trentino and Alto Adige). The affinities of Friulian, spoken around Udine in north-western Italy but classified by many linguists as belonging to the Rhaeto-Romance grouping (represented also in the Grisons area of Switzerland), are moot, as are those of Sardinian, which has many distinctive structural features, yet also much in common with southern Italian dialects. From the point of view of linguistic structure, it is notoriously the case that the so-called Italo-Romance dialects have no single feature which distinguishes all of them from all other Romance dialects, and that there are rarely sharply defined boundaries separating 'Italo-Romance' and other Romance varieties. A degree of linguistic unity exists, however, in dialects to the south of a line running roughly between La Spezia and Rimini (cf. Ch.5: 2), among them those of

Tuscany. Tuscan dialects (of which Florentine is one) have been notably conservative in their linguistic evolution, and have failed to acquire many of the distinguishing features of the remaining dialects of central and southern Italy. The geographical distribution and structure of the Romance dialects of Italy will be examined more closely in Chapter 5. But to seek to impose the geographical label 'Italo-Romance' on the Romance of Italy (or on part of it) is simply to do violence to the linguistic facts, to impose rigid and discrete divisions on a continuum. In so far as we use this label in the rest of this book, it should be remembered that it is just a useful shorthand for something essentially ill-defined. Mention should be made of an alternative approach to the classificatory problem, in which the label 'Italian dialects' is more appropriate than 'Italo-Romance', which involves taking a wholly 'external' perspective and recognizing as Italian dialects those Romance varieties for which (or rather for whose speakers), the standard Italian language, based on the dialect of Florence, constitutes a 'guiding' (cf. Pellegrini (1975b: 56f.)), prestigious, superordinate speech variety.[4] For further exploration of the nature of the relationship between 'standard languages' and 'their' dialects, readers might consult the work of Muljačić (e.g., 1986).

The profundity of the linguistic difference between Italian dialects (however we define these) should not be underestimated. For nearly two millennia there has been very little to restrain the dialects from divergence. Measurement of degrees of linguistic difference is a tricky enterprise, not least because of the problem of deciding what relative 'weight' to give to different divergent features, but it is by no means far-fetched to assert that the difference between some Italian dialects, especially those more geographically distant from each other (say Turinese and Potentino), is equal to or greater than that between modern Italian and modern Spanish, and anecdotes of incomprehension between speakers of different Italian dialects abound (cf. also Pellegrini (1970: 222f.)).

2.2 Some observations on linguistic variety in ancient Italy

Regional linguistic variation within spoken Latin was probably present from the moment Latin became diffused among the various peoples of Italy and the wider Roman Empire. The languages spoken by the inhabitants of ancient Italy included a number of now extinct sisters of Latin (belonging, like Latin, to the 'Italic' family of Indo-European languages), notably the Umbrian of the upper Tiber valley, and Oscan of much of southern Italy, the Celtic languages (another branch of the Indo-European family, once spoken over vast areas of Europe and surviving in modern Irish, Scots Gaelic, Welsh and Breton) of much of northern Italy (excluding what is now the Veneto). Greek , once widely spoken in Sicily, Calabria and southern Puglia, may well have survived in these regions into the early Middle Ages, and there are still Greek-speaking villages in Salento and southern Calabria. Etruscan, a language of uncertain linguistic affinities, generally held not to be of Indo-European origin, was spoken in an area bounded roughly by the Arno to the north and the Tiber to the south and east. For a succinct account of the various languages of Italy at the time of the expansion of Latin, see Devoto (1977: 38–64).

It is difficult to imagine that the native speech habits of the populations newly speaking Latin would not have impinged on their use of Latin. However, it is also virtually impossible, at a remove of some two thousand years, to say which features of Italo-Romance dialects might be attributable to the influence of such early linguistic 'substrates'. This is not because such influence is implausible, but because it is almost impossible to verify, and the possibility that the relevant developments are due to spontaneous 'internal' linguistic change can rarely be reasonably excluded. We have consequently given little attention to 'substratist' explanations of linguistic phenomena in this book (but see Ch.2: 7).[5] Another external source of regional variation is the influence of languages with which Romance speakers in Italy have, over the centuries, come into contact. A distinction is sometimes made between 'adstrate' influences, arising from contact between neighbouring speech communities, and 'superstrate' influences reflecting the language of some conquering or dominant social group. A possible example of an 'adstrate' influence, with some interesting structural repercussions, is the syntactic influence of Greek on certain dialects of southern Italy (Ch.5: 2.3.2.9). The various Germanic invaders (Goths, Longobards and Franks) who, from the third to the ninth century held power in Italy, also left their linguistic stamp on the Italo-Romance dialects, although the influence of Germanic is almost exclusively a matter of introducing new *words*, rather than grammatical or phonological structures, into Italo-Romance dialects (but see Ch.2: 5.1). For further details of Germanic influences on Italo-Romance see Devoto (1977: 205–12) and Migliorini and Griffith (1984: 50–4).

2.3 From Florentine dialect to Italian

The political and cultural fragmentation of Italy favoured linguistic fragmentation not only negatively, in failing to provide any centripetal force which might restrain linguistic divergence, but also positively, in that the rise of municipal centres of power, during the late Middle Ages, tended to confer prestige on the speech of the relevant towns, which speakers throughout the respective spheres of influence sought to imitate, thereby accentuating the linguistic differences between rival areas of political and cultural influence. Political and economic power often favoured the blossoming of influential literature in the relevant dialects. But in the first half of the thirteenth century Florentine still did not stand tall in the crowd of Romance dialects, and as yet enjoyed none of the cultural importance, as a *literary* language, of Sicilian or Bolognese, whose influence had spread widely beyond their place of origin,[6] or of non-Italo Romance varieties such as French and Provençal.

What primarily determined the pre-eminence of Florentine in Italy was the flowering of Florentine culture, and particularly the literary prestige – rapidly diffused throughout Italy and beyond – of writers such as Dante, Petrarch and Boccaccio, who wrote in Florentine. Florence's status as a major commercial power undoubtedly also served to promote and diffuse its speech. But the acceptance of Florentine as the basis of the Italian language, and its codification (e.g., the production of dictionaries, and of grammars, serving to fix and prescribe norms of correct usage) is of rather later date. Long after the Latin of imperial Rome had ceased to be anybody's native language, it continued to be universally accepted, and employed, in literature, philosophy, theology, history, medicine and other intellectual activities, as well as the writing of legal and administrative documents. By the early sixteenth century, there had emerged a general recognition in Italy that some form of the 'lingua volgare' (i.e., some form of the indigenous spoken language of Italy, as opposed to Latin) should supplant Latin as the medium of written cultural discourse. The *Questione della Lingua*, the debate about *which* form of the 'lingua volgare' should be employed for this purpose, was a complex one which continued, in various forms, well into the nineteenth century.[7]

The view which prevailed was that espoused by the Venetian Pietro Bembo (see particularly his *Prose della Volgar Lingua* (1525)), who proposed Florentine.[8] But, believing it inappropriate for a literary language to be too close to everyday speech, Bembo favoured as the basis of the literary language not the Florentine of his time, but the prestigious literary language of two centuries earlier. In other words, Bembo (and his followers), helped fix as the literary language a variety which, already in the sixteenth century, was structurally divergent from all contemporary Italian dialects, even from Florentine. Indeed, the 'Florentineness' of literary Italian in the sixteenth century should not be overstated – as has been acutely observed by Weinapple (1983). Already in the fifteenth century a literary language was gaining ground throughout Italy whose basis was undoubtedly Florentine, but which had acquired general characteristics which could be said to be 'Italian', but were *not* typical of Florence, and which on occasion were capable of opposing and ousting features exclusive to Florence (among these are, probably, the change from the type *lo mi dà* 'he gives it to me', to *me lo dà* (Ch.3: 9.4.2), the triumph of the structure *non facendolo* 'not doing it' over *non lo facendo* (Ch.3: 9.4.1), the establishment of the type *presero* 'they took' over *presono* (Ch.3: 8.3.3), and other phenomena).

Over the ensuing four centuries, the gulf between the literary language of Italy, and the speech of the Italians, tended to widen. Calculation of the proportion of the Italian people that could have been said to know Italian in the 1860s, at the time of the political unification of Italy, is fraught with difficulty.[9] In so far as Italian was principally a written language, only the functionally literate – a minute proportion of the populace – were likely to be able to acquire a full command of the language. On the other hand, any native speaker of an Italo-Romance dialect, and particularly those who spoke Tuscan or another central Italian dialect, would have been able, given sufficient attention, to understand at least something of the Italian language, so that a degree of *passive* knowledge of Italian need not have been the exclusive preserve of the literate. Estimates of the numbers of those able to speak Italian at the time of Unification range between 2.5% of the population, according to De Mauro (1976), through 9.52% (or about two and a quarter million persons), according to Castellani (1982), to 12%, suggested by Serianni (1990: 18 n6). It should be added that a small proportion of Italians used speech varieties other than Italo-Romance. Indeed, their numbers increased after the First World War, due to border changes: De Mauro (1976: 10f.) estimates them at 2.1% of Italians (or about 800 000 souls) in 1921. In addition to the other Romance varieties (Ladin, Occitan, Franco-Provençal), there were also German dialects (spoken in Val Canale (Udine), parts of Trentino, and the Val de Gressoney (Aosta)), Slovenian (around Gorizia, Val di Resia and the upper Torre and Natisone valleys, and the area around Trieste), Greek (in clusters of villages in Salento to the south of Lecce and the Aspromonte area of Calabria), Albanian (scattered in villages in Abruzzo, Puglia, Basilicata, Calabria and Sicily), and Serbo-Croat (in a few villages in Molise). At Alghero in Sardinia a variety of Catalan was spoken. These speech communities all persist to this day.[10]

The perception of a linguistic gulf between the literary language and the speech of the Italian people, particularly where vocabulary is concerned, is keenly articulated in the nineteenth century by the Milanese Alessandro Manzoni, for whom the *Questione della Lingua* was no longer a debate about a *literary* language, but about the best means of extending knowledge of the language to the Italian people at large. But not only was Italian structurally remote from the everyday speech of most Italians, it was also functionally remote, in that it had remained elevated above the needs of everyday life, and was ill-equipped for use in everyday discourse. Part of Manzoni's solution was to propose that contemporary spoken Florentine (or a cultivated variety thereof), rather than archaic literary Florentine, should form the basis of the national language, and the final version of his novel *I promessi sposi* (1840) was intended, among other things, as an exemplar thereof. The culmination of a lifetime's meditation on this problem was Manzoni's report, commissioned by the Ministry of Education and published in 1868, on the unity of the Italian language and means of diffusing it, in which he proposed, *inter alia*, the teaching of Florentine in schools, and the publication of a modern Florentine dictionary. When the latter, even the first word of whose title – *Novo vocabolario della lingua italiana secondo l'uso di Firenze* – was distinctively Florentine (Ch.2: 4.2), began to appear in 1870, it provoked a memorable and insightful response from a scholar of linguistic history, Graziadio Ascoli. Ascoli (1873) cogently pointed out the impracticalities of a number of Manzoni's proposals, and above all that of overturning the established literary tradition in favour of a variety of Florentine many elements of whose structure were unfamiliar to the great majority of educated people. Ascoli also expressed his opposition to the imposition of inflexible linguistic models of any kind, whether archaic or modern. For him, the traditional literary language must be the basis of Italian, but its evolution as the national language of the Italians could only be the *product* of an increased and intensified cooperative intellectual activity on the part of the Italian people, a condition which he regarded as still lacking.[11]

In fact, political unification helped promote the expansion of Italian (the Italian of the literary tradition – not contemporary Florentine) along two major dimensions. The first was social: the Italian language was gradually acquired by the Italian populace at large. The mechanisms of this expansion, and the roles variously played by migration, military service, the educational system, the mass media, and other factors, have been explored, for example, by De Mauro (1976).[12] In the late twentieth century, we find that the overwhelming majority of Italians understand and use Italian, although the *way* in which they use Italian may be divergent from the standard language based on the literary tradition, as we shall see. It is very difficult to obtain a true estimate of the proportion of the populace which remains substantially ignorant of the language, but we may safely say that it is minute, restricted to rural areas (especially of the far south and Sardinia), and to older generations. Perhaps the most telling indicator of the penetration of Italian among the Italians is whether they use the language at home, that is to say in the most intimate sphere of their lives. A recent survey (Doxa (1988)), in which a sample of Italians were asked to report on their own linguistic behaviour, suggests that about 34.4% of the population use only Italian, even in the home, while the remainder continue to use dialect at least with some members of their families, in addition to Italian. The proportion of those claiming to employ Italian at home (as well as in the wider world) at least some of the time was 60.4%.

The second, accompanying, type of expansion concerns the domains of discourse in which Italian is used. As the language was acquired by the populace at large, so Italian was put to use in an ever widening range of domains, in casual conversation, in military life, in bureaucracy, in civil administration, and so forth. These expansions of Italian have resulted in structural diversity within Italian. The once remote and relatively homogeneous literary language has begun to show systematic variation according to region, social group, topic and context of discourse, and so forth. It is with such variation that shall be concerned in Chapter 5.

3 Chronology and historical sources

3.1 Chronology

It is as difficult to divide Italian into chronological periods as it is to divide Italo-Romance dialects into geographical areas. From an 'internal' perspective we are inclined to think that such division is a counterproductive distraction. We shall not, then, be particularly concerned with periodization here, although we would not wish to deny the importance of this complex issue from a perspective which is primarily 'external'. See particularly Weinapple (1983) and D'Achille (1991) for further discussion of problems of periodization. In this book we have preferred simply to state the (approximate) date for which the linguistic phenomena in question are attested. From an internal perspective, there is no historical moment of dramatic, structural upheaval which would allow us to distinguish 'old' and 'modern' Italian. Indeed, it is probably better for our purposes in this book to avoid the term 'old Italian' altogether, and to date the emergence of 'Italian', with quite deliberate vagueness, from the 'fifteenth or sixteenth centuries', the centuries during which a form of Tuscan dialect (based principally on Florentine) was becoming generally accepted as the literary language of Italy. In the history of 'Italian' thus defined, there is little need for further periodization. It would be a gross exaggeration to say that the structure of modern Italian had already assumed its present form by the fourteenth century. Indeed, we shall be at pains to underline the many changes – such as the rise of the progressive tense form of the type *sto facendo* 'I am doing', or the abandonment of interrogative structures of the type *viene egli?* 'is he coming?' (Ch.4: 3), etc. – which have occurred in Italian ever since the fifteenth century. But it is also true that Italian – primarily a literary idiom remote from spontaneous, everyday, language – has changed strikingly little since the time of Boccaccio and Petrarch, particularly in the domains of phonology and morphology. Before the fifteenth century, it might be more accurate to talk of 'old Tuscan' rather than of 'old Italian',[13] since Tuscan was not universally accepted as the Italian *lingua*, even though the perception of the prestige and primacy of Tuscan was gathering ground from the time of Dante onwards. In the fifteenth century we find the terms *fiorentino*, *toscano* and *italiano* being used sometimes interchangeably. And, so far as one can determine, there was relatively little divergence between written Tuscan dialect and spoken Tuscan dialect.

3.2 Early texts

The earliest concrete attestations of Italo-Romance are, of course, written texts. The first surviving continuous texts uncontroversially written in an Italo-Romance dialect, and not in Latin, are certain brief, formulaic, legal depositions dating from the 960s (the so-called *Placiti cassinesi*), written in a variety of Campanian.[14] There is a hiatus of a century before the appearance, towards the end of the eleventh century, of the next Italo-Romance texts which have come down to us from Sardinia and central Italy. Romance texts (usually of a practical or religious nature) become increasingly frequent through the twelfth century, but our direct knowledge of OTuscan only commences with a text (a Pisan naval account register) written no earlier than the early twelfth century, while the first surviving text from Florence is a bankers' book of 1211. It is only from the mid thirteenth century that Tuscan texts (including the first literary texts, for example, the *Novellino*) begin to appear with any frequency.

3.3 'Proto-Romance' and 'Classical Latin'

For our knowledge of the Romance of Italy as it emerged before the year 1000, we are dependent principally on reconstruction of 'Proto-Romance'[15] forms on the basis of comparison of the modern dialects, supported by our knowledge of their Latin antecedents, and of certain general principles of linguistic change. We cannot enter here into a critical discussion of the technique of comparative reconstruction. Suffice it to say that there are many cases where it is beyond reasonable doubt that a particular change in the structure of Latin underlies all or most of the modern Romance varieties of Italy, and that systematic differences between those varieties are wholly consistent with the postulation of a common historically underlying system; the evolution of the 'western' Romance vowel system, discussed in (Ch.2: 2.1) is a nice case in point. We follow in this book the convention of signalling forms whose existence is postulated, but unattested, by means of an asterisk; note that a double asterisk denotes some putative linguistic form whose existence is *denied.*

The most convenient historical starting point, in terms of which to consider the subsequent evolution of Tuscan and other Italo-Romance dialects, is Classical Latin. But some caveats are in order. It is easy to fall into the trap of treating Classical Latin as if it represented a primordial state of linguistic neatness and cohesion which subsequently fragmented into the various Romance dialects. In reality, the Latin of the Roman Empire already displayed a vast range of variation according to region, social stratum, register of speech, and so forth. It is extremely unlikely that Classical Latin as represented by writers such as Vergil, Cicero or Caesar is the *direct* ancestor of Romance. While we are unconvinced by the hypothesis that Proto-Romance might have existed as a structurally distinct 'sister' of Classical Latin spoken in southern Italy already in the imperial period (cf. Hall (1950)), it seems very probable that Romance descends from the everyday, uncultivated, and already regionally variant, Latin of the Empire. That is to say that it has its origins in speech forms by no means wholly identical to those of Classical Latin. We shall take Classical Latin as the 'starting point' of our analysis, but it should always be borne in mind that we do this *faute de mieux*, because Classical Latin is probably the best approximation we have to the structure of the forebear of the Romance languages.[16]

4 A note on phonetic transcription

In this book, where possible, we have given Latin and Italian words in their conventional orthography. When, as is often the case, this is inadequate for our purposes, we have transcribed into the International Phonetic Alphabet. However, certain phonological characteristics can be represented by means of minor adjustments to orthography. Latin orthography represents neither stress nor vowel length; we have signalled these by giving stressed syllables in bold type, and marking length with a colon (:) after the vowel. Stress in Italian words has been indicated, where necessary, by placing a grave accent over the stressed vowel (e.g., *àmano* **'aːmano** 'they love'); where no stress is indicated, it should be assumed that the penultimate syllable is stressed (e.g., *ama* **'aːma** 'he loves'). As is conventional, stress in IPA transcriptions is indicated by the symbol ' immediately to the left of the stressed syllable (e.g., **man'daːre**).

Particular attention should be drawn to a transcriptional practice followed in this book which deviates from standard practice, and reflects our methodological scepticism (explained in our comments on the 'phoneme' in section 5.4) about the value of the traditional distinction between 'phonemic' and 'phonetic' representations. We shall not use at all the slashes (/ /) normally associated with the representation of 'phonemes'. Transcriptions of speech sounds will be indicated in bold face, and square brackets ([ ]), normally associated with 'phonetic' or 'allophonic' (and, therefore, 'non-phonemic') transcriptions. They will be used only where speech sounds are cited in isolation from the words in which they appear. In other words, '[**e**]' means 'this is the speech sound **e** (and not the *letter* 'e')'.

5 Some concepts in linguistic change

Without attempting to provide even an outline of the theory and principles of language change (see, for example, McMahon (1994)), we sketch here, with some very brief illustrations, certain concepts which will be particularly useful in studying the history of Italian. Among these are

- The inherent variability of language
- The notion of 'learnèd' forms
- Hypercorrection
- The regularity and irregularity of sound change
- Phonetically conditioned variation in speech sounds
- Allomorphy
- Grammaticalization (including morphologization)
- Analogy
- Emergence of analytic structures
- Spoken vs. written language

5.1 Variation

That language is spoken by human beings in human societies should be a statement of the obvious, but it is all too easy in charting the 'internal' linguistic history of a language, to talk as though the structural changes which have taken place were the result of ineluctable laws on a par with those of physics, operating on an abstract and homogeneous linguistic structure in which humans were merely the mindless conduit of change. Indeed, it is difficult not to talk in this way when discussing historically remote periods in the history of a language, of which our knowledge is, perforce, sketchy. But in reality, the way in which a speaker uses language may vary according to a wide range of factors (e.g., speed of speech, formality of the speech situation, and so forth); and social groups within a wider speech community may be distinguished by the systematically different ways in which their members use a common language. Speakers can be extremely sensitive even to minute patterns of variation, both within their own speech, and between social groups, and can choose to adopt, reject or modify aspects of the variation they hear about them. In short, no living language is homogeneous, and speakers are potentially active participants, not just passive automata, in the unfolding of linguistic change.

Except perhaps for the inhabitants of the most remote and isolated localities, all Italians over the past two millennia must have been, at least, *aware* of the existence of varieties of language other than their own, ranging from the relatively minor perceptible speech differences between neighbouring villages, through the major differences in the language of Romance-speakers coming from more distant regions, and finally to Latin, and latterly Italian, as prestigious varieties of language superordinate to local dialect. Speakers who are aware of variation are also capable of imitating, often by adopting ('borrowing') into their own speech structural or lexical features of some other variety. We shall see that Florentine, for example, seems to have borrowed a variety of pronunciations and grammatical features from other Italo-Romance dialects – e.g., the pronunciation of 's' as [**z**] between vowels in words like *francese* 'French' (Ch.2: 7.2) seems to have been taken from northern dialects, and the ordering of clitic pronouns *me lo dà* instead of OFlorentine *lo mi dà*, appears to be a matter of imitation of Sienese and of other dialects to the south of Florence (Ch.3: 9.4.2). The centuries of cultural prestige accorded to written Latin has meant that Latin has constituted a practically inexhaustible reservoir of 'learnèd' vocabulary for use in cultured discourse. Much of the learnèd vocabulary of Italian, i.e., words introduced into the language by an educated elite, is of Latin origin (Classical Greek is another major source), transmitted into Italian by intellectuals, clerics, lawyers, and others who possessed an active knowledge of Latin. Sometimes Latin words are adopted into Italian alongside the indigenous Italo-Romance words of which they are the historical source. This often has the effect of reintroducing into the language the historically underlying form of words which are already part of the native linguistic tradition. The word *cosa* 'thing' (from Latin CAUSA(M)) is the result of a continuous linguistic development going back to Roman times, displaying, for example, the characteristic monophthongization of the Latin diphthong [**aw**] (Ch.2: 4.4). But *causa* 'cause', is a learnèd borrowing into Italian from written Latin which, because it has not been continuously on the lips of Italians, has not undergone the sound changes to which its 'indigenous' counterpart has been subject. Such pairs of popular and learnèd words arising from a common source are termed *etymological doublets*. Imitation of prestigious linguistic models is not, of course, limited to the lexicon.

5.2 Hypercorrection

Attempts to imitate varieties considered, for whatever reason, more prestigious or desirable, often result in hypercorrection: in their endeavours to reproduce the desired pattern of speech, speakers can, in effect, 'overstretch' themselves, producing novel structures which do not exist in the variety of speech which they are attempting to produce. We shall see that hypercorrection has played a major role in the linguistic history of Italian. An extreme, and potent, form of hypercorrection, is the exaggerated reinforcement of characteristic features of one's own speech as an assertion of local identity, while eschewing others which are in reality indigenous, but are perceived as 'foreign'.[17] Some changes in the history of Tuscan, including such historical puzzles as the unexpected appearance of the middle vowel [**a**] in *cronaca* 'chronicle' from Latin CHRONICA(M), or of [ŋg] in parts of the verb *tenere* 'to hold' (e.g., *tengo* 'I hold'), where we would expect to find [ɲɲ] (*tegno*), etc., are probably the results of hypercorrection (see Ch.2: 4.6.4.1 and Ch.3: 8.4.1).

5.3 Sound change and allomorphy

Variation is inherent in the pronunciation of a language. Some variation is random and unsystematic, but if a variant articulation is systematically adopted by speakers, we say that a sound change has taken place. This is not the place to explore the intricate question of why sound changes occur, or how they spread through speech communities, but the adoption of variant pronunciation is often connected with a preference for relative ease of articulation. A potentially countervailing force is ease of perception: an easier articulation may obscure the identity of a speech sound, and so a potential change may be blocked, or changes may occur which serve to reinforce the identity of the intended sound. A nice example of both is the story of reduction and (hypercorrect) 'restoration' of unstressed vowels in Tuscan, discussed in (Ch.2: 4.6.4.1). Sound changes are not like physical laws, in the sense of blindly and automatically applying to all the sounds potentially subject to the change – although often, from the foreshortening perspective of history, it may look as if they have done so. Some sound changes do eventually operate on all occurrences of the sounds potentially subject to them but usually there is tension between a conservative norm and an innovatory pronunciation, and a speaker may apply the new pronunciation in some words but not in others, and in casual more than formal speech, and even in certain grammatical categories but not others, and so on. Some incipient changes may never become fully established because of the influence of competing linguistic varieties in which the relevant change does not occur, or occurs in a different way. An example is the story of palatalization by yod, discussed in Ch.2: 5.2, where 'borrowing' of the output of sound changes which have regularly taken place in other dialects has played a role. Probably the most helpful way to approach sound changes is to realize that they *tend* to affect every occurrence of the relevant sounds and in this respect are 'regular'. But where those sound changes produce results which are systematically and perceptibly different from the pronunciation of other varieties of the language (for example, of more conservative speech patterns, or of the varieties spoken in other regions), there is a tendency for the influence of these coexistent and competing models to produce exceptions to otherwise general phonetic changes, and in this respect sound changes are often, perhaps usually, 'irregular'.

We shall pay particular attention in this book to the way in which sound changes have impinged on the grammatical structure of Italian. Some changes may result in a sound becoming identical to some other sound from which it was originally distinct: in this case we speak of *merger*. A very common scenario is that a sound changes only when a certain other sound precedes or follows it. Where this phonetic context is not present, the change does not take place. Contextually conditioned phonetic changes of this kind are usually *assimilations* – that is to say that the sound which changes adopts some phonetic characteristic of a neighbouring sound. A classic example in the history of Italo-Romance (Ch.2: 6), and of a great many other languages, is that velar consonants ([**k**] and [**g**]) tend to change into palatal consonants (articulated with raising of the tongue body towards the palate) in anticipation of the raised tongue position inherent in the articulation of a following front vowel [**i**] or [**e**]. Where no [**i**] or [**e**] followed, the change did not take place. This contextually conditioned split of one sound into different articulations has left its mark in the grammatical structure of Italian in the distinction between **ˈdiːtʃi** 'you say', which displays the results of palatalization of an original [**k**] before a front vowel [**i**], and **ˈdiːko** 'I say', where the velar consonant has remained intact, because a back vowel [**o**] follows. We can see that the sound change has impinged on the morphological system of Italian, in that the single meaning 'say', which in the Latin present tense was just **diːk**, is now represented by two forms, **diːk** in the first person singular, and **diːtʃ** in the second person singular. Where a particular meaning is expressed in this way by more than one form – a state of affairs which arises usually, but not necessarily, as a result of sound change – we speak of *allomorphy*.

5.4 A note on the 'phoneme'

For methodological reasons, we have felt compelled in this book to deviate from certain usually held assumptions about the importance of the 'phoneme' in historical phonological description. This is not the place for a lengthy theoretical digression (for more detailed argumentation, see Maiden (1991)), but a few general remarks (which some readers may prefer to skip) are in order here.

A point all too often neglected in historical linguistics is that we do not know at what point in the history of a sound change a resulting phonetic differentiation ceases to be merely a matter of more or less mechanical articulatory habit, and begins to be connected with the expression of the different grammatical categories with which the resulting differences are (at first accidentally) associated (e.g., first vs. second persons of the verb *dire*).[18] There is no reason to identify this point – as many historical linguists of a structuralist bent do – with the moment at which a sound change becomes *phonemic*, that is when it is no longer exclusively and uniquely predictable from its phonetic context, and where the relevant sound difference can function on its own, independently of context, to distinguish the meaning of words which are in all other respects identical. Such minimally differentiated words are called 'minimal pairs', and constitute the principal diagnostic for phonemic opposition. For example, in modern Italian it is not the case that every [**ʧ**][19] can be derived from [**k**] preceding a front vowel (cf. *cioccolato* **ʧokko'la:to** 'chocolate' where [**ʧ**] occurs before [**o**], and no [**i**] was ever present in the history of Italian), and not every [**k**] before a front vowel becomes [**ʧ**] (e.g., *chilo* **'ki:lo** 'kilo'); moreover, [**ʧ**] vs. [**k**] can function alone, and independently of context, to distinguish the meaning of words: e.g., *dici* **'di:ʧi** vs. *dichi* **'di:ki**, the former being the second person singular present indicative of *dire*, and the latter being a *popular* form of the present subjunctive of *dire* 'to say' (readers can find for themselves hundreds of other minimal pairs of this kind). Therefore, [**ʧ**] and [**k**] (or rather /**ʧ**/ and /**k**/, to present them in traditional phonemic representation, cf. section 4, above) are separate phonemes.

When a once phonetically conditioned difference results in sounds which are phonemically distinct, and cannot be derived exclusively from their phonetic environment, we know that speakers must by now be associating the phonetic difference with differences of meaning. But speakers are perfectly capable of perceiving systematically occurring phonetic differences long before these cease to be exclusively predictable from their phonetic environment, and speakers are therefore perfectly capable of interpreting and using such phonetic differences – even while they are still motivated by articulatory factors – as additional expressions of associated differences in meaning. There is good evidence that this is precisely what does happen (cf. Maiden (1991)) and indeed we suspect that this is *normally* the case. Many linguistic histories make much of the distinction between phonetic (or 'allophonic') variation on the one hand and the emergence of phonemic opposition on the other. While the notion of distinctive opposition is of absolutely fundamental importance, it is far from evident that phonemic opposition defined in terms of minimal pairs deserves to be given much weight. We think that far less violence is likely to be done to the linguistic facts if the classification of sound differences into 'phonemic' and 'allophonic' is not overemphasized, and there will be little mention of the 'phoneme' in what follows.

Overemphasis on the 'phoneme' defined in terms of minimal pairs can also be a distraction in another respect: a fertile imagination is needed to conceive of any circumstances under which the small handful of minimal pairs involving opposition between voiced and voiceless sibilants in Tuscan (such as **ˈkjɛːse** 'he asked' vs. **ˈkjɛːze** 'churches' (Ch.2: 7.2)), could function to distinguish meaning in normal discourse. The origins, and connotations for native speakers, of these distinct, voiced and voiceless, pronunciations are extremely interesting, as we shall see; but that minimal pairs may be found – with some effort on the part of the researcher – is much less so.

5.5 Morphologization and grammaticalization

What is usually understood by morphologization is the integration of the effects of some sound change into the morphology of a language. 'Morphology' is concerned, in broad terms, with the relationship between the phonological shape of words and the meanings expressed by words: important factors in Romance morphology are the inflectional endings which express grammatical meanings, and the relationship between differences in the 'stem' (Ch.3: 1) of words, and the grammatical categories they express. We saw above how the results of palatalization of velar consonants can become part of the morphological person and number system of the verb, in addition to the inflectional endings. Another type of morphologization occurs when originally different words become the 'same' as far as lexical meaning is concerned, but are associated with different grammatical categories within the word: for example, we find *and-* in most persons of the verb *andare* 'to go', but *va(d)-* in the singular and third person plural forms of the present tense. These two forms were originally the stems of independent words, of different lexical meaning. Extreme allomorphy of this kind, where there is no phonological similarity between the alternating forms, is termed *suppletion*.[20]

Morphologization is a form of 'grammaticalization', but the term *grammaticalization* is commonly reserved for that development whereby an originally autonomous lexical word gradually loses its distinctive meaning, and becomes a mere indicator of grammatical categories. For example, the ending *-mente*, which in modern Italian is used to form the grammatical class of adverbs, originated as an independent word meaning 'mind', and the person and number endings of the future tense (e.g., *finirò* 'I shall finish', *finirai* 'you will finish'), originate as present tense forms of the Latin verb HABERE, meaning 'to have', 'to possess'.

5.6 Analogy

Linguistic form often becomes reorganized in such a way that it constitutes a more perspicuous and diagrammatic expression of meaning. One mechanism by which this happens is termed 'analogy'. The most prominent type of analogical change we encounter in the history of Italian occurs in morphology and takes the form either of *analogical levelling*, or of analogical creation of alternation. Allomorphy (see Ch.3: 0.2) tends to contradict the 'normal' expectation that each meaning will be signalled by just one linguistic form. That a single meaning should be expressed by two or more different forms involves, on the face of things, a wholly redundant complication of the grammar, and the relationship between form and meaning becomes 'opaque', while a one-to-one form-meaning relationship is maximally 'transparent'. Where such allomorphic 'complications' are eliminated, by substitution of a single invariant form, where previously multiple forms indicated a single meaning, we speak of analogical levelling. For example, the OTuscan verb 'to reap' *miètere* displayed, as a result of sound change (Ch.2: 4.2), a diphthong wherever the (first) syllable was stressed (*mièto* 'I reap') but not where that syllable was unstressed (*metèmo* 'we reap'). The discrepancy between the single meaning 'reap', and this duality of form, was resolved by generalizing the form containing the diphthong to all parts of the verb, whence modern Italian *mièto*, *mietiàmo*.

Some grammatical differences may be expressed in certain parts of the grammar, but not in others. In OTuscan, the categories first and third persons singular in present tense, first conjugation, verbs were distinguished, respectively, by the endings *-o* and *-a* (*parlo* 'I speak' vs. *parla* 'he speaks'); in the imperfect tense, however, the inflectional endings did not distinguish these persons (*parlava* 'I spoke' vs. *parlava* 'he spoke'). Subsequently, on the analogy of the present tense, the *-o* vs. *-a* distinction was introduced into the imperfect (*parlavo* vs. *parlava*). In such cases we speak of analogical creation of alternation. Sometimes, this may even have the effect of disrupting one-to-one matchings between sound and meaning. For example, in OTuscan the verb *fuggire* had an invariant stem **ˈfuddʒ-**, meaning 'flee' (e.g., *fuggio* **ˈfuddʒo** 'I flee', *fuggi* **ˈfuddʒi** 'you flee', etc.), but on the model of alternation between first person singular *leggo* **ˈlɛggo** 'I read', and *leggi* **ˈlɛddʒi** 'you read' (etc.), a new alternation has been created in *fuggire*, yielding *fuggo* **ˈfuggo** 'I flee' vs. *fuggi* **ˈfuddʒi** 'you flee'. Analogical changes can also operate in other parts of the grammar. For example, the extensive historical reorderings in the syntax of clitic pronouns in relation to the verb. In modern Italian we say *lo vedo* 'I see it' and *vederlo* 'to see it', but in OTuscan both *vedolo* and *lo vedo* and *lo vedere* or *vederlo* were, within certain constraints, possible. This change probably reflects an analogical generalization of the fact that in OTuscan the clitic *tended* to precede finite verbs, and *tended* to follow infinitives (Ch.3: 9.4.2).

5.7 The emergence of 'analytic' structures

A major trend in the history of Italian (and of other Romance languages) is the emergence of so-called 'analytic' structures. Much of Latin morphology was 'synthetic', that is to say that the expression of lexical meaning ('dog', 'do', 'tall', etc.) was tightly 'bound', within a single word, with the expression of grammatical meaning ('plural', 'genitive', 'first person', 'perfect tense', etc.). Grammatical meaning was usually expressed by means of an inflectional ending inseparable from the verb, noun or adjective (e.g., CANIUM 'of dogs', FECI 'I did', etc.). In the emergence of analytic structures, the expressions of lexical and grammatical meaning get, so to speak, 'unpacked': in the history of Italian this has usually involved the assignment of grammatical meanings and lexical meanings to separate and originally autonomous words. Some of the functions of the Latin genitive inflections are taken over by a separate word, the preposition *di* (e.g., *di cani* 'of dogs'), and some of the functions of the perfect tense are replaced by a structure comprising the verb *avere* 'to have', which bears information about person and number, and the past participle of the verb, which bears the lexical meaning of the verb (e.g., *ho fatto* 'I have done'). What is particularly fascinating to trace in the history of Italian is the way in which the originally autonomous elements of the analytic structure (particularly in the verb) may become 'grammaticalized' (see above) in that they gradually lose the characteristics of semantically, syntactically and phonologically independent words, and become more and more like the 'bound' elements of the synthetic structures they originally replaced (e.g., Ch.3: 8.8).

5.8 Written and spoken language

It is a fundamental principle of linguistic analysis that writing is secondary to speech. Suffice it to observe that the majority of languages that have ever been spoken have not been written down by their native speakers. And, until this century, the overwhelming majority of native speakers of Italo-Romance were illiterate, but no less fluent and accurate in their native speech for that. Virtually all the phonetic and other changes we chart in this book originated in the speech of the unlettered.

Having made this clear, it is important to add that we should not underestimate the influence of writing in the history of Italian. For the last two thousand years, and probably longer, the Italians have lived in the shadow of the written word, not least because it was the medium of religious texts, and of legal and commercial language. Illiterate as the populace may have been, it is doubtful whether even the humblest peasant in the remotest village in the darkest moment of the Dark Ages did not know what reading and writing were, and did not recognize the prestige accorded to the written word. And in the Renaissance the proportion of literate males in the population sometimes reached surprisingly high levels in major urban centres, possibly higher than those reached in the nineteenth century.[21]

Where there is a discrepancy between speech and othography, there has long been a tendency among the literate to adapt pronunciation to spelling ('spelling pronunciation'). And spelling has sometimes exercised a 'distorting' influence on the otherwise regular implementation of sound change. Since, for many centuries, the language of writing was *par excellence* Latin, and since Italian vocabulary has been continually replenished from written Latin, there have entered into Italian a great many Latin words pronounced, letter for letter, as they are spelled.[22] This is one of the main sources of the rise of etymological doublets, such as *causa* 'cause' vs. *cosa* 'thing' (Ch.2: 13). The Roman alphabet, adapted for the writing of Latin, is ill-equipped to represent some of the sounds of Italian: for example, it offers no orthographic distinction between the open and closed mid vowels (Ch.2: 2.1), both spelled with 'e' and 'o', nor between [s] and [z] (both spelled 's') and [ʦ] and [ʣ] (both spelled 'z').[23] Such ambiguities in the relation between sounds and letters have played a role in the emergence of 'popular' Italian pronunciation in this century (Ch.5: 3.1.3), with speakers failing to make those distinctions which are not unambiguously indicated in standard Italian orthography, but also sometimes pronouncing letters which in modern Italian have no phonetic value (such as the 'i' in *giallo* 'yellow' – where 'i' is a 'diacritic' sign, indicating that the preceding 'g' is pronounced [ʤ], not [g], or in *cielo* 'sky', where the 'i' is not pronounced in modern standard Italian).

There are other respects in which writing and speech are different. Spoken language is usually more spontaneous and less carefully meditated than written language. Written language is permanent, and is usually that medium in which norms of 'correct' linguistic usage are first laid down. Spoken language tends to favour innovation in linguistic structure, whereas the written word is more conservative. The permanency of writing allows the reader to look back over what has been written, and this fact facilitates the use of syntactically far more complex structures than tend to be used in spoken language. Complex syntactic structures in spoken language tend to place a heavy burden both on the speaker's and on the hearer's memory, and simpler structures tend, accordingly, to be preferred. We shall see many examples in what follows of structural differences between written and spoken Italian, ranging from the use of personal pronouns (Ch.3: 9.1.2), to the basic ordering of elements in the sentence (Ch.4: 1).

Notes

1. See Varvaro (1984: 25–7; 33f.; 38–40) for an analysis of the history of this distinction.
2. On this point see also Varvaro (1984: 45–7). But the present work is closer in kind to what he describes as a 'sophisticated form of structural diachrony' than to his conception of a 'history of the language'.
3. To mention but a few, there are Migliorini and Griffith (1984); Bruni (1987); and the new multivolume series *Storia della lingua italiana*, emerging under the general editorship of F. Bruni, which combines rich textual documentation with detailed linguistic analysis. A succinct and up-to-date account of the rise of Italian as a 'standard' language since the Renaissance appears in Muljačić (1988).
4. This definition clearly includes Sardinian and Friulian, but excludes Franco-Provençal, for which the 'guiding' language is French. Unfortunately, it also tends to exclude Corsican, which is patently a variety of Tuscan (introduced to the island around 1000), yet most of whose speakers would now recognize French, not Italian, as their 'guiding' language (see also Dalbera-Stefanaggi (1991: 27–30)).
5. Substratist accounts are on much firmer ground where the lexicon is concerned. Words such as *verna* 'elm' and *brüc* 'heather' in northern dialects are known to be of Celtic origin. The *attrufu* 'October' of Basilicata can be shown to be of Oscan origin. See Rohlfs (1972b: 17–19).
6. For an account of early flowerings of Italo-Romance dialects as literary languages, see, for example, Migliorini and Griffith (1984, Chapter 4).
7. For a historical account see particularly Vitale (1984), and the succinct account in Hall (1942a). Menocal (1991) gives a sober assessment of the importance of the *Questione* for the history of Italian.
8. It is likely that the structural conservatism of Florentine, making it apparently more similar to Latin than are other Italo-Romance varieties, may also have served to promote its acceptance as a worthy successor to Latin.
9. See, however, Pellegrini (1975b: 64f.).
10. For further details see, for example, Bruni (1987: 287f.). Note that Val d'Aosta has two official languages, Italian and French. The number of German speakers increased greatly through the incorporation of the Austrian Südtirol (Alto Adige) after the First World War.
11. For the nineteenth century *Questione della Lingua*, and especially the debate between Manzoni and Ascoli, see Vitale (1984), also Serianni (1990: 41–67).

12. See also Serianni (1990: 23–6).
13. If the term 'old Italian' can be used at all, it is in the essentially geographical sense of all the various dialects used in the Middle Ages in the territory of what is now Italy, and in which Italian is now used and accepted as standard language (see also Varvaro (1984: 48 n155)).
14. For analysis of the earliest Italo-Romance texts see, for example, Castellani (1973).
15. Since there was never any break in continuity of transmission between the spoken Latin of Italy in the Imperial period, and modern Italo-Romance, we see little advantage in distinguishing 'Vulgar Latin' from 'Proto-Romance', or in trying to identify the point when Latin 'ended' and Romance 'began'.
16. A very useful introductory sketch of Latin for Romance linguists is Vincent (1988b).
17. For a discussion of the type of concepts mentioned here, see, for example, Hudson (1980: 195–201) and Chambers and Trudgill (1980: 87f.).
18. The same arguments given here can apply to cases of 'lexicalization', where the result of some sound change becomes analysed as a primary element of the phonological shape of a word: the initial palatal [**ʧ**] of *cena* **'ʧeːna** 'dinner' is the result of historical palatalization rules affecting an original velar consonant *[**k**] before a front vowel. But nothing rules out the possibility that, at some stage in its history, the palatal consonant could be *both* the 'allophonic' result of a 'live' phonetic process of palatalization, *and* part of the lexical representation of a word. In other words, we do not accept that the phonological representation of words must be 'phonemic'.
19. See section 4 above for the value of square brackets.
20. Similar to morphologization is lexicalization, discussed in note 18.
21. For an account of the extent of literacy in early modern Italy, see Burke (1987).
22. It may not always have been so. Wright (1982) develops the stimulating and still controversial thesis that, until the time of Charlemagne, in France, and the twelfth century in Spain, written Latin and spoken Romance were not perceived as separate languages, and Latin was not pronounced 'one sound for one letter'. Rather, written Latin was simply the writing system of spoken Romance. In principle, it might also have been the case in the Italy of the first millennium that, for example, one *wrote* UIRIDIS, but said **'verde** 'green', and perhaps even wrote IGNIS, but *said* **'fwɔːko** 'fire'. What is certain is that there were some respects in which written Latin was adapted to native pronunciations in Italy: Latin CT was generally pronounced [**tt**], TI + vowel was pronounced [**tsj**] + vowel, and GN was pronounced [**ɲ**] (e.g., SECTA > **'sɛtta** *setta* 'sect'; UITIUM > **'vittsjo** *vizio* 'vice'; IGNORO > **iɲ'ɲɔːro** *ignoro* 'I am unaware').
23. For an account of attempts, in the sixteenth century, to distinguish these sounds orthographically, see Migliorini and Griffith (1984: 228–30). The orthographical treatises of Trissino and others are gathered in Richardson (1984). For subsequent attempts at spelling reform, see Migliorini and Griffith (1984: 323; 374; 423).

Chapter 2

History of the sound system

0 Introduction

In the development of the the Italian sound system from Latin, the losses have been few, the innovations many. Some of the latter, notably the enrichment of vowel quality distinctions, and the emergence of palatal consonants, have had a major impact on the morphological structure of Italian. For this reason, the following account of Italian historical phonology has a strongly morphological bias, in that it explores in particular those changes which have helped to confer on the language its characteristic morphological shape. Sections 1 to 3 of this chapter summarize the principal phonological developments from Latin[1] to Italian. Thereafter, a number of sound changes which have had a major impact on morphological structure will receive a more detailed investigation.

1 The prosodic system

Prosodic (or *suprasegmental*) phonology is concerned with domains or 'stretches of sounds', greater than the single consonant or vowel segment. Among these are the *syllable*, *stress* (the relative loudness of syllables within some domain – usually the word), and *length* (concerning the relative duration of a vowel or consonant). If we conceive the chain of speech sounds as comprising a series of segmental 'slots', then *long* vowels or consonants might be viewed as those whose articulatory features are spread over more than one such 'slot'.[2]

1.1 The syllable

Of the syllable we need only say, for the moment, that in CL, as in modern Italian, it always comprises a *nucleus* constituted by a vowel, which *may* be preceded by a consonantal *onset*, and *may* be followed by a consonantal *coda*. Clusters of up to three consonants are admitted in the onset. The last consonant of an onset cluster must be a liquid ([**r**] or [**l**]), the first a sibilant ([**z**] or [**s**]), and the middle one an obstruent.[3] In the coda up to two consonants are admitted, but the first must be either a liquid or a nasal. Some examples are: SPLEN-DET 'it shines'; STRIC-TUS 'squeezed'; MULC-TUS 'milked'; PROMPT-SI 'I produced'; FARC-TUS 'stuffed'. The *preferred* syllable structure, in CL as in Italian, and as in a great many other of the world's languages, is *open*, which is to say that there should be no consonant in the coda. This preference is apparent in the fact that, in sequences of a single consonant followed by a vowel (or by a liquid, [**r**] or [**l**], followed by a vowel), the consonant always forms a syllable with the following vowel, never with a preceding vowel (e.g., CL A-MA-BA-TIS 'you loved'; PA-TREM 'father' and not **AM-AB-AT-IS; **PAT-REM/**PATR-EM. We show in sections 8 and 9 below that such preferred syllable structures have played a considerable role in various consonantal changes in Italian.

1.2 Stress

In CL, stress was *proparoxytonic* (i.e., it fell on the the last syllable but two of a word of three or more syllables), unless the penultimate syllable was *heavy* in which case stress was *paroxytonic* (i.e., it fell upon the penultimate syllable of a word). The definition of a heavy syllable is that it contains either a long vowel or a vowel, whether long or short, followed by a consonant. The operation of stress placement can be conveniently illustrated from the following morphological forms (1):

(1)

COL-LI-GO: 'I gather'	COL-**LEC**-TUM 'gathered'	COL-**LE:**-GI: 'I gathered'
A-MAT 'he loves'	A-**MA:**-BAT 'he loved'	A-MA-**BA:**-MUS 'we loved'
A-MANT 'they love'	A-**MAN**-TUR 'they are loved'	
DO-MI-NA 'mistress'	DO-MI-**NA:**-RUM 'of mistresses'	
POR-TA 'door'	POR-**TA:**-RUM 'of doors'	

As a rule, the stressed syllables of Latin words[4] are continued as stressed syllables of Italian words,[5] although their relative position in the word may have altered as a result of other changes. Syncope (the deletion of non-final unstressed vowels, discussed in 4.6.4.1), has made **CO**LLIGO and **DO**MINA into paroxytones (*colgo*; *donna*). A stress pattern almost unknown[6] to Latin is *oxytonic* (last syllable) stress, which has arisen in the history of Italian usually as a result of deletion of a final vowel or a final syllable: AM**A**UIT > Proto-Romance ***a'maw(t)** > *amò* 'he loved'; CIUITATE(M) > OTuscan *cittade* > *città* 'city'; UIRTUTE(M) > OTuscan *virtude* > *virtù* 'virtue'.

1.2.1 Stress in Italian

Latin stress placement was entirely predictable on the basis of phonological information. The position of Italian stress is, in contrast, often impossible to predict without reference to non-phonological information. Practically all that remains of the Latin system is the constraint debarring placement of stress to the 'left' of the antepenultimate syllable (and even this is violated by certain third person plural verb forms, such as *telèfonano* 'they telephone', which will be analysed further in Ch.3: 8.3.3). Otherwise, stress may fall on any syllable from the antepenultimate rightwards, regardless of syllable structure. This new freedom of stress (shared, historically, by all Romance varieties) has allowed the emergence of meaningful distinctions between stress patterns, such as *presentò* 'he presented' vs. *presènto* 'I present', or *càpito* 'I turn up'; *capìto* 'understood' and *capitò* 'he turned up'. However, stress is generally not admitted to the left of the penultimate syllable if that syllable is closed (i.e., if it ends in a consonant). Thus we have *presentò* and *presènto*, but not ***prèsento*. This is a remnant of the CL 'heavy penultimate' rule and, while it is indisputable that the overwhelming majority of Italian words happen to conform to this stress, and that modern Italians tend to assume that this rule operates when they pronounce unfamiliar words, it is questionable whether, in the modern language, this rule constitutes a particularly powerful constraint on stress-placement. After all, violations of this principle are found in what are, historically, loanwords (especially those originally taken from Greek), and in certain placenames (*màndorla* 'almond'; *pòlizza* 'insurance policy'; *còrizza* 'coryza'; *àrista* 'chine of pork'; *Tàranto*; *Lèpanto*; *Àgordo*) but these show no sign of being corrected in favour of the 'normal' pattern.

Italian displays a relationship between stress and syllable structure which is an inversion of that obtaining in CL. Whereas CL stress was predictable partly on the basis of syllable structure, syllable structure in Italian (as, historically, in other Romance varieties) becomes partly predictable from stress, and from certain other aspects of word structure. The modern Italian rule is that *all stressed syllables must be heavy*. An important qualification is that open stressed syllables in oxytones are light before a pause or a vowel (**par-'lɔ** *parlò* 'he spoke'; **par-'lɔ-'aŋ-ke** *parlò anche* 'he also spoke'). Open syllables which were not originally heavy have become heavy by means of 'segment lengthening': **'aː-ma-no** *amano* 'they love'; **'faː-tʃi-le** *facile* 'easy'; **de-'tʃiː-ze-ro** *decisero* 'they decided', etc. The formulation 'segment lengthening', rather than the more traditional 'vowel lengthening', is deliberate, since we shall be suggesting in 8.2 that both lengthening of vowels and lengthening of consonants were historically available to make up the 'weight' of a stressed syllable, and that the type of historical consonant lengthening detectable in proparoxytones such as *fèmmina* 'woman' < FEMINA(M), or after the stressed syllable of oxytones when a consonant follows (e.g., **par-'lɔ** *parlò*, but **par-'lɔb-'bɛː-ne** *parlò bene* 'he spoke well') represents an alternative strategy for the formation of heavy stressed syllables. We shall see below that vowel length, once a partial determinant of stress placement, is now exclusively determined by stress and syllable structure, with long vowels appearing solely in stressed open syllables.

1.3 Length

Distinctions of length (or 'quantity') played a central role in the CL vowel and consonant system, and minimal pairs, distinguished only by the opposition between long and short vowels or consonants, were common (e.g., POPULUS 'people' vs. PO:PULUS 'poplar'; FRICTUS 'rubbed' vs. FRI:CTUS 'fried'; GRADUS 'step' vs. GRADU:S 'steps'; FALLAM 'I shall deceive' vs. FALAM 'scaffolding'; AGER 'field' vs. AGGER 'embankment', etc.). Unlike modern Italian, vowels could be distinctively long or short, irrespective of the structure of the syllable in which they occurred (cf. Allen (1978: 64–77)). Not only are CL long consonants generally preserved intact in Italian (MITTO 'I send' > *metto* 'I put'; PASSU(M) 'step' > *passo*, etc.), but some originally short consonants have become lengthened (e.g., HABEAT 'let him have' > *abbia*), in circumstances which will be explored in 8.2. Preservation of distinctive consonant length is a characteristic which sets Italian (and other central and southern Italian dialects, together with Sardinian), apart from all other modern Romance varieties. Vowel length evolves quite differently. CL differences in vowel length have been lost, but not necessarily without trace, since they have usually been transformed into differences of vowel *aperture* – see 2.1). At some stage *after* the loss of CL vowel length, there appeared a new, phonologically determined, differentiation of vowel length, which is continued into modern Italian, and underlies most Italo-Romance and Gallo-Romance varieties. The new distributional principle for vowel length is that all vowels are short, unless they occur in a stressed and open syllable, in which case they are long. These length variations are especially apparent in the verb stem, which may be stressed or unstressed (Ch.3: 8.1), and where, in some cases, an open-syllable stem may alternate with a closed-syllable stem. Thus the third person present indicative, passato remoto, and imperfect indicative forms of the modern Italian verbs *dire* 'to say'; *valere* 'to be worth'; *tradurre* 'to translate' are (2):

(2)

Stressed Open Syllable	Stressed Closed Syllable	Unstressed Syllable
'diː-tʃe	**'dis-se**	**di-'tʃeː-va**
'vaː-le	**'val-se**	**va-'leː-va**
tra-'duː-tʃe	**tra-'dus-se**	**tra-du-'tʃeː-va**

This distinction between the long vowels of stressed open syllables and the short vowels of all other syllables plays a particularly important role in the history of Gallo-Romance and Italo-Romance vocalism, since the long vowel of open syllables is often subject to further differentiation (particularly diphthongization) with respect to its short counterparts. A putative case in point, whose nature and origin will be reviewed at length in 4.2, are the diphthongs [**jɛ**] and [**wɔ**], which have arisen in stressed open syllables in Italian, as in many Gallo-Romance dialects (e.g., Italian *muore* 'dies' vs. *morto* 'dead', *moriva* 'died'; *siede* 'sits' vs. *seduto* 'sat'; *uomo* 'man' vs. *omino* 'little man', etc.).

2 Vowels

2.1 Loss of vowel length, and expansion of aperture distinctions

The CL vowel system comprises five vowels, each of which can be distinctively long or short, so that there is a '5 × 2' vocalic system (3):

(3)

	BACK				FRONT
HIGH	**u/uː**				**i/iː**
MID		**o/oː**		**e/eː**	
LOW			**a/aː**		

Latin vowel length has been lost in all Romance varieties. At one extreme, Sardinian (supposedly with certain dialects of southern Basilicata) has lost vowel length distinctions without trace, with long and short vowels simply merging: e.g., MU:RU(M) 'wall' > **'muːru**, CRUCE(M) 'cross' > **'ruːke**, SO:LA(M) 'alone' > **'soːla**, ROTA(M) > **'rɔːta**, CARU(M) FEL 'gall' > **'fɛːle**, UE:RA(M) 'true' > **'vɛːra**, NIUE(M) 'snow' > **'niːve**, FI:LU(M) 'thread' > **'fiːlu**, etc. The vowels of Romanian (and, apparently, of a tiny pocket of southern Basilicata, near Potenza) have followed the 'Sardinian' development so far as [**a**], and back vowels, are concerned. The front vowels of Romanian continue to distinguish original long and short realizations, as in Italian.[7] Italian, in common with the great majority of Romance dialects, has lost only the distinction between Latin long and short [**a**]. The other vowel length differences have been transformed into differences of vowel quality, with an attendant expansion of the range of vowel qualities.

Latin short vowels were pronounced with a more open articulation than their long counterparts; (cf. Allen (1978: 48f.)). In the vowel system historically underlying Italian, the short vowels (other than the already maximally open [**a**]) enhanced these aperture distinctions, so that, while long [**iː**] and [**uː**] retained their quality, short [**i**] and [**u**] opened to [**e**] and [**o**], thereby *merging* with the reflexes of Latin long [**eː**] and [**oː**]. Short [**e**] and [**o**], however, assumed a low mid articulation ([**ɛ**] and [**ɔ**]), in stressed syllables. The result was a system with *seven* vowels (4):

(4)

	BACK						FRONT
HIGH	**u**						**i**
HIGH MID		**o**				**e**	
LOW MID			**ɔ**		**ɛ**		
LOW				**a**			

These changes can be seen in: MU:RU(M) 'wall' > **ˈmuːro**, LU:CTU(M) > 'mourning' > **ˈlutto**, UO:LUIT 'he wanted' > **ˈvolle**, SURDU(M) 'deaf' > **ˈsordo**, *ROTA(M) 'wheel' > **ˈrwɔːta**, PORTO 'I bear' > **ˈpɔrto**, CA:RU(M) 'dear' > **ˈkaːro**, CAPUT 'head' > **ˈkaːpo,** UENIT 'he comes' > **ˈvjɛːne**, PERDIT 'he loses' > **ˈpɛrde**, UE:NIT 'he came' > **ˈvenne**, DICTU(M) 'said' > **ˈdetto**, DI:CIT 'he says' > **ˈdiːtʃe,** UI:XIT 'he lived' > **ˈvisse**. The same seven-vowel system probably underlies the modern vowel system of Sicilian (with Calabrian and Salentino), where [**e**] and [**o**] have been further raised, to merge with [**i**] and [**u**] (e.g., Sicilian **ˈmuːru**, **ˈluttu**, **ˈsurdu**, **ˈdiːtʃi**, **ˈvissi**, **ˈdittu**).

2.2 Loss of Latin diphthongs

Of the three Latin diphthongs, Æ [**ai**], Œ [**oi**], AU [**aw**], only the last survived into Italo-Romance (its later monophthongization as [**ɔ**] in Italian will be discussed in 4.4). All three were already subject to occasional monophthongization in the classical period, especially in rustic speech (cf. Allen (1978: 60–2)). In Proto-Romance the diphthongs [**ai**] and [**oi**] had merged, respectively, with reflexes of Latin short [**e**] and long [**eː**]. Thus, CÆLU(M) > **ˈtʃɛːlo** 'sky', and PŒNA(M) > **ˈpeːna** 'grief'.

2.3 Stress and vowel quality

The Latin '5 × 2' vowel system has been resolved as a seven vowel system only in *stressed* syllables. In unstressed syllables, [**ɛ**] and [**ɔ**] do not appear. Rather, short O and E merge with their long counterparts, to give [**o**] and [**e**]: e.g., PORTAT and PORTATIS > **'pɔrta** 'he carries', but **por'ta:te** 'you carry'; PERDIT and PERDEBAT > **'pɛrde** 'he loses', but **per'de:va** 'he lost'. The result is a system of five unstressed vowels: [**u**] [**o**] [**a**] [**e**] [**i**]. This differential development of stressed and unstressed vowels is amplified in the subsequent history of Tuscan: while the vocalism of stressed syllables is enriched by the emergence, in stressed open syllables, of the diphthongs [**jɛ**] and [**wɔ**] from [**ɛ**] and [**ɔ**] (see 4.2), the range of unstressed vowels *tends* to be further reduced to four or even three, in a variety of ways, to be examined in 4.6.1.

3 Consonants

3.1 Loss of [h]

The list of phonological 'losses' in the evolution of the consonant system is brief indeed. The one complete loss is that of Latin [**h**]. This sound, already subject to deletion in the classical period (cf. Allen (1978: 43f.)), has disappeared without any trace in all Romance languages. Thus, in Italian, HABEBAT > *aveva* 'he had'; PER HOC > *però* 'however', etc. The consonant [**h**] may have been reintroduced in later loans from Germanic, but even so, it subsequently disappeared from all Italo-Romance varieties: e.g., ***'haŋka** > *anca* 'hip'; ***'haspa** > *aspa* 'reel'. It does not appear in learnèd borrowings from Latin (or Greek): e.g., HORRIBILEM 'horrible' and HABITARE 'to dwell' are borrowed as **or'ri:bile** and **abi'ta:re**.

3.2 Emergence of the voiced fricative [v]

Latin possessed the voiceless fricative [**f**], but lacked its voiced counterpart [**v**] (fricatives are consonants uttered by expelling air between speech organs, in this case the lips and the teeth, which are brought close together, thereby producing turbulence). There are two major sources of [**v**] in Romance. One of them is Latin [**w**] in syllable-initial position (e.g., UIUO > *vivo* 'I live' – a development to be discussed in 8.1); the other is Latin word-internal intervocalic [**b**], which gave [**v**] in common Proto-Romance, probably via the fricative [**β**]: FABA(M) > *fava* 'bean'; HABEBAT > *aveva* 'he had'; DEBET > *deve* 'he must'. In the perfect tense of the verb, however, intervocalic U was deleted; AMAUI > *amai* 'I loved'; AMAUISTI > *amasti* 'you loved'. Latin word-initial [**b**] remains intact in Italian; *barba* 'beard'; *battere* 'to beat'; *bene* 'well'; *bere* 'to drink', etc., are examples. The Italian forms *bevo* 'I drink' < BIBO; *vivo* 'I live' < UIUO and *serva* 'maid'< SERUA(M); *erba* 'grass' < HERBA(M), illustrate how the outcomes of Latin [**b**] and [**w**] coincide in word-internal intervocalic position, but remain distinct elsewhere. There are occasional occurrences of [**rb**], rather than [**rv**]: NERUU(M) > *nerbo* 'sinew'; SERUAT > *serba* 'he keeps'.

3.3 Postconsonantal [l] > [j]

In virtually all Italo-Romance varieties, the liquid consonant [**l**] has become [**j**] when preceded by a tautosyllabic consonant (i.e., by a consonant that occurs in the same syllable – cf. 8.2) (5).

(5)

Proto-Romance	Italian	
***ˈplenu**	**ˈpjeːno**	‘full’
***ˈtɛmplu**	**ˈtɛmpjo**	‘temple’
***ˈdoplu**	**ˈdoppjo**	‘double’
***ˈblaŋku**	**ˈbjaŋko**	‘white’
***ˈflore**	**ˈfjoːre**	‘flower’
***koɱˈflare**	**goɱˈfjaːre**	‘swell’
***ˈklaru**	**ˈkjaːro**	‘clear’
***ˈklave**	**ˈkjaːve**	‘key’
***ˈglanda**	**ˈgjanda**	‘acorn’

The cluster [**sl**] is resolved as [**skl**], which then yields [**skj**]: ***ˈslavu** > ***ˈsklavu** > *schiavo* ‘slave’. The incidence of original consonant + [**l**] sequences is augmented by syncope of unstressed vowels (see 4.6.4.1), notably in the originally diminutive suffix -ULUS. Note that *[**tl**] > [**kl**]:

(6)

CL	Proto-Romance	Italian	
FIBULA(M)	***ˈfibla**	**ˈfibbja**	‘brooch’
OCULU(M)	***ˈɔklu**	**ˈɔkkjo**	‘eye’
UNGULA(M)	***ˈuŋgla**	**ˈuŋgja**	‘nail’
UETULU(M)	***ˈvɛklu**	**ˈvɛkkjo**	‘old’

The change of postconsonantal [**l**] to yod is relatively minor, since it does not give rise to morphological alternations. It attracts attention because it comes close to constituting the sole common and distinctive characteristic of Italo-Romance dialects. But the phenomenon is also represented, in various phonetic forms, outside Italy (although only in Italo-Romance is the palatal realization of [**l**] attested after *all* preceding consonants in the same syllable); and within the Italo-Romance domain, there are dialects of north-eastern Lombardy, and of Abruzzo where postconsonantal [**l**] survives. In the relevant parts of

Abruzzo, while the change has taken place in the original clusters [**kl**] and [**gl**], [l] has been maintained after other consonants: e.g., Bellante **cɛf** 'key' < *'**klave**; '**viccə** 'old' < *'**vɛklu**; **blɛŋk** 'white' < *'**blanku**.

The mechanism of this development is explored in detail, from a comparative Romance perspective, by Repetti and Tuttle (1987), who argue that the change of postconsonantal [l] to [**j**] (via a postulated stage *[**ʎ**]) was originally limited to consonant clusters comprising velar + lateral (i.e., just [**gl**] and [**kl**]). This initial phase of the development is conserved in some modern varieties of Abruzzese and is apparent in OPaduan and medieval Romagnol and Marchigiano. Elsewhere, it extended to other consonantal environments.

The intervocalic cluster [**gl**] has sometimes yielded [**ʎʎ**], rather than [**ggj**] in Tuscan: STRIG(I)LE(M) > '**striʎʎa** 'currycomb'; UIG(I)LARE > **veʎ'ʎaːre** 'to stay awake'; TRIGLA(M) > '**triʎʎa** 'red mullet'; TEG(U)LA(M) > '**teʎʎa** 'baking tray' (also '**teggja**). Castellani (1954) assumes that the original Tuscan development was [**ggj**], and that the emergence of [**ʎʎ**] is a hypercorrection motivated by the merger, in less prestigious Tuscan varieties, of both [**ʎʎ**] and [**ggj**], yielding the voiced palatal affricate [**ɟɟ**] (e.g., '**fiɟɟa** < '**fiʎʎa** 'daughter'). On this account, speakers purportedly tended to 'correct' *every* incidence of [**ɟɟ**] in favour of [**ʎʎ**], regardless of its origin. A different view is that of Repetti and Tuttle (1987: 81), who opine that [**ʎʎ**] is the result of phonetic changes affecting [**g**] before [**ʎ**].

3.4 Emergence of the palatal and affricate consonants

Palatal consonants are those articulated by making contact between the body of the tongue and the hard palate; affricate consonants are those produced by completely blocking the flow of air through the mouth, then gradually releasing the air, so that friction, or 'turbulence' is produced. Although rather different in nature ('palatal' refers to a point of articulation, and 'affricate' to a manner of articulation), it is appropriate to discuss them together here because of the common elements in their origin in Italo-Romance. Latin had neither type of consonant, although it is probable that, before a vowel, what was written 'I' was pronounced as a 'yod' – that is, a palatal glide [**j**] produced without actual contact between tongue body and palate: IAM = *__jam__ 'already'; PEIUS = *__pejjus__ 'worse', etc. In contrast, all Romance varieties have, or have had at some time in their history, a range of palatal and affricate consonants, which arose in Proto-Romance principally where a consonant was immediately followed by a yod. The emergence of this yod in Romance will be discussed in 5.2. In most Romance varieties, original velar consonants ([**k**] or [**g**]) have become palatal consonants wherever they were immediately followed by front vowels ([**i**], [**e**] or [**ɛ**]): e.g., CENA(M) > *'**kena** > '**ʧeːna** 'dinner'.

The palatal and affricate consonants of modern Italian are the following. Palatals: [**ɲ**] (e.g., in *gnocco* 'dumpling'), [**ʎ**] (e.g., in *gli* 'to him'), [**ʃ**] (e.g., in *scelto* 'chosen'). Affricates: [**ʦ**] (e.g., in *alza* 'he lifts'), [**ʣ**] (e.g., in *orzo* 'barley'). Dental-alveolar[8] affricates: [**ʧ**] (e.g., in *vince* 'he wins'), [**ʤ**] (e.g., in *sorge* 'it rises') The emergence of these palatals and affricates, which accounts not only for the distinction between, say, **'lɛggo** 'I read' and **'lɛdʤi** 'you read', but, ultimately, for that between **'vɛŋgo** 'I come' and **'vjɛːni** 'you come' (see Ch.3: 8.4.1), will be discussed in section 6.

3.5 Voicing

'Voiced' consonants are those, like [**g**], [**d**], [**b**], [**v**], etc., which are articulated with vibration of the vocal chords, and often with less muscular tension than their voiceless counterparts; 'voiceless' consonants, such as [**k**], [**t**], [**p**], [**f**], etc., lack such vibration, and often involve stronger muscular activity. When any consonant is situated between two vowels it is said to be 'intervocalic'.

Most Latin voiceless intervocalic consonants appear to have survived intact into Italian: *amato* 'loved'< AMATU(M), *ape* 'bee' < APE(M), *dico* 'I say' < DICO. Yet a handful of exceptions, such as *strada* 'street' < STRATA(M), *riva* 'bank' < RIPA(M), *lago* 'lake' < LACU(M), display voicing, and we shall see in section 7 that such cases are just the tip of a very large historical phonological iceberg.

An innovation in the Romance phonological inventory, almost entirely absent from CL (but see Allen (1978: 45f.)), is [**z**], the voiced counterpart of the sibilant [**s**]. The sound [**z**] arises in all Italo-Romance varieties as an assimilated, contextually conditioned, phonetic variant of [**s**] occurring in the environment of a following voiced consonant: cf. Italian **'zbatto** *sbatto* 'I slam' vs. **'spakko** *spacco* 'I split', or **sten'taːto** *stentato* 'hard earned' vs. **zden'taːto** *sdentato* 'toothless'. But in northern Italo-Romance dialects, as in the history of Gallo-Romance and Ibero-Romance dialects generally, [**s**] was regularly voiced to [**z**] in intervocalic position (e.g., Venetian **'naːzo** 'nose'; **'kaːza** 'house', etc.). This intervocalic [**z**] is alien to central and southern Italian dialects, where [**s**] is maintained (e.g., Tuscan **'naːso**; **'kaːsa**), but it appears in some Tuscan (and therefore in Italian) words, such as **'kjɛːza** *chiesa* 'church'. Its origins in Italian, discussed in 7.2, are mainly to be sought in borrowing from northern Italian dialects.

4 Major vowel changes

4.1 Major vowel changes, and their morphological effects

The historical evolution of the Italian vowel system has left its mark on the modern language in the form of extensive patterns of morphological alternation (Ch.3: 0.2), notably in the verb. The following verb forms recapitulate virtually all of the major historical changes affecting vowels, namely diphthongization, monophthongization of [**aw**], anaphonesis, reduction and deletion of unstressed vowels; we give the present indicative and past participle of the verbs *perdere* 'to lose', *portare* 'to carry', *tenere* 'to hold', *morire* 'to die', *udire* 'to hear', *stringere* 'to squeeze', (*gittare* 'to throw'), *dovere* 'to owe'; in (7)–(14), the infinitive, first person singular future, and third person singular *passato remoto*, of *parlare* 'to speak' in (15), and the infinitive and first person singular future of *sapere* 'to know' in (16). The forms given in parentheses are now considered archaic.

(7)	(8)	(9)	(10)
'pɛrdo	'pɔrto	'tɛŋgo	'mwɔːjo
'pɛrdi	'pɔrti	'tjɛːni	'mwɔːri
'pɛrde	'pɔrta	'tjɛːne	'mwɔːre
per'djaːmo	por'tjaːmo	te'njaːmo	mo'rjaːmo
per'deːte	por'taːte	te'neːte	mo'riːte
'pɛrdono	'pɔrtano	'tɛŋgono	'mwɔːjono

'pɛrso	por'taːto	te'nuːto	'mɔrto

(11)	(12)	(13)	(14)
'ɔːdo	'striŋgo	'ʤɛtto	'deːvo
'ɔːdi	'striɲʤi	'ʤɛtti	'deːvi
'ɔːde	'striɲʤe	'ʤɛtta	'deːve
u'djaːmo	striɲ'ʤaːmo	(ʤit'tjaːmo)	dob'bjaːmo
u'diːte	striɲ'ʤeːte	(ʤit'taːte)	do'veːte
'ɔːdono	'striŋgono	'ʤɛttano	'deːvono

u'diːto	'stretto	(ʤit'taːto)	do'vuːto

(15)	(16)
par'laːre	**sa'peːre**
parle'rɔ	**sa'prɔ**
par'lɔ	

4.2 Diphthongization of low mid vowels

Examples 7–10 illustrate the major lines of development of the mid vowels. The low mid vowels [**ɛ**] and [**ɔ**] appear only in stressed syllables. In *open* syllables, these vowels were subject to a process of diphthongization, involving the production of a palatal glide [**j**] before [**ɛ**] and a labial glide [**w**] before [**ɔ**]. This development is apparent also in **'pjɛː-de** 'foot' < ***'pɛ-de**; **'fjɛː-le** 'gall' < ***'fɛ-le**; **'vwɔː-le** 'he wants' < ***'vɔ-le**; **'bwɔː-na** 'good' < ***'bɔ-na**, etc. The effects of this STRESSED OPEN SYLLABLE DIPHTHONGIZATION (henceforth, SOSD) are also observable (17) in many Gallo-Romance dialects (e.g., French, and the Gallo-Italian dialects of Emilia, Liguria and the Po Plain). In some Gallo-Romance varieties, the original diphthongs have become monophthongized giving [**e**] (or [**i**]) and [**ø**].

(17)

Proto-Romance	Italian	Milanese	
***'fɛ-le**	**'fjɛː-le**	**fel**	'gall'
***'pɛ-tra**	**'pjɛː-tra**	**'peː-dra**	'stone'
***'mɛː-le**	**'mjɛː-le**	**mel**	'honey'
***'sɛt-te**	**'sɛt-te**	**sɛt**	'seven'
***'pɛl-le**	**'pɛl-le**	**pɛl**	'skin'
***'nɔ-va**	**'nwɔː-va**	**'nøː-va**	'new'
***'kɔ-re**	**'kwɔː-re**	**kør**	'heart'
***'fɔ-ra**	**'fwɔː-ri**	**'føː-ra**	'outside'
***'kɔr-nu**	**'kɔr-no**	**kɔrn**	'horn'
***'ɔs-su**	**'ɔs-so**	**ɔs**	'bone'

The origin of SOSD is one of the most controversial and complex issues in the historical phonology of Italian, and as such deserves detailed examination. Two major lines of explanation have been offered. One ascribes the diphthongization to a development of phonetically lengthened stressed vowels which is 'unconditioned' or 'spontaneous', in the sense that it is a change naturally affecting stressed vowels in open syllables which is not triggered either by following or by preceding sounds; the other sees the origin of SOSD in an assimilatory phonetic process called metaphony. The balance of evidence, as we shall see below, favours the latter, metaphonic, explanation. To anticipate the elements of the argument, we may say that SOSD is likely to be of metaphonic origin because the diphthong is identical to the type of diphthong produced by metaphony, and because metaphony, like SOSD, seems originally to have been limited to open syllables.

The view that SOSD is a matter of spontaneous diphthongization is championed, albeit from very different perspectives, by Castellani (1962; 1967; 1970a; 1970b), who claims that SOSD arose in Tuscany independently of any external influence, and by Wartburg (1967), who sees the diphthongization as spontaneous, but due to the influence of Germanic speech habits upon Romance. The 'spontaneous' accounts seem to be supported by the fact that, in Gallo-Romance dialects, the *high* mid vowels [**e**] and [**o**] are also subject to unconditioned diphthongization when they occur in stressed open syllables. But the principal objection to linking diphthongization of high mid vowels with SOSD, articulated particularly by Schürr (1980: 19–36; 142–4), is that diphthongization of high mid vowels gives rise to *falling* diphthongs,[9] that is, diphthongs that decrease in loudness as they are uttered, such as [**ei**] and [**ou**] (e.g., **ˈseira** 'evening' <***ˈse-ra**; **meis** 'month' <***ˈme-se**; **fjour** 'flour' <***ˈflo-re**; **ˈsoula** 'alone' <***ˈso-la**); in contrast, the diphthongs [**jɛ**] and [**wɔ**] derived from low mid vowels are *rising*, i.e., they *increase* in loudness as they are uttered. And while high mid vowel diphthongization and SOSD often coexist in Gallo-Italian dialects, in Tuscan *only* SOSD occurs.

Schürr has focused instead on the fact that the rising diphthongs are phonetically identical to the output of *metaphony* of low mid vowels. Metaphony is a phonetic assimilatory process (cf. Ch.1: 5.3) involving total or partial raising of stressed vowels in anticipation of following unstressed high vowels [**i**] or [**u**]. There are good reasons to ascribe SOSD to a metaphonic origin, since metaphony appears originally to have been present in virtually all Italo-Romance dialects. Metaphony of low mid vowels appears to have yielded initially a rising diphthong [**jɛ**] or [**wɔ**] – later monophthongized as [**e**] and [**o**] in some dialects. Less commonly (cf. Maiden (1987)), stressed [**a**] also underwent metaphonic raising (usually to give [**ɛ**]). The following noun/adjective and verbal paradigms (18) display a typical central Italian pattern of metaphony of mid vowels (see also Ch.5: 2.3.1.2); metaphony occurs before unstressed [**i**] and [**u**], but not before [**a**], [**e**] or [**o**].

(18)

	Sg.	Pl.	
M.	'su:lu	'su:li	'alone'
F.	'so:la	'so:le	

M.	'ni:ru	'ni:ri	'black'
F.	'ne:ra	'ne:re	

M.	'grwɔssu	'grwɔssi	'large'
F.	'grɔssa	'grɔsse	

M.	a'pjɛrtu	a'pjɛrti	'open'
F.	a'pɛrta	a'pɛrte	

1Sg.	2Sg.	
'korro	'kurri	'run'
've:do	'vi:di	'see'
'mɔ:ro	'mwɔ:ri	'die'
'pɛrdo	'pjɛrdi	'lose'

A further similarity between SOSD and metaphony is their *asymmetry*. In most of Tuscany, with the exception of the province of Arezzo in the south-east, and Lunigiana and Garfagnana in the north, SOSD affects principally, or exclusively, the front vowel [ɛ], but not [ɔ]. Rohlfs (1966: 106; 134) and Schürr (1980: 52) concur that the absence of SOSD of [ɔ] is primitive, i.e., that it is not the case that this vowel was first diphthongized then somehow became, again, a monophthong. And there is reason to suspect that the [wɔ] which has become established in literary Italian is not indigenous to Tuscany, but has been taken from outside – a view corroborated by the hypercorrect extension of the diphthong, in some medieval texts (cf. Rohlfs (1966: 136)), into environments where it could not have occurred as a result of regular phonetic change, such as closed syllables. A tendency for [ɔ] not to undergo SOSD is also apparent in some Alpine dialects (see Maiden (1988a: 13–16)). A similar asymmetry appears in the northern Umbrian dialect of Città di Castello as described by Bianchi (1888), with SOSD for front vowels, but SOSD of [ɔ] restricted to (original) metaphonic environments. In some dialects (e.g., in parts of Salento, and in the Garfagnana region of Tuscany, metaphony is restricted principally to [**ɛ**]).[10] There appears, by the way, to be no Italo-Romance variety in which SOSD affects [**ɔ**] but not [**ɛ**].

Thus far, the Tuscan diphthongs are consistent with a metaphonic origin. But there are some major apparent inconsistencies: Tuscan SOSD shows no correlation with following unstressed [**i**] and [**u**], the conditioning environments for metaphony: the Tuscan diphthongs occur in stressed open syllables, regardless of the nature of the final vowel. Moreover, metaphony is generally believed to operate regardless of the structure (closed or open) of the stressed syllable, but SOSD is, of course, restricted to *open* syllables.[11] To account for the appearance of SOSD outside metaphonic environments, Lausberg (1965: 248) invokes analogy: forms such as the feminine *nuova*, *nuove* 'new' represent analogical extensions of metaphonic diphthongs which were at first present only in the corresponding masculines, whose final vowels (-**u** was originally a masculine singular inflection) would have triggered metaphony: *nuovo*, *nuovi* < ***ˈnwɔːvu ˈnwɔːvi**. This hypothesis is supported by the fact that the diphthong is *absent* from some morphologically invariant words in which the conditioning environment for metaphony was never present, such as *bene* **ˈbɛːne** 'well' and *nove* **ˈnɔːve** 'nine' (< CL BENE and NOUEM). It is perfectly plausible that morphological analogy *contributed* to generalization of the diphthong (see Maiden (1988a: 26f.)), but this hypothesis fails to account for the *presence* of the diphthong in many words which would never have possessed metaphonically conditioned diphthongs to begin with, for lack of original inflectional forms containing the conditioning vowels (e.g., *dietro* 'behind' < ***de rɛtro**; *ruota* 'wheel' < ***ˈrɔta**).

A worse defect is that Lausberg's account offers no explanation of the apparent expulsion of the metaphonic diphthong from closed syllables.[12] Schürr (1980) seeks to overcome this problem by appeal to the principle of *syllabic isochrony* – a general shortening of long vowels in closed syllables, and a lengthening of short vowels in stressed open syllables, purportedly originating in central Gaul. The distinction between the metaphonic diphthongs and the corresponding monophthongs was supposedly reanalysed as a distinction between long and short vowels, and the diphthongs (counting as 'long' vowels) were consequently expelled from closed syllables, while the monophthongs [**ɛ**] and [**ɔ**] (counting as 'short' vowels) were ousted from all stressed open syllables in favour of the diphthongs. A major plank of Schürr's argument is the existence of geographically 'lateral' dialects of Tuscany, namely medieval Aretine[13] and central Garfagnana, in which the diphthong is restricted to open syllables, yet occurs in a predominantly metaphonic environment (e.g., OAretine *vene* 'he comes' vs. *vieni* 'you come'; *-uolo* (suffix < -***ɔlu**) vs. *sola* 'sole of shoe' (< ***sɔla**)). And the dialect of Città di Castello has generalized [**jɛ**] to all open syllables, but [**wɔ**], while restricted to open syllables, still occurs exclusively in originally metaphonic environments. For Schürr, these dialects conserve a transitional phase in the passage from SOSD to metaphony.

But why should original diphthongization in closed syllables, supposedly indigenous, and therefore extensively represented in the language, ever have become 'intolerable' in the face of what, after all, was supposed to be an alien innovation?[14] In fact, the evidence of northern Italian dialects is that SOSD and metaphonic diphthongization in closed syllables were never incompatible. For example, in the archaic Gallo-Italian dialect of Trecchina (spoken in Basilicata, near the Gulf of Policastro), we have SOSD (**'fuora** 'outside', **'tiene** 'he holds') and also diphthongization in closed syllables before palatal consonants and in original metaphonic environments (**'muorti** 'dead', **a'pierti** 'open').[15]

The problem of reconciling SOSD with metaphony may have a surprisingly simple solution: the diphthongs are indeed of metaphonic origin, but are restricted to open syllables because metaphony was itself originally restricted to open syllables. In most dialects having SOSD (but not in Tuscan) metaphony subsequently penetrated closed syllables as well. The Tuscan dialects which Schürr identifies as a transitional phase in the emergence of SOSD may in fact be seen as conserving original open syllable metaphony. There are no grounds to postulate that, in these dialects, metaphony was ever present in the closed syllables. There are various other dialects in which metaphony shows clear signs of having been restricted to open syllables;[16] such restrictions on low mid vowel metaphony occur in parts of Puglia (e.g., Torremaggiore and Lesina),[17] and of Lazio.[18] In parts of the Gargano promontory,[19] metaphony of high mid vowels by [**u**] appears to be sporadically blocked in closed syllables. Significantly, no Italian dialect has yet come to light in which metaphony occurs in closed, but not in open, syllables.

Restriction to open syllables may, after all, be consistent with a metaphonic origin, but how are we to explain the generalization of the diphthong outside the metaphonic environment? A valuable clue is furnished by a number of northern Italian dialects, in areas of Piedmont and Lombardy roughly bounded by Lake Maggiore, Cuneo, Turin, Milan and Biella: here there is evidence[20] that the spread of the diphthong took place by a gradual simplification in the conditioning environment for the metaphony, such that diphthongization extended from the environment of high *non-mid* vowels [**i**] and [**u**] to that of high vowels *in general* (so as to include the unstressed mid vowels [**e**] and [**o**]). The resulting wholesale replacement of [**ɛ**] and [**ɔ**] by the diphthongs then provided a model for generalization of the diphthongs before unstressed [**a**] as well. In these dialects, SOSD shows a clear sensitivity to the quality of the final atonic vowel, such that it occurs regularly in the original environment for metaphony yet also, rather less consistently, before [**e**] and [**o**]. But it is often absent before the most open of the unstressed vowels, [**a**]. In the Val Mesolcina, for example,[21] we find: [**e**] – a regular reflex in these dialects of an original diphthong [**wɔ**] – before original [**i**] and [**u**] (**fek** 'fire' < *'**fwɔku**; **nef** 'nine' < *'**nwɔvu**); frequent but inconsistent diphthongization before original final [**e**] and [**o**] (**mef** 'he moves' and 'I move' < *'**mɔve** and *'**mɔvo**; **pjof** *or* **pjef** 'it rains' <*'**plɔve**); frequent absence of the diphthong before original [**a**] ('**rɔːda** 'wheel' < *'**rɔta**; '**mɔːla** 'whetstone' < *'**mɔla**; '**ʃkɔːla** or '**ʃkeːla** 'school' < *'**skɔla**). While no particular sensitivity to unstressed vowel quality is detectable in Tuscan SOSD, it is the case that the majority of exceptions to SOSD found in Tuscan dialects (see Rohlfs (1966: 103f.) and Castellani (1962)) appear before [**e**], [**o**] and [**a**]: e.g., '**bɛːne** 'well'; '**ɛːra** 'he was'; '**mɛːle** 'honey'; '**fɛːle** 'gall'; '**sɛːde** 'he sits'; '**sɛːmo** 'we are'; '**sɛːte** 'you are'; '**sɛːpe** 'hedge'; '**vɛːne** 'he comes', etc.

This fact, taken with the Gallo-Romance evidence, supports the view that SOSD originated as a gradual generalization of the conditioning environment for open syllable low mid vowel metaphony. Given the presence, to a greater or lesser degree, of metaphony in virtually every other mainland Italian dialect, it is inherently plausible that the metaphonic process might also have been indigenous to Tuscany. But the question which, given the available evidence, can only remain open, is whether SOSD evolved in Tuscany, or emerged in northern[22] or other dialects, for its effects then to be imported into Tuscany.

4.3 Other developments of the low mid vowels

When immediately followed by a vowel other than [**i**], the diphthongs [**jɛ**] and [**wɔ**] were monophthongized in Tuscan as [**i**] and [**u**], whence the alternations observable between these vowels and diphthongs in the modern possessive adjectives: *mio mia mie* vs. *miei* 'mine'; *tuo tua tue* vs. *tuoi* 'your'. Also *bue* 'ox' vs. *buoi* 'oxen' < ***bwɔe**, ***bwɔi**, and the first person singular pronoun *io* < ***jɛo** < EGO.

Romance [**ɔ**] from Latin short O was regularly subject in Tuscan to raising to [**o**] before a nasal occurring within the same syllable: '**pon-te** 'bridge' < PONTE(M); '**kon-tro** 'against' < CONTRA; '**soɲ-ɲo** 'dream' < SOMNIU(M); '**oɲ-ɲi** 'every' < OMNE(M); '**kom-pra** 'he buys' < COMPARAT, etc. The only instances of [**ɔ**] before a syllable-final nasal appear before [**nn**]: '**dɔnna** 'lady'; '**gɔnna** 'skirt'.

4.4 The evolution of [aw]

Example 11 above ('**ɔːdo**, '**ɔːdi**, etc., from Latin AUDIO, AUDIS, etc.), and the perfect tense form in 15 (**par'lɔ** from PARABOLAUIT), illustrate the evolution of the Latin diphthong [**aw**] as [ɔ]. In the dialects of northern and central Italy, this sound has been monophthongized, yielding in *stressed* syllables the back round low mid vowel [ɔ]: **'ɔːro** 'gold' < AURU(M); **'kɔːsa** 'thing' < CAUSA(M); **'ɔːka** 'goose' < ***'awka**; **'tɔːro** 'bull' < TAURU(M), etc. Comparative and internal evidence indicates that this monophthongization was of relatively late date, because:

(i) The diphthong persists in many Italo-Romance dialects from the Abruzzi and northern Campania southwards (e.g., Campanian **'tawru**) as well as in Romanian, Rhaeto-Romance, Occitan and Portuguese.[23]
(ii) In those Romance varieties, such as northern Italian dialects, in which intervocalic voiceless consonants were voiced (cf. section 7), voicing did not occur after [ɔ] derived from [**aw**]: e.g., northern Italo-Romance **'poːka** 'not much' < PAUCA(M). This indicates that the (semiconsonantal) glide [**w**] was still present at the time when consonants were being voiced, and blocked the process.
(iii) [ɔ] derived from [**aw**] is not subject to, and therefore must postdate, diphthongization of [ɔ] (cf. **'lwɔːgo** 'place' < LOCU(M) vs. **'pɔːko** 'not much' < PAUCU(M)).
(iv) Monophthongization affects not only Latin [**aw**], but also new instances of [**aw**] arising from other sources in Proto-Romance: e.g., **pa'rɔːla** 'word' < ***pa'rawla** < PARABOLA(M).

In unstressed syllables, [**aw**] yielded [**o**], and sometimes [**u**]: *orecchia* 'ear' < AURICULA(M); *udite* 'you hear' < AUDITE; *uccello* 'bird' <***aw'kɛllu**. Forms such as *ascoltare* 'to listen' < AUSCULTARE and *agosto* 'August' < AUGUSTU(M), reflect an occasional tendency (cf. Tekavčić (1980 I: 78)), for unstressed [**aw**] to become [**a**] before a following [**u**].

4.5 Anaphonesis

The stressed vowel of the past participle *stretto* (example 12 above) reflects the regular phonetic development, namely [**e**], of Latin short I (< STRICTU(M)). In contrast, forms like the present indicative first person singular *stringo* (< STRINGO) show [**i**] instead of the expected [**e**]. *Stringo* is an example of what Castellani (1952=1980) has termed 'anaphonesis' ('anafonesi'), a peculiarity of northern and western Tuscan – and particularly of Florence and region[24] – such that the reflexes of Latin [**eː**] and [**i**], and of [**oː**] and [**u**] appear, respectively, as [**i**] and [**u**], rather than as the regular [**e**] and [**o**] (e.g., *lingua* 'tongue' < LINGUA(M); *unghia* 'fingernail' < UNGULA(M)). Anaphonesis appears very consistently in the environment of a nasal followed by a velar consonant; in all of the following examples, a short [**i**] or [**u**] was present in CL:[25] *vinco* 'I win'; *tinca* 'tench'; *tingo* 'I dye'; *fingo* 'I feign'; *cingo* 'I gird'; *spingo* 'I push'; *ungo* 'I grease'; *pungo* 'I prick'; *mungo* 'I milk'; *giungo* 'I join'; *fungo* 'mushroom'; *giunco* 'reed'; *chiunque* 'whoever'; *dunque* 'so'; *lungo* 'long', etc.). Front vowel anaphonesis, with [**i**] for [**e**], also appears before [**ɲ**] and [**ʎ**] derived from Proto-Romance [**nj**] and [**lj**] (e.g., *gramigna* 'couch grass'; *famiglia* 'family'; *miglio* 'millet'; *striglia* 'currycomb'; *piglia* 'he takes'; *consiglio* 'counsel'; *tiglio* 'lime tree'; *triglia* 'red mullet'; *ciglia* 'eyelashes') and before the consonant cluster [**skj**] (e.g., *mischia* 'he mixes'; *fischia* 'he whistles'; *ischio* 'holm oak'; *vischio* 'mistletoe'). There is, however, no anaphonesis of back vowels in these environments (e.g., *vergogna* 'shame'; *moglie* 'wife'). Forms such as *grongo* 'conger eel', *tronco* 'trunk', *carbonchio* 'carbuncle', exempt from anaphonesis, possibly indicate a lesser susceptibility of back vowels in the environment nasal + velar.

The origins of anaphonesis, and the reasons for its occurrence solely in the region of Florence, remain to be explained. Might we postulate a kind of assimilatory raising akin to metaphony, and triggered by yod? In various dialects metaphony has indeed been triggered by yod, or by palatal consonants arising from contact with yod;[26] and Franceschini (1991: 262–5) relates anaphonesis before yod to a wider Romance tendency to raise vowels before yod. The greater susceptibility of the front vowel to anaphonesis also recalls the kind of front-back asymmetry observable in metaphony.[27] But raising in the environment of [**skj**], and before prevelar nasals (i.e., [**ŋg**], [**ŋk**]), has no parallel in metaphony.

4.6 Unstressed vowels

The evolution of the Italo-Romance unstressed vowel system displays two major characteristics:

(i) The inventory of five unstressed vowels (cf. 2.3) tends to be reduced, as a result of phonetic merger or assimilation.
(ii) Such reduction is often asymmetrical, in that there are differences between posttonic syllables (i.e., those to the right of the stressed syllable) and pretonic syllables (those to the left of the stressed syllable).

Merger (or *paradigmatic neutralization*) involves originally distinct vowel qualities becoming identical. Commonly in Italo-Romance, the unstressed vowels yield [**ə**] (this is the case in much of mainland southern Italy), or disappear altogether (a development widely observed in Gallo-Italian varieties). Many dialects tend to preserve a three or four vowel system in pretonic syllables, but to display only two vowels in posttonic syllables. It is a generalization valid for all Italo-Romance dialects that [**a**] never systematically merges with other vowels in pretonic position, although it may so merge – in some southern varieties – in posttonic syllables. For example, the dialect of Agnone (Molise) has three pretonic vowels [**a**], [**u**] and [**ə**], but usually only [**ə**] in posttonic position: **'femmənə** 'woman' < FEMINA(M); **fa'tiːjə** 'toil' <***fa'tika**; **'fiːkərə** 'figs' <***'fikora**; **'kandələ** 'sing it' <***'kantala**; **lə'moːsənə** 'alms' < ELEMOSINA(M); **və'dajmə** 'we see' <***ve'demo**; **pu'tajmə** 'we can' <***po'temo**, etc. Assimilatory (or *syntagmatic*) neutralization of unstressed vowels involves partial or total assimilation of the vowel to the vowel of a following syllable. It operates in many dialects of central and extreme southern Italy[28] whose unstressed vowel system is, *prima facie*, fairly conservative. In central Italy, such merger is often *asymmetrical*: complete assimilation to the following vowel (for example, around Cortona and in the southern Marche) characterizes posttonic syllables only, while pretonic syllables are either immune to assimilation or, as is the case in parts of Lazio and the Marche, subject to a partial assimilation involving raising of [**e**] and [**o**] to [**i**] and [**u**] before a high vowel. The following examples of asymmetrically differentiated assimilation types are from the dialect of Servigliano (Marche). Complete assimilation of posttonic vowels: **te'neːte**, **te'neːtala**, **te'neːtulu** 'you hold, hold her, hold him'; **dom'meːnaka**, **dom'meːneke** 'Sunday, Sundays'; **'prɛːdoko**, **'prɛːdiki**, **'prɛːdaka** 'I preach, you preach, he preaches'; raising assimilation of pretonic vowels in **kummuni'kiːmo**, **kommo'nekeːte** 'we communicate, you communicate'; **durmi'rɔ**, **dorme'reːte** 'I will sleep, you will sleep', etc.

4.6.1 Asymmetrical merger of Tuscan unstressed vowels

Most varieties of Tuscan have neither systematic paradigmatic merger nor systematic assimilatory merger.[29] But the asymmetry between pretonic and posttonic syllables is detectable: in native vocabulary (excluding words of learnèd origin), Tuscan presents five vowels in pretonic syllables ([**i e a o u**]), but in posttonic syllables only four ([**i e a o**]). Yet there is a tendency for Proto-Romance *pretonic* [**o**] to be raised to [**u**]: *ubbidire* 'to obey' (or *obbedire*); *mulino* 'mill'; *udire* 'to hear'), and similarly, *pretonic* [**e**] is sometimes raised to [**i**]: *misura* 'measure'; *finestra* 'window'; *cipolla* 'onion'. All of these words contained unstressed [**e**] or [**o**] in their etyma. Here also belong certain unstressed clitic forms such as *di* 'of' (< ***de**), and the first, second and third person pronouns *mi*, *ti*, *si*, alternating with stressed *me*, *te*, *sé*. Meyer-Lübke (1972: 62; 1974: 299) and Monaci (1955: 95) attribute such raising to an original assimilation before following [**u**] or [**i**], of the type described above for central Italian dialects. It is true (cf. Rohlfs (1966: 162)) that there are many examples in Tuscan in which raising has occurred before mid and low vowels, as well (e.g., *cipolla*; *finestra*;

bisogno 'need'; *rimane* 'he stays'), but this need not exclude the possibility that raising commenced, as in other dialects of central Italy, as an assimilatory process, only to be generalized later outside its original phonetic environment – rather in the manner suggested above for SOSD. We shall see in 4.6.4 that in *posttonic* syllables there is a tendency for even more radical types of paradigmatic merger of unstressed vowels.

4.6.2 *Rounding and backing of front vowels*

Our example in 14 above (*dobbiamo*, *dovete* 'we/you must' alternating with *devo* 'I must') is representative of occasional rounding and backing (i.e., rounding of the lips combined with retraction of the tongue body) of unstressed front vowels when they are followed by a labial consonant [**b**], [**v**], [**p**] or [**m**], yielding [**o**] or [**u**]. This is to be seen also in *domandare* 'to ask' < DEMANDARE; *ubriaco* 'drunk' < EBRIACU(M); *lumaca* 'slug' <***li'maka**; *dopo* 'after' < DE POST; *mènomo* 'slightest' < MINIMU(M); *rovesciare* 'to overturn' < ***revers'jare**; *indovinare* 'to guess' < ***indivi'nare**. A hypercorrect reaction to this tendency is *dimesticare* instead of *domesticare* 'to tame, make familiar'.

4.6.3 *Raising of unstressed [**a**]*

Raising of unstressed [**a**] to [**e**] before [**r**] (compare the first conjugation infinitive and future forms *parlare* 'to speak' and *parlerò* 'I shall speak', in example 15) deserves particular attention, since it constitutes a distinctive characteristic of Florentine, and is one of the phonological features which clearly identifies the Florentine basis of standard Italian. The development is most conspicuous in the future stems of first conjugation verbs, but may also be observed in suffixal alternations such as *sellàio* 'saddler', *selleria* 'saddlery'; *macellàio* 'butcher', *macelleria* 'butcher's shop', (cf. also *margherita* 'daisy' < MARGARITA(M)).[30]

4.6.4 *Deletion of unstressed vowels*

Deletion of unstressed vowels is relatively rare in Tuscan. Unstressed [**i**] and [**e**] are sometimes suppressed after [**l**] and [**r**], regularly so in adjectives followed by the adverbial suffix *-mente* (Ch.3: 0.1), such as *naturalmente* 'naturally'; *regolarmente* 'regularly' from *naturale* and *regolare*; also in OTuscan *corca* = *corica* 'he goes to bed'; *merta* = *merita* 'he deserves'. Unstressed [**e**] and [**i**] are sporadically subject to deletion before [**r**], notably in certain future tense forms (cf. Ch.3: 8.8.5): *sapere* 'to know' vs. *saprò* 'I shall know'; *vedere* 'to see' vs. *vedrò* 'I shall see'; *comperare* or *comprare* 'to buy'; *diritto* or *dritto* 'straight'.

Unstressed vowels at the beginning of words were also sometimes subject to deletion, a process known as APHERESIS. A common cause of this in the history of Italian is the morphological reanalysis of a word-initial vowel as the final element of a preceding word, particularly the definite article: *l'omicidio* > *lo micidio* 'the murder'; *l'arena* > *la rena* 'the sand'; *l'alesina* > *la lesina* 'the awl'.

4.6.4.1 Syncope of the penultimate vowel of proparoxytones

There is evidence that Tuscan may once have tended to syncopate (delete), the penultimate vowel of proparoxytones,[31] a tendency against which speakers may subsequently have reacted by *restoring* a vowel.

The evidence for this claim is the existence of a series of words in which the penultimate vowel of proparoxytones displays a curiously irregular substitution of the original vowel (cf. Rohlfs (1966: 173f.)), e.g.: *sèdano* 'celery' < **SE**LINON; *cronaca* 'chronicle' < **CHRO**NICA(M); OTuscan *stròlago* 'astrologer' < **ASTRO**LOGU(M); *nèspolo* 'medlar tree' < **ME**SPILU(M); *dèbole* 'weak' < **DE**BILE(M); *sèmola* 'semolina' < **SI**MILA(M); *àttimo* 'moment' < **A**TOMU(M), etc. This substitution cannot be accounted for in terms of regular sound change. Tuttle (1974), who also reviews some earlier attempts to resolve this problem, suggests that these unexpected vowels conceal earlier deletion (syncope),[32] and that, from about the beginning of the second millennium, the pattern of a phonologically more conservative group of words, which had retained intertonic vowels in proparoxytones, began to serve as a model for *restoration* of syncopated intertonic vowels. The motivation for this phonological volte-face is a matter for speculation, but it might be seen as a reaction, concomitant with the rise in cultural and economic prestige of Tuscany, against a phonological habit which was perceived as characteristic of northern Italian dialects (cf. Romagnol **'tɔʃk** 'poison' < **TO**XICU(M); **'pegra** 'sheep' < **PE**CORA, etc.). In contrast, retention of the proparoxytonic pattern, with the penultimate vowel preserved, was a characteristic both of central and southern Italian dialects in general, and of a great many Greek and Latin elements in learnèd, or semi-learnèd, vocabulary.

In Tuscan, [**a**] seems always to have survived intact in the penultimate vowel of proparoxytones: e.g., *càlamo* 'pen' < **CA**LAMU(M); *òrfano* 'orphan' < **OR**PHANU(M); *sàbato* 'Saturday' < **SA**BATU(M). This fact is consistent with our observation, above, that unstressed [**a**] is generally preserved in Italo-Romance dialects. The penultimate vowel of proparoxytones was also generally maintained, with occasional modifications (Latin [**u**] becomes [**o**]), in learnèd or semi-learnèd vocabulary (e.g., *cìrcolo* 'circle' < **CIR**CULUM; *vìncolo* 'bond' < **UIN**CULUM; *tègola* 'tile' < **TE**GULAM, alongside popular *cerchio*; *vinchio* and *tegghia*; also *ànima* 'soul' < **A**NIMAM; *ùltimo* 'last' < **UL**TIMUM. Now it is one thing to feel that insertion of an intertonic vowel is desirable – according, perhaps, to some notion of what sounds 'Tuscan' and 'not northern' – quite another to know *which* vowel to insert in those proparoxytones where the penultimate vowel had been deleted or was at best very weakly articulated. The result is that the inserted vowel often does not correspond to the original vowel, but instead follows the model of the surviving proparoxytones characterized either by intertonic [**a**] (whence the profusion of forms such as *crònaca*, *sèdano*, with [**a**]) or, in the environment of a following [**l**], of the suffix *-olo* (whence forms such as *sèmola*; *dèbole* and OTuscan *ùtole* for *ùtile* 'useful'; *àngiolo* for *àngelo* 'angel'). Occasionally, a vowel may even be inserted where none was present historically: *battèsimo* 'baptism' < BAPTISMU(M); *Còsimo* (a name), for *Cosmo*. If this analysis of the counteretymological vowels is correct, then we have here a type of hypercorrection which might be perhaps be labelled 'hypertuscanization'.

Such instability of the unstressed vowel may, in reality, have been a property of posttonic vowels in general (as it is in many northern dialects), rather than of non-final posttonics alone. Counteretymological outcomes are also found among Tuscan word-final unstressed vowels, especially when these vowels have no morphological function, that is to say when they are not inflectional desinences. We find a final [**i**] in *oggi* 'today'; *lungi* 'far', *fuori* 'outside', *domani* 'tomorrow', *avanti* 'forward', *dieci* 'ten' from Latin HODIE, LONGE, FORAS, MANE, ANTE, DECE(M); [**o**] in *contro* 'against', *entro* 'within' from Latin CONTRA, INTRA, and [**e**] in *oltre* 'beyond', from Latin ULTRA. The adverbial suffix -MENTE, generally conserved as *-mente*, presents a final [**i**] in *altrimenti* 'otherwise'; *parimenti* 'likewise'. The transformation into -**i** of the first conjugation present subjunctive inflectional ending -**e** (Ch.3: 8.4) (*'**kante**; *'**ame** > *canti* 'let him sing'; *ami* 'let him love') may also belong here, since -**i** vs. -**e** has no morphologically distinctive function in the signalling of mood. The source of these substitutions is often obscure: the final vowel of CONTRA may have been reanalysed as a separate word, namely the preposition *a*, leaving ***kontr**, which needed to be furnished with some final vowel. Some of the forms with final [**i**] possibly reflect the analogical influence of words such as *ieri* 'yesterday' and *venti* 'twenty' (cf. Rohlfs (1966: 142)).

Where final vowels have an inflectional function, they are generally well preserved, and are relatively immune from neutralizing influences. A major problem is presented, however, by the evolution of the plural and second person singular inflection -**i**, and by the feminine plural inflection -**e**. Since a discussion of this leads naturally into considerations of morphological structure, and also requires reference to the question of palatalization of velars (section 6, below), it has been placed towards the end of this chapter (section 11).

4.6.5 The prosthetic vowel [**i**]

Many Romance dialects (notably Ibero- and Gallo-Romance varieties) have introduced a 'prosthetic' vowel before word-initial [**s**] + consonant (cf. Castilian *estrella* 'star' < STELLA(M); *escudo* 'shield' < SCUTU(M)). The same process, yielding [**i**], is observable in thirteenth century Tuscan (e.g., *ispediti* 'sent'; *istamane* 'this morning'; *iscudi* 'shields', etc.), and survives here and there in western Tuscan dialects. It persists notably in Corsican. In modern Italian it is wholly restricted to the literary language, and occurs notably after certain prepositions ending in a consonant, where its retention perhaps serves the function of breaking up abnormal consonant clusters, such as [**nzv**], [**rzb**], [**nsk**], [**nsp**], etc.: e.g., *in Isvizzera* 'in Switzerland'; *in iscatola* 'in a box'; *per isbaglio* 'by mistake'; *non ispostare* 'not to move'. The disappearance of prosthetic [**i**] carried with it some instances of word-initial [**i**] which are not the result of prosthesis: HISTORIA(M) > *istoria* > *storia* 'history'; INSTRUMENTU(M) > *istrumento* > *strumento* 'instrument'. Sporadic instances of prosthetic [**i**] before initial [**ɲ**] are also found in the literary language: e.g., *ignudo* for *gnudo* 'naked'; *ignocco* for *gnocco* 'dumpling'.

5 The glides [j] and [w], and their effects

Latin unstressed high vowels, written 'I' and 'U', when followed by a vowel, were probably pronounced, respectively, as palatal and labial *glides* [**j**] and [**w**] (cf. Allen (1978: 37–42)): e.g., IANUARIUS = ***janwarjus** 'January'. They certainly acquired these values in Proto-Romance. An early effect of these glides, (see section 8), was to induce lengthening of preceding consonants. Thereafter, their development is divergent.

5.1 The fate of [w]

The glide [**w**] (< U (+ vowel)) was generally deleted after a consonant (19):

(19)

Latin	Proto-Romance	Italian	
FUTUO	***'fotwo**	**'fotto**	'I copulate'
HABUI	***'abwi**	**'ebbi**	'I had'
UOLUI	***'volwi**	**'volli**	'I wanted'
JANUARIU(M)	***jan'warju**	**ʤen'naːjo**	'January'

The sounds [**kw**] and [**gw**], the latter restricted in CL to the environment of a preceding nasal consonant, behave slightly differently (20):[33]

[**gw**] is maintained in Tuscan; [**kw**] loses its labial glide before the front vowels [**e**] and [**i**], but not before [**a**]. 'Delabialization' of [**kw**] before a front vowel is by no means complete throughout Italo-Romance (cf. Rohlfs (1966: 221)), and it apparently postdates the palatalization of velar consonants before front vowels (datable to about the fifth century, see section 6), since the resulting [**ki**] and [**ke**] are not palatalized.

(20)

CL	Proto-Romance	Italian	
QUÆRIT	***ˈkɛre**	**ˈkjɛːde**	'he asks'
QUI	***ki**	**ki**	'who'
QUANDO	***ˈkwando**	**ˈkwando**	'when'
QUATTUOR	***ˈkwattro**	**ˈkwattro**	'four'
ANGUILLA(M)	***aŋˈgwilla**	**aŋˈgwilla**	'eel'
SANGUEN	***ˈsaŋgwe**	**ˈsaŋgwe**	'blood'

Occurrences of the sound [**gw**] have been increased in Italo-Romance by certain words of Germanic origin, originally with [**w**]. Such are *guadagnare* 'to gain'; *guida* 'guide'; *guerra* 'war'; *guastare* 'spoil'; *guado* 'ford'.[34] New instances of [**kw**] + front vowel arise from Proto-Romance [**ku**] or [**ko**] + front vowel: *'**ɛkku 'estu** > *questo* 'this'; *'**ɛkku 'ellu** > *quello* 'that'.

5.2 Palatalization and affrication by [j]

The Proto-Romance palatal glide yod ([**j**]) – which arose from Latin unstressed E or I immediately followed by a vowel – was to have radical consequences for the Romance consonant system, in that it triggered an assimilatory palatalization of immediately preceding consonants, and thereby gave rise to a series of new, palatally articulated, consonants. In addition to palatalization, yod produced an *affricate* articulation of preceding [**t**], and sometimes also [**d**], yielding the affricates [**ʦ**] and [**ʣ**] (see Tekavčić (1980 I: 187f.) for early documentation of these effects of yod).[35] The emergence of yod from [**e**], [**i**] + vowel, and its subsequent palatalizing effects on preceding consonants, are illustrated in (21). Some of the archaic verb forms cited in (21), (22), (23) and (24) below, such as *vegno* 'I come', *tegno* 'I hold' and *seggio* 'I sit', etc., have disappeared from modern usage. Their replacement by *vengo*, *tengo* and *siedo*, etc., will be explained in Ch.3: 8.4.1 .

(21)

CL	Proto-Romance	Italian	
UINEA(M)	*'vinja	'viɲɲa	'vine'
UENIO	*'vɛnjo	'vɛɲɲo	'I come'
FILIA(M)	*'filja	'fiʎʎa	'daughter'
SOLEO	*'sɔljo	'sɔʎʎo	'I am wont'
DIURNU(M)	*'djornu	'ʤorno	'day'
SEDEO	*'sɛdjo	'sɛdʤo	'I sit'
MEDIU(M)	*'mɛdju	'mɛddzo	'middle'
HORDEU(M)	*'ɔrdju	'ɔrdzo	'barley'
FORTIA(M)	*'fɔrtja	'fɔrtsa	'strength'
PUTEU(M)	*'potju	'pottso	'well'
LANCEA(M)	*'laŋkja	'lanʧa	'lance'
FACIO	*'fakjo	'fatʧo	'I do'
FAGEU(M)	*'fagju	'fadʤo	'beech'
REGIA(M)	*'regja	'redʤa	'palace'
BASIU(M)	*'basju	'baːʧo	'kiss'
CASEU(M)	*'kasju	'kaːʧo	'cheese'

Palatalization by yod occurred at an early date (in, or before, the second century), and has left traces in all Romance varieties. In addition to creating an entirely new series of consonants, it produced patterns of morphological alternation (22) which were to play a major role in the grammar of the Italian verb.

(22)

	CL	Italian	CL	Italian
1Sg.Ind.	SOLEO	**'sɔʎʎo**	UENIO	**'vɛɲɲo**
2Sg.Ind.	SOLES	**'swɔːli**	UENIS	**'vjɛːni**
3Sg.Ind.	SOLET	**'swɔːle**	UENIT	**'vjɛːne**
1Sg.Subj.	SOLEAM	**'sɔʎʎa**	UENIAM	**'vɛɲɲa**
2Sg.Subj.	SOLEAS	**'sɔʎʎa**	UENIAS	**'vɛɲɲa**
3Sg.Subj.	SOLEAT	**'sɔʎʎa**	UENIAT	**'vɛɲɲa**
1Sg.Ind.	SEDEO	**'sɛdʤo**	TENEO	**'tɛɲɲo**
2Sg.Ind.	SEDES	**'sjɛːdi**	TENES	**'tjɛːni**
3Sg.Ind.	SEDET	**'sjɛːde**	TENET	**'tjɛːne**
1Sg.Subj.	SEDEAM	**'sɛdʤa**	TENEAM	**'tɛɲɲa**
2Sg.Subj.	SEDEAS	**'sɛdʤa**	TENEAS	**'tɛɲɲa**
3Sg.Subj.	SEDEAT	**'sɛdʤa**	TENEAT	**'tɛɲɲa**

All consonants were modified by yod, except for the labials (e.g., **'abbja** 'let him have' < HABEAT; **ven'demmja** 'vintage' < UINDIMIA(M); **'sappja** 'let him know' < SAPIAT, etc.),[36] and for [**r**] (see below). Proto-Romance [**nj**] and [**lj**] regularly yielded [**ɲ**] and [**ʎ**].

The evolution of [**sj**] is more complex. The regular development in Tuscan is a *short* [**ʃ**]: ***'basju** > **'baːʃo** 'kiss'; ***ka'misja** > **ka'miːʃa** 'shirt'; ***'kasju** > **'kaːʃo** 'cheese'. Where originally preceded by a consonant, this [**ʃ**] is maintained, with assimilation of the preceding consonant: ***rever'sjaːre** > **roveʃ'ʃaːre** 'to overturn'. But the result of original *intervocalic* [**sj**] is [**ʧ**] in the modern *standard* language: **'baːʧo**; **ka'miːʧa**; **'kaːʧo**. Another frequent reflex of intervocalic *[**sj**], beside [**ʃ**] (or [**ʧ**]), is the voiced [**ʒ**] (giving [**ʤ**] in standard Italian): e.g., **fa'ʒaːno** *fagiano* 'pheasant' < ***fa'sjanu**; **fa'ʒwɔːlo** *fagiuolo* 'bean' < **fa'sjɔːlu**; **ka'ʒoːne** *cagione* 'cause' < ***okka'sjone**; **pi'ʒoːne** *pigione* 'rent' < ***pe'sjone**; **ʧi'ljɛːʒo** *ciliegio* 'cherry < ***ke'rɛsju**. These developments present two problems: (i) Why have the intervocalic fricatives [**ʃ**] and [**ʒ**] become [**ʧ**] and [**ʤ**] in standard Italian?; (ii) Why does the voiced [**ʒ**] or [**ʤ**] sometimes occur instead of intervocalic [**ʃ**] or [**ʒ**]?

The first problem is probably a matter of hypercorrection. We shall see in section 6 that in the dialects, and the regional Italian, of Tuscany, intervocalic affricates [**ʧ**] and [**ʤ**] (arising from original [**k**] or [**g**] + front vowel) have lost their occlusion, becoming fricatives [**ʃ**] and [**ʒ**]: e.g., ***'dike** > **'diːʧe** 'he says' > **diːʃe**; ***la 'gente** > **la 'ʤente** 'the people' > **la 'ʒɛnte**. This innovation may have met resistance in more conservative models of pronunciation, where [**ʧ**] and [**ʤ**], from original [**k**] and [**g**], were maintained; Tuttle (1977: 610f.; 1979: 95) proposes that such reaction in favour of conservative and more prestigious varieties may have coincided with the rise in cultural, economic and political prestige in the Florence of the fourteenth century. Less conservative speakers, anxious to 'correct' their speech, but uncertain as to which cases of popular [ʃ] and [ʒ] corresponded to [**ʧ**] and [**ʤ**], and which did not, used the simple equation 'popular intervocalic [ʃ] and [ʒ] = "correct"/conservative intervocalic [**ʧ**] and [**ʤ**]', substituting intervocalic [**ʧ**] and [**ʤ**] wholesale for reflexes of original intervocalic [**sj**], whence the pronunciations **'baːʧo**, **fa'ʤwɔːlo**, etc. The lack of any clear method of spelling the fricative sounds may also have hindered their absorption into more prestigious varieties of Tuscan, and their subsequent acceptance into standard Italian (cf. De Mauro (1976: 320)): both *bascio* and *bacio* were possible spellings in OTuscan, but *sci* usually signals *long* intervocalic [ʃʃ] (e.g., *fascio* **'faʃʃo**), while *ci* also indicates [**ʧ**] (e.g., *città* **ʧit'ta**), and [ʒ] was variously rendered as *sci* (which was also used for [ʃ] and [ʃʃ]), as *gi* (which also represented [**ʤ**]), or occasionally *sgi*.

Some instances of intervocalic [ʒ] (or [**ʤ**]) are probably loans from Gallo-Romance dialects, and reflect historically underlying [**tj**], as well as [**sj**] (e.g., *servigio* 'favour' < ***ser'vitju**; *ragione* 'reason' < ***ra'tjone**; *pregio* 'virtue' < ***'prɛtju**; *segugio* 'hound' < ***se'kutju**; *rugiada* 'dew' < ***ro'sjata**). But the majority of cases of [ʒ] (or [**ʤ**]) from *[**sj**] belong to basic, everyday, vocabulary (see the examples above, and Castellani (1960)), and cannot be readily attributed to borrowing. The voiced fricative is also often observable in Tuscan placenames (e.g., *Fregiano* < ***fre'sjanu**; *Pugiano* < ***apu'sjanu**; *Bugiana* < ***bu'sjana**; *Carigio* < ***ka'risju**), and placenames are most unlikely candidates for lexical borrowing. Castellani attributes this pronunciation to imitation of northern speech habits, rather than to lexical borrowing from Gallo-Romance. That voiced [ʒ] ([**ʤ**]) should occasionally appear in native Tuscan words, in place of [ʃ] (or [**ʧ**]) is wholly consistent with the tendency, which we examine in detail in 7.2, for Tuscan voiceless intervocalic consonants – including sibilants – to become voiced. As we shall see, such voicing may result both from an *indigenous* tendency to voicing and, in some cases, from northern Italian linguistic influences.

The evolution of the dental and velar consonants before [**j**] constitutes one of the more intricate and problematic chapters of Italian historical phonology, of which we can do little more here than sketch the elements. The group [**gj**] consistently develops into the palatal affricate [**ʤ**][37] (23).

(23)

Proto-Romance	Italian	
ˈfagju	**ˈfaddʒo**	‘beech’
ˈregja	**ˈreddʒa**	‘palace’
ˈfugja	**ˈfuddʒa**	‘let him flee’

But [**kj**], [**tj**] and [**dj**] all have dual outcomes (24), sometimes resulting in etymological doublets (underlined):

(24)

Proto-Romance	Italian	
(i) [**kj**]	[**tʃ**] (occasionally [**ts**])	
*****ˈ**fakjo**	**ˈfattʃo**	‘I do’
*****ˈ**lakju**	**ˈlattʃo**	‘lace’
*****ˈ**fraŋkja**	**ˈfraɲtʃa**	‘France’
*****-ˈ**akju**	**-ˈattʃo**	(pejorative suffix)
*****ˈ**laŋkja**	**ˈlaɲtʃa**	‘lance’
*****ˈ**oŋkja**	**ˈoɲtʃa**	‘ounce’

*****fa**ˈkjɔlu**	**fatˈtswɔːlo**	‘handkerchief’
*****ˈ**kalkja**	**ˈkaltsa**	‘sock’
*****-ˈ**akju**	**-ˈattso**	(pejorative suffix)
*****bi**ˈlaŋkja**	**biˈlaɲtʃa**	‘scales’

(ii) [**tj**]	[**ts**] (occasionally [**tʃ**])	
*****ˈ**tɛrtju**	**ˈtɛrtso**	‘third’
*****ˈ**platja**	**ˈpjattsa**	‘square’
*****ˈ**vetju**	**ˈvettso**	‘habit’
*****ˈ**noptje**	**ˈnɔttse**	‘wedding’
*****-ˈ**antja**	**-ˈantsa**	(noun suffix)

*****kap**ˈtjare**	**katˈtʃaːre**	‘to hunt’
*****ko**ˈmintjo**	**koˈmiɲtʃo**	‘I begin’
*****eks**ˈkwartjo**	**ˈskwartʃo**	‘I rend’
*****ˈ**gottja**	**ˈgottʃa**	‘drop’

(iii) [dj] > [ddʒ] and [ddz] in intervocalic position; [dʒ] in initial position; [dz] in postconsonantal position.		
*ˈvedjo	ˈveddʒo	'I see'
*ˈradju	ˈraddʒo	'ray'
*ˈmɔdju	ˈmɔddʒo	'bushel'
*-ˈedja	-ˈeddʒa	(verb suffix)
*ˈɔdje	ˈɔddʒi	'today'
*ˈpodju	ˈpoddʒo	'hill'
*ˈmɛdju	ˈmɛddzo	'middle'
*ˈrodju	ˈroddzo	'rough'
*ˈradju	ˈraddzo	'spoke'
*ˈmɔdju	ˈmɔddzo	'hub
*-ˈedja	-ˈeddza	(verb suffix)

The appearance of [ts] instead of [tʃ] is, in some cases, attributable to borrowing from other dialects: [ts] was[38] the regular outcome of [tj] in northern Italy (e.g., OPaduan *brazzo* 'arm' < *ˈ**brakkju**; OMilanese *faça* 'face' < *ˈ**fakja** where *zz* and *ç* represent [ts]). As the examples in (24) show, such borrowing could give rise to etymological doublets. 'Hypertuscanization' (in this case, the creation of etymologically erroneous 'Tuscan' forms, on the basis of an equation "Northern [ts] = Tuscan [tʃ]") may have played some role in the occurrence of [tʃ] in place of [ts]. But there is also reason to suspect that [tʃ] was an alternative, indigenous, phonetic reflex of [tj]. The alveolar-palatal affricate [tʃ] probably developed via an earlier stage *[tsj], and since the regular development of [sj] in Tuscan is [ʃ], then [tʃ] – which is, in effect, [t] + [ʃ] – is a plausible outcome of [tsj]. Now [tʃ] for [ts] occurs principally where a consonant immediately precedes, especially after original [s], where it is the sole outcome: ***aŋˈgostja** > ***aŋˈgoʃtʃa** > **aŋˈgoʃʃa** 'anxiety'; *ˈ**ostju** > *ˈ**uʃtʃo** > ˈ**uʃʃo** 'doorway' (for the change [stʃ] > [ʃtʃ] > [ʃʃ], see section 6). This partial phonological predictability of [tʃ] lends weight to the view that [tʃ] is also an indigenous development of [tj] arising in postconsonantal position.

The dual evolution of [dj] also shows a degree of phonological regularity which suggests an indigenous evolution, rather than piecemeal lexical borrowing from other dialects: the result is *always* [dz] after a consonant;[39] *always* [dʒ] in word-initial position, and *usually* [dʒ] intervocalically, beside a number of cases of intervocalic [dz] (including some etymological doublets). No such differentiation exists in northern Italian dialects. Moreover, the intervocalic resolution, [ʤ], became deeply rooted in the morphological structure of some very common verbs (e.g., **'sɛdʤo** 'I sit'; **'vedʤo** 'I see'), which are most unlikely candidates for dialect borrowing (see Ch.3: 8.4.1 for their subsequent replacement by *siedo* and *vedo*). It appears, then, that the phonetically regular Tuscan development of intervocalic and initial [**dj**] is not [**ʣ**] (the voiced counterpart of [**ʦ**]), but rather [**ʤ**]. This [**ʤ**] is identical not only to the outcome of [**gj**], but also to that of the word-initial and intervocalic glide [**j**] (25).

(25)

Proto-Romance	Italian	
***'peju**	**'pedʤo**	'worse'
***'maju**	**'madʤo**	'May'
***ja**	**ʤa**	'already'
***jan'warju**	**ʤen'naːjo**	'January'

This proposed *asymmetrical* evolution of [**tj**] and [**dj**] is exactly consistent with what we find in southern Italian dialects, where [**tj**] gives [**ʦ**] or [**ʧ**], while [**dj**] merges with [**gj**] and [**j**] to give [**j**] (cf. Rohlfs (1966: 411; 413; 393f.)).[40] It is likely that in Tuscan, as in southern Italy, [**dj**], like [**gj**], originally merged with [**j**], subsequently yielding [**ʤ**]. As for [**ʣ**], it was the regular outcome of [**dj**] (and [**gj**] and [**j**]) in northern Italy. Over wide areas of the north (except some mountain dialects of Liguria and Piedmont) [**ʣ**] has yielded [**z**] (cf. Rohlfs (1966: 392f.)). For example, Bolognese (where final [**z**] > [**s**]) (26):

(26)

Proto-Romance	Bolognese	
***'jɔku**	**zuk**	'game'
***'radju**	**ras**	'ray'
***'mɛdja**	**meza**	'half' (F.)

Some Tuscan forms with intervocalic [**ʣ**] may be loanwords: Rohlfs (1966: 391) proposes that **'radʣo** 'spoke', and **'mɔdʣo** 'hub' are borrowed from northern Italian dialects and reflect northern expertise in cart building, a hypothesis about which Bolelli (1980) is, however, most sceptical. The [**ʣ**] of the verbal suffix -**ed'ʣaːre** (vs. -**ed'ʤaːre**) is plausibly of northern origin in **batted'ʣaːre** 'to baptize', given that northern linguistic influence is detectable in other areas of religious terminology (cf. 7.2), but there is nothing religious, nor culturally prestigious, about **spetedˈʣaːre** 'to break wind'. And there is no clear motivation for borrowing in **ˈmɛdʣo** 'middle' or **ˈrodʣo** 'rough', although Rohlfs suggests hypercorrection in the direction of a more prestigious 'northern' pronunciation. It is noteworthy that there are no examples of [**ʣ**] in word-initial position, although initial [**ʣ**] is perfectly common in the northern dialects. These facts suggest that [**ʣ**] may have been an alternative, indigenous, Tuscan resolution of intervocalic [**dj**]. We are forced to leave open the very considerable problem of explaining why Tuscan [**dj**] should have evolved differentially in postconsonantal, intervocalic and initial position.

In most Italo-Romance varieties, yod apparently produces no palatalizing effect on preceding [**r**]. It is a distinctive characteristic of Tuscan, and one that has left its mark on the morphological structure of Italian, that the resolution of original [**rj**] is [**j**]. The following are examples from the verbs *morire* 'to die' and *parere* 'to seem' (27):

(27)

	Proto-Romance	Italian	Proto-Romance	Italian
1Sg.Ind.	***ˈmɔrjo**	**ˈmwɔːjo**	***ˈparjo**	**ˈpaːjo**
2Sg.Ind.	***ˈmɔris**	**ˈmwɔːri**	***ˈpares**	**ˈpaːri**
3Sg.Ind.	***ˈmɔre**	**ˈmwɔːre**	***ˈpare**	**ˈpaːre**
3Pl.Ind.	***ˈmɔrjo(n)**	**ˈmwɔːjono**	***ˈparjo(n)**	**ˈpaːjono**
1Sg.Subj.	***ˈmɔrja**	**ˈmwɔːja**	***ˈparja**	**ˈpaːja**

etc.

There are also alternations involving reflexes of the agentive suffix *-**ˈarju** and its derivative, indicating the place where some activity is carried out, *-**aˈria**: **maʧelˈlaːjo** 'butcher' vs. **maʧelleˈriːa** 'butcher's shop'.

In many other Italo-Romance dialects, the outcome is [**r**]: Veroli (Lazio) -**ˈaro**, **ˈmɔro**, and the suffix -**ˈaːro** is the hallmark of a non-Tuscan origin (cf. Italian *calamaio* 'inkpot' vs. *calamaro* 'squid' – both from ***kalaˈmarju**). A common resolution in Ibero-Romance, and Gallo-Romance dialects (e.g., Piedmontese), and sporadically in Calabrian, Lucanian, Neapolitan and Pugliese, is metathesis, i.e., inversion of [**r**] and [**j**], as in Piedmontese ***ˈarja** > **ˈajra** 'threshing floor' (cf. Rohlfs (1966: 402f.)). The early stages of the development of [**rj**] are difficult to reconstruct, but we might postulate that [**j**] originally *palatalized* a preceding [**r**], giving *[**r'**], just as [**sj**] originally gave palatal [**ʃ**]). This proposed palatalized *[**r'**], may subsequently have evolved in one of three ways, according to region: (i) loss of the fricative element, leaving the glide [**j**], as in Tuscany; (ii) loss of the palatal element, leaving [**r**], as in central and southern Italy; (iii) linearization (or 'separating out') of the palatal and fricative elements of the consonants, yielding [**jr**], as in Gallo- and Ibero-Romance.

5.3 Other sources of [ɲ] and [ʃ] from yod

Palatalization of [**n**] and [**s**] was sometimes also triggered by a *preceding* yod, the source of which was a velar consonant [**g**] or [**k**] (28).[41]

(28)

[**gn**]	* [**jn**]	[**ɲɲ**]	
LIGNU(M)	*'**lejnu**	'**leɲɲo**	'wood'
COGNATU(M)	*'**kojnatu**	**koɲ'ɲaːto**	'brother-in-law'
PIGNUS	*'**pejnu**	'**peɲɲo**	'pawn'
AGNELLU(M)	***aj'nɛllu**	**aɲ'ɲɛllo**	'lamb'

The postulated yod is preserved in parts of Basilicata, Puglia, Campania and the Abruzzi, for reflexes of [**gn**][42]: e.g., Ischitan '**lejnə** 'firewood'; '**ajnə** 'lamb'; '**pujnə** 'fist', < LIGNA; AGNU(M); PUGNU(M). Elsewhere, the [**g**] undergoes assimilation (Sardinian '**mannu** 'big' < MAGNU(M)), is deleted (Sora '**lena**), or becomes (in parts of Calabria, Campania, Puglia and Basilicata) a labial glide [**w**], (e.g., Calabrian '**liwna**; '**awnu**).[43]

The sequence [**ks**] (spelled X in Latin) generally yields [**ss**] by assimilation (see 8.2), but sometimes also [**ʃʃ**] (29):

(29)

[**ks**]	[**ss**] or [**ʃʃ**]	
TEXERE	'**tessere**	'to weave'
FRAXINU(M)	'**frassino**	'ash tree'
CONDUXI	**kon'dussi**	'I led'
REXI	'**rɛssi**	'I held'
COXIT	'**kɔsse**	'he cooked'
AXILLA(M)	**aʃ'ʃɛlla**	'armpit'
COXA(M)	'**kɔʃʃa**	'thigh'
EXIT	'**ɛʃʃe**	'he goes out'
EXHALARE	**ʃa'laːre**	'to squander'

Again, a probable intermediate stage is *[**js**], subsequently giving [**ʃʃ**]. Note that, unlike the the outcome of [**sj**], this [**ʃ**] is *long* when intervocalic. Palatalization of [**k**] before a following obstruent is a feature of Gallo-Italian dialects (and of general Gallo- and Ibero-Romance). But the outcome [**ʃ**] (or [**ʃʃ**]) coexists with [**s**] (or [**ss**]) in southern and central dialects as well as in the Gallo-Romance dialects of northern Italy (see Hall (1942b) for the geographical distribution). Indeed, in the north [**ʃ**] is characteristic of Liguria and Piedmont only. But there is nothing notably 'exotic', nor specifically north-western, about those words in which [**ʃ**] occurs in Tuscan (cf. Rohlfs (1966: 317)), and no particular reason why instances of [**ʃ**] found south of Tuscany should be ascribed to borrowings from Tuscan (cf. Hall (1942b)). In short, it remains unclear whether the dual outcomes in Tuscan, central dialects and southern dialects is or is not indigenous.

6 Palatalizing effects of the front vowels

6.1 Palatalization of velars

In about the fifth century, there occurred a further variety of palatalization, affecting velar consonants ([**k**] and [**g**]) when immediately followed by a front vowel ([**i**], [**e**] or [**ɛ**]), which has left traces in all Romance varieties except the Logudorese and Nuorese dialects of Sardinian, and in Dalmatian, where palatalization did not occur before [**e**]. Palatalization of velars is extensively reflected in modern Italian morphological alternations (30).[44]

(30)

1Sg.	2Sg.	3Sg.	
ˈdiːko	**ˈdiːʧi**	**ˈdiːʧe**	'say'
ˈlɛggo	**ˈlɛdʤi**	**ˈlɛdʤe**	'read'

Sg.	Pl.	
ˈpɔrko	**ˈpɔrʧi**	'pig'
aˈmiːko	**aˈmiːʧi**	'friend'

The modern Italian reflex of original [**k**] before front vowels is [**ʧ**]: **ˈʧeːna** 'dinner' < ***ˈkena**; **ˈʧiŋkwe** 'five' < ***ˈkiŋkwe**; **ˈpaːʧe** 'peace' < ***ˈpake**; **viˈʧiːno** 'neighbour' < ***viˈkinu**; **ˈkarʧere** 'jail' < ***ˈkarkere**. There is an asymmetry in the palatalization of [**k**] and [**g**], in that [**g**] appears to have yielded, at first, a glide identical, or closely similar, to [**j**];[45] its development thereafter is (almost) identical to that of Proto-Romance [**j**] (and of [**gj**] – see section 5). It gives [**ʤ**] in word-initial position, and [ʤ] intervocalically: **'ʤɛnte** 'people' < ***'gente**; **'ʤiːro** 'tour' < ***'giru**; **'leʤʤe** 'law' < ***'lege**; **'ruʤʤine** 'rust' < ***'rugine**; **sud'ʤɛllo** 'seal' < ***se'gɛllu.** In intervocalic position, when followed by a stressed front vowel, the glide has sometimes been deleted: ***re'gina** > OTuscan *reina* 'queen'; ***sa'getta** > ***sa'jetta** > **sa'etta** 'arrow', 'lightning'; ***pa'gese** > ***pa'jeːse** > **pa'eːse** 'village'; ***ma'gestro** > ***ma'jestro** > **ma'estro** 'schoolmaster'.

A characteristic of Tuscan which has not entered the literary language, is loss of occlusion in *intervocalic* [ʧ] and [ʤ], yielding [ʃ] and [ʒ]. This occurs across word boundaries as well as within words (31).

(31)

'paːʧe >	**'paːʃe**	'peace'
di'ʧeːva >	**di'ʃeːva**	'said'
la 'ʧeːna >	**la 'ʃeːna**	'the dinner'
a'ʤiːre >	**a'ʒiːre**	'to act'
la 'ʤɛnte >	**la 'ʒɛnte**	'the people'

The resulting *short* [ʃ] is distinct from the *long* [ʃʃ] which arises from [**sk**] + front vowel, as can be seen in such minimal pairs as: **'paːʃe** *pace* 'peace' vs. **'paʃʃe** *pasce* 'it grazes'; **'peːʃe** *pece* 'pitch' vs. **'peʃʃe** *pesce* 'fish'. The change [ʧ] > [ʃ] is shared by many other central and southern dialects; in contrast, these other dialects usually pronounce [ʤ] where Tuscans say [ʒ] (examples in Ch.5: 2.3.1.5).

6.1.2 Palatalization of velars in consonant clusters

The cluster [**ɲg**] + front vowel displays a geographically differentiated development. In eastern Tuscany (and in OFlorentine), in common with virtually all of southern Italy, it evolves like [**nj**], to yield [**ɲɲ**]; however, in the west, including modern Florentine, the cluster emerges as [**nʤ**], a resolution which also probably underlies the [**nʣ**] or [**nz**] encountered in modern northern dialects. OFlorentine exhibits both outcomes: *piange* and *piagne* 'he cries'; *spegnere* and *spengere* 'to extinguish'. It is [**nʤ**] which has generally prevailed in Italian (*spegnere* is an exception). The reasons for this preference for an originally non-Florentine pronunciation have yet to be explained satisfactorily, but perhaps the similarity of [**nʤ**] with the northern Italian development, plus the fact that this development was, apparently, native also to a large part of Tuscany, favoured its selection over [**ɲɲ**]. The resolution of [**rg**] + front vowel as [**rj**] is a characteristic of southern Italy; in Tuscany the outcome is consistently [**rʤ**] (**'sorʤere** 'to arise'; **ar'ʤilla** 'clay'; **'sparʤe** 'he scatters'). An exception is

OTuscan *ariento* 'silver' which existed alongside *argento*. The relatively rare cluster [**lg**] + front vowel evolves in the same manner as [**lj**] (see above), to give [ʎ]: **'kɔʎʎe** 'he plucks' < ***'kɔlge**; **'ʃeʎʎe** 'he chooses' < ***ek'selge**.

The cluster [**sk**] + front vowel evolves, via *[**stʃ**], then *[ʃtʃ], to [ʃʃ] in intervocalic position, and to [ʃ] elsewhere: ***'kreski** > **'kreʃʃi** 'you grow'.

6.2 Palatalization of other consonants

The front vowels have a palatalizing effect principally on velar consonants. An exception is the sporadic palatalization of [**s**] apparent in **'ʃimmja** 'monkey' < SIMIA(M); **veʃ'ʃi:ka** 'bladder' < UESSICA(M).

The modern second person singular form *vuoi* 'you want' (alternating with third person singular *vuole*), the now archaic third person singular masculine pronoun *ei* (= *egli*), the masculine plural adjectives *bei* 'beautiful' and *quei* 'those' and the masculine plural article *i* (OTuscan *ei*) (with *dei* 'of the'), are remnants of a tendency, sporadically attested in the medieval language, for [**l**] to become palatalized before final [**i**], and thereafter to be subject to deletion: OTuscan *capegli* 'hairs' (< ***ka'pelli**); *cavagli* 'horses' (< ***ka'valli**); *tai* 'such' (< ***'ta:li**); *animai* 'animals' (< ***ani'ma:li**); modern Italian *egli* / *ei* (pronouns) and *i* (definite article) (< ***'elli**); *vuoi* (< ***'vɔli**); *bei* (< ***'bɛlli**); *quei* (< ***'kwelli**). See also Rohlfs (1968: 306; 326).

7 Consonantal weakening

7.1 The fate of the intervocalic voiceless consonants

The Latin voiceless stop consonants [**k**], [**t**] and [**p**], in intervocalic position (or when preceded by a vowel and followed by [**l**] or [**r**]), are usually maintained in Italian. All of the examples in (32) contained voiceless consonants in CL (e.g., DICO 'I say'; NEPOTE(M) 'nephew'; APERTU(M) 'open', etc.).

(32)

dico 'I say'	*fico* 'fig'	*cieco* 'blind'	*pecora* 'sheep'
poco 'not much'	*fuoco* 'fire'	*amico* 'friend'	

nipote 'nephew'	*ruota* 'wheel'	*dito* 'finger'	*sete* 'thirst'
catena 'chain'	*potere* 'power'	*amate* 'you love'	

aperto 'open'	*apre* 'he opens'	*cipolla* 'onion'	*ape* 'bee'
capo 'head'	*ripa* 'bank'	*sapete* 'you know'	

Italian and the modern Tuscan dialects present a number of cases in which original voiceless consonants [**k**], [**t**] and [**p**] have, in intervocalic position, undergone voicing to yield, respectively, [**g**], [**d**] and [**v**]: e.g., Latin ACU(M) 'needle'; MUTARE 'change'; EPISCOPU(M) 'bishop', etc. The change [**p**] > [**v**] may be assumed to have passed through a stage *[**b**], which regularly became [**v**] (see 3.3). All of the intervocalic voiced stop consonants in (33) were voiceless in Latin.

(33)

ago 'needle'	*lago* 'lake'	*drago* 'dragon'
bottega 'shop'	*spiga* 'ear of corn'	*luogo* 'place'
fegato 'liver'	*lattuga* 'lettuce'	*segare* 'to saw'
pregare 'to pray'	*annegare* 'to drown'	*affogare* 'to smother'

strada 'road'	*contrada* 'district'	*rugiada* 'dew'
medesimo 'same'	*cadauno* 'each one'	*codesto* 'this'
badessa 'abbess'	*podestà* 'mayor'	*podere* 'smallholding'
budello 'intestine'	*parentado* 'relatives'	*mudare* 'to moult'

povero 'poor'	*vescovo* 'bishop'	*riva* 'bank'
ricevere 'to receive'	*ricoverare* 'to give refuge'	*scovolo* 'cannon brush'

The picture is complicated yet further by the Tuscan dialects. Some of these, including the dialect of Florence, also show occasional voicing of word-internal intervocalic consonants, but otherwise conserve voicelessness. However, in these dialects voiceless intervocalic [**k**], [**t**], [**p**] have been subject to *spirantization* (also called *gorgia*). In phonetic terms, spirantization involves incomplete closure of the vocal tract in production of the consonants, retaining sufficient constriction to produce turbulence as air passes through. In geographical extent, the heartland of the phenomenon reaches from the north of the province of Florence to a point about 25 kilometres south of Siena, and from Empoli and Volterra in the west to at least the Casentino area in the east. It is present, to a lesser degree, in western Tuscany as well.[46] Unlike intervocalic voicing, whose effects are generally restricted to word-internal position, spirantization also operates across word boundaries. It is a productive phonetic process, whose realization is *variable*, both as regards the range of voiceless stops subject to it, and as regards the degree of phonetic constriction. Table (34) illustrates some common effects of spirantization, together with the standard Italian orthography of the words cited.

(34)

'di:ho *dico* 'I say'	**'ʧɛ:ho** *cieco* 'blind'	**la 'ɸɛ:hora** *la pecora* 'the sheep'
'fɔ:ho *fuoco* 'fire'	**a'mi:ho** *amico* 'friend'	**la 'ha:sa** *la casa* 'the house'

ni'ɸo:θe *nipote* 'nephew'	**'rɔ:θa** *ruota* 'wheel'	**'pra:θo** *prato* 'meadow'
a'ʃe:θo *aceto* 'vinegar'	**ka'θe:na** *catena* 'chain'	**la 'θorre** *la torre* 'the tower'

'lu:ɸo *lupo* 'wolf'	**a'ɸɛrto** *aperto* 'open'	**ʧi'ɸolla** *cipolla* 'onion'
ko'ɸɛrto *coperto* 'covered'	**la 'ɸarte** *la parte* 'the part'	**i 'ɸi:ni** *i pini* 'the pines

The origins of voicing and spirantization have aroused intense speculation among dialectologists. Two widely held views are (i) that voicing is not indigenous, but the result of dialect borrowing from northern Italy, or (ii) that spirantization reflects the influence of the Etruscan linguistic substrate on the Latin of Tuscany. But it is increasingly clear that appeal to external influences is not only redundant, but in many respects implausible. Both voicing and spirantization are likely to be indigenous to Tuscany, and to have evolved independently of any external linguistic influence. Moreover, they may be viewed as divergent realizations of a single phenomenon: *weakening* of intervocalic consonants.

7.2 Word-internal voicing

Voicing of intervocalic short voiceless consonants is a characteristic of northern Italian dialects, together with other Gallo- and Ibero-Romance varieties: e.g., modern Milanese **fur'mi:ga** 'ant' < ***for'mika**; **sal'va:dega** 'wild' < ***sel'vatika**; **'rø:da** 'wheel' < ***'rɔta**; **'se:da** 'silk' < ***'seta**; **sen'ti:da** 'felt' < ***sen'tita**; **'ka:vra** 'goat' < ***'kapra**; **'sko:va** 'broom' < ***'skopa** (and Castilian *hormiga*; *rueda*; *seda*; *sentida*; *cabra*; *escoba*). That some instances of intervocalic voicing in Tuscan may be attributable to borrowing from northern Italian dialects of words containing voiced consonants is entirely plausible. From the sixth century, Tuscany became a dependency of northern Italy, with Lucca as its ecclesiastical and political capital. Into the twelfth century, Tuscany continued to be linked politically with the north, and as late as the fourteenth century Lucca, and to a lesser extent Pisa, remained part of a political entity centred on northern Italy and, presumably, particularly susceptible to northern Italian linguistic influence. It is likely that officials both of the church and of civil government were sent down from the north, and that the lesser cities of Tuscany (among them, at first, Florence) may have sought to imitate the speech of Lucca. Words such as *vescovo* 'bishop', *badessa* 'abbess', *podere* 'smallholding', *podestà* 'mayor', clearly belong to the realms of clerical and civil administration. The influence of northern seafaring powers, such as Genoa, is possibly reflected in *cavo* 'cable', *coverta* 'deck', *scovolo* 'cannon brush' and, perhaps, *riva* 'bank'.

Other examples of voicing in standard Italian, while not obviously of northern origin, are not indigenous to Tuscany, either: *segare* 'to saw'; *sbadigliare* 'to yawn'; *aguzzare* 'to hone', correspond to the native Tuscan *serrare*, *alare*, *amolare*, while the literary *rugiada* 'dew' corresponds to Tuscan *guazza*. The words *povero* 'poor' < PAUPERU(M), *arrivare* 'to arrive' connected with Latin RIPA(M) 'bank', *scodella* 'bowl' < SCUTELLA(M), *padella* 'frying pan' < PATELLA(M), *ricevere* 'to receive' < RECIPERE, while probably of northern origin, are found, with voiced consonants, in most Italian dialects, and are not peculiar to Tuscan.

A number of words showing intervocalic voicing are so rooted, semantically, in the ground of everyday life that an exotic origin is implausible: e.g., *ago* 'needle'; *fegato* 'liver'; *lago* 'lake'; *luogo* 'place'; *codesto* 'that'; *budello* 'intestine'. *Fegato* (< FICATU(M)) is additionally problematic, in that the [**k**], but not the [**t**], has undergone voicing (cf. also the form *asegutore*, for *esecutore* 'executor', in the fifteenth century Macinghi Strozzi letters). In northern dialects, no such differential susceptibility to voicing is detectable. The demonstrative *codesto* is characteristically Tuscan, and exists alongside voiceless *cotesto*; indeed, it encodes proximity to the addressee, an aspect of the deictic system which is notably absent from most northern Italian varieties (Ch.3: 6).

A further argument against the hypothesis of a northern origin for consonant voicing is the striking absence of words displaying that shortening of long consonants (see section 8) which characterizes all northern dialects, and which some scholars group with northern Italian voicing under the general label of 'lenition'.[47] Shortening in northern Italy is certainly of great antiquity.[48] It is therefore curious that it should not have been imported into Tuscan at the same time as words containing voiced consonants. Moreover, the geographical distribution of voiced and voiceless consonants is not always consistent with absorption into Tuscany from the north via Lucca: Lucchese *statea* 'steelyard' (a weighing device); *mortatella* 'baloney', correspond to *stadera*; *mortadella*, elsewhere in the region. These facts do not, of course, license the contrary suggestion (cf. Merlo (1933)) that voicing must be the indigenous development in Tuscany, since the overwhelming majority of clearly native lexical items, including grammatical formatives such as the second person plural and past participle endings, contain voiceless consonants: *ruota* 'wheel'; *sete* 'thirst'; *aceto* 'vinegar'; *capo* 'head'; *apre* 'he opens'; *fuoco* 'fire'; *dico*

'I say'; *dito* 'finger'; *amato* 'loved'; *venite* 'you come', etc. So the problem of intervocalic voicing remains unsolved.[49]

7.2.1 Voicing of intervocalic sibilants

The hypothesis of lexical borrowing from the north as one source of voiced consonants is supported by the treatment of intervocalic sibilants (see Franceschi (1965)), which in northern dialects are regularly subject to voicing. Latin [**s**] is generally preserved in native Tuscan words (e.g., in *asino* 'donkey'; *mese* 'month'; *naso* 'nose'; *casa* 'house'), although it must be recognized that many Tuscan placenames, such as *Fiesole* or *Cesana*, unlikely to be loans from other dialects, also display voicing of [**s**] (cf. Castellani (1960: 67–70)); we have already discussed in section 6 the voicing of reflexes of [**sj**]. Significantly, the incidence of [**z**] is highest in the north of Tuscany (especially around Lucca and Pisa), and lowest in the far south. Among words with [**z**] we find ecclesiastical and religious items such as *quaresima* 'Lent', *chiesa* 'church', *paradiso* 'heaven', *cresima* 'confirmation', *Gesù* 'Jesus', *diocesi* 'diocese', *elemosina* 'alms', *fariseo* 'pharisee', *battesimo* 'baptism'. The suffix *-ese* has a voiceless sibilant, save in *francese* 'French' (a word whose transmission via northern Italy is quite plausible) and *marchese* 'marquis'. The association of sibilant voicing with 'elevated' and relatively 'exotic' vocabulary seems to have been such, that learnèd and exotic words in general are pronounced with sibilant voicing: e.g., *fantasia* 'fantasy'; *fase* 'phase'; *fisica* 'physics', etc. Even *quasi* 'almost', is in origin a loan from Latin, and correspondingly displays [**z**]. It is probably this association of voiced sibilant pronunciations with that which is learnèd and culturally prestigious which accounts also for the fact that the voiced affricate [**ʣ**], instead of [**ts**], is characteristic of learnèd vocabulary: *Zebedeo* 'Zebedee'; *zinco* 'zinc'; *romanzo* 'novel'; *rizoma* 'rhizome', etc. See also Ch.5: 3.1.3.4.

7.3 Tuscan spirantization

7.3.1 The theory of the Etruscan substrate

No less problematic than the voicing of voiceless stops is their spirantization in Tuscan. Spirantization is unique to Tuscany,[50] and an excessive preoccupation with its phonetic and geographical uniqueness has favoured a vogue (of which Merlo (1927) is the foremost example) for attributing its origin to the linguistic habits of the ancient Etruscans. The evidence for an Etruscan substrate in Tuscan is extremely tenuous:[51] there is a very rough geographical correspondence between the extent of spirantization and the ancient territory of the Etruscans, and there is evidence (particularly from the way in which Greek and other loanwords were transliterated into the Etruscan alphabet), that Etruscans tended to *aspirate* voiceless stop consonants. Opponents of the Etruscan hypothesis (e.g., Hall (1949); Rohlfs (1966); Izzo (1972)) have variously objected that: (i) the territories of the ancient Etruscans (comprising modern Tuscany roughly from the Arno southwards, and parts of modern Umbria and Lazio to the north and west of the Tiber) and the geographical extent of modern spirantization are far from coextensive – it is not found, for example, in most of Lazio and Umbria, which were the areas most densely populated by the Etruscans in pre-Roman times; (ii) there is no unequivocal attestation of spirantization of [**k**] until Tolomei alludes to it in 1525, and none for [**t**] and [**p**] before the eighteenth century; (iii) the varieties of Tuscan imported to Corsica (and to parts of Sardinia) around the year 1000 show no sign of spirantization; (iv) if spirantization were of Etruscan origin, its operation would presumably have antedated the palatalization of [**k**] before front vowels (see section 6): we should expect, therefore, to encounter ****'diːhi**; ****'paːhe** < CL DICIS 'you say'; PACE(M) 'peace', rather than the actually occurring Tuscan dialect forms with a palatal consonant (**'diːʃi**; **'paːʃe**); (v) the epigraphic evidence suggests that the changes attested in Etruscan involved *aspiration* (i.e., a delayed release of closure, resulting in a loud expulsion of air after release) not *spirantization*; (vi) Etruscan *aspiration* can, in any case, be shown not to have been restricted to the intervocalic position; (vii) the structure of Tuscan is otherwise devoid of remnants of a putative Etruscan linguistic substrate (although Rohlfs (1972b) discusses some possible lexical remnants in Tuscan dialects).

None of these objections is fatally damaging to the 'Etruscan hypothesis', as Giannelli (1983) has demonstrated. Phonetic changes spread through space as well as time, so that discrepancies in geographical domain are to be expected. Lack of attestation before the sixteenth century is simply 'neutral': spirantization may long have been associated with the lower social classes, without 'surfacing' in written forms. The varieties of Tuscan imported into the Tyrrhenian islands originate from western Tuscany – a region chiefly characterized, as we shall see later, by *voicing*, rather than spirantization, of the relevant consonants. The affricate [**ʧ**] is realized as [**ʃ**] in intervocalic position in Tuscany (section 6), and we cannot rule out the *possibility* that [**ʃ**] reflects a palatalized variant of an original *[**h**], occurring in the environment of a front vowel (cf. Giannelli (1983: 62)). A change from aspirate to spirant articulation is a simple and plausible diachronic change, attested in the history of many languages. And if, as is possible, aspiration was a 'tendency' in Etruscan, with variable realizations (cf. Agostiniani (1983: 58)), then it might have come to establish itself preferentially in intervocalic position. Indeed, Giannelli and Savoia

(1978; 1980) have shown that Tuscan spirantization remains a phonetic *variable*, whose degree of articulatory constriction, and range of input consonants, vary according not only to locality and to the age of speakers, but to such factors as tempo, register and information content. In short, nothing excludes the possibility that spirantization, or the phonetic tendencies giving rise to it, might have survived as a phonetic variable in Tuscany since Etruscan times. But, as Giannelli's sober review of the arguments (1983) demonstrates, this possibility is at best a remote one, sorely wanting for cogent corroboration.

7.4 Spirantization and voicing as 'weakenings'

A resolution of these problems is promised by a perspective, also assumed (in somewhat different forms) by Weinrich (1958) and Contini (1960), which concentrates not on the uniqueness of Tuscan spirantization, but on its complementarity – both geographical and phonological – within the framework of Italo-Romance 'weakening' of Latin short voiceless occlusives. 'Weakening' describes any kind of attenuation of the maximal blockage of airflow and cessation of vibration of the vocal chords which is inherent in the articulation of voiceless stop consonants. Italo-Romance displays at least two major varieties of weakening: (i) spirantization and (ii) lenition. The latter is a relaxation of muscular tension during the articulation of intervocalic consonants. If this relaxation includes slackening of the vocal chords, these may continue to vibrate, giving rise to actual *voicing* of the consonants. Lenition (and concomitant voicing) is characteristic of much of upper southern, and central, Italy: e.g., Umbrian **le pa'ta̬ːt̬e 'k̬ɔtte** or **le ba'daːde 'gɔtte** 'the cooked potatoes'. It is also encountered over much of the periphery of Tuscany.[52] The remainder of western Tuscany (a zone bounded by Viareggio and San Marcello in the north, extending beyond Empoli and Volterra to the east, and including Grosseto to the south) displays an intersection of lenition and 'central' Tuscan spirantization. In sum, virtually the whole of Tuscany manifests either spirantization or lenition (including voicing), and an intersection of the two patterns in the west. There are close structural parallels between the two weakening processes. Both operate across word boundaries (**la 'haːsa** and **la 'gaːsa** 'the house'), and both show a propensity to affect [**k**] to a greater degree than [**p**] and [**t**]: in some marginal areas (e.g., Firenzuola and around Pistoia) spirantization affects [**k**] with greater frequency, and often with a greater degree of opening, than the dental and the labial; in the west, voicing of velars is more frequent than that of dentals (which, in turn, is more frequent than that of labials – see Giannelli and Savoia (1978: 25; 1980: 43).

These properties make Tuscan weakening superficially unlike northern Italian voicing of consonants, which is predominantly word-internal and does not privilege velar consonants over others. Also, northern Italian voicing was blocked where the diphthong [**aw**] preceded the consonant (e.g., *ˈ**awka** > ˈ**oːka** 'goose'), but Tuscan lenition/voicing (and spirantization) display no such sensitivity (e.g., ˈ**ɔːga** (ˈ**ɔːha**)). It is unlikely that Tuscan voicing could have been 'borrowed' from the north, but the geographical contiguity of northern and central-southern Italian voicing raises the strong suspicion that they share a common origin, in the kind of lenition which remains live in central and upper southern Italy. The reason why voicing in northern Italy is confined almost entirely to word-internal position may be that, in this position, the consonant is *always* intervocalic and therefore maximally exposed to lenition. Word-initial consonants, in contrast, are not always intervocalic (they may be preceded by a pause, or by another word ending in a consonant), and consequently would have displayed both voiced and voiceless variants (e.g., ***la** ˈ**garne** 'the meat' vs. ***iŋ** ˈ**karne** 'in meat'), a variation ultimately resolved in favour of the voiceless consonant (**la** ˈ**karne**).[53] Giannelli and Savoia's fine-grained study[54] of modern Tuscan spirantization and lenition leads them to postulate (1980: 87–94) an original situation throughout Tuscany in which voiceless consonants were subject to varying degrees of weakening, with at least two possible realizations: spirantization or lenition. They suggest that the two weakenings stood in a complementary relationship (1980: 57f.) such that one of them tended to operate in the absence of the other. In modern Florentine, while spirantization is the norm, whenever it is avoided – for example, for reasons of style or register – lenition is likely to operate in its stead (Giannelli and Savoia (1978: 43f.)).

Spirantizing variants seem to have found particular favour in Florence and surrounding area. We can only speculate on the reasons for this local preference. Perhaps the growing cultural and linguistic prestige of Florentine induced in speakers a greater resistance to deviations from prestigious linguistic norms:[55] the spirants represent a less glaring deviation from the occlusive articulations in that the voiced sounds [**d**], [**g**] and [**b**] were already part of the phonological inventory of Tuscan (and could enter into phonemic oppositions with the voiceless stops), whereas the spirants were merely 'allophonic' variants. This preference might have been reinforced by orthographical considerations: voicing would have produced consonants with a distinct orthographic representation (the letters *g*, *d* and *b*); the spirants, in contrast, were not represented by any distinct letters of the alphabet. Elsewhere in Tuscany (and other parts of central Italy), lenition (with resulting voicing) prevailed. We would attach little importance to any consideration that voicing might have been avoided in order to eschew loss of a phonemic opposition with original [**d**], [**g**] and [**b**]. After all, in many Tuscan, and other, dialects, such merger did occur! At some date, possibly the mid sixteenth century (see Giannelli and Savoia (1980: 63f.)), Florentine spirantizations were extended into areas of Tuscany previously characterized by lenition.

The assumption of an indigenous lenition, often resulting in voicing, and originally present, alongside spirantization, throughout Tuscany, offers a satisfactory account not only of its presence in indigenous vocabulary, and of the asymmetry of voicing in a word like *fegato*, but also of the fact that voiced, but not shortened, consonants were sometimes imported from northern Italy. The voiced sounds would have been consistent with the local Tuscan tendency to voicing, but shortened consonants found no counterpart in indigenous phonetic developments. That standard Italian conserves the voiceless intervocalic occlusives may be due in part to the failure of the orthography to indicate spirantization, but also to a tendency for the more cultured and conservative Tuscan (and particularly Florentine) speech, to minimize the effects of weakening of any kind.

8 Consonant lengthening, and syllable structure

The dialects of central and southern Italy, and Sardinian, are distinguished among the Romance varieties in that they have retained Latin long consonants. Elsewhere (including the northern Italian dialects), consonantal length has been lost (35).

(35)

CL	Venetian	Tuscan	
TERRA(M)	**ˈtɛra**	**ˈtɛrra**	‘earth’
ANNU(M))	**ˈɑno**	**ˈanno**	‘year’
PASSU(M)	**ˈpaso**	**ˈpasso**	‘step’
MITTO	**ˈmeto**	**ˈmetto**	‘I put’
CABALLU(M)	**kaˈvalo**	**kaˈvallo**	‘horse’

This phonological rift between central and southern Italo-Romance (with Sardinian) and the rest of the Romance world is widened by the fact that the former not only conserves consonantal length, but acquires *new* long consonants, from two major sources,[56] namely, syllable-initial strengthening, and regressive assimilation.

8.1 Syllable-initial strengthening

Proto-Romance consonants were lengthened before the glides [**j**] and [**w**] (see section 5), and also before the liquid [**l**] (36).

(36)

LATIN	P-R glide	P-R lengthening	Italian	
SAPIAT	*'**sapja**	*'**sappja**	'**sappja**	'he knows'
SIMIA(M)	*'**simja**	*'**simmja**	**ʃimmja**	'monkey'
FUTUO	*'**fotwo**	*'**fottwo**	'**fotto**	'I copulate'
HABUI	*'**abwi**	*'**abbwi**	'**ebbi**	'I had'
UOLUI	*'**volwi**	*'**vollwi**	'**volli**	'I wanted'
IANUARIU(M)	***jan'warju**	***jan'nwarju**	**ʤen'naːjo**	'January'
FOLIA	*'**fɔlja**	*'**fɔllja**	'**fɔʎʎa**	'leaf'
AQUA(M)	*'**akwa**	*'**akkwa**	'**akkwa**	'water'
OCULU(M)	*'**ɔklu**	*'**ɔkklu**	'**ɔkkjo**	'eye'
FIBULA(M)	*'**fibla**	*'**fibbla**	'**fibbja**	'brooch'
TEGULA(M)	*'**tegla**	*'**teggla**	'**teggja**	'baking tray'

Lengthening before yod explains why, in intervocalic position, the consonants palatalized by yod are also invariably long (see section 5), and that before the glide [**w**] explains the lengthening of stem-final consonants observable in the passato remoto of many irregular verbs, into which [**w**] has frequently been introduced as a result of the morphological analogies discussed in (Ch.3: 8.5): e.g., *caddi* 'I fell' < *'**kadwi**; *seppi* 'I knew' < *'**sapwi**; *stetti* 'I stood' < *'**stetwi**.

Lengthening before the glides reflects a principle of syllable structure which has more extensive manifestations in the history of Italian phonology. The fundamental syllable structure in Italo-Romance dialects is CV (consonant + vowel). This is also, incidentally, the syllable structure that children acquire first when learning their native language (cf. Jakobson (1968)), and is extremely widespread among the world's languages. By saying that the fundamental syllable structure is CV we mean that the onset of the syllable involves maximal constriction of the vocal tract, and is maximally 'strong', while the coda is maximally 'weak', in that vocal tract constriction is minimal. Among consonants, the obstruents are 'stronger', and at the top of the 'consonantal strength scale' are occlusives, in that they involve complete or partial blockage of airflow. At the 'weaker' end of the scale are liquids, and glides (significantly also known as 'semivowels'), which involve minimal constriction, and are most 'vowel-like'. The following strength hierarchy may be projected for consonants (37):[57]

(37)

⇓	⇓
glides	**j/w 'weaker'**
liquids	**r/l**
nasals	**n/m**
voiced fricatives	**v/z**
voiceless fricatives and voiced stops	**f/s/d/g/b**
voiceless stops	**t/k/p 'stronger'**
⇓	⇓

A consequence of the tendency for syllable onsets to be maximally 'consonantal' (or 'strong'), and for syllable codas (or 'ends') to be maximally vowel-like ('weak') is, that in chains of syllables, a syllable-final consonant is generally not 'stronger' than an immediately following syllable-initial consonant. Lengthening before glides and [l] in Italo-Romance is interpretable as a strategy for removing violations of this syllable-boundary constraint.

Initially, the syllable boundary is likely to have fallen in between the consonant and the glide: e.g. *ˈ**fɔl-ja** 'leaf'; *ˈ**ab-ja** 'may she have'; *ˈ**fot-wo** 'I copulate'. The alternative, **ˈ**fɔ-lja**; **ˈ**a-bja** and **ˈ**fo-two** would have been less likely, since Latin had no precedent for syllable-initial **Cj** or **Cw**,[58] but plenty of examples of syllable-initial [**j**] and [**w**] (UENIT [ˈ**wɛnit**] 'he comes', IACET [ˈ**jaket**] 'he lies', etc.). Such a syllable division would, however, have violated the general principle that syllable onsets should not be weaker than the preceding coda. This violation may have been subsequently remedied by projection (lengthening) of the preceding consonant into the onset of the following syllable: *ˈ**fot-wo** > *ˈ**fot-two**; *ˈ**fɔl-ja** > *ˈ**fɔl-lja**; *ˈ**ab-ja** > *ˈ**ab-bja**, etc.

This analysis, proposed for Italian[59] by Vennemann and Murray (1983) (also Vennemann (1988: 45f.)), is not without difficulties. Why could the putative violation of syllable boundary strength properties not have been resolved simply by transferring the consonant into the following syllable (*ˈ**ab-ja** > **ˈ**a-bja**)? One possible explanation, like that given by Vennemann and Murray for similar phenomena in Germanic, invokes stressed syllable 'weight' conditions (see section 1). Briefly, a Proto-Romance stressed syllable was always 'heavy', that is, it contained either a long vowel, or a short vowel + syllable-final consonant. Now Proto-Romance [**j**] and [**w**] very frequently followed a stressed syllable, so that shifting the final consonant of the stressed syllable into the following one would have violated the weight condition, by leaving a 'light' stressed syllable. A solution accommodating both stressed syllable weight conditions, and syllable boundary strength conditions, is *extension*, rather than resyllabification, of the consonant. The same strategy can be seen to apply in modern Italian words having final consonants: intervocalically, such word-final vowels are projected into the following syllable, rather than undergoing resyllabification (e.g., *tram elettrico* 'electric tram' is **'tram-me-'lɛt-tri-ko**, not ****'traː-me-'lɛt-tri-ko**). As for the lengthening effects of [**l**], virtually all instances of word-internal intervocalic [C + l] arose from syncope of an intervening vowel (e.g., NE-BU-LA(M) 'mist' > ***'neb-la**; UE-TU-LU(M) 'old' > ***'vɛk-lu**), where [**l**] had been *syllable-initial*. It is therefore plausible that ***'nebla** and ***'vɛklu** at first retained the syllabification ***'neb-la** and ***'vɛk-lu**, so that strengthening of the onset of the second syllable was achieved, as with the glides, by extension of the preceding consonant: ***'neb-la**; ***'vɛk-lu** > ***'neb-bla**; ***'vɛk-klu** > **'neb-bja**; **'vɛk-kjo**. That the other liquid, [**r**], did not usually condition lengthening of a preceding consonant[60] is entirely consistent with this general hypothesis, since word-internal syllable-initial [C**r**], unlike [C**l**], was perfectly common in Latin (e.g., NI-GRU(M) 'black', PA-TRE(M) 'father'). The derivation of the Italian forms **'neːro** 'black' < ***'negru** < NIGRU(M); **in'tɛːro** 'whole' < ***in'tɛgru** < INTEGRU(M); **peri'taːre** 'to hesitate' < ***pegri'tare** < PIGRITARE; **'beːre** 'to drink' < ***'bev(e)re** < BIBERE, suggests that in the consonant clusters [**gr**] and [**vr**] the first segment was deleted.

Evidently, lengthening of a preceding consonant is not an available option where no consonant precedes (for example, in word-initial position). Initial and intervocalic 'weak' syllable onsets also tend, already in common Proto-Romance, to undergo strengthening, by increasing their degree of consonantality. Intervocalic and word-initial [**w**] is strengthened to the labiodental fricative [**v**]: UADIT > ***'wade** > *va* 'he goes'; UIUO > ***'wiwo** > *vivo* 'I live'; LAUARE > ***la'vare** > *lavare* 'to wash'. In loanwords of Germanic origin, initial [**w**] was strengthened to [**gw**]: *guerra* 'war', *guisa* 'guise', *guadagno* 'gain'. In word-initial position, [**j**] was strengthened by the introduction of an alveolar occlusive (giving rise to a voiced palatal affricate): IAM > ***ja** > **ʤa** 'already'; IANUARIU(M) > ***jan'warju** > **ʤen'naːjo** *gennaio* 'January'; IUNIU(M) > ***'junnju** > **'ʤuɲɲo** *giugno* 'June'. In intervocalic position, Latin I (> Proto-Romance [**j**]) was already subject to lengthening (attested in inscriptions such as MAIIUS 'May', PEIIUS 'worse'); Proto-Romance [**j**] from intervocalic [**g**] + front vowel (see section 6 below), converging with [**j**] from Latin, is similarly lengthened. The resulting long glide is then subject to the same affrication rule observable for this glide in word-initial position: MAIU(M) > MAIIU(M) > ***'majjo** > **'madʤo** *maggio* 'May'; REGIT > *'**reje** > *'**rɛjje** > '**rɛddʒe** *regge* 'he holds'.[61]

The strengthening principle is not ineluctable in the historical phonology of Italian. Intervocalic [**g**] before a stressed front vowel was often subject to deletion (SAGITTA(M) > *saetta* 'arrow'), creating a vowel-initial syllable. Also, Tuscan syllables commencing with vowels do not generally acquire a 'strengthened' onset. The position is different in various southern dialects (see Rohlfs (1966: 473–7)), where vowel-initial syllables often acquire an initial consonant. Tuscan occasionally develops [**v**] in semi-learnèd forms where [**o**] is immediately followed by another vowel (cf. Rohlfs (1966: 415)): RUINA(M) > ***ro'ina** > *rovina* 'ruin'; UICTUALIA > ***vetto'aːlja** > *vettovaglia* 'victuals'; GENUA > *'**dʒeːnoa** > *Genova*. OTuscan showed a tendency to insert [**j**] before stressed [**e**] in hiatus: *Bartolomejo*, *Andreja*, *cimineja* 'chimney'. The deletion of original [**j**] (derived from [**g**]) in *saetta* 'arrow', *maestro* 'schoolmaster', *paese* 'village', etc., is perhaps interpretable as a hypercorrect reaction against such insertion of yod. We also find [**g**] in OTuscan *Pagolo* (= *Paolo*); *pagone* 'peacock' < ***pa'one** <***pa'vone**; *sego* 'tallow' < *'**seo** < *'**sevo**; OSienese *aguto* 'had' < ***a'uto** < ***a'vuto**.

Unlike its counterpart [**l**], [**r**] is not susceptible to projection into the following syllable before [**j**] or [**w**]. The sequence *[**rw**] is therefore resolved as [**rv**]: *parvi* 'I seemed' < *'**par-wi** < PARUI; *serve* 'he serves' < *'**sɛr-we** < SERUIT. Similarly, with the exception of a small enclave of northern Calabria (cf. Rohlfs (1966: 403)), yod has no lengthening effect on preceding [**r**]. The failure of [**r**] to undergo lengthening possibly reflects the fact that it is almost as low on the strength hierarchy as [**j**]; little advantage would therefore have accrued from projecting it into the following syllable.

8.2 Regressive assimilation of consonants

In regressive assimilation, a consonant in syllable-final position, becomes identical in position of articulation to an immediately following consonant (38). The result, in intervocalic position, is a lengthened version of that following consonant.

(38)

CL	Italian		CL	Italian	
DIXIT	**'disse**	'he said'	FRIG(I)DU(M)	**'freddo**	'cold'
AD+BATTUO	**ab'batto**	'I fell'	FRAG-MENTU(M)	**fram'mɛnto**	'fragment'
DICTU(M)	**'detto**	'said'	RUPTU(M)	**'rotto**	'broken'
AUT+UERU(M)	**ov'vɛːro**	'or'	NEC+MINUS	**nem'meːno**	'not even'

The strength hierarchy alluded to above is relevant here, too. Consonants at the weaker end of the hierarchy do not assimilate, except to following consonants that are equally weak, or weaker. The liquid [**r**] does not assimilate (e.g., **'parto** 'I leave'; **'parko** 'park'; **'parlo** 'I speak'; **'karne** 'flesh'; **'vɛrme** 'worm'; **'pɛrso** 'lost')[62]; [**l**] assimilates only before [**r**]; the nasals assimilate only before [**r**] and [**l**]. The sequences [**nl**], [**lr**] and [**nr**] are, in any case, rare. They did not occur within Latin words, but arose in Proto-Romance as a result of syncope of atonic vowels. Assimilation of [**nr**] and [**lr**] is the source of a major variety of stem allomorphy in the future tense forms of some verbs (e.g., *rimanere* 'to stay' – *rimarrò* 'I shall stay'; *valere* 'to be worth' -*varrà* 'it will be worth'), where the vowel preceding [**r**] is deleted (39).

(39)

Proto-Romance	Syncope	Assimilation	
***veni'ra**	***ven'ra**	**ver'ra**	'he will come'
***tene'ra**	***ten'ra**	**ter'ra**	'he will hold'
***vole'ra**	***vol'ra**	**vor'ra**	'he will want'
***dole'ra**	***dol'ra**	**dor'ra**	'it will hurt'

Other examples are OTuscan *orrare* (= *onorare* 'to honour'), *merrò* (= *menerò* 'I will lead') and *possiallo* (*possiamlo* = *possiamolo* 'we can (do) it'); *pialla* 'plane'< PLAN(U)LA(M); *spilla* 'pin' < SPIN(U)LA(M).

8.2.1 Assimilation and the problem of rafforzamento sintattico

The most dramatic structural effect of lengthening lies not in inflectional morphology, but in the phenomenon known as *rafforzamento sintattico* or *raddoppiamento (fono)sintattico* (hereafter RS), whereby a word-initial consonant is lengthened when preceded, within the same syntactic phrase,[63] by (i) a word ending in a vowel which is stressed (or, more accurately, 'not unstressed'),[64] or (ii) by certain lexical items specified as triggering RS (40). Such lengthening is not represented in orthography except when, by convention, the triggering word and the word undergoing RS are joined in writing as a single word. A structurally and orthographically prominent case of RS is constituted by lengthening of the initial consonant of enclitic pronouns preceded by stressed second person singular imperatives.

(40)

(i)

ʧit'ta p'pɛrsa	*città persa*	'lost city'
sa'ra b'bɛllo	*sarà bello*	'it'll be nice'
vener'di p'prɔssimo	*venerdì prossimo*	'next Friday'
koli'bri b'blu	*colibrì blu*	'blue humming bird'
o'blɔ k'kjuːso	*oblò chiuso*	'closed porthole'
par'lɔ f'fɔrte	*parlò forte*	'he talked loudly'
kaf'fɛ t'turko	*caffè turco*	'Turkish coffee'
vir'tu nnatu'raːle	*virtù naturale*	'natural virtue'

(ii)

'sopra mmi'laːno	*sopra Milano*	'over Milan'
'sopra t'tutto	*soprattutto*	'above all'
'kome l'lui	*come lui*	'like him'
'kwalke v'vɔlta	*qualche volta*	'sometimes'
a m'me	*a me*	'to me'
da k'kaːpo	*da capo (or daccapo)*	'from the start'
'iːo e tte	*io e te*	'I and you'
'io o l'lui	*io o lui*	'I or he'
se k'kanti	*se canti*	'if you sing'
ma s'sai	*ma sai*	'but you know'

fallo	*fallo!*	'do it!'
'ditʧelo	*diccelo!*	'tell us it'
'dammi	*dammi!*	'give me'

It is undisputed that some instances of RS arise from regressive assimilation, where the triggering word originally terminated in a consonant: A(D) > *a* 'to'; *SUPER AD > *sopra* 'above'; *DE AD (or *DE AB) > *da* 'from'; ET > *e* 'and'; AUT > *o* 'or'; *QUOMODO ET > *come* 'how'; NEC > *né* 'nor'. However, oxytones, virtually unknown in Latin, are a Romance innovation (see 1.2), arising usually through loss of a final syllable, leaving a stressed final vowel. Their lengthening effect cannot therefore be attributed to a historically underlying final consonant. Some other words triggering RS, such as *ho* 'I have', *do* 'I give', *sto* 'I stand', *so* 'I know', *tu* 'you', *se* 'if', *sé* 'self', *te* 'you', *me* 'me', never terminated in a consonant.

The main controversy is between two hypotheses:

(i) RS originates exclusively as a consonantal assimilation. The original conditioning final consonant is eventually lost (see section 9), but the property of provoking a lengthening of a following initial consonant remains. The conditioning environment for RS thereby becomes opaque (i.e., it can no longer be determined from the phonological form of the conditioning word, which now ends in a vowel). Since RS now occurs after vowels, it is possible to generalize the property of triggering RS analogically to other vowel-final words, and particularly to all oxytones, which did not originally terminate in an assimilating consonant.

— or —

(ii) Lengthening triggered by oxytones arises independently of assimilation, as a consequence of the principle that all stressed syllables that occur within a phrase (i.e., do not occur at the end of a sentence, or before a pause) must be *heavy* (i.e., must contain either a long vowel, or a short vowel + consonant). In Proto-Romance, final vowels, whether stressed (in oxytones) or unstressed, had all been short. RS might therefore be viewed as a phonological 'make-weight' strategy, producing a heavy word-final stressed syllable, by projecting or extending into it the initial consonant of a following word.

The major objection to (ii) is that it fails to explain why syllable weight should be made up by consonant lengthening, rather than by vowel lengthening. After all, in the stressed syllables of paroxytones it is (cf. Tekavčić (1980 I: 13–15)) the *vowel* that is lengthened: from Latin LATUS 'side' we have **'laːto** not **'latto, and from MARE 'sea' **'maːre**, not **'marre. However, Vincent (1988a) proposes that consonant lengthening was the *normal* strategy for creation of heavy syllables, that it applied both in oxytones and in proparoxytones, and that vowel lengthening in paroxytones was an *exception* to this procedure. Vincent cites a number of Italian proparoxytones in which the vowel has not been lengthened, as is attested by the occasional absence of diphthongization of the low mid vowels [ɛ] and [ɔ]; we should recall that diphthongization is the normal fate of lengthened low mid vowels in stressed open syllables. For example, the diphthong is absent in: *pècora* 'sheep'; *mèdico* 'doctor'; *òpera* 'work'; *pòpolo* 'people'; *vòmere* 'ploughshare'.[65] In this respect the proparoxytones are identical to the oxytones, in which diphthongization is also blocked: *no* 'no' (**nɔ**); *però* 'however'; *ciò* 'that', etc. In addition, originally short consonants are sometimes lengthened after the stressed syllable of proparoxytones: *legìttimo* 'legitimate' < LEGITIMU(M); *àttimo* 'moment' < ATOMU(M); *àbbaco* 'abacus' < ABACU(M); *màcchina* 'machine' < MACHINA(M); *fèmmina* 'woman' < FEMINA(M).

These facts suggest that, in proparoxytones, consonants, not vowels, tended to be lengthened. In this respect, proparoxytones may be seen as behaving identically to oxytones, and it becomes possible to assert that consonant lengthening might be the *normal* method of making a syllable heavy, so that the exceptional case would be constituted by paroxytones, in which the *vowel* is normally lengthened. Significantly for Vincent's argument, there are cases of consonant lengthening even in paroxytones (*tutto* 'all' < TOTU(M); *succo* 'juice' < SUCU(M); *brutto* 'ugly' < BRUTU(M); *coppa* 'cup' < CUPA(M)). The first person plural ending of the passato remoto, in *-mmo*, seems to have arisen via deletion of an original syllable [**i**] (FUIMUS > *'**fuimo** > *fummo* 'we were'; cf. also CIUITATE(M) > ***ʧi'itate** > **ʧit'ta** *città* 'city'). It appears, then, that the resulting proparoxytonic open stressed syllable is made heavy by lengthening of the consonant, rather than the vowel. It is significant that shortening of long consonants in favour of lengthened vowels is never attested.[66] We argued in 8.1 that 'strengthening' of syllable onsets containing glides was achieved by extension of the final consonant of the preceding syllable into the onset of the following syllable, rather than by simply re-assigning that consonant to the following syllable (e.g., from *'**ab-ja** we have '**ab-bja**, not **'**aː-bja**). If this analysis is correct, then it also suggests a preference for maintaining syllable weight by the presence of a syllable-final consonant, rather than by vowel lengthening.

But why should vowel lengthening be the normal result in paroxytones? Vincent (1988a: 429f.) points out that early Latin stress always fell on the initial syllable of a word, regardless of syllable weight; subsequently, and for reasons which remain unclear, stress is known to have been attracted on to the penultimate syllable of a word, whenever that syllable was heavy. In this way, all stressed *open* penultimate syllables contained long vowels, and the structural model for the creation of syllable weight by vowel lengthening in open penultimate syllables was established.

Loporcaro (1988a) favours the alternative view that RS originated in consonantal assimilation, citing many dialects of central and southern Italy (and Sardinia) where RS is demonstrably and exclusively linked to the presence of an original preceding final consonant. As a rule, in the centre-south RS is not triggered by final stressed syllables. According to Loporcaro, RS subsequently evolved differentially from region to region: it has all but disappeared in Umbria, the southern

Marche and the province of Arezzo. The operation of RS after oxytones in Tuscan occurred because 'the vowel preceding the empty consonantal position happened to be stressed in the majority of cases [. . .] this originally redundant feature of the context became pertinent, and a reinterpretation took place, leading the rule to depend on a more transparent phonological condition' (Loporcaro (1988a: 366)). In this view, the sporadic consonantal lengthening observable in proparoxytones, which is the focus of Vincent's attention, is purely accidental, and historically unconnected with RS.

The two perspectives are not incompatible. One might argue, for example, that in Tuscan there was a tendency to achieve syllable weight by a rule of consonant lengthening, which was especially characteristic in proparoxytones but also, occasionally, found in paroxytones, and that the model of consonantal assimilation at *word boundaries* particularly favoured this solution for words stressed at the word boundary (i.e., oxytones). Whatever approach we take, the thorny question remains why RS should occur after oxytones in Tuscan, but not in other central and southern dialects.

9 Syllable-final weakening

In the history of Tuscan there have been relatively few examples of the counterpart to syllable-initial strengthening, namely syllable-final weakening. Examples of syllable-final assimilation to following consonants have already been discussed in 8.2. A pan-Romance development is deletion of syllable-final nasal before a sibilant: MEN-SE(M) > *mese* 'month'; CON-STARE > *costare* 'to cost'; PEN-SARE > *pesare* 'to weigh'. The effects of this change are particularly apparent in parts of the verbal paradigm: *spendere* 'to spend' vs. *speso* 'spent' (SPEN-SU(M)); *scendere* 'to go down' vs. *sceso* 'gone down' (SCEN-SU(M)); *rimanere* 'to stay' vs. *rimasi* 'I remained' (RE-MAN-SI). Forms such as *denso* 'dense' and, perhaps surprisingly, *pensare* 'to think' (an etymological doublet of *pesare* 'to weigh'), reveal a learnèd origin. However deletion of [**n**] has continued to operate, even in learnèd words, in the cluster [**nsC**]: IN-STRU-I-RE > *istruire* 'to instruct'; IN-STI-TU-TUM > *istituto* 'institute'; TRAN-SPOR-TA-RE > *trasportare* 'to transport'; IN-STI-GA-RE > *istigare* or *instigare* 'to instigate', etc.

A form of syllable-final weakening attested in a number of dialects, and sporadically in Tuscan, is a tendency to vocalize syllable-final [**l**], pronouncing it as [**w**]. After [**a**] the result is [**aw**] (whence [**ɔ**], see 4.4). Both retention of [**l**] and vocalization are represented by the pair *talpa* 'mole' and *topa* or *topo* 'mouse' (cf. Rohlfs (1966: 37f.)). OTuscan forms such as *aldo* (= *odo* 'I hear'), *altore* (= *autore* 'author'), *altentico* (= *autentico* 'authentic') are hypercorrect orthographic reactions to this tendency. Speakers of many modern Tuscan dialects, including that of Florence, tend to pronounce syllable-final [l] as [i] (e.g., **ˈvɔitta** 'time' < **ˈvɔlta**; cf. Rohlfs (1966: 344f.)).

10 The word-final consonants

It is a distinctive characteristic of Italian, among the Romance languages, that no native word capable of occurring at the end of a phrase terminates in a consonant. Loanwords (e.g., *sport*; *gas*; *tilt*, etc.), and those grammatical function words which, by their nature, never occur phrase-finally (e.g., *il* 'the'; *con* 'with'; *per* 'for'; *un* 'a'), are the only forms which admit final consonants. Latin, in contrast, admitted almost the full range of consonant sounds in word-final position. The erosion of final consonants may be seen as a particularly strong case of the tendency towards a CV syllable structure. It is notable that those native words which do conserve final consonants end in sonorants, i.e., in 'weak' sounds low on the scale of consonantality. Correspondingly, deletion of final unstressed vowels only applies where the resulting final consonant is [**l**], [**r**] or [**n**] (*aver fatto* 'to have done'; *vuol farlo* 'he wants to do it'; *ben visto* 'well seen'; *l'amor di Dio* 'the love of God', etc.). In central and southern varieties of popular Italian, loanwords in final consonants often acquire a final vowel, usually [**e**]: **ˈspɔrte**; **ˈgasse**, etc. The conservation of final [**d**] from Latin AD in *ad Anna* 'to Anna', etc. (also OTuscan *ched era* 'which was' < CL QUID ERAT) is possible because the [**d**], while at the end of the *word*, is at the beginning of the *syllable*. This [**d**] seems to have been extended analogically to *e* (*ed è* 'and it is'), or it may represent an intervocalic voicing of the final [**t**] of Latin ET. The prevocalic [**d**] was extended, in OTuscan, into certain forms which never terminated in a dental consonant (*sed* for *se* 'if'; *ned* for *né* 'nor'; *mad* for *ma* 'but', etc.).

The exceptions to the general deletion of Latin final consonants are [**s**] (which subsequently yielded [**i**], as in *poi* 'then' < POS(T), *dai* 'you give' < DAS – see section 12), and word-final [**l**] and [**r**] which acquired a following vowel, either by metathesis (SEMPER; QUATTUOR > *sempre* 'always'; *quattro* 'four'), or, in the case of original third declension neuter nouns, by addition of [**e**] (SAL > *sale* 'salt'; COR > *cuore* 'heart'), probably on the analogy of third declension masculines and feminines in -[**e**] (*mese* 'month'; *voce* 'voice', etc.). Also crucial for the morphological evolution of Italo-Romance is loss of final [**t**] (the third person inflectional marker in the verb), and of the final nasal [**m**] (an inflectional marker of the first person singular in some moods and tenses, and of the accusative singular in the noun and adjective). Deletion of the final dental can be seen in the (third person) verb forms *ama* 'he loves' < AMAT, *amano* 'they love' < AMANT, *viene* 'he comes'

< UENIT, *vengono* 'they come' < UENIUNT, *dà* 'he gives' < DAT. Also *o* 'or' < AUT, *e* 'and' < ET, *capo* 'head' < CAPUT. The word-final nasal has survived only in some monosyllables (e.g., *con* 'with' < CUM; *non* 'not' < NON; *son(o)* 'I am' < SUM, but also *già* 'already' < IAM). There is abundant evidence (cf. Allen (1978: 30f.)) that, already in CL, final [**m**] tended to not be pronounced, although its presence was reflected in lengthening and nasalization of the preceding vowel. At any rate, the final nasal consonant is lost in *figlia* 'daughter' < FILIAM; *padre* 'father' < PATREM; *mano* 'hand' < MANUM, also *nome* 'name' < NOMEN; *seme* 'seed' < SEMEN, and the first person singular forms *venda* 'I sell' (subjunctive) < UENDAM; OTuscan *amava* 'I loved' < AMABAM, etc.

11 Dissimilation and metathesis

11.1 Dissimilation

Sequences of identical sonorant consonants (notably [**l**] and [**r**], but also [**n**] and [**m**]), in successive syllables, have been subject to sporadic dissimilation throughout the history of the language: e.g., COLUCULA(M) > *conocchia* 'distaff'; MERCURI DIE(M) > *mercoledì* 'Wednesday'; RARU(M) > *rado* 'scarce'; ARMARIU(M) > *armadio* 'cupboard'; UENENU(M) > *veleno* 'poison'; CANONICU(M) > OTuscan *calonago* 'canon'. The apparent dissimilation of sequences of [**r**]s through substitution of the *first* [**r**] by [**d**] is unique to the verb: e.g., QUÆRERE > *chiedere* 'to ask'; FERIRE > OTuscan *fedire* 'to strike/wound' (modern *ferire*); INTERERE > *intridere* 'to knead'; CONQUIRERE > OTuscan *conquidere* 'to conquer'. But in these verbs the [**d**] appears in all persons and tenses (except for the past participle and passato remoto, *chiesto*, *conquiso*; *chiesi*, *conquisi*), not merely where [**r**] follows (e.g., *intride*; *chiede*; *intrideva*; *chiedeva*, etc.). It is therefore more likely that we have here a case of morphological analogy (see Ch.1: 5.6) where, on the model of verbs in which a passato remoto in [**s**] alternates with other tense forms in [**d**] (e.g., *rise* 'he laughed' vs. present *ride* 'he laughs', imperfect *rideva* etc.), passato remoto forms such as *chiese* and *intrise* have given rise to *chiede*, *chiedeva*; *intride*, *intrideva*, etc., in other tenses.[67] Dissimilation may take the form of deletion of one of the consonants: DE RETRO > *dietro* 'behind'. The segments subject to dissimilation need not be wholly identical. We have dissimilation between two different nasal consonants in NUMERU(M) > *novero* 'number', and in the proper name HIERONYMU(M) > *Girolamo*, of labial consonants in MESPILU(M) > *nespolo* 'medlar tree', and of a palatal and non-palatal lateral in *giglio* (**'ʤiʎʎo**) 'lily', from LILIU(M). That the word for 'July' is *luglio* (**'luʎʎo**), rather than the expected ****'ʤuʎʎo**, from IULIU(M), may be a case of hypercorrection of an initial consonant [ʤ] wrongly assumed to be, like the initial consonant of *giglio*, the result of a dissimilation before a following lateral.

11.2 Metathesis

The lateral consonant [**l**], when preceded by a word-internal consonant, is sometimes subject to metathesis (inversion of position with respect to an adjacent consonant), displaying a marked tendency to migrate into the stressed syllable: FABULA(M) > *ˈ**fabla** > ***flaba** > *fiaba* 'fairy tale'; COMULA(M) > *ˈ**komla** > *ˈ**kloma** > *chioma* 'head of hair'; FUNDULA(M) > *ˈ**fondla** > *ˈ**flonda** > *fionda* 'sling'; POPULU(M) > *ˈ**poplu** > *ˈ**popplu** > *ˈ**ploppu** > *pioppo* 'poplar' (see also Tekavčić (1980: 147f.; 165)). Another kind of metathesis involves reversal of the glide [**j**] and the initial consonant of a following syllable: BAI(U)LA(M) > *ˈ**bajla** > *balia* 'wet nurse'; PAGINA(M) > *ˈ**pajna** > *pania* 'bird lime'; OTuscan *sieda* > *sedia* 'chair'. The motivation for this change is unclear.[68]

12 The phonetic sources of inflectional -e and -i

The origins of these inflectional endings, characteristic of the plurals of nouns and adjectives, and of the second person singular of verbs, are problematic and controversial. Two possibilities have been suggested, one morphological, the other phonetic.[69] The balance of evidence favours the latter view and, anticipating our own conclusion, we have included our discussion in the chapter dedicated to phonology. To summarize briefly, we propose that -**e** and -**i** evolve phonetically from word-final -**as** and -**es**, via a putative intermediate stage *-**ai** and *-**ei**, – although morphological analogy has also played a part in the development of the masculine plural inflection. Since what follows makes crucial reference to the inflectional systems of the Latin noun, adjective and verb, readers unfamiliar with them may find it useful to consult the relevant parts of Chapter 3, sections 1, 3 and 8, first.

At first sight, it might appear that the modern plurals *capre* 'goats'; *asini* 'donkeys' directly continue the Latin nominative plurals CAPRÆ (recall that unstressed Æ, pronounced [**ai**], became [**e**]), and ASINI:). As for second person singular *dormi* 'you sleep', its inflectional ending could continue the long [**iː**] of the Latin DORMI:S (a fourth conjugation verb form). But how are we to explain the following?:

(i) CAPRÆ and ASINI are nominatives, but it is generally the *accusative* which is continued in Italian (see Ch.3: 1.2).

(ii) The nominative plural inflections -Æ (> [**e**]) and -I would have been expected to trigger palatalization of a preceding velar consonant (see section 6). But feminine plural -**e** *never* does so, and palatalization before masculine plural **-i** is rare.

(iii) Modern second person singular **-i** also corresponds to Latin second conjugation ending -ES (SEDE:S > *siedi* 'you sit'), and to the third conjugation ending -IS (UENDIS > *vendi* 'you sell'), where no long [**iː**] is historically underlying. The long E: of SEDE:S, and the short I of UENDIS, would have been expected to yield -***e**.

(iv) The OTuscan inflection *-e*, corresponds to Latin -AS, not only in the plural of nouns and adjectives, but also in the second person singular indicative of first conjugation verbs, and in the second person singular subjunctive of non-first conjugation verbs: e.g., indicative AMAS > *ame* 'you love'; PORTAS > *porte* 'you carry'; subjunctive UENDAS > *vende* 'you buy'.

(v) The modern plural inflection **-i** replaces the Latin third declension plural inflection -ES (CANES > *cani* 'dogs; UOCES > *voci* 'voices').

According to Rohlfs, loss (see section 10) of word-final [**m**] and [**s**], and the merger (see 4.6.1) of final unstressed [**u**] with [**oː**], would have led to the obliteration of the distinction between the accusative singulars CAPRA(M) 'goat', ASINU(M) 'donkey', CANE(M) 'dog', etc., on the one hand, and their corresponding plurals CAPRAS, ASINOS, CANES, etc., on the other. To obviate such obscuration of the inflectional number distinction, the distinctive nominative inflections -Æ and -I were purportedly preferred over the accusatives. This explains *capre* and *asini*, but not *cani* (whose nominative plural was CANES), for which Rohlfs invokes analogical generalization of the plural inflection -**i**.

Rohlfs (1968: 247f.) invokes a similar principle of disambiguation of a neutralization occasioned by loss of word-final inflectional consonants, to account for the development of the second person singular of the verb. Loss of second person -**s** and third person -**t** would have yielded **'sjɛːde** 'you sit' identical to **'sjɛːde** 'he sits' (< SEDES, SEDET), although there is no incontrovertible evidence for this in OTuscan, and Rohlfs himself suggests that some apparent examples in OSienese may have a different explanation. This loss of distinction was supposedly remedied by analogical extension of the fourth conjugation second person singular inflection **-i** (on the model of *dormi* 'you sleep'). But in the first conjugation, the identity of ***'aːma** 'you love' and ***'aːma** 'he loves' was supposedly remedied by the introduction of the *second conjugation* second person singular inflection -**e**, as in *tu siede* (cf. Rohlfs (1968: 248 n2)). What is undisputed is that inflectional -**i** in the first conjugation was introduced analogically, on the model of the second person singular of the other conjugations.

Rohlfs' analysis presents various problems. Appeal to avoidance of neutralization is always risky, since Italo-Romance dialects (and languages in general) can and do tolerate obscuration of inflectional distinctions; indeed, there are areas of northern Tuscany (Garfagnana and Lunigiana) in which neutralization of the accusative singular and plural inflections, and of the second and third person plural inflections, has actually occurred (cf. Rohlfs (1968: 28f.; 247f.)). While generalization of the fourth conjugation second person singular inflection -**i** into the second and third conjugations might seem at least conceivable, it is not at all clear why a second and third conjugation second person singular inflection -**e** should have been extended into the first conjugation. After all, such an -**e** (unlike -**i**) would not have been a *distinctive* second person singular inflection, since -**e** also characterized the third person singular (e.g., *perde* 'he loses'; *dorme* 'he sleeps'); and if the more distinctive -**i** could be extended analogically into the third conjugation, why should it not have been extended into the first conjugation as well?

An alternative, and in our view more plausible, approach is to view inflectional -**e** and -**i** as *phonetic* developments of the unstressed vowels, triggered by original final [**s**]. Inflectional -**s** survives intact in Ibero-Romance, Gallo-Romance and Sardinian. Traces of inflectional -**s** also appear in some northern Italian dialects.[70] After a *stressed* vowel, [**s**] has generally become [**i**] in Italo-Romance: *noi* 'we' < NOS; *voi* 'you' < UOS;[71] *poi* 'then' < POS(T); *crai* 'tomorrow' < CRAS (in southern dialects); *stai* 'you stand' < STAS. This lends weight to the view, proposed, for example, by Reichenkron (1939) and Lausberg (1965: 431–3), that unstressed final [**as**] and [**es**] yielded *[**ai**] and *[**ei**] (Lausberg actually proposes *[**ai̯**] and *[**ei̯**]), which subsequently monophthongized,[72] to [**e**] and [**i**]: TERRAS > *'**tɛrrai** > '**tɛrre** 'lands'; CANTAS > *'**kantai** > '**kante** 'you sing'; UIDES > *'**vedei** > '**veːdi** 'you see'; CANES > *'**kanei** > '**kaːni** 'dogs'. For a succinct survey of this, and similar, views, see Tekavčić (1980 II: 50). Some scholars, such as Sabatini (1965), opine that final [**s**], rather than a putative *[**i**], has a closing effect on the preceding vowel, raising unstressed [**a**] and [**e**] to [**e**] and [**i**]; the conditioning [**s**] was then deleted. That final [**s**] might have produced some closing effect is by no means impossible,[73] but the evidence for the change of final [**s**] to [**i**], and the very high degree of plausibility of a subsequent monophthongization in unstressed syllables (Italo-Romance normally admits diphthongs only in *stressed* syllables), lead us to favour Lausberg's hypothesis. The same process in the second declension should have yielded *?'**asinui**, then *?'**asinu**, from ASINOS 'donkeys'. It is not impossible that *?'**asinu** actually existed: given that posttonic [**u**] is replaced by [**o**] in Tuscan (section 4.6.1), we might have expected *?'**aːsino**, identical to the singular (cf. fourth declension plural MANUːS > OTuscan *mano* 'hands'), and thus a prime candidate for disambiguation by introduction of a more distinctive inflection. That is speculation; however it may be, the presence of inflectional -**i** in *asini* is probably due to analogical extension from the *cani* type.[74]

The plural inflection **-i**, derived from Latin -ES, characterizes both feminine and masculine forms (e.g., masculine *i cani* 'the dogs' and feminine *le voci* 'the voices'). Why, then, should analogical extension of this **-i** be restricted to *masculine* nouns?[75] That this development is limited to the masculine may reflect vestigial survival of the Latin second declension *masculine* plural inflection -I. It is significant, in this regard, that **-i** was not at first extended into the plural of *mano* 'hand', a *feminine* survivor of the CL fourth declension, which in OTuscan was invariant (*la mano*, *le mano*). Postulation of a system in which the CL feminine plural inflection -Æ has given way completely to a continuant of -AS, while a nominative -I was vestigially retained is, by the way, entirely consistent with the inflectional system known to have existed in early Gallo-Romance. Various Rhaeto-Romance dialects also show evidence (see Haiman and Benincà (1992: 116–19)) of coexistent masculine plural inflections in **-s** and **-i**.

Palatalization of velar consonants before front vowels (see section 6) has an important bearing on the problem. If the inflections **-e** and **-i** directly continue the Latin nominative inflections -Æ and -I, then we would expect to find regular palatalization of stem-final velars before these inflections. But if these inflections are successors of inflectional -AS and -OS (respectively, by phonetic development of the former to **-e**, and by analogical substitution of the latter, consequent on the phonetic change -ES > **-i**), then they might have come into being *later* than palatalization of velars. After all, palatalization of velars is common to virtually all Romance dialects, while the change of final -AS to **-e** (and of -ES to **-i**) is peculiar to Italo-Romance (and to Romanian),[76] suggesting a more recent innovation.

The facts are strongly consistent with the hypothesis that inflectional **-e** and **-i** do not directly continue Latin inflections containing front vowels. There is *no* palatalization whatsoever of velar consonants before the feminine plural inflection (nor before the second person singular indicative inflection *-e* of the OTuscan first conjugation)[77]: e.g., **a'miːka** 'friend', **a'miːke**; **'grɛːka** 'Greek', **'grɛːke**; **'fiːzika** 'physical', **'fiːzike**; **'larga** 'broad', **'large**; **'bjaŋka** 'white', **'bjaŋke**. This absence of alternation in the feminine is repeated throughout the modern Italo-Romance dialects.[78] As for the exiguous muster of possible medieval examples of such palatalization (those where no orthographic *h* is present), Parodi (1896: 121) shows that feminine plurals such as *biece* 'surly' and *piage* 'wounds' in the Divine Comedy only appear in *rhyme* with words in *-ce* and *-ge* (the learnèd *metafisice* 'metaphysical' and *fisice* 'physical' are the sole exceptions).[79] Throughout the attested history of the dialects, non-palatalization has been the rule in the overwhelming majority of feminine plurals. The same is broadly true for the masculine plurals: there are only three palatalized masculine plural words in modern Italian which are unambiguously native and non-learnèd: **a'miːko** 'friend', **a'miːtʃi**; **ne'miːko** 'enemy', **ne'miːtʃi**; **'pɔrko** 'pig', **'pɔrtʃi.** All others have invariant plural roots: **'luŋgi** 'long'; **'laːgi** 'lakes'; **'kaːriki** 'loaded'; **'vaːliki** 'mountain passes', **'pittsiki** 'pinches'; **'bjaŋki** 'white', etc., although it is true that the range of palatalized forms must once have been rather greater than it is now (evidence of palatalized plurals in reflexes of ***'bruki** 'caterpillars', and ***'fuŋgi** 'mushrooms' can be seen in the AIS maps 481 and 621 for Tuscany and southern Italy; also Goidanich (1940: 176f.)).

The remaining examples of palatalization are all words of learnèd origin, notably those with the unstressed suffixes *-ico*, *-aco* and *-ologo*: **'grɛːko** 'Greek', **'grɛːtʃi**; **'fiːziko** 'physical', **'fiːzitʃi**; **'sindako** 'mayor', **'sindatʃi**; **'maːgo** 'wizard', **'maːdʒi**; **'bjɔːlogo** 'biologist', **'bjɔːlodʒi**; **ki'rurgo** 'surgeon', **ki'rurgi**; **as'paːrago** 'asparagus', **as'paːradʒi**; **'bɛlga** 'Belgian', **'bɛldʒi**. Alternation of root-final [g] is marginal, even in learnèd words: the *-ologo* suffixes alternate only optionally (*biòloghi* (etc.) is also admitted). Other words in *-logo* do not alternate at all (*catàloghi* 'catalogues', *diàloghi* 'dialogues'), with the exception of *asparagi*. The plural *chirurgi* also occurs. *I Magi* are 'the Magi' (the plural of *mago* meaning 'wizard' is *maghi*); *i Belgi*, until recently, denoted only the Belgæ, a Celtic tribe of antiquity; all of the *-logo* words are learnèd borrowings from Greek. The phonological evidence also shows these forms not to be indigenous: we saw in section 6 that the regular development of word-internal intervocalic [g] followed by a front vowel in Tuscan is either [ddʒ] or complete deletion, but in any case *not* [dʒ]. By no means all *-aco* words alternate: *stòmaco* 'stomach', *fòndaco* 'warehouse', *intònaco* 'plaster' have invariant roots for many speakers, and there has been considerable vacillation, historically, between alternation and invariance in words ending in *-ico* (cf. Goidanich (1940)).

In this light, it looks as if palatalization in such forms is not the result of a phonetic process of palatalization; the palatal alternants are attributable to orthographically based pronunciations of *ci* and *gi*, rather than to spontaneous sound change. Overall, the incidence of palatalization before the plural inflections is strongly consistent with the hypothesis that feminine plural **-e** evolved phonetically from original **-as**, and that second declension masculine plurals originally terminated in a non-palatalizing **-os**. The fact that a handful (and no more) of masculine plurals which are clearly not of learnèd origin none the less display palatalization is consistent with the view expressed above, that traces of nominative plural -ɪ, (triggering palatalization) may also have survived in early Italo-Romance.

13 A note on 'learnèd' phonology

The extensive 'borrowing' into Italian of learnèd vocabulary, particularly from Latin, has led to the introduction of words which have failed to undergo the regular phonological development of indigenous words, and often preserve, more or less intact, phonological structures which were long ago modified in Italian. Among the phonological hallmarks of learnèd borrowing are:

– Preservation of the unstressed, prevocalic, vowels I and E where, in indigenous words, these have been lost, usually after modifying a preceding consonant: *vizio* 'vice' vs. *vezzo* 'habit', both from Latin UITIUM. Note, however, that 'TI' + vowel in Latin words is usually pronounced [**tsj**] + vowel.
– Appearance of [**i**] and [**u**] corresponding to Latin *short* I and U, instead of the phonologically regular [**e**] and [**o**]: *vitreo* 'vitreous' < Latin UITREUM, but *vetro* 'glass' < Latin UITRU(M) 'glass'; *assurdo* 'absurd' < Latin ABSURDUM, but *sordo* 'deaf' < Latin SURDU(M).[80]
– Preservation of the diphthong [**aw**] (see 4.4): *aureo* 'golden' < Latin AUREUM, but *oro* 'gold' < ***awru** < Latin AURU(M).
– An additional phonological trait of the vocalism of learnèd and borrowed words is that stressed mid vowels are pronounced open. This applies even to mid vowels that in Latin were *long*, and would therefore have been expected to emerge as closed vowels: cf. **ˈkrɛːdo** 'creed' vs. **ˈkreːdo** 'I believe', both from Latin CREːDO; **mɔtto** < French *mot*.
– Preservation of postconsonantal [**l**] (cf. 3.3): *florale* 'floral' < Latin FLORALEM, but *fiore* 'flower' < ***ˈflore** < Latin FLOS
– Retention of word-internal intervocalic [**b**] (cf. 3.2): *plebeo* 'plebeian' < PLEBEUM, but *pieve* 'parish' < ***ˈplɛbe** < PLEBE(M)
– Preservation of nasals before sibilants (cf. section 9): *mensile* 'monthly' < Latin MENSILEM, but *mese* 'month' < Latin MENSE(M).

Sometimes, only the more recondite learnèd borrowings resist native phonological habits. Loanwords from Latin and Greek are usually subject to consonantal assimilation (see 8.2): *attitudine* 'aptitude' < CL APTITUDINEM; *deissi* 'deixis' < Greek ΔΕΙΞΙΣ, etc. But some do resist: *ctonico* 'chthonic'; *incapsulare* 'to crown (teeth)', etc. Among other non-assimilated consonants clusters in learnèd vocabulary are *bdellio* 'bdellium', *opzione* 'option', *mnemonico* 'mnemonic', *atmosfera* 'atmosphere', *eczema*, etc. For the pronunciation of such words in popular speech, see Ch.5: 3.1.1.

Notes

1. We take as our starting point the sound system of CL, of which Allen (1978) gives a particularly lucid survey. Our examination of CL inevitably focuses on those sound differences which form minimal pairs (cf. Ch.1: 5.4), since we cannot know for sure which other, distributionally 'allophonic', sound differences, also functioned to distinguish meaning.
2. Long consonants are often described as 'geminates' in studies of Italian phonology. This description might be taken to imply a succession of 'twin' separate identical articulations, which is not the case. In our phonetic transcriptions of long consonants, however, we have followed the established tradition of representing them by two successive consonants (e.g., **'gatto** 'cat'). Some studies represent long consonants by means of a colon (e.g., **'gatːo**).
3. An obstruent is a consonant produced with blockage, or considerable constriction, of the airflow, such as [**t**], [**k**], [**p**], [**v**], etc.
4. In Latin the position of stress within the word can shift when certain *clitic* particles are attached to the word: cf. CL PO-PU-LUS 'the people' vs. POPULUSQUE 'and the people' with a heavy, and therefore stressed, penultimate syllable. In Tuscan word-stress is not sensitive to the attachment of clitics (for which see Ch.3: 9.4): cf. *mandàndo* 'sending', but *mandàndogli* 'sending (to) him' (phonetically **man-'dan-doʎ-ʎi**) with a heavy but unstressed penultimate syllable.
5. For the shift of stress between INTEGRU(M) and Italian *intèro* see Tekavčić (1980 I: 215f.). In CL sequences of stressed I or E + unstressed vowel, the accent shifted in Proto-Romance to the second vowel FILIOLU(M) >* FILIOLU(M) > Proto-Romance ***fi'ljɔlu** 'son'.
6. A small handful of oxytones did exist in the CL, mainly as a result of deletion of a vowel in the final syllable (see Allen (1978: 87)). What did not occur, it seems, is stressed vowels at the end of words.
7. For an illustration of the various Romance vowel systems, see Vincent (1988b: 32–4). See also Lausberg (1939) for a detailed survey of these four systems as they are represented, in close proximity, in a small area of southern Basilicata and adjacent parts of Calabria.
8. The 'alveolum' is the hard ridge between the teeth and the palate.
9. Castellani (1962) cites one apparent case of spontaneous *rising* diphthongization of low mid vowels in the Occitan dialect of Quérigut.
10. For details see Maiden (1988a: 23f.), and Venturelli (1979: 101), who records that metaphony in closed syllables is restricted to [**ɛ**] in parts of the Garfagnana region.
11. Another seeming inconsistency is that, in most Italo-Romance dialects, metaphony affects *all* mid vowels, and sometimes also [**a**], while in Tuscan, there is no trace of metaphony affecting high mid vowels or [**a**]. This objection is less serious than it seems, since it is the case (cf. Maiden (1987: 63–6)) that there are various central Italian dialects in which metaphony itself is restricted to low mid vowels.
12. For a survey of some other approaches to this problem, see Tekavčić (1980 I: 33).

13. See also Castellani (1986: 123–5).
14. A completely unconnected (and relatively recent) phenomenon is elimination of the onglide after a complex syllable onset ending in [**r**]: OTuscan *brieve* 'brief'; *truova* 'he finds' > *breve*; *trova*. Vennemann (1988: 13f.; 16) suggests an explanation in terms of syllable structure conditions (see 8.1).
15. See also Maiden (1988a: 10–12). The patterns of metaphony found in Trecchina are of a typically northern Italian kind (triggered only before [**i**]) and do not significantly reflect the influence of the surrounding southern Italian dialects.
16. Maiden (1987; 1988a: 19–21).
17. Stehl (1980: 58; 97).
18. Vignoli (1925: 11f; 14f.).
19. Melillo (1926).
20. Maiden (1988a: 15–19).
21. Camastral (1959: 128ff.).
22. The view that SOSD was imported from the north was held by Rohlfs and, for most of his scholarly career, by Schürr. But see Schürr (1972: 320f; 1980: 60), and the discussion in Maiden (1988a: 27f.).
23. See Tekavčić (1980 I: 59f.) and Lausberg (1965: 277–9) for a more detailed account.
24. For a discussion of its medieval and modern geographical diffusion, see Franceschini (1991).
25. It so happens that nearly all of the examples cited contained short [**u**] and [**i**] in Latin. The example of *lungo* from Latin LONGU(M) 'long', with short [**o**], is revealing, since it shows that anaphonesis is a matter of raising, and not of conservation of the height value of Latin short [**u**] and [**i**]. The intermediate underlying form would have been ***ˈlongu**, displaying regular raising of [**ɔ**] to [**o**] before syllable-final nasals (cf. **ˈponte** 'bridge' < PONTE(M)). However, see also Castellani (1980: 76 n16).
26. See, for example, Rohlfs (1966: 72).
27. For a possible absolute chronology of the varieties of anaphonesis, see Castellani (1980: 86), who dates the emergence of anaphonesis before the velar nasal from around the late fourth century, and other kinds of anaphonesis from some point between the second and the eighth centuries.
28. See Maiden (1988b). The central Italian territory stretches across northern Lazio, southern and eastern Umbria, parts of Tuscany (e.g., Cortona and region, and parts of north-western Tuscany above Lucca), the southern Marche and adjoining parts of Abruzzo.
29. There are sporadic examples of assimilation of pretonic [**e**] before [**a**]: *danaro* 'money' = *denaro*; OTuscan *sanza* 'without'= *senza*; *maraviglia* 'wonder' = *meraviglia*.
30. For evidence of a tendency in OTuscan to raise unstressed [**a**] to [**e**] after [**i**] and also before [**l**] (e.g., *diemànte* for *diamànte* 'diamond') see Poppe (1966).
31. Some Latin intertonic vowels had already undergone syncope in common Proto-Romance: *caldo* 'hot'; *freddo* 'cold'; *felce* 'fern'; *lardo* 'bacon'; *vecchio* 'old'; *macchia* 'stain', < CALIDU(M); FRIGIDU(M); FILICE(M);

LARIDU(M); UETULU(M); MACULA(M). The date of syncope is uncertain in some other words: *pesca* 'peach'; *posto* 'put'; *prete* 'priest', < PERSICA(M); POSITU(M); PRESBYTERU(M).

32. Or perhaps just a very weak and indistinct articulation, with occasional deletion. If we assume complete deletion, it is difficult to see how it is that (with just a few exceptions) a new vowel is introduced *only* where there had previously been a vowel sound.
33. There is debate as to whether they should be properly analysed in CL as labially articulated velars, or as a velar + labial glide (cf. Tekavčić (1980 I: 100f.)), but the balance of evidence favours the former view (cf. Allen (1978: 16–20; 25)).
34. The last two examples are actually hybrids of Latin and Germanic words. See Rohlfs (1966: 230).
35. For reasons not directly connected with the palatalization process, the new consonants are long in intervocalic position, and short elsewhere. The sole exception is [**ʧ**] < [**ʃ**] < [**sj**] (see below).
36. The change of [**bj**] to [**ʒ**] or [**ʤ**], and of [**pj**] to [**ʧ**] is a characteristic of Gallo-Romance and of some southern Italian dialects (cf. Rohlfs (1966: 386f.; 400)). OTuscan *cangiare* 'to change' (beside *cambiare*) is a Gallicism. The OTuscan verbal forms *deggio* 'I must' and *aggio* 'I have' were probably formed on the analogy of *seggio* 'I sit' and *veggio* 'I see'.
37. The apparent parallelism between the evolution of [**kj**] (> [**ʧ**]) and [**gj**] (> [**ʤ**]) may in reality be an historical accident. We suggest below that [**gj**] originally became [**j**], which only later gave [**ʤ**].
38. While [**ʦ**] survives in some modern Ligurian and Alpine dialects, it has yielded [**s**] in many modern northern varieties (e.g., Romagnol **bras**).
39. Except for ***vere'kondja > ver'goɲɲa** 'shame'.
40. Modern Italian forms in intervocalic [**j**] betray a non-Tuscan source: **zdra'jaːre** 'to stretch out' < ***eksdera'djare** is probably of southern origin; **anno'jaːre** 'to bore' < **eno'djare** is from Provençal.
41. The postulated mechanism, whereby a preconsonantal velar yields [**j**], which subsequently palatalizes the following consonant, is supported by an overview of 'western' Romance dialects, where [**kt**], as well as [**ks**], [**gn**] and [**gl**] is subject to palatalization. In some Romance varieties (e.g., Piedmontese, Portuguese, OFrench) [**jt**] < [**kt**] is retained (Piedmontese **lajt**; **nøjt**; Portuguese *leite* 'milk'; *noite* 'night' < ***'lakte**; ***'nɔkte**). Elsewhere (for example in Lombard and Castilian), the palatal and dental element of [**jt**] merge, yielding a palatal affricate [**ʧ**] (Lombard **latʃ**; **notʃ**; Castilian *leche*; *noche*).
42. We need not subscribe to the view (cf., Tekavčić (1980 I: 201f.)) that the cluster spelled GN, in CL was pronounced [**ŋn**] in Proto-Romance (although there may have been some degree of nasalization in the velar): it is very hard to see how the attested glide [**j**] could have emerged from [**ŋ**]. But there is plenty of Italo-Romance evidence (e.g., Rohlfs (1966: 366f.)) for [**g**] > [**j**] before following consonants. See also Allen (1978: 23–5)
43. See Rohlfs (1966: 368f.), Tekavčić (1980 Vol. 1: 207f.).
44. Martinet's suggestion (repeated in Tekavčić (1980 I: 116–19)) that palatalization of velars is motivated by the avoidance of merger with [**ke**],

[**ki**] derived from Latin [**kwe**], [**kwi**] (a change supposedly motivated in turn by encroachment of [**kwe**] and [**kwi**] from Latin [**kui**] and [**kue**]) is less than convincing: in Sardinian there has been delabialization but not palatalization; delabialization seems to postdate palatalization, and unlike palatalization, is incomplete; palatalization of velars before front vowels is a common occurrence across a wide range of languages, and has no special need of putative 'structural pressures'. And why *should* speakers avoid phonological merger here, when they have allowed it in so many other cases? See also Vincent (1978: 411f.).

45. See Tekavčić (1980 Vol. 1: 121) for some early orthographic evidence.
46. Roughly from Viareggio and S. Marcello in the north, to Grosseto and Montalcino in the south.
47. For an overview of the various structuralist theses proposed to account for the relationship between shortening and voicing in northern Italy, see Tekavčić (1980 I: 125–7).
48. Although it is probably of more recent date than voicing – the earliest written attestations date from the eighth century.
49. For further documentation of this problem, with useful bibliographical references, see Izzo (1980), who argues against the hypothesis of an indigenous origin for Tuscan voicing.
50. Similar, but not identical, phenomena appear in some other Italo-Romance varieties, such as that of Chioggia (Veneto), or of Dorgali in Sardinia.
51. Agostiniani (1983) gives an extensive critical documentation of the 'Etruscan' arguments.
52. From north of Poppi and Sansepolcro to Orbetello and Grosseto in the south, including Elba; in the Garfagnana region in the north-west.
53. The northern dialects, and Italian, retain sporadic examples of voicing in word-initial position: Milanese *galavrò* 'hornet'; *gavana* 'shed' (< ***kala'brone**; ***ka'panna**). It is significant that the handful of cases of voicing of initial voiceless stops in Italian (and in other Tuscan varieties) all involve that consonant which in Tuscany is most susceptible to voicing, namely the velar (e.g., *gonfiare* 'to swell' < CONFLARE; *gastigare* 'to punish' (or *castigare*) < CASTIGĀRE); *gomito* 'elbow' < CUBITU(M). See Rohlfs (1966: 197f.; 220; 226f.).
54. We cannot begin to do justice here to this subtle and complex study. Among its most interesting findings is that weakening in modern (and presumably ancient) Tuscany is not wholly restricted to voiceless occlusives, nor to intervocalic position.
55. This hypothesis might lead us to expect to find cases of *hypercorrection*, in which voiceless consonants sometimes appeared in place of original voiced consonants (e.g., ***cota* for *coda* 'tail'). We have to recognize, as Izzo (1980: 144f.) points out, that there are no examples clearly interpretable in this way. But absence of hypercorrection does not, of itself, undermine our hypothesis.
56. Italian also displays a handful of forms where the source of lengthening is less evident: e.g., *cioccolata* 'chocolate'; *pellicano* 'pelican'; *coccodrillo* 'crocodile'; *caffè* 'coffee'; *tabacco* 'tobacco'. Now these are all loanwords from languages (mainly Spanish) in which there is no distinction between

long and short consonants, and in which the articulation of [**k**], [**t**], [**p**], may have been perceived as similar to Italian long consonants. As for the [**kk**] of *accademia* 'academy' (< ACADEMIAM), this may reflect the large number of words in Italian commencing with *acc-* (*accadere* 'to happen'; *accorgersi* 'to realize', etc.).

57. For the theoretical bases of strength hierarchies and their relation to syllable structure, see Hooper (1976).
58. See 5.1 for the original status of (syllable-initial) velar consonants + labials in Latin.
59. See also the unpublished study by Vincent, summarized in an appendix to Vennemann and Murray (1983).
60. Examples of lengthening before [**r**] are confined to the labial [**b**]: *labbro* 'lip'; *febbre* 'fever'. This may reflect the general propensity, observable in various central and southern Italian dialects, for word-internal [**b**] to be lengthened. The occasional *Affrica* for *Africa*, is more likely to be a case of proparoxytonic lengthening, discussed below.
61. For strengthening of word-initial [**r**] in certain dialects, including some varieties of Tuscan, see Rohlfs (1966: 223f.).
62. There is occasional assimilation of [**r**] to [**s**]: **'dorsu** > *dosso* 'back'; **'persika** > *pesca* 'peach', and, in the language of the fourteenth to sixteenth centuries (Macinghi Strozzi, Petrarch, Boccaccio, Pucci, Ariosto, Tasso and others) of [**r**] before clitic [**l**] or [**ʎ**]: *vedella* 'to see her'; *volegli* 'to wish him', etc.
63. The prosodic domain within which RS operates is broadly identifiable with the syntactic *phrase* (e.g., noun phrase or verb phrase). That this specification of the domain of RS is in need of further refinement, is demonstrated by Nespor and Vogel (1986).
64. The oblique negative formulation given here is necessitated by the fact that word-internal stress is *relative*. That is to say that it refers to that syllable which is *louder* than any other within a word. Given this definition, which presupposes that a word must contain more than one syllable, we cannot say that monosyllables, many of which trigger RS (e.g., *ha* 'he has'; *va* 'he goes'; *dà* 'he gives'; *sta* 'he stands', etc.), are 'stressed'. They may however be distinguished from clitic (cf. Ch.3: 9) monosyllables, such as *di*; *la*; *i*; *si*; *ci*; *mi*, etc., which do not trigger RS, and part of whose definition is that they are inherently *unstressed* in relation to the host word to which they are attached.
65. There is even evidence for *shortening* of originally long vowels in proparoxytones, in some central and southern Italian dialects. See Rohlfs (1966: 23f.).
66. Loporcaro (1988a: 383 n57) interprets consonant lengthening in paroxytones as undermining Vincent's case. But the essence of the latter's argument is not that there is a necessary dichotomy between the stressed syllables of paroxytones and other stressed syllables, but rather that consonant lengthening is the default 'make-weight' strategy.
67. Malkiel (1973: 214–25) gives a more detailed account of the possible analogical origins of these forms. He also suggests that this analogical substitution of [**d**] for [**r**] may have provided a stimulus for substitution of

[**r**] by [**d**] in genuine phonological dissimilations, such as *rado*; *armadio*.

68. *Pace* Vennemann (1988: 66f.) this cannot be a strategy to avoid disfavoured falling (or 'narrowing') diphthongs, since the example of *sedia* 'chair' shows that [**jɛ**], too, is involved (cf. also Tuscan dialect **'sɛːpje** = *siepe* 'hedge').
69. For a review of the various theoretical positions concerning this problem, see Tekavčić (1980 II: 46–53). Lüdtke (1980), by a series of arguments somewhat different from ours, also derives feminine -**e** from the accusative plural, but does not investigate plural -**i**.
70. Inflectional -**s** is rare in the dialects of northern Italy. It survives in a few lexical 'fossils', such as the modern Venetian monosyllabic interrogatives *astu*? 'do you have?'; *vastu*? 'do you go?'; *sastu*? 'do you know?'. However, inflectional -**s** only exists in non-final position (when the clitic pronoun *tu* follows), otherwise, -**s** is dropped (e.g., *Ti va via?* 'Are you going away?'). Forms in inflectional -**s** survived in Old Lombard, and some dialects on the periphery of Provençal or Ladin speaking areas maintain a second person singular inflectional -**s** (cf. Rohlfs (1968: 247)).
71. Sornicola (1991) adduces some persuasive evidence, at least for parts of northern Italy, that the second vowel of Latin dative/ablative NOBIS and UOBIS may be the origin of final -**i** in *noi* and *voi*. But she leaves open the question whether *noi* and *voi* continue ablative/dative forms everywhere in Italy.
72. Note that this monophthongization seems only to have affected unstressed diphthongs.
73. Aebischer (1960; 1961) adduces evidence from eighth, ninth and tenth century Latin texts from Italy to indicate such closing. The difficulty lies in determining what phonetic value the written 's' had: was it [**s**], or perhaps [**ʃ**] or [**ç**], both closer to [**i**], or was it already [**i**]?
74. It may be objected that inflectional -**s** did not, apparently, change -**e** to -**i** in the second person plural endings derived from Latin -TIS. Thus AMATIS 'you love' > *amate*; AMAUISTIS > *amaste*, etc. This may simply reflect early deletion of -**s**, facilitated by the fact that, in this case, the consonant was functionally unimportant (second person plural was indicated by the whole syllable -TIS). In some Italo-Romance dialects (cf. Rohlfs (1968: 254)), and consistently in Romanian, -TIS gave rise to *-**ti**: e.g. Neapolitan **a'vitə** 'you have', Romanian **a'vetś**, both of which can be shown, on phonological grounds, to derive from ***a'veti**.
75. For sporadic instances of introduction of -**i** into feminines, see Ch.3: 3.
76. We suggest that the relevant Romanian inflections evolved in the same way. It must be recognized, however, that in Romanian inflectional -**e** and -**i** *always* trigger palatalization of a preceding velar, in noun and verb alike. But a tendency towards palatalization, even of labial consonants, before front vowels, is a recurrent feature of the history of Romanian (cf. Rosetti (1986: 572f.)), and it may well be the case that the phonetic tendency towards palatalization of velars before front vowels persisted much longer in Romanian than it did in Italo-Romance, thereby operating before -**e** from original -**as**, and before analogically extended -**i**. It is significant in this regard that Romanian palatalizes original [**k**] from original [**kw**], while

Italian does not: Latin QUÆRIT > Italian **'kjɛːde**, Romanian **'ʧere**, 'he asks' (cf. Rosetti (1986: 116f.)).

77. For the absence of palatalization in the first conjugation subjunctive as well, see Ch.3: 8.4.1.
78. Goidanich (1940: 181) cites a few supposed examples of feminine plural palatalization, but the palatal is also present in the corresponding singular forms, and there is little to support Goidanich's hypothesis that these singulars represent analogical levelling in favour of the plural root.
79. The (apparently palatalized) feminine plurals *lunge* 'long' and *pesce* 'peaches' appear in the *Cento Novelle*. Jacopone da Todi has *amice* and *formice*. For the occasional *biance* 'white' (and perhaps we might include here the *blançe* used by Giacomino da Verona), Parodi considers the possibility of contamination from French *blanche*. See also Goidanich (1940: 192).
80. The source of 'popular' and learnèd noun and adjective forms is identifiable as the Latin accusative (cf. Ch.3: 1.2). In giving the etyma of words directly inherited from Latin, we mark the accusative case-ending -M in parentheses, since it was probably only weakly pronounced, even in the classical language. But in the medieval and Renaissance sources of learnèd borrowings, this -M *was* pronounced, and accordingly it is appropriate not to mark it in parentheses.

Chapter 3

Structural evolution of nouns, adjectives and verbs

0 Structure of words

All Italian words contain a lexical *root*, which expresses the basic meaning of the word (e.g., meanings such as 'dog'; 'love'; 'sing'; 'happy'; 'large'; 'from'; 'for', and so forth). Most roots are unanalysable, which is to say that they cannot be further broken down into meaningful elements. Some words (particularly prepositions and conjunctions, but some nouns and adjectives as well) consist solely of roots; e.g., *bene* 'well'; *radio* 'radio'; *già* 'already'; *blu* 'blue'; *ma* 'but'; *e* 'and'; *quando* 'when'; *scimpanzé* 'chimpanzee'; *di* 'of'; *con* 'with'; *contro* 'against'; *da* 'from', etc. All verbs contain a *stem*, which comprises a root together with, in some parts of the verb system, a semantically empty thematic vowel (see 8.1) attached at the end of the root. The overwhelming majority of nouns and adjectives, and all verbs, have an inflectional ending (or 'inflectional desinence') following the stem or the root. The function of the inflectional desinences is to express grammatical categories such as person, number, mood, tense and gender. For example, *ross-i* ('red' + masculine plural inflection); *cant-a-te* ('sing' + thematic vowel [**a**] + second person plural present indicative inflection), and so forth. The inflections possess a very low degree of structural *autonomy*. They are obligatorily attached, or *bound*, to the right of the stem or of the root, unable to stand in isolation from it, and cannot be moved in relation to it. Words whose internal structure consists of a stem or root bound in this way to an inflectional desinence are described as *synthetic*. All synthetic word forms constitute tightly cohesive, indivisible units, in that no syntactic material can be intercalated inside them: we can say *cantate anche voi* 'you sing too', or *anche voi cantate*, but never ****cant-anche-voi-ate*.

This sketch of Italian word structure holds for CL as well. But a major development in Romance historical morphology is the emergence, particularly in the verb system, of complex, so-called 'analytic' or 'periphrastic', structures composed of historically independent words, but whose synchronic meaning and function cannot be exhaustively derived from their component parts. For example, in a structure such as the 'passato prossimo' tense form *ho fatto* 'I have done', there is only one verb with full lexical meaning, namely *fare* 'to do', while the role of the auxiliary verb *avere* 'to have' is not to indicate possession (the normal meaning of the lexical verb *avere*), but to function rather like an inflectional marker of person, number and mood – in this case 'first person singular indicative'. We shall see that such analytic structures have acquired some of the properties of synthetic words, yet still retain, to a greater or lesser degree, characteristics of the independent origins of their components.

0.1 The example of the adverb

A simple example of the historical principles involved is provided by the evolution of the adverb. CL adverbs are usually formed from the adjectival stem + adverbial ending -E or -ITER (e.g., DULC-E 'sweetly'; FORT-ITER 'bravely'). The structure originally in -E is continued in Italian *bene* 'well'; *male* 'badly'; *tardi* 'late'; *lungi* far' (cf. Ch.2: 4.6.4.1); that in -ITER is wholly extinct. CL also uses neuter forms (see section 4) of the adjective in adverbial function. Such neuters are the source of Italian *molto* 'much' (< MULTU(M)); *poco* 'not much' < (PAUCU(M)), etc. The western Romance languages (including northern Italian dialects, together with Tuscan) acquired new adverbial structures derived from the CL phrases having the structure ADJECTIVE + MENTE. MENTE is the ablative singular (see 1.2) of the feminine noun MENS 'mind', e.g., LÆTA MENTE means 'with a happy mind'. The adjective and noun are, semantically and syntactically, autonomous words. They have separate dictionary entries, and they may be separated or inverted; MENTE LÆTA 'with a happy mind'; LÆTA ET FELICI MENTE 'with a happy and glad mind'; LÆTA CANIT MENTE 'he sings with a happy mind' are all possible. In Italian adverbs, such as *lietamente*, -*mente* is a bound form attached to the right of the adjectival form: its position cannot be changed, nor can any material be intercalated between adjective and adverbial suffix (we cannot say ***mentelieta* or ***lieta canta mente*). There is also some reduction in the phonological autonomy of the adjective, in that adjectives in *-le*, and *-re* appear without their final *-e* before adverbial *-mente* (*naturale* 'natural', *regolare* 'regular' but *naturalmente*, *regolarmente*). The form *-mente* has been wholly evacuated of its original lexical meaning 'mind', and functions simply as a grammatical marker of the category adverb. Consequently, it can be combined with adjectives which could not normally qualify the word 'mind' (*lungamente* from *lungo* 'long'; *ripetutatmente* from *ripetuto* 'repeated', etc.), and can modify verbs whose grammatical subjects are inanimate and therefore could not be said to possess a 'mind' (e.g., *l'albero cresce lentamente* 'the tree grows slowly').

However, the components of the adverb retain vestiges of their autonomous origins in that, in the medieval language, but not today, *-mente* could modify conjoined adjectives: *villana ed aspramente* 'basely and roughly' (from the thirteenth century Novellino) – a construction still found in Castilian. The adjectival stem also remains, as a rule, identical to the feminine form of the adjective. Phonologically, however, the adjectival stem has lost some of its autonomy, since it cannot contain the vowels [**ɛ**] and [**ɔ**], which can occur only in the primary stressed syllables of *words* (cf. Ch.2: 2.1): since the primary stressed syllable of *apertamente* 'openly' falls on the ending, not on the adjectival stem, we have the adverb **aperta'mɛnte**, despite the feminine adjective **a'pɛrta**. To the extent that *-mente* has become an inflectional marker of grammatical category, we say that it has become *grammaticalized* or *morphologized*. Other analytical structures which will be seen to inhabit the zone between independent wordhood and synthetic forms are those comprising AUXILIARY VERB + PARTICIPLE, collocation of adjectives in relation to nouns, and combinations of verbs and clitic pronouns.

0.2 The paradigmatic dimension

Word structure also has what may be termed a paradigmatic dimension, in that the relationship between meaning and the elements of word structure is not always 'one-to-one'. A single meaning may be expressed by more than one form, as is the case in the following examples from *tenere* 'to hold'. Here, both the root, meaning 'hold' and the inflection signalling first person singular, have multiple realizations: **'tɛŋgo** 'I hold'; **'tenni** 'I held', **ter'rɔ** 'I shall hold', etc. Where a single meaning is represented by multiple forms, we speak of *allomorphy* or, in cases of extreme allomorphy, *suppletion*. For definitions of these terms, see Ch.1: 5.3.

It is also the case, especially in inflectional endings, that one form may simultaneously express more than one meaning. This state of affairs may be labelled 'cumulative exponence' – a phenomenon particularly well represented in the inflectional morphology of Latin and Italian: the Italian inflection *-o* in *amo* 'I love', *parto* 'I leave', etc., cumulatively expresses 'first person', 'singular' and 'indicative'. It is impossible to analyse [**o**] into component elements each expressing one of these grammatical meanings. Latin and Italian inflectional morphology is also characteristically *syncretistic*, in that distinct grammatical categories are expressed by a phonologically identical form. For example, in Italian there is syncretism between the first person singular ending of the passato remoto, and the second person singular inflection of the present tense (both [**i**]): e.g., *vidi* 'I saw', *vedi* 'you see', etc.

1 Inflectional morphology of the noun and adjective

The inflectional system for the noun and adjective in CL signals gender, number and case.[1] Nearly all Latin nouns and adjectives belong to one of five declensions, characterized by the presence, in certain parts of the paradigm, of an essentially meaningless *thematic* vowel. Three of these declensions (conventionally labelled 'first', 'second' and 'third') comprise both nouns and adjectives. The fourth and fifth contain only nouns (1).

(1)
First Declension

	Sg.	Pl.
Nom.	**CASA** (F.) 'hut'	**CASÆ**
Acc.	**CASAM**	**CASA:S**
Gen.	**CASÆ**	**CASA:RUM**
Dat.	**CASÆ**	**CASI:S**
Abl.	**CASA:**	**CASI:S**

Second Declension

	Sg.	Pl.	Sg.	Pl.
Nom.	**GALLUS** (M.) 'cock'	**GALLI:**	**FOLIUM** (N.) 'leaf'	**FOLIA**
Acc.	**GALLUM**	**GALLO:S**	**FOLIUM**	**FOLIA**
Gen.	**GALLI:**	**GALLO:RUM**	**FOLII:**	**FOLIO:RUM**
Dat.	**GALLO:**	**GALLI:S**	**FOLIO:**	**FOLII:S**
Abl.	**GALLO:**	**GALLI:S**	**FOLIO:**	**FOLII:S**
(Voc.	**GALLE**)			

Third Declension

	Sg.	Pl.	Sg.	Pl.
Nom.	**CA**NIS (M.) 'dog'	**CA**NE:S	**LA**TRO: (M.) 'thief'	LA**TRO:**NE:S
Acc.	**CA**NEM	**CA**NE:S	LA**TRO:**NEM	LA**TRO:**NE:S
Gen.	**CA**NIS	**CA**NIUM	LA**TRO:**NIS	LA**TRO:**NUM
Dat.	**CA**NI:	**CA**NIBUS	LA**TRO:**NI:	LA**TRO:**NIBUS
Abl.	**CA**NE	**CA**NIBUS	LA**TRO:**NE	LA**TRO:**NIBUS

Nom.	PARS (F.) 'part'	**PAR**TE:S	**MA**RE (N.) 'sea'	**MA**RIA
Acc.	**PAR**TEM	**PAR**TE:S	**MA**RE	**MA**RIA
Gen.	**PAR**TIS	**PAR**TIUM	**MA**RIS	**MA**RIUM
Dat.	**PAR**TI:	**PAR**TIBUS	**MA**RI:	**MA**RIBUS
Abl.	**PAR**TE	**PAR**TIBUS	**MA**RI:	**MA**RIBUS

Nom.	**TEM**PUS (N.) 'time'	**TEM**PORA
Acc.	**TEM**PUS	**TEM**PORA
Gen.	**TEM**PORIS	**TEM**PORUM
Dat.	**TEM**PORI:	**TEM**PORIBUS
Abl.	**TEM**PORE	**TEM**PORIBUS

Fourth Declension

	Sg.	Pl.
Nom.	**A**CUS (F.) 'needle'	**A**CU:S
Acc.	**A**CUM	**A**CU:S
Gen.	**A**CU:S	**A**CUUM
Dat.	**A**CUI:	**A**CUBUS
Abl.	**A**CU:	**A**CUBUS

Fifth Declension

	Sg.	Pl.
Nom.	**DIE**:S (F.) 'day'	**DIE**:S
Acc.	**DIEM**	**DIE**:S
Gen.	DIE:I:	DIE:RUM
Dat.	DIE:I:	DIE:BUS
Abl.	**DIE**:	DIE:BUS

Lexical roots are generally phonologically invariant, except in the so-called 'imparisyllabic' nouns and adjectives of the third declension (such as LATRO and PARS), where the nominative singular root (and the accusative singular root, in neuter forms) is phonologically differentiated in a variety of ways from all other case forms. In particular, the imparisyllabic nominative singular is one syllable shorter than other members of the paradigm and, in some nouns, such as LATRO, there are stress differences between the nominative singular and all other case forms. It will be seen from the above that the inflectional system is multiply *opaque*: each case is expressed by an array of inflectional endings varying according to number and case; and most inflectional endings syncretistically express more than one case. To take just the example of the genitive, it is expressed variously by -Æ, -ARUM, -I, -ORUM, -IS, -IUM, -UM, -US, -UUM, -EI, -ERUM; and several of these forms have multiple functions: for example, -Æ expresses genitive and dative singular, and nominative plural, while -I expresses genitive singular, dative singular, and nominative plural, and so forth.

The inflectional signalling of gender and of number persists in Italian, albeit with radical modifications. The declensional classes have been reduced from five to three, the morphologically distinct gender classes from three to two; the intricate and opaque system of inflectional case desinences has virtually disappeared.

1.1 Declension

The fourth and fifth declensions are not directly continued in modern Italian. The close formal similarity (notably in the nominative and accusative singulars, where both declensions manifested the inflections -US and -UM) between the fourth declension and the second declension favoured the reassignment of most fourth declension words to the second. Since the second declension was predominantly non-feminine (we shall see in section 4 that it comprised masculines and neuters which generally coalesced into a single gender, characterized in Tuscan by the singular inflectional ending **-o**), original fourth declension feminines were often assigned masculine gender (e.g., feminine accusative ACU(M) > masculine ***ako** > *ago* 'needle'). Feminine fourth declension nouns denoting persons were allocated to the (overwhelmingly feminine) first declension, characterized by inflectional **-a** (e.g., SOCRU(M) 'mother-in-law' > ***sɔkra** > *suocera*). Certain feminine fourth declension nouns were not at first incorporated into the (usually masculine) second declension. The feminine singular accusative MANU(M); FICU(M), plural MANUS; FICUS, appear in the medieval language, and in some modern central Italian dialects, as the invariant *mano mano* 'hand'; *fico fico* 'fig'. For the plurals we may reconstruct the development MANUS > ***manui** > ***manu** > ***mano** (cf. Ch.2: 12 and Ch.2: 4.6.4.1 for the phonetic development). Fifth declension nouns, of which the majority were feminine, were generally incorporated into the first declension (RABIE(M) 'rage' > ***rabja** > *rabbia*; FACIE(M) 'face' > ***fakja** > *faccia*). First declension nouns and adjectives are generally continued in Italian feminine forms of the type singular *porta*, plural *porte* 'door'; singular *aperta*, plural *aperte* 'open'. Second declension masculines, into which many of the Latin second declension neuters are absorbed, are continued in the type singular *gallo*, plural *galli* 'cock'; singular *aperto*, plural *aperti* 'open'. The third declension masculine and feminine forms survive in the type singular *cane*, plural *cani* 'dog'; singular *parte*, plural *parti* 'part'; singular *verde*, plural *verdi* 'green'.

1.2 The case system

The modern Italian nouns and adjectives are morphologically invariant so far as the signalling of case is concerned (although vestiges of a case system persist in the personal pronouns – see 9.1). The overwhelming majority of modern nouns and adjectives appear to derive from Latin *accusative* forms. The vocative, which has a distinctive inflectional form only in the second declension masculine singular (e.g., GALLE 'O cock'), is wholly extinct. A few remnants of ablative forms survive in the prepositions *senza* 'without' (< ABSENTIA 'in the absence'); *durante* 'during' (< DURANTE '(while) lasting'); *nonostante* 'despite' (< NON OBSTANTE 'not withstanding'); *ora* 'now' (< HORA '(at the) hour'), and the adverbial suffix *-mente* (< MENTE '(with a) mind').

That the majority of modern Italian nouns and adjectives derive from forms most closely identifiable with the Latin *accusative* may not be immediately obvious. Inspection of Table (1) will show that loss of final [**m**] (cf. Ch.2: 10), together with the merger of long and short [**a**], of [**u**] with [**oː**], and (in unstressed syllables) of short [**i**] with both [**e**] and [**eː**] (cf. Ch.2: 2.1), would have had the effect of effacing the distinction between nominative, accusative and ablative singular in the first declension, that between accusative, dative and ablative (and neuter nominative) singular in the second declension, and that between singular accusative and ablative singular (and neuter nominative of nouns like MARE) in the third declension. These changes would have yielded the modern singular forms **'ka:sa**; **'gallo**; **'ka:ne**, etc. That the accusative historically underlies most Italian noun and adjective forms can be deduced by a process of elimination. Clear evidence for not identifying the source of the Italian forms as the genitive, dative or ablative comes from the plurals – where **'ka:se** 'houses' and **'ka:ni** 'dogs' cannot be derived phonologically from CASARUM, CASIS and CANIUM, CANIBUS – and from the third declension imparisyllabic neuter singulars, where **'tɛmpo** 'time' or **'ka:po** 'head' could continue the nominative/accusative forms TEMPUS, CAPUT, but not TEMPORIS, TEMPORI, TEMPORE or CAPITIS, CAPITI, CAPITE. This leaves either the accusative or the nominative as possible sources. Some reasons for deriving the modern *plural* inflections from the accusative (with possible influence also from the masculine plural nominative) have been discussed in Chapter 2:12. The development of the imparisyllabic third declension singulars assists in the choice between the nominative and the accusative. Recall that in this category the nominative singular contains one syllable less than all other case forms, and is often further distinguished by a variant stress pattern and by certain types of consonantal alternation. Modern forms such as *parte* 'part'; *notte* 'night'; *monte* 'mountain'; *piede* 'foot' are disyllabic, and reflect the consonantal structure of the CL accusatives PARTE(M); NOCTE(M); MONTE(M); PEDE(M), rather than nominatives PARS; NOX; MONS; PES.

Some lexicalized remnants of case forms other than the accusative have survived. The endings and stress patterns of original imparisyllabics such as *uòmo* 'man', *sàrto* 'tailor', *làdro* 'thief', *suòra* 'nun' (originally 'sister'), *mòglie* 'wife', *prète* 'priest' reflect nominatives (**HO**MO; **SAR**TOR; **LA**TRO; **SO**ROR; **MU**LIER; **PRES**BYTER) rather than accusatives (**HO**MINEM; SAR**TO**REM; LA**TRO**NEM, MULI**E**REM, PRES**BY**TERUM). The survival of the nominative in such examples may be explicable by the relatively high frequency of the nominative forms of nouns denoting human beings, which in turn reflects the fact that the nominative is the case form of the grammatical subject of transitive verbs. And one of the principal roles of the transitive subject is that of indicating *agent* or instigator of the verb's action, a role characteristically performed by human referents.[2]

The proparoxytonic stress pattern of *confratèrnita* '(religious) brotherhood', from nominative CONFRA**TER**NITAS rather than accusative CONFRATERNI**TA**TEM, and the pronunciation of *Spirito santo* 'Holy Ghost' as **'spi:ritos'santo** (< SPIRITUS SANCTUS), probably both reflect nominative forms encountered in the Latin of the Church; the phrase 'SPIRITUS SANCTUS', would have been heard repeatedly in mass.

Remnants of the genitive are the names of the weekdays *lunedì*; *martedì*; *mercoledì*; *giovedì; venerdì* 'Monday; Tuesday; Wednesday; Thursday; Friday' (< LUNÆ 'of the moon'; MARTIS 'of Mars'; MERCURI 'of Mercury'; IOUIS 'of Jupiter'; UENERIS 'of Venus' + DIES 'day'). Structures of the type *Por Santa Maria* 'St. Mary's gate'; *Piazza San Giovanni* 'St. John's Square', still found in modern placenames, may continue (syntactically, but not morphologically) earlier genitive structures (e.g., PORTA SANCTÆ MARIÆ, OFlorentine *Porta Sante Marie*). A syntactic remnant of a genitive structure survives in Tuscan after *casa* (e.g., Compagni *in casa i Frescobaldi* 'at the Frescobaldis' house'; Macinghi Strozzi *in casa Marco* 'at Marco's house'). The genitive endings in *-e* and *-i*, attested in the earliest surviving Italo-Romance texts, the *Placiti Cassinesi*, are probably deliberate imitations of Latin (cf. Castellani (1973: 68)), as are constructions such as *fratello Rinucini* 'Rinucini's brother'; *figliastro Buonfantini* 'Buonfantino's stepson', found in the early thirteenth-century Florentine bankers' book.

1.2.1 The expression of the case functions

As the inflectional case endings declined, alternative means of expressing the same grammatical functions came to assume an increasingly important role – see Harris (1978: 37–48) for a detailed account of these developments in Romance. The distinction between grammatical subject and grammatical object was expressed by the device, common to all Romance languages, of placing the subject before the verb, and placing the object after it. The order of subject and object in relation to the verb will be discussed further in the following chapter. Other case functions are indicated in Romance by the increased deployment of a structure already available in CL, namely PREPOSITION + NOUN PHRASE, which has the major advantage, over the allomorphic and syncretistic inflectional case endings of CL, of expressing the semantic relationship of noun phrases to other parts of the sentence by means of a morphologically *invariant* form. In all Italo-Romance varieties, a continuant of the preposition AD, namely *a*, functions to indicate the indirect object, in place of the CL dative case: *do una lettera a Marco* 'I give a letter to Marco', etc. It is also AD which expresses motion towards (often expressed by the bare accusative in CL): *vado a casa* 'I go home' (= CL EO DOMUM). Many of the functions of the genitive, notably that of expressing possession, or the dependency of one noun upon another, are taken over by reflexes of CL DE (originally 'from'): *il libro di Marco* 'Marco's book'; *l'amor di Dio* 'the love of God'. The functions of the ablative inflectional ending are often performed by reflexes of CUM (> *con* 'with') in expressions of means or accompaniment (*ruppe la finestra con un martello* 'he broke the window with a hammer'; *venne con un amico* 'he came with a friend'), or by *da* (< *DE A(B) or *DE A(D)) in expressions of agency, such as *la finestra è stata rotta da un ragazzo* 'the window was broken by a boy'. This represents a generalization of structures already available in CL: the prepositions CUM and A(B), selecting the ablative, are regularly deployed in CL in expressions of accompaniment, or where the agent noun denoted a person. The dative was often used in Latin to express 'advantage' or 'benefit'. In Italian, this function is often performed by *per* (< CL PER 'through'): *lo faccio per i miei amici* 'I do it for my friends'. The structural evolution of prepositions in Italian will be discussed in section 10.

2 Invariance and inflectionlessness

Before embarking on a history of the inflections, a word should be said about morphologically invariant forms of Italian. Most of these are 'inflectionless'. Since the gender and number inflections of Italian nouns and adjectives are *unstressed word-final vowels*, any noun or adjective lacking an unstressed final vowel cannot inflect for number and gender. Absence of the final vowel may come about for various reasons: it is absent in acronyms or in loanwords which lack final vowels in their source language (*il bar i bar*; *lo sport gli sport*; *il gas i gas*; *la colf le colf* 'home help'; *la Fiat le Fiat*, etc.); it has been discarded, along with the whole of the final syllable, in certain oxytones which were originally paroxytonic (*la virtude le virtudi* 'virtue'; *la cittade le cittadi* 'city' > *la virtù le virtù*; *la città le città*). The ranks of these invariant oxytones have been further swollen by words, often borrowings from foreign languages, containing original final stressed vowels: *gli oblò* 'the portholes'; *gli scimpanzé* 'the chimpanzees'; *i papà* 'the dads'; *i caribù* 'the caribu', etc.

Thus far, invariance is wholly predictable from phonological form. Another type of truncation of word-endings, much of it dating from this century, results in final unstressed vowels which are not inflections: e.g., *l'automobile le automobili* 'automobile' > *l'auto le auto*; *la motocicletta le motociclette* 'motorcycle' > *la moto le moto*; *il cinematografo i cinematografi* 'cinema' > *il cinema i cinema*. These forms contradict the general rule that words with final unstressed vowels inflect for number. A handful of other words also belong to this category: learnèd borrowings from the CL fifth declension in final [**je**], follow the CL model of invariance between the (nominative) singular and plural: e.g., singular SERIES, plural SERIES; singular CONGERIES, plural CONGERIES > *la serie le serie* 'series'; *la congerie le congerie* 'congeries', etc. That plural *superfici* 'surfaces' and *speci* 'species' is admitted as well as *superficie*, *specie* reflects the fact that, although these words are learnèd borrowings from the fifth declension SUPERFICIES and SPECIES, *phonetically* they end not in [**je**], but in [**e**] (**superˈfiːtʃe**, **ˈspeːtʃe**). Another class of invariant words having final unstressed vowels is proper names (e.g., *gli Amato* 'the Amatos'); included here is *il sosia i sosia* 'identical twin', originally the name of a theatrical character. Forms whose inflectional endings were not (originally) noun or adjective inflections are also invariant: thus *il vaglia i vaglia* 'postal order', from an old third person singular present subjunctive form of the verb *valere*, meaning, literally, 'let it be worth'.[3]

3 Number in the noun and adjective

The modern Italian system of number inflection presents a drastic simplification of the Latin system. The great majority of Italian nouns and adjectives form their plural as follows:

(i) With the exception of clause (ii) below, noun and adjective plurals are characterized by substitution of the inflection *-i* for the inflectional vowel of the singular, including where the latter is itself *-i*: *bello belli* 'beautiful'; *ragazzo ragazzi* 'boy'; *mano mani* 'hand'; *verde verdi* 'green'; *mese mesi* month'; *rete reti* 'net'; *pessimista pessimisti* 'pessimist'; *poeta poeti* 'poet'; *aroma aromi* 'aroma', etc. We may include here words such as *crisi crisi* 'crisis', *brindisi brindisi* 'toast', whose singulars are also characterized by final *-i* .

(ii) Nouns and adjectives that are feminine, and have the inflection *-a* in the singular, form their plurals in *-e* (*bella belle* 'beautiful'; *ragazza ragazze* 'girl'; *pessimista pessimiste*; *spia spie* 'spy'; *guida guide* 'guide', etc.).

We saw in Ch.2: 12 that the origins of plural *-i* and *-e* are probably to be sought in regular *phonetic* developments of the Latin accusative endings -ES and -AS. It was suggested that the plural -I replaced the second declension plural -OS by an analogy which was possibly favoured by the CL second declension *nominative* ending -I. The characteristic masculine ending *-i* has also been extended analogically to masculine nouns in singular *-a* (POETA(M) POETAS > *poeta poeti* 'poet'). Such is the predominance of inflectional *-i*, that in medieval Tuscan (cf. Rohlfs (1968: 24)) it tends to encroach on feminine *-e* (e.g., *le porti* 'the doors'; *le spesi* 'the expenses'). Remnants of this substitution are Italian *ala ali* and *arma armi*. The plural inflection *-i* establishes itself, as well, in the previously invariant feminine plural *mano*. But (perhaps as a reaction against the encroachments of *-i*) the feminine plural inflection *-e* was often extended into third declension feminine nouns and adjectives, giving rise to invariance (*la chiave le chiave* 'key'; *verde verde* 'green', etc.) a state of affairs persisting in many modern dialects, including Tuscan. The occasional plural *poete*, used by Dante, is probably a Latinism, continuing nominative POETÆ (cf. Rohlfs (1968: 30)).

3.1 Nouns that are masculine in the singular, and feminine in the plural

A small, and now wholly unproductive, class of masculine singular nouns in *-o* has the exceptional property of displaying grammatically feminine plurals, characterized by an inflection identical to that of the first declension feminine, namely *-a*. Among these are (2):

(2)

MSg.	FPl.	
uovo	*uova*	'egg'
corno	*corna*	'horn'
lenzuolo	*lenzuola*	'sheet'
osso	*ossa*	'bone'
dito	*dita*	'finger'
vestigio	*vestigia*	'trace'
centinaio	*centinaia*	'hundred'
grido	*grida*	'shout'

The source of this inflectional pattern (more widespread in the medieval language than the modern – e.g., OTuscan *il castello le castella* 'castle'; *il mulino le mulina* 'the mills') is the Latin second declension neuter type OUU(M) – OUA; OSSU(M) – OSSA, etc. The assignment of feminine gender to the plural is attributable to the identity between neuter plural -**a** and the inflection -**a** characteristic of the feminine singular. In certain cases, indeed, CL neuter plurals have been reinterpreted as feminine singulars: *foglia* 'leaf'; *legna* 'firewood'; *pera* 'pear'; *arma* 'weapon', are originally neuter plurals (FOLIA; LIGNA; PIRA; ARMA). Those words in which *-a* remains restricted to the plural acquire a peculiar grammatical status, in that they have a special 'collective' plural inflection identical to the feminine singular *-a*. They remain, however, grammatically plural, and the categories 'plural' and 'feminine' are expressed through syntactic agreement of determiners and adjectives (e.g., *queste lenzuola bianche* 'these white sheets'). An interesting intermediate development is represented by the word for 'eyelash', which comes from CL CILIU(M) – CILIA: in standard Italian it is continued as *ciglio – ciglia*, but for many speakers, its singular, like its plural, is feminine *ciglia*. Here the plural has been reanalysed as a feminine singular, while inflectional *-a* has remained in the plural.

The CL third declension neuter plural ending -ORA (e.g., TEMPUS, TEMPORA 'time'; CORPUS, CORPORA 'body') does not survive in Italian. But in OTuscan it not only persisted in forms such as *il corpo le còrpora* , but was sometimes extended into masculine nouns that were not, historically, neuters (e.g., *càmpora* 'fields'; *òrtora* 'orchards'; *fuòcora* 'fires'; *bòscora* 'woods'); this inflection, like *-a*, carries feminine gender. Whereas northern dialects and Tuscan have lost this ending, it has enjoyed considerable fortune in southern Italy,[4] where it has established itself as a common marker of the plural of masculine *inanimate* nouns, with no necessary connotation of collectivity: e.g., Amaseno (Lazio) **ˈljɛttə ˈlɛttəra** 'bed'; **ˈwɔrtə ˈɔrtəra** 'orchard'; **ˈraːmə ˈraːməra** 'branch'; **ˈkaːpə ˈkaːpəra** 'head'.

3.2 Number, and allomorphy in the root

We have already considered (Ch.2: 12) the evolution of palatal alternation in masculine plurals (e.g., **aˈmiːko aˈmiːtʃi** 'friend'; **neˈmiːko neˈmiːtʃi** 'enemy'; **ˈpɔrko ˈpɔrtʃi** 'pig'. Given our observation that palatalized masculine plural forms possibly reflect the influence of the *nominative* case ending, and (section 1.3) that words denoting *persons* are sometimes continued by original nominative, rather than accusative, forms, we perhaps have an explanation of why palatal alternation should persist in *nemico* 'enemy'; *amico* 'friend', and *greco* 'Greek'. As for the plurals *porci* 'pigs', and *asparagi* 'asparagus', the persistence of the palatal alternants in these words may owe something to a semantic factor, 'set-reference', which we explore in section 3.3.

The characteristically Tuscan change of *intervocalic* [**rj**] to [**j**] (Ch.2: 5.2) gave rise to alternation in reflexes of the singular suffix -*ˈ**arju** vs. its plural -*ˈ**ari**.[5] OTuscan has *notaio notari* 'lawyer'; *acciaio acciari* 'steel'; *danaio danari* 'money'. These alternations have been analogically levelled in favour of the singular roots (*notai*; *acciai*), except for *danaro*, which has been levelled in favour of the plural. The OTuscan alternation *cavallo cavai* 'horse'; *animale animai* 'animal', now extinct, arises through palatalization and subsequent deletion of root-final [**l**] (see Ch.2: 6).

We shall see in Ch.5: 2.3.1.2 that, in most Italo-Romance dialects, inflectional alternations for number are accompanied by alternations in the root vowel, generally triggered by metaphony. But in Tuscan nouns and adjectives vocalic alternations are almost unknown, except that, as a result of monophthongization of [**jɛ**] and [**wɔ**] in hiatus with vowels other than [**i**] – cf. Ch.2: 4.3 – we have *mio miei* 'my'; *bue buoi* 'ox'; *tuo tuoi* 'your'. The plural of *dio* 'god', namely *dei*, is a learnèd form (cf. also feminine *dea*).

3.3 Properties of irregular plurals

At first sight, the irregular plurals of Italian form a motley collection with very different historical origins. But a question which should always be asked in cases of stable structural irregularity is 'Why has it lasted so long?' A survey of the meanings of the irregular plurals suggests the possibility of a unified account of their stability over time, in terms of a kind of 'semantic rift' between singular and plural. In a monotheistic culture, *dei* must be something other than the plural of *dio* (or, at any rate, of *Dio*), namely 'pagan gods'. In many cases, the plural expresses more than mere 'plurality': it represents a group, set or pair, a collectivity, which amounts to 'more than the sum of its parts'. *Ali* 'wings'; *labbra* 'lips'; *braccia* 'arms'; *corna* 'horns'; *calcagna* 'heels' form pairs, while *buoi* 'oxen' are usually yoked in pairs. *Armi* 'weapons'; *uova* 'eggs'; *lenzuola* 'sheet'; *ciglia* 'eyelashes'; *dita* 'fingers'; *membra* 'limbs'; *vestigia* 'traces' all occur in sets or groups. *Asparagi* 'asparagus', the only word in *-go* retaining an obligatory palatalized root-final velar, probably also belongs here. Preservation of plural *-a* (and of *-i* in *armi* and *ali*) in such words probably originates in the relatively high frequency of the plural forms, a direct consequence of the characteristic occurrence of the referents in sets or groups of more than one. The list of words bearing the feminine plural inflection *-i* was formerly more extensive (cf. Rohlfs (1966: 25f.)), but many of its members, such as words for 'veins'; 'thorns'; 'doors'; 'pages' (of books); 'shoulders'; 'expenses'; 'papers'; 'herbs'; 'feastdays', were characterized by similar semantic properties. That *-a* is analysed as the inflectional marker of collectivities is manifested in the fact that the originally neuter plural inflection *-a* has been generalized to certain collective plurals historically in *-i*: e.g., *le urla* 'the screams'; *le frutta* 'the fruits'; *le dita* 'the fingers'; *le strida* 'the yells'; *le grida* 'the shouts'. Used non-collectively, most nouns in plural *-a* have the masculine plural inflection *-i*. Plurals such as *centinaia* 'hundreds'; *migliaia* 'thousands'; *paia* 'pairs' do not denote sets, but they, too, might be seen as reflecting an abnormal relationship between singular and plural. These words are 'plurals of plurals', rather than 'plurals of singulars', in that the corresponding grammatical singulars are, semantically, also plurals.

A further indication of the association between inflectional *-a* and the characteristic occurrence of the reference in pairs is provided by the evolution of Latin AURICULA(M) 'ear': the phonetically regular development, *orecchia*, appears to have been reanalysed as a collective plural like *corna* 'horns', with the consequent creation of an analogical singular form *orecchio* . The unique number alternation which this word displays in modern Italian (*l'orecchio le orecchie*) reflects a fusion between the historically regular *orecchia orecchie* and the analogical *orecchio orecchia*, the result of which is to widen yet further the formal rift between singular and plural.[6]

There exists considerable dialectal evidence for the special morphological status of 'set plurals'. The modern Lazio dialects of Subiaco and Ascrea have a wider range of *-i* plurals than does Italian but, significantly, words for such things as 'stairs'; 'goats'; 'turnips'; 'shoes'; 'rooms'; 'beans' and 'wasps' make up much of the list. In the northern Italian dialects of the Po plain, metaphonic alternation for number has largely disappeared, but tends to persist precisely among set-reference words (e.g., **pe pi** 'foot'; **ka'vel ka'vi** 'hair'; **bɔ bø** 'ox'; **fa'soe̯o fa'sui** 'bean').[7]

4. Gender

In Italian, as in CL, the grammatical gender of a noun is largely arbitrary: there is little correlation between meaning and gender, and little correlation between gender and morphological form. Gender is primarily a matter of *morphological agreement* between nouns and their modifiers. To say that a noun is 'masculine', 'feminine' (or, in CL, 'neuter'), is to say that its modifiers must be selected from the inflectional class conventionally labelled 'masculine', 'feminine' (or 'neuter'). We say in Italian *la luce bianca* 'the white light' and *il volume bianco* 'the white volume', but not ***il luce bianco*; ***il luce bianca*; ***la volume bianca* or ***il volume bianca*; because *la* and *bianca* are feminine, *il* and *bianco* masculine, and *luce* and *volume* are specified as selecting, respectively, either the former or the latter category of articles and adjectives. The labels 'masculine' and 'feminine' have only an approximate correlation with the sex of the referent, and are therefore quite different from 'singular' and 'plural', which involve inflectional endings expressing semantic properties of the referent. Most names of females are feminine (but cf. *il donnone* 'the great big woman'; *il soprano* 'the soprano'), and most names of males are masculine (but cf. *la guardia* 'the guard'; *la spia* 'the spy'), yet words with 'asexual' referents belong to either one or the other gender (*il sasso* 'the rock'; *la pietra* 'the stone'; *la mano* 'the hand'; *il piede* 'the foot', etc.).

We shall see that there is, in fact, a more consistent correlation between gender distinction and the semantic distinction between trees and their fruits, than there is between gender and sex. Nor is gender predictable from the inflectional endings of nouns: nouns and adjectives in *-a* are predominantly, but not always, feminine (cf. *il programma* 'the programme'; *il boia* 'the executioner'); those in *-o* are overwhelmingly, but not necessarily, masculine (cf. *la mano* 'the hand'); nouns with inflectional *-e* may be either masculine or feminine (cf. *il mese* 'the month', but *la rete* 'the net'). A major distinction between feminine and masculine is that the latter is the 'default' or 'unmarked' gender; that is to say that the masculine is the gender to which are assigned most loanwords and neologisms (*il gas*; *lo sport*; *il gulag*), adjectives, verbs and other parts of speech when they are substantivized (used as nouns): e.g., *il verde* 'the (colour) green'; *il difficile* 'that which is difficult'; *il volare* '(the fact/action) of flying'; *il 'sì'* 'the 'yes''; *dare il via* 'to give the go ahead', from feminine *via* 'road', probably via the exclamation *via!* 'off you go!'. In cases of agreement with conjoined masculine and feminine nouns, a masculine adjective is usually selected (*Carolina, Giovanni, Patrizia e Silvia sono partiti* 'Carolina, Giovanni, Patrizia and Silvia have left').

Much the same situation obtained in CL. With greater consistency than in Italian, names of females were feminine, and names of males were masculine. While the 'neuter' gender was characterized almost exclusively by 'asexual'[8] referents (except rare cases where a neuter noun may be used figuratively to refer to a human), it is certainly not the case that all semantically asexual referents were neuter, as we see in MENSA (F.) 'table'; NASUS (M.) 'nose', etc.). From the morphological perspective, first declension nouns in nominative singular -A are overwhelmingly feminine, although we find NAUTA (M.) 'sailor', AGRICOLA (M.) 'farmer'; second declension nouns in nominative singular -US are overwhelmingly masculine, although the names of trees in this declensional class are *feminine*: e.g., MALUS ALTA 'tall apple tree', PIRUS ALTA 'tall pear tree'; second declension nouns in nominative singular -UM are all neuter; third declension nouns in nominative singular -S contain both masculines and feminines, and make no morphological distinction between them; third declension nouns in nominative singular -E, or ending in a consonant, are neuter; fourth declension nouns in nominative singular -US are either masculine or feminine (a few, in nominative singular -U, are neuter); fifth declension nouns are either masculine or feminine, without morphological distinction. Neuter is the gender to which substantivized parts of speech are assigned; in cases of gender conflict, where nouns of different genders are conjoined, neuter modifiers are selected for impersonal referents, while masculine is selected as the default gender where conjoined nouns of different genders have personal referents.

The historical reorganization of the gender system in the history of Italian must be understood against this background of relatively arbitrary, and inherently labile, connections between meaning, inflection and gender.

4.1 The fate of the neuter gender

The major event in the development of the Romance gender system from Latin is the collapse of the inflectional distinction between masculine and neuter. Whereas CL has three genders, Italian, in common with most other Romance varieties, has only two: feminine and 'non-feminine'. The merger in Latin of the masculine and the neuter into a common non-feminine gender, conventionally labelled 'masculine', is largely a consequence of the extensive formal identity already existing in CL between masculine and neuter, augmented by independent phonetic and morphological adjustments in Romance. In CL second declension singulars, masculine and neuter are distinct only in the nominative (see Table 1). In the second declension plural, and in the third declension singular and plural, they are distinct in the nominative and accusative. Masculine and neuter were also distinct in the fourth declension nominative, and dative singular. Bearing in mind that Italian generally continues the accusative forms, the distinction between neuter and masculine would have been wholly lost in the second declension singular forms. The loss of final [**m**] (see Ch.2: 10) entails loss of distinction between third declension singular accusatives in -M and neuter forms in -E (masculine MENSE(M) > *mese* 'month'; neuter MARE > *mare* 'sea'). The formal distinction between neuter and non-neuter seems at this point to have become so far eroded that neuter accusative singulars ending in a consonant also merged formally either with the original second declension masculines or with third declension masculines and feminines: TEMPUS; LATUS; CORPUS > *tempo* 'time'; *lato* 'side'; *corpo* 'body'; LAC; SAL; MEL > *latte* 'milk'; *sale* 'salt'; *miele* 'honey'. A consequence of this merger is that there is no longer a distinct morphological class with exclusively 'asexual' referents, and the new 'non-feminine' (or 'masculine') gender inherits the 'default' function of the CL neuter.

What of the neuter plural forms in -A? Here we observe an intricate interplay between formal and semantic factors. In all adjectives, and frequently in nouns, the formal identity of the originally neuter and non-neuter inflections -**o** or -**e** in the *singular* leads to the replacement of neuter -A (etc.) by -**i** in the *plural* (e.g., MARIA > *mari* 'seas'). The occasional survival of inflectional -A is due, in part, to its distinctness from all other plural inflections. We have seen (3.3) that where original neuter plural -A (or -ORA) persists, it often becomes an inflectional marker of collectivity. But while -A is formally distinct from all other plural inflections, it is identical to the characteristic first declension feminine singular inflection, a fact which has two consequences. Forms in inflectional -A are reanalysed as grammatical feminines, and therefore are modified by feminine adjectives and determiners: *le uova crude* 'raw eggs', etc. Sometimes they are even reanalysed as feminine *singulars*: the modern singulars *arma* 'weapon'; *foglia* 'leaf'; *pera* 'pear'; *legna* 'firewood'; *frutta* 'fruit'; *ferraglia* 'scrap iron', all originate as neuter plurals. The fact that many of these plurals designated a collectivity or a set (and continue to do so in the case of *frutta*; *legna*; *ferraglia*) possibly also favours their reanalysis as singulars – a process already under way in CL (cf. Ernout (1927: 3f.)).

It is *perhaps* this association of feminine gender with collectivity which is at the root of the correlation in Italian, unprecedented in CL, between feminine gender and *size* – because collectivities are necessarily larger than their single members. At any rate, the masculines *coltello* 'knife' and *buco* 'hole' have acquired feminine counterparts *coltella* 'kitchen knife' and *buca* 'large hole'. The feminines *gamba* 'leg'; *manica* 'sleeve'; *mestola* 'ladle' have acquired masculine diminutive counterparts *gambo* 'stalk of wine glass or plant'; *manico* 'broomhandle'; *mestolo* 'small ladle' – there are, of course, other semantic differences between the members of some of these gender pairs, in addition to size. The correlation between gender and size is also apparent in a series of masculine diminutives formed from feminine base words by suffixation: *finestra* 'window', *finestrino*; *cucina* 'kitchen', *cucinino*; *festa* 'feast/celebration', *festino* 'party'; *rana* 'frog', *ranocchio*; *aquila* 'eagle', *aquilotto*, etc.[9]

4.2 The gender of names of fruits and trees

Italian also associates masculine gender with names of cultivated trees, and feminine gender with those of the corresponding fruits (*il melo la mela* 'apple'; *il pero la pera* 'pear'; *il noce la noce* 'nut'; *il pesco la pesca* 'peach'; *il prugno la prugna* 'plum'; *il ciliegio la ciliegia* 'cherry'; *l'ulivo la uliva* 'olive'; *il castagno la castagna* 'chestnut'; *il banano la banana* 'banana', etc.). In CL, the names of trees were usually second declension feminines, while the names of the associated fruits were second declension neuters (3):

(3)

	Sg.	Pl.	
F.	PIRUS	PIRI	'pear tree'
N.	PIRUM	PIRA	'pear'

F.	MALUS	MALI	'apple tree'
N.	MALUM	MALA	'apple'

These second declension feminines in -US constitute an anomalous conjunction of gender and inflectional class, comprising only a handful of words. In Proto-Romance they were made congruent with one of two prevailing patterns. In some dialects, feminine gender is preserved, and the nouns are assigned to the characteristically feminine first declension, but in Tuscan, the declensional class is preserved and the gender is changed to masculine. In addition, the neuter plural PIRA, etc., is reanalysed as a feminine singular, (with the consequent creation of a new feminine plural *pere*, etc.).[10] Hence the modern Italian system (4):

(4)

	Sg.	Pl.	
M.	*pero*	*peri*	'pear tree'
F.	*pera*	*pere*	'pear'

M.	*melo*	*meli*	'apple tree'
F.	*mela*	*mele*	'apple'

The gender distinction does not remain confined to second and first declension words, nor to the name of indigenous fruits: third declension feminine *noce* gives rise in Tuscany to an analogical masculine *il noce* (which means 'walnut tree'); the original first declension feminines *uliva* and *castagna*, and the exotic *banana*, acquire new masculine forms *ulivo*, *castagno* and *banano* to designate the tree; *fico* 'fig', originally a fourth declension feminine (FICUS), was reanalysed in OTuscan as a second declension masculine, with corresponding *fica* for the fruit.[11]

4.3 Gender and hyponymy

Assignment of grammatical gender of some proper names seems to have been governed, in certain cases, by relationships of hyponymy: nouns acquire the gender of that noun of which they are hyponyms (or 'subordinate terms', as 'pig' and 'cat' are hyponyms of 'animal'). The feminine gender of the names of cars (*la Fiat*, *la Ferrari*, *la Mercedes*), and the change to feminine of the originally masculine *automobile* 'automobile' may be attributable to the feminine gender of *macchina* 'car' (and *vettura* 'car', 'carriage'). As *fiume* 'river' is masculine, so are most river names (*il Tamigi* 'the Thames', *il Tevere* 'the Tiber') although those in *-a* tend to remain feminine (*la Loira* 'the Loire', *la Dora* 'the Dora'). As *città* 'city' is feminine, so are virtually all city names (e.g., *A mio avviso, Milano, Bristol e Bruxelles sono tutte e tre brutte* 'In my opinion, Milan, Bristol and Brussels are all ugly'). The position in OTuscan, as in many modern dialects, is less clear: city names, other than those in *-a*, were often masculine (see Hasselrot (1945: 221f.)).

4.4 Absence of semantic and formal motivation

Where there are neither formal nor semantic clues (such as sex) as to gender assignment, nouns have tended to vacillate diachronically between masculine and feminine. This is especially the case with the original third declension neuters (e.g., MARE 'sea'; MEL 'honey'; SAL 'salt'; FLOS 'flower'; NOMEN 'name'; FEL 'gall'; LAC 'milk'). In Tuscan, all of these words have been assigned to the masculine (*il mare*; *il miele*; *il sale*; *il fiore*; *il nome*; *il fiele*; *il latte*). In northern Italian dialects they are often feminine (Piedmontese *la sal*; *la mel*; *la fjur*; *la luit* – but *el mar*). Modern Italian *la fonte* 'source, fount' and *la palude* 'marsh' were masculine in OTuscan and CL. CL masculine CARCER 'jail' has predominantly masculine gender in modern Italian (*il carcere*), although a femine form is sometimes found in literary usage, and the plural is commonly *le carceri*. The gender of *fine* (CL masculine FINE(M)) vacillated considerably before the establishment of the modern semantic distinction between *il fine* 'end, aim' and *la fine* 'end, termination'. Modern Italian *fine settimana* 'weekend' may take either gender.

4.5 Sex, form and gender

In third declension nouns having male or female referents, gender is generally determined by the sex of the referent, and has remained historically stable. Some Latin agent nouns in the suffix -TOR (accusative -TOREM) had distinct feminines in -TRIX (accusative -TRICEM), a distinction which persists in *imperatore* 'emperor' *imperatrice* 'empress'; *accusatore accusatrice* 'accuser', etc. Some nouns in *-e* with human referents have acquired the distinctively feminine inflection *-a* where the referent is a female: *signore* 'gentleman' *signora* 'lady'; *pastore* 'shepherd' *pastora* 'shepherdess'; *ghiottone ghiottona* 'glutton'. The assignment of gender is sometimes determined by morphological form. Despite the usually masculine gender of loanwords, loans bearing suffixes which are transparently cognate with Italian feminine suffixes (e.g., French, *-té*, *-ance*, *-tion*, *-ie*, English *-ty*, *-tion*, *-ance*, *-y* = Italian *-tà*, *-anza*, *-zione*, *-ia*) are assigned to the feminine.

Feminine nouns with predominantly male referents generally originated as abstract nouns denoting the activity performed by those persons: e.g., *la spia* 'spy'; *la guida* 'the guide'; *la guardia* 'the guard'.

5 Adjectives

5.1 Morphology of comparative and superlative adjectives

CL forms the comparative and superlative of adjectives by means of the suffixes -IOR (neuter -IUS) and -ISSIMUS (FORTIS, FORTIOR, FORTISSIMUS). The following adjectives form their comparative and superlative suppletively (5):

(5)

	Comparative	Superlative	
BONUS	MELIOR	OPTIMUS	'good'
MALUS	PEIOR	PESSIMUS	'bad'
MAGNUS	MAIOR	MAXIMUS	'big'
PARUUS	MINOR	MINIMUS	'small'

There existed also *analytic* comparative structures in CL. 'Less' is expressed by the analytic structure MINUS + adjective, continued as Italian *meno* + adjective. 'More' may also be expressed by MAGIS (continued in Castilian *más*, Romanian *mai*) or PLUS + adjective. The latter is continued in Italian: *più bello* 'more beautiful'; *più corto* 'shorter', etc. Only the suppletive synthetic comparatives have survived: *migliore* 'better'; *peggiore* 'worse'; *maggiore* 'greater'; *minore* 'lesser'. The last two coexist in standard Italian with *più grande*; *più piccolo*. The adverbs MELIUS and PEIUS are continued in *meglio* 'better' and *peggio* 'worse'. The modern adjectival suffix *-issimo*, and the adjectives *pessimo* 'very bad'; *ottimo* 'excellent'; *massimo* 'greatest', and *minimo* 'least', are all learnèd forms, in origin. They function as intensifiers, rather than as absolute superlatives (*lunghissimo* means 'extremely long', not 'longest'). There survives no formal distinction between the comparative and the superlative: *il ragazzo più alto* means both 'the taller boy' and 'the tallest boy', and *questa ragazza è la più alta* means both 'this girl is tallest' and 'this girl is the taller'. The construction of the superlative adjective by obligatory anteposition of the definite article (e.g., *il ragazzo il più alto*), sometimes encountered in the literary language of the eighteenth and nineteenth centuries, is probably an imitation of French (see Migliorini and Griffith (1984: 328); Tekavčić (1980 II: 114–31)).

5.2 Possessive adjectives

The possessive adjectives of Italian require little comment. Unlike French or Castilian, which have developed special, phonologically reduced possessive adjectives which are usually proclitic (cf. 9.4) to the noun phrase, the Italian possessives are the phonologically regular continuants of CL MEU(M) 'my', TUU(M) 'thy', SUU(M) 'his/her/its/their', NOSTRU(M) 'our', UOSTRU(M) 'your', namely *mio tuo suo nostro vostro*. CL SUUS expresses both singular and plural possessors, a double function continued in modern Tuscan dialects (e.g., **i ssu a'miːho** is both 'his/her friend', and 'their friend'). The Italian third person plural possessive *loro* distinguishes the number of its possessor but, true to its origins as a genitive plural (< ILLORUM 'of those ones'), not the gender or number of its head noun. It is probably of Gallo-Romance origin (cf. Rohlfs (1968: 122)), and the dialectal evidence indicates that it is not indigenous in central and southern Italy, including Tuscany. Italian, like many other Romance languages, has lost the distinction made in CL between third person SUUS (possessor identical to the subject of the clause) and EIUS (indicating a possessor distinct from the clause subject): *legge il suo libro* can mean either 'he reads his (own) book', or 'he reads his (somebody else's) book'. The possessive adjectives have much the same syntactic distribution as other adjectives (although they usually precede their noun in the modern language), and may be modified by determiners and even by adverbs: *la mia macchina* 'my car'; *la macchina mia*; *questi miei amici* literally 'these my friends'; *una cosa molto sua* literally 'a very his thing' – 'something typical of him', etc. The absence of the definite article where possessive adjectives modify the singular names of relatives (*mio padre* 'my father'; *vostra madre* 'your mother', etc.) probably reflects lexicalization of these phrases earlier than the extension of the definite article to nouns having unique referents (see 7.2); in such cases, if the noun is in any way modified, or the adjective is postposed, the article is duly required (*la figlia vostra* 'your daughter'; *la mia cara madre* 'my dear mother', etc.). In southern dialects and OTuscan, another type of lexicalization of such expressions is manifested in the use of a specialized enclitic singular possessive adjective: *mogliata*, 'your wife', *signorto* 'your master', appear in the Decameron (cf. Rohlfs (1968: 124f.) and Ch.5: 2.3.2.4).

In the literary language of the fifteenth and sixteenth centuries (as in Tuscan dialect), the forms *mia*, 'my' *tua* 'thy', and *sua* 'his' are often employed as plural possessives (e.g., Cellini *a' mia figliuoli* 'to my children'; *i figliuoli tua* 'your children'). Note also *dua* for *due* 'two' (Cellini: *io gli resi i vasi, che ve n'era dua mia. . .* 'I gave him back the vases, and there were two of mine among them'). The origin of the final *-a* has yet to be satisfactorily explained: Rohlfs (1968: 121) offers a phonetically based account.

5.3 Syntax of the adjective

The position of the CL adjective in relation to the noun it modifies is fairly free, at least in literary usage – cf. Vincent (1988b: 28). Adjectives usually precede the noun, although a tendency is discernible, already in the classical period, for adjectives to follow, particularly where they predicate an unfamiliar or unexpected property of the noun. In Italian, as in other Romance languages, there has emerged a rigidification of adjective position:[12] adjectives normally follow the noun, and in this case the adjective is 'semantically autonomous' with respect to the noun, in that it predicates some property of the noun which is not inherent in the noun's meaning. But adjectives (and certain other modifiers, such as quantifiers and determiners) collocated to the left of the noun are 'non-autonomous', in that they merely make explicit some inherent or logically necessary property of the referent. Thus we have *la neve rossa* 'the red snow' (redness is not an inherent property of snow, and the adjective therefore asserts something new about the snow) but usually *la bianca neve* 'the white snow' (because snow is inherently white). Similarly, *il Dante fiorentino* refers to a (person called) Dante from Florence (as distinct from, say, Dante da Maiano); *il fiorentino Dante* expresses of Dante the well-known property of his being Florentine. Other modifiers which do not predicate some property of the noun, among them quantifiers (*troppo* 'too much'; *poco* 'not much'; *alcuni* 'some'; *tutto* 'all'; *molto* 'much'; *tanto* 'so much'; *ciascuno* 'each'; *nessuno* 'none'; *qualche* 'some'; *qualsiasi* 'any'; *ogni* 'each'; *primo* 'first'; *ultimo* 'last'; *terzo* 'third' and other ordinal and cardinal numerals) and determiners such as the demonstratives (*questo*; *quello*) and definite and indefinite articles are also collocated to the left of the noun.

In general, the 'left-hand' position is occupied by items having a very low degree of semantic autonomy with respect to the noun they modify. In this light, the semantic differentiation between preposed and postposed occurrences of adjectives such as *certo* 'certain'; *diversi* 'sundry'; *vari* 'various'; *unico* 'sole'; *nuovo* 'new'; *vecchio* 'old', becomes intelligible. Preposed, they have been evacuated of almost all of their original lexical meaning, and function as quantifiers. The first three, when preposed (*certe idee* 'certain ideas' etc.), are indefinite quantifiers; postposed (*idee certe* 'ideas which are certain', etc.), they have the independent lexical meanings 'sure', 'different', 'varied'. Preposed *unico* is semantically identical to *solo uno* 'just one'; following the noun it means 'unique'. Preposed *nuovo* is close in meaning to *altro* 'other' (also always preposed, like its antonyms *medesimo* and *stesso*[13] 'same'); postposed, it means 'new'. Preposed *vecchio* (*un vecchio amico* 'an old friend') might be described as a temporal quantifier, meaning 'one who has been a friend for a long time', but *un amico vecchio* is a 'friend who is old'. As for preposed *povero*, and *grande* 'great', both express inherent qualities, although preposed *povero* connotes 'pitiableness', rather than financial poverty, and *grande* greatness of mind or achievement; following the noun, these words possess their full lexical meaning of 'poor' (not rich) and 'big'. Precisely because a preposed adjective expresses inherent properties of the noun, such positioning is often associated with the expression of value judgements: *Ammiro i magnifici politici italiani* 'I admire the magnificent Italian politicians' suggests that I believe that Italian politicians are, by their very nature, magnificent.

6 The demonstratives

CL possessed a three-term demonstrative system. The demonstrative adjective and pronoun ILLE designated referents 'external to the speech situation' (in proximity neither to the speaker nor to the addressee). The other two terms correspond roughly to 'first person' (speaker-focused) – HIC, and 'second person' (addressee-focused) – ISTE. In Italian vestiges of the ternary system survive, but a binary system is that most widely used, in which there is a simple distinction between speaker-focused and non-speaker-focused deixis. In almost every case, the demonstrative forms of CL have not been directly continued in their demonstrative function in Italian. There has also been some differentiation of adjectival and pronominal forms. The latter are examined in 9.5.

Conservation of a ternary system characterizes the dialects of central and southern Italy, southern Gaul and Iberia. Example (7) is from Amaseno (Lazio)

(7)

	1Pers.	2Pers.	Other
M.	**ˈkiʃtu**	**ˈkissu**	**ˈkiʎu**
F.	**ˈkeʃta**	**ˈkessa**	**ˈkella**

In the remaining areas (e.g., French, northern Italian dialects, Rhaeto-Romance, Romanian) a binary system generally obtains.[14] Thus Milanese:

(8)

	1 and 2 Pers.	Other
M.	**kest**	**kel**
F.	**ˈkesta**	**ˈkela**

The modern standard language employs principally the binary system *questo* vs. *quello*. Tuscan dialects, the Tuscan regional variety of Italian, and the literary language, possess a third term (*cotesto* or, particularly in Florence, *codesto*) corresponding to the second person. For many speakers outside Tuscany, *cotesto* has an archaic, and even pejorative, ring (cf. Durante (1981: 166)). Berruto (1990: 78) observes that contemporary *questo* and *quello* may be losing some of their deictic force, and asssuming some of the functions of the definite articles – compare the evolution of the Romance definite articles from CL demonstratives (see section 7).

The modern *questo* and *quello* are derived, respectively, from a combination of the Proto-Romance presentative particle ***'ɛkko** (Italian *ecco*) < CL ECCE, with the forms ***'estu** (< CL ISTU(M)) and ***'ellu** (< CL ILLU(M)). Hence *esto* (found in the medieval language, and continued in the modern, non-literary *sto*) and modern *questo* < ***'ɛkko 'estu**, and *quello* < ***'ɛkko 'ellu**. Forms of the demonstrative pronoun in *co-* (e.g., *costui*, *costei*, etc.) apparently derive from Proto-Romance structures in which the initial vowel of ***'estu**, etc., was deleted (***'ɛkko (e)'stui**, etc.). The type *codesto* or *cotesto*, unique to Tuscany and some neighbouring areas of central Italy (cf., Umbrian **'testo**), is derived in the same way as *questo*, with the intercalation of a second person pronoun ***te**: ***'ɛkko te 'estu** literally 'behold (for) you this' > *cotesto*.

There has been considerable functional and structural readjustment in the demonstrative system.[15] ISTE is continued with first, not second person reference, while HIC has been discontinued (but see 9.5). In the binary system, a reflex of ILLE assumes the functions both of CL ILLE and of ISTE. In ternary systems, the second person term is furnished, outside Tuscany, by **'kwesso** or **'esso** (or local variants thereof), reflexes of the Latin adjective and pronoun IPSE 'the self same' (accusative IPSU(M) > **'esso**): Proto-Romance ***'ɛkko 'essu** > **'kwesso**. The form **'kwesso** occurs in some Tuscan dialects (e.g., Elba), and *esso* appears in OTuscan, where it retains some of its original anaphoric function: *esso libro* = 'the said/self same/aforementioned book.' Another remnant of this function survives in *stesso* < Proto-Romance ***'estu 'essu** < ISTU(M) + IPSU(M), i.e., 'that one itself', 'that very one', 'the same'. The source of the literary *medesimo*, is reconstructable as a combination of -MET, which was an intensifying suffix attached to pronouns, e.g., EGOMET 'I', with a superlative form of IPSE, namely IPSIMU(M): *MET IPSIMU(M) > OTuscan *medesmo*, *medesimo*.[16] For the old anaphoric form *desso* (< ID IPSUD), see Rohlfs (1968: 210f.).

Like the demonstrative adjectives and pronouns, the locative adverbs occur both in a binary and a ternary system. Unlike the demonstratives, the three CL terms are continued in their original function, combined with ***'ɛkko**: HIC/HAC > *(**'ɛkko**) **i**/*(**'ɛkko**) **a** > *qui* /*qua* ; ISTIC/ISTAC >

*(ˈ**ɛkko**) **sti**/ *(ˈ**ɛkko**) **sta** > *costì* / *costà*; ILLIC/ILLAC > ***li**/ *(ˈ**ɛkko**) **la** > *lì* /*(co)là*. The forms in [**i**] and [**a**] are practically synonymous, although the variants with [**a**] tend to indicate location in a general area, while [**i**] is associated with precise, punctual location. Hence *al di là* 'beyond', not ***al di lì*.

7 The articles

7.1 Morphology of the articles

Italian, like all Romance languages, has definite and indefinite articles. CL had neither. The source of the Italian definite article is the Latin demonstrative ILLU(M) 'that one' (in Sardinian, medieval Catalan, and modern Balearic Catalan the definite article continues IPSU(M) 'the self same': e.g., Sardinian *su*, *sa*, *sos*, *sas*); that of the indefinite article, in all Romance languages, is the numeral UNU(M), 'one'.

The phonological and morphological history of these forms is relatively unproblematic. ILLU(M), ILLA(M), ILLOS, ILLAS, apparently stressed (like the related clitic pronouns) on the final syllable, give OTuscan *lo la li le*. With divers local variations, this system persists in most southern Italian dialects (cf. Rohlfs (1968: 106f.)). The final vowel is regularly deleted before words beginning with a vowel, a situation which persists in the modern language, (e.g., *l'orso* 'the bear') and optionally for the feminine (*l'orsa* or *la orsa*). In the modern language, feminine singular *l'* is retained principally before following [**a**]: *l'arte*. Masculine plural *l'* is extinct, however, and the feminine plural is now almost always *le*, although plurals such as *l'arti* 'the arts' survive in the literary language into the nineteenth century. The masculine definite article (in common with the adjectives *bello* 'beautiful' and *quello* 'that') has acquired a series of forms which vary according to the phonological character of the beginning of the following word. Before vowels the singular is *l'* and the plural *gli* (pronounced [**ʎ**]): *l'orso gli orsi* 'bear'. Before a heterogeneous set of phonological environments (namely [**ts**], [**dz**]; [**s**] + consonant; [**ʃ**]; [**ks**]; labial occlusive + obstruent; [**ɲ**]; [**j**]), we have singular *lo* and plural *gli* ([**ʎi**]): *lo zio gli zii* 'uncle'; *lo spacco gli spacchi* 'split'; *lo scatto gli scatti* 'click'; *lo stato gli stati* 'state'; *lo sfregio gli sfregi* 'slash'; *lo scemo gli scemi* 'idiot'; *lo xilofono gli xilofoni* 'xylophone'; *lo pneumatico gli pneumatici* 'tyre'; *lo psichiatra gli psichiatri* 'psychiatrist'; *lo bdellio* 'bdellium'; *lo gnocco gli gnocchi* 'dumpling'; *lo yacht gli yacht*, etc. Since most cases of initial [**ʃ**] (as in *lo scemo*) derive from [**stʃ**] (Ch.2: 6), this, too, can perhaps be counted as an (original) [**s**] + consonant environment. In the modern spoken language it is before [**s**] + consonant that *lo* and *gli* most consistently occur.[17] In all other environments, we have singular *il* and plural *i*: *il gatto i gatti* 'cat'; *il passo i passi* 'step'.

In OTuscan, *lo* could appear regardless of phonological environment: e.g., Dante *era lo loco* 'it was the place'; *Lo giorno se n'andava* 'The day was dying'; *a rimirar lo passo* 'to look at the pass again', etc. Its allomorph *il* or *'l* appeared *only* where preceded by a vowel and followed by a word-initial consonant (e.g., Dante *m'avea di paura il cor compunto* 'had struck my heart with fear'; *e il sol montava* 'and the sun rose'), and its origin may have been a continuant of CL ILLU(M) stressed on the first syllable, giving Proto-Romance ***'ellu**, and Tuscan *il 'l* (or *el*).[18] The form [l] persists in the modern *dal* 'from the', *sul* 'on the', *al* 'to the', etc., and in the spoken language as a postvocalic variant of *il*: cf. **il 'kaːne 'vjɛːne** 'the dog comes' vs. **'vjɛːne l 'kaːne**. But already in the thirteenth century, *il* is becoming phonologically autonomous, in that it can occur in exactly the same environments as *lo*, except that *lo* at first continues to be preferred after a preceding consonant, particularly [**r**]. This preference for *lo* after [**r**] is reflected in the modern set phrases *per lo meno* 'at least' and *per lo più* 'mostly'. Throughout the fourteenth and fifteenth centuries, *il* steadily gains ground over *lo*.

It is difficult to account for the modern distribution of *lo* in terms of some general phonological principle, such as avoidance of undesirable consonant clusters that might arise in contact with [**l**]. After all, *il* is used before [**r**] (*il ramo* 'the branch'), even though [**lr**] is an avoided consonant cluster in Italian (see Ch.2: 9); and *lo* appears before [**ts**], even though [**lts**] is perfectly admissible (e.g., **'altsa** *alza* 'he raises'). However, the sequence [**lr**] may be a pronunciation based on orthography, since in many areas of Tuscany [**lr**] is regularly assimilated to [**rr**] across word boundaries, as in **ir re** *il re* 'the king', so that no unnatural cluster arises in pronunciation. As late as the eighteenth century, *il* is the predominant form in front of initial *z*, and the occurrence of *lo* in this position is by no means consistent, even in the modern language. Although *lo* is the prescribed form (*lo psicologo* 'the psychologist'; *lo pneumatico* 'the tyre'; *lo gnomo* 'the gnome'; *lo yacht; lo xilofono* 'the xylophone'), these initial consonants are also commonly preceded by *il* in modern usage (see Brunet (1979)).

The position in which *lo* is most firmly established is before [**s**] + consonant, and here a clear phonological motivation is available: *lo* is preferred because it furnishes a prosthetic vowel.

We have shown in Ch.2: 4.6.5 that initial [**s**] + consonant sometimes developed a prosthetic vowel ([**i**]); this initial vocalic element could equally be provided by the final vowel of preceding *lo*. Indeed, in OTuscan initial [**i**] is sometimes deleted where *lo* precedes: *inganno* 'deception' but *lo 'nganno*; *ispecchio* 'mirror' but *lo specchio*; *ignudo* 'naked' but *lo 'gnudo*. Generalization of *lo* to words in initial [**ts**] and [**dz**] (a change in which prescriptive grammarians have had a major hand) seems to represent a simplification in the phonological environment for *lo* such that it is selected before any word-initial consonant cluster containing a sibilant. The ultimate stage in generalization of the rule is that *lo* tends to be employed before all unusual (alien) word-initial consonant clusters, and also before initial [**h**][19] in certain foreign words (*lo Hegel*; *lo Heine*). The final vowel of *uno* (and of its derivatives *alcuno* 'some'; *nessuno* 'none') survives in the same environments as *lo* and for the same reasons: deletion of its final [**o**] before a vowel and before other consonants reflects the tendency for deletion of final unstressed vowels after [**n**], [**l**] and [**r**], discussed in Ch.2: 4.6.4.

The masculine plural form used before a vowel *gli* (pronounced [**ʎ**]), is a regular reflex of [**li**] + vowel (Ch.2: 5.2). For preconsonantal *i* (OTuscan *ei*), *bei* and *quei*, via palatalization, and subsequent deletion, of [**l**] before final [**i**], see Ch.2: 6.2. All three stages survive, as late as the eigtheenth century, in the alternative preconsonantal masculine plural forms *i*, *gli* and *li*. *Li* survives to this day in parts of Tuscany (especially Elba), and in the formulaic *li 20 maggio* 'the 20th of May', used in dating letters. The ultimate triumph of *i* may have been favoured by its similarity – it lacks initial [**l**] – to the singular *il*. That *gli* (pronounced [**ʎi**]) has become established as the plural form corresponding to *lo* is probably due to the analogical influence of prevocalic masculine singular *l'* whose is plural *gli* ([**ʎ**]).

7.2 Semantic development of the articles

An overview of the uses of the articles in the modern language is not possible here – see Brunet (1979); Renzi (1988: Ch.7). We can, however, trace some of the stages in the 'desemantization', or gradual loss of lexical meaning, of the demonstrative ILLE and the numeral UNUS 'one'.

CL ILLE has the following characteristics: (i) it expresses distance from speaker and addressee; (ii) like all deictic terms it individuates (singles out) an entity or set of entities; (iii) like all deictic terms, it presupposes 'shared cognition' between speaker and addressee: the addressee is assumed to recognize, or to be capable of recognizing, the entity designated. In the history of Italian there has been considerable attenuation of deictic force, while the feature of 'shared cognition' has assumed increasing importance. In Proto-Romance, continuants of ILLE are already losing their association with spatial distance from the interlocutors, becoming (like IPSE,[20] which is the source of the definite article in Sardinian) principally *anaphoric*, which is to say that they serve to point to some noun or noun phrase within the discourse, and usually already mentioned (cf. Tekavčić (1980 II: 101)). The function of individuating from among a set of entities is still reflected in the medieval language in that the definite article is not generally employed with referents which could not, by virtue of their being unique, abstract or generic, be 'singled out': e.g., *sole* 'sun'; *luna* 'moon'; *cielo* 'sky'; *terra* 'earth'; *pane* 'bread'; *ferro* 'iron'; *lana* 'wool'; *legno* 'wood'; *Puglia*; *Francia* 'France'; *amore* 'love'; *odio* 'hatred'; *giustizia* 'justice', etc. Modern remnants of this state of affairs survive in some lexicalized expressions such as: *tra cielo e terra* 'between heaven and earth'; *ho fame* 'I'm hungry' (literally 'I have hunger'); *ho sete* literally 'I have thirst'; *ho paura* literally 'I have fear', etc.

It is 'shared cognition' which becomes the *predominant* factor in selection of the definite article: Renzi (1976: 31–4) identifies what he terms 'presupposizione comune' ('shared presupposition') as a determinant of the selection of ILLE already in sixth century Latin texts, and an early Italo-Romance attestation of this usage appears in the ninth or tenth century inscription of the catacomb of Commodilla: NON DICERE ILLE SECRITA A BBOCE 'do not say the secret prayers out loud' (cf. Castellani (1973: 31–7)). Any referent assumed to be part of the common universe of experience of interlocutors, regardless of whether it is unique or generic, comes eventually to require the definite article: *il sole è lontanissimo* 'the sun is very far away'; *l'oro è prezioso* 'gold is precious'; *viva la libertà* 'long live freedom'; *amo la giustizia* 'I love justice'. This includes inalienable and necessary or normal attributes (such as singular parts of the body, e.g., *mi batte il cuore* 'my heart is beating'). The names of rivers and countries (except *Israele*), but not of towns or small islands, have also acquired the definite article. The article is still not employed with singular names of countries after the preposition *in* (*in Francia*), and may be omitted, with feminine names, after *di* (*il cielo di Francia* or *il cielo della Francia* 'the sky of France'). Personal names denote unique individuals and to this day do not normally admit an article, even though occasional uses of the article with masculine names can be detected already in the medieval language – cf. Del Popolo (1991). For the optional use of the article with proper names in the modern language, (e.g., *il Manzoni* and, especially in Tuscany, *la Maria*), see Renzi (1988: 391–8). The continued individuating function of the article is apparent in the fact that all nouns require it when they are qualified by expressions of type, variety, or aspect: *ho odiato la Milano degli anni ottanta* 'I hated the Milan of the 1980s'; *non riconosco il Luigi che tu mi descrivi* 'I don't recognize the Luigi you're describing to me', etc.

The definite article is not employed with referents whose identity is assumed to be unknown to the addressee, that is, where there is no 'shared cognition'. Included here are partitive constructions, expressing indeterminate parts, numbers or quantities of some larger whole. In the earliest Italo-Romance texts, such forms appear without an article, a state of affairs conserved in the modern plural (*vedo gatti* 'I see cats'; *mangia mele* 'he eats apples'), and in proverbial locutions and set phrases such as *a caval donato non si guarda in bocca* 'don't look a gift horse in the mouth'; *gatta ci cova* 'something's up' (literally 'a she-cat is brooding on it'); *fare onore* 'to do honour'; *andare in carrozza* 'to travel by carriage', etc.

The indefinite article establishes itself later in Romance than its definite counterpart. In the language of the thirteenth century, structures such as *donami kavallo da cavalcare* 'give me a horse to ride', *brigata di chavalieri cienavano* 'a band of knights was dining' (Novellino) are still encountered. True to its origins as the numeral 'one', it can only be employed with singular referents, and tends to be omitted with negated referents: *mangio mele* 'I eat apples'; *la mia lettera è rimasta senza risposta* 'my letter did not get a reply'; *non c'è (uno) studente che lo sappia* 'there is no student who knows it'. Like the definite article it has an individuating function, but it implies *lack of cognition* on the part of the addressee (which may or not be shared by the speaker as well), and thereby serves to introduce something *new* into the discourse. It cannot be used with referents of which, because they are unique or generic, there cannot be more than one. Thus *riso* is 'rice', but *un riso* is a particular variety of rice, as distinct from other varieties. The property of non-specification or indefiniteness has been extended to novel use in expressions of approximation: e.g., *un tre metri* 'about three metres', *avrà un quarantadue anni* 'he must be about forty-two'.

A relatively recent innovation is the formation of a 'partitive' article by combination of the preposition *di* with the definite article: *mangio del pane* 'I eat bread'; *ci sono degli studenti* 'there are some students'; *legge dei giornali* 'he reads newspapers'. These structures are significantly less well established in the modern language than are the definite and indefinite article. In standard Italian, and in southern Tuscan and central and southern dialects in general (cf. Rohlfs (1968: 116)), the partitive may be expressed by the unmodified noun; e.g., *mangio mele* 'I eat apples', etc.[21] The articulated partitive is characteristic, instead, of northern Italian dialects, and of the regional Italian of northern Italy. In the standard language, the articulated partitive has not penetrated negative constructions: e.g., ***non mangio del pane*; ***non ci sono degli studenti*.[22] Nor has the partitive established itself after prepositions, particularly *di* and *da*: *un bicchiere di vino* 'a glass of wine' not ***un bicchiere di del vino*; *sparavano da finestre* 'they were shooting from windows' not ***sparavano da delle finestre*. The partitive originates in the extension of the definite article to generic and partitive nouns (see above), and in its combination with an already existing partitive structure *di* + NOUN, continuing a CL structure DE + (ablative) NOUN. For example, in the Decameron *ho di belli gioielli e di cari* 'I have some beautiful and expensive jewels'. Once the definite article becomes generalized in front of generic nouns (*acqua* 'water' > *l'acqua*), the OTuscan partitive construction *bevo di acqua* 'I drink some water' (CL BIBO DE AQUA) becomes *bevo dell'acqua*. Traces of the older partitive construction survive in Tuscan dialects, especially where the noun is modified by preceding adjectives: e.g., *di belle patate* 'nice potatoes'; *di bon vino* 'good wine'.[23] The articulated partitive is already frequent in Tuscan by the late thirteenth century.[24]

8 The verb

8.1 The CL verb

The verb, in CL as in modern Italian, is a category whose complexity and intricacy is unmatched elsewhere in the grammar. Its broad characteristics may be outlined as follows. With the marginal exceptions of the perfect passive, all CL verb forms are synthetic and have the canonical structure ROOT (+ THEMATIC VOWEL) + INFLECTION. The root expresses the lexical meaning of the verb. The theme vowel, a semantically arbitrary marker of conjugation, is affixed to the root in certain verb forms, among them the infinitive: first conjugation AMA:RE 'to love'; second conjugation UIDE:RE 'to see'; third conjugation MITTERE 'to send'; fourth conjugation DORMI:RE 'to sleep'. A major morphological cleavage within the CL verb stem is that between forms expressing imperfective aspect and perfective aspect (the former expresses the event or state indicated by the verb as viewed 'from within', the latter expresses them as viewed 'from without', and focusing on their temporal limits – see Ch.4: 8.1 for further discussion). Perfective stems of the first, fourth and of most second conjugation verbs are characterized by a stem-final [**w**] 'U': e.g., AMAUI 'I have loved' (past perfect) AMAUERAM 'I had loved' (pluperfect) AMAUERO 'I shall have loved' (future perfect). Third conjugation verbs (and a number from the second and fourth) display root allomorphy between perfective and imperfective (e.g., present MITTO 'I send' vs. past perfect MI:SI 'I sent'). The inflectional endings, bound morphemes attached to the right of the stem, express mood, tense, person and number. The inflections are usually monosyllabic or bisyllabic, and characteristically cumulative. Tense and person are mutually implicational: signalling of one entails signalling of the other. The infinitive, the gerund, and the present and past participles do not indicate person. The present participle is active, the past participle is neutral as to voice. The remaining participial forms of CL, the supine (e.g., AMATUM) and the future participle (e.g., AMATURUS) (cf. Ernout (1927: 359–62; 362–4)), are not continued into Romance. In CL, as in Italian, stress in some parts of the verb may be *rhizotonic* (stressed on the root) and in others *arhizotonic* (not stressed on the root).

8.2 Participial and infinitive forms

8.2.1 The infinitive

The CL infinitive marker -RE is continued into Italian, and generalized (together with the thematic vowel [**e**]) to the handful of infinitives which in CL terminated in -SE and -LE: AMARE; ESSE; UELLE > *amare* 'to love'; *essere* 'to be'; *volere* 'to want'. The CL perfective infinitive (AMA(UI)SSE, etc.) is extinct, having been replaced by analytic syntagms of the *aver amato* 'to have loved' type (see 8.8). Some originally arhizotonic infinitives have become rhizotonic in Italian: MOUERE > *muòvere* 'to move'; RIDERE > *rìdere* 'to laugh'; RESPONDERE > *rispòndere* 'to answer'. Some rhizotonic infinitives are subject to syncope (see Ch.2: 4.6.4.1), and subsequent consonantal assimilations, giving rise to allomorphy (see Ch.1: 5.3) in the root: PONERE 'to place'; PONET 'he places' > *'**ponre**; *'**pone** > *porre*; *pone*. A consonantal assimilation appears also to have operated in the syncopated infinitives *-durre* (-DUCERE); *trarre* 'to draw' (< *'**tragere** < CL TRAHERE). *Dire* 'to say' and *fare* 'to do' (< DICERE and FACERE) have modelled their infinitives on the *-ire*, *-are* type. It is likely that *fare* has been remodelled on *dare* 'to give', while *dire* is possibly refashioned on the OTuscan verb *gire* 'to go' (see 8.4.1).

8.2.2 The present participle

The CL present participle declines for gender, number and case, like an adjective, and has the basic structure ROOT + THEMATIC VOWEL + (E)NT + INFLECTION (e.g., nominative AMANS, accusative AMANTEM 'loving'; nominative HABENS, accusative HABENTEM 'having'; nominative AUDIENS, accusative AUDIENTEM, 'hearing'). It has been lost from the Italo-Romance verb system, although some present participle forms have survived as verbal adjectives, often with considerable semantic differences from their corresponding verbs: e.g., *abbiente* 'wealthy' (cf. 8.2.3 for the use of the subjunctive stem in this form) as well as *avente* 'having' vs. *avere* 'to have'; *potente* 'powerful' vs. *potere* 'to be able'; *ubbidiente* 'obedient' vs. *ubbidire* 'to obey'; *errante* 'wandering', 'errant' vs. *errare* 'to wander'. Others are more commonly used as nouns: e.g., *un amante* 'a lover' vs. *amare* 'to love'; *un credente* 'a believer' vs. *credere* 'to believe', *un perdente* 'a loser', etc. A remnant of the participle's verbal status survives in structures such as *le note riferentisi al discorso* 'the notes referring (themselves) to the speech', bearing a clitic reflexive pronoun (*si*) which, as we shall see in 9.4, occurs almost exclusively with verbs.

8.2.3 The gerund

The CL gerund (AMANDUM 'loving'; UENDENDUM 'selling'; DORMIENDUM 'sleeping') is a verbal noun which is complementary to the infinitive, in that it provides the genitive, dative, ablative and, after a preposition, accusative forms of the infinitive. The morphologically similar gerundive, is a – usually passive – verbal adjective (AMANDUS; UENDENDUS; DORMIENDUS) agreeing in gender, number and case with the noun it modifies. It is the gèrund which survives in Italo-Romance, in the morphologically invariant form *amando* 'loving'; *vendendo* 'selling', *dormendo* 'sleeping', etc. OTuscan occasionally employed the present subjunctive stem in the formation of the gerund: e.g., *sappiendo* 'knowing'; *faccendo* 'doing'; *veggendo* 'seeing'; *vogliendo* 'wanting' – cf. the subjunctives *sappia*; *faccia*; *veggia*; *voglia*.

The meaning of the Italian gerund remains close to that of the Latin ablative gerund ('while/by doing something'). In the modern language, and rather less consistently in the medieval, its grammatical subject must always be the subject of the main verb of the clause. So, *vidi l'uomo camminando lungo la strada* means 'I saw the man while I walked along the road', not 'I saw the man walking along the road'. The gerund assumes a particular importance in the syntactic history of Italian, through its combination with auxiliary verbs, notably *stare* – to be discussed in 8.8.3.

8.2.4 The past participle

The CL past participle originated as a kind of verbal adjective, whose meaning might be expressed roughly as 'having performed, or having undergone, the action expressed by the verb'. In Italian it survives as a verbal adjective expressing, broadly, the quality of having 'undergone' the action, and as an integral structural element in the formation of certain tense forms, of the type AUXILIARY + PP (*ho fatto* 'I have done'; *sono arrivato* 'I have arrived', etc.).[25]

The Italian first and third conjugation past participles perpetuate the structure (ROOT + THEMATIC VOWEL + TUS) of their CL antecedents: AMATU(M) > *amato* 'loved'; DORMITU(M) > *dormito* 'slept'. The past participle of *morire* 'to die' is *morto* (< CL MORTUU(M)); that of *venire* 'to come' is *venuto* (= CL UENTU(M)), analogical on *tenuto* 'held'. For the OTuscan first conjugation past participle forms *cerco* 'sought'; *salvo* 'saved'; *tocco* 'touched'; *porto* 'carried', etc. = *cercato*; *salvato*; *toccato*; *portato*, probably attributable to the analogical influence of non-first conjugation rhizotonic past participles like *fuso* 'melted' and *messo* 'put', see Rohlfs (1968: 375–7).

The third conjugation participles deviate markedly from this pattern. All of them were originally rhizotonic; many formed their past participles in -SUS, sometimes accompanied by allomorphic modification of a preceding root-final dental, a pattern extensively conserved in Italian (8):

(8)

MITTERE	MISSU(M)	*mettere* 'to put'	*messo*
RIDERE	RISU(M)	*ridere* 'to laugh'	*riso*
TORQUERE	TORTU(M)	*torcere* 'to wring'	*torto*
FUNDERE	FUSU(M)	*fondere* 'to melt'	*fuso*
OCCIDERE	OCCISU(M)	*uccidere* 'to kill'	*ucciso*
MORDERE	MORSU(M)	*mordere* 'to bite'	*morso*
CLAUDERE	CLAUSU(M)	*chiudere* 'to close'	*chiuso*
ACCENDERE	ACCENSU(M)	*accendere* 'to light'	*acceso*
PREHENDERE	PREHENSU(M)	*prendere* 'to take'	*preso*
REMANERE	REMANSU(M)	*rimanere* 'to remain'	(OTuscan) *rimaso*
CURRERE	CURSU(M)	*correre* 'to run'	*corso*

etc.

The majority form their past participle in -TUS, but lack a thematic vowel. In addition to conserving existing patterns of allomorphy (e.g., NASCI, NATU(M) > *nascere* 'to be born', *nato*), new forms of allomorphy have arisen as a result of regular phonetic processes, especially assimilation (Ch.2: 8.2) (9):

(9)

FACERE	FACTU(M)	*fare* 'to do'	*fatto*
REGERE	RECTU(M)	*reggere* 'to hold'	*retto*
SCRIBERE	SCRIPTU(M)	*scrivere* 'to write'	*scritto*
DUCERE	DUCTU(M)	*-durre*	*-dotto*
LEGERE	LECTU(M)	*leggere* 'to read'	*letto*
COQUERE	COCTU(M)	*cuocere* 'to bake'	*cotto*
IUNGERE	IUNCTU(M)	*giungere* 'to join'	*giunto*
PLANGERE	PLANCTU(M)	*piangere* 'to cry'	*pianto*
ASSUMERE	ASSUMPTU(M)	*assumere* 'to assume'	*assunto*

etc.

On the analogy of other parts of the paradigm (*pingere* 'to paint' and *vincere* 'to win'), a nasal consonant has been introduced into *pinto* (CL PICTU(M)) and *vinto* (CL UICTU(M)). Probably on the analogy of the past participle *chiesto* 'asked' (< QUAESITU(M)) and *posto* 'put' (< POSITU(M)), a number of new past participles in *-sto* have arisen: *visto* 'seen'*; risposto* 'answered'; *rimasto* 'remained'; *nascosto* 'hidden' (= CL UISU(M); RESPONSU(M); REMANSU(M); (IN)ABSCONSU(M)). Other changes show introduction of the endings in *-so* (see above): *mosso* 'moved' (CL MOTU(M)); *valso* 'having been worth' (CL UALITU(M), OTuscan *valuto*); *parso* 'seemed' (CL PARITU(M), OTuscan *paruto*). The emergence of past participle forms *porto* 'proffered'; *accorto* 'realized'; *colto* 'plucked'; *scelto* 'chosen' (replacing CL PORRECTU(M); ACCORRECTU(M); COLLECTU(M); EXELECTU(M), where one might have expected ****por'rɛtto**, etc.) appears to be due to the fact that the infinitives of these verbs are stressed on the root (e.g., *pòrgere*; *accòrgere*; *cògliere*; *scègliere*), and that most other rhizotonic infinitives in *-ere* have correspondingly rhizotonic past participles.

Certain CL verbs lack a past participle, but with the incorporation of the past participle into the tense and aspect system of the verb, through the creation of analytical verb structures of the type *ho amato* 'I have loved'; *sono venuto* 'I've come', there arises a need to create a past participle for every verb – although there remain some gaps in Italian, in a few verbs, among them *divergere* 'to diverge' and *stridere* 'to squeak'. The verbs STARE 'to stand' (lacking a past participle in Latin) simply follows the model of other -ARE verbs, giving *stato*.[26] In the second conjugation, to which the majority of verbs lacking a past participle belong, no obvious pattern presents itself: most other CL second conjugation verbs have rhizotonic past participles, accompanied by often idiosyncratic stem allomorphy. What speakers appear to have sought is a pattern that preserves an arhizotonic and morphologically invariant stem, and this is provided by a small class of verbs ending in -UI in the perfect, with past participle -UTU(M): SOLUERE 'to pay' SOLUI, perfect SOLUTU(M); FUTUERE 'to copulate', perfect FUTUI FUTUTU(M). The verbs UELLE 'to want', perfect UOLUI; TENERE 'to hold', perfect TENUI; POSSE 'to be able', perfect POTUI; SAPERE 'to taste', perfect SAP(I)UI, all lacking a past participle in Latin, thus acquire the past participle forms continued in modern Italian *voluto*; *tenuto*; *potuto*; *saputo*. The same ending helped to form a past participle for ESSE 'to be', namely *(es)suto* or *suto* (later replaced by *stato*). A class of proparoxytonic past participles in -ITU(M) (some of them already possessing perfect forms in -UI, such as HABUI and DEBUI) were also replaced by the arhizotonic -UTU(M): DEBITU(M); POTU(M) (or BIBITU(M)); CREDITU(M); UENDITU(M); PERDITU(M); NOCITU(M); COGNITU(M); UALITU(M); PARITU(M); TACITU(M); DOLITU(M) yield, respectively, *avuto* 'had'; *dovuto* 'owed'; *bevuto* 'drunk'; *creduto* 'believed'; *venduto* 'sold'; *(perduto* 'lost'); *nuociuto* 'hurt'; *conosciuto* 'known'; *(valuto* 'having been worth'); (*paruto* 'seemed'); *taciuto* 'fallen silent'; *doluto* 'ached'. The items in parentheses, attested in the medieval language, have been replaced by the forms *valso*; *parso*. The literary language still has both *perso* and *perduto*, although the latter is most commonly used in northern Italy. Other additions to the *-uto* class are *veduto* 'seen' (beside *visto*) (CL UISU(M)); *goduto* 'enjoyed' (CL GAUISU(M)); *mietuto* 'reaped' (CL MESSU(M)); *ceduto* 'yielded' (CL CESSU(M)); *cresciuto* 'grown' (CL CRETU(M)). *Vissuto* 'lived' (CL UICTU(M)) is an unusual case of attachment of the participial ending *-uto* to the root of the passato remoto (*vissi*) – cf. Rohlfs (1968: 369f.). The *-uto* ending has also enjoyed some success as an adjective-forming suffix: *nasuto* 'long-nosed'; *nerboruto* 'sinewy'; *baffuto* 'moustachioed'.

The past participles of *esigere*; *scindere*; *espellere*; *esistere*; *consistere*, namely *esatto* 'demanded'; *scisso* 'cleft'; *espulso* 'expelled'; *esistito* 'existed'; *consistito* 'consisted', are probably learnèd imitations of CL EXACTUS; SCISSUS; EXPULSUS; EXISTITUS; CONSISTITUS.

8.3 Person and number

8.3.1 The first person

Latin first person singular present indicative -O is preserved (e.g., *amo* 'I love'; *vendo* 'I sell'; *sto* 'I stand/am'). The first person singular imperfect indicative ending -BA(M) is continued as *-va* (*amava*, etc.) in most Italo-Romance dialects. It persists in the literary language (particularly as used by non-Tuscans) into the nineteenth century, but the analogy of the present indicative inflection *-o* had given rise, already in the fifteenth century, to the type *amavo*, which occurs consistently in the late fifteenth century Florentine Macinghi Strozzi letters; none the less, both inflections appear a century and a half later in the correspondence of Galileo. The CL perfect ending -I is continued as *-i* (AMAUI > *amai* 'I loved'; UIDI > *vidi* 'I saw'). The imperfect subjunctive ending -E(M) (e.g., AMA(UI)SSE(M)) gave *-e* in OTuscan (*amasse*), which has been analogically replaced by the first person singular inflection *-i* characteristic of the passato remoto (e.g., *amassi*).

The first person plural ending is *-mo* (< -MUS), in all moods and tenses. The lengthened consonant of *-mmo* in the passato remoto (and conditional) seems to reflect compensatory lengthening of [**m**] in response to deletion of a preceding segment (probably [**i**]): AMAUIMUS > ***a'maimo** > *amammo* 'we loved' (Ch.2: 8.2).

It is a peculiarity of Tuscan, firmly established in Florentine by the fifteenth century (and one of the hallmarks of the Tuscan origin of Italian), that the first person plural present indicative and subjunctive are characterized by the ending *-iamo*. In most central and southern dialects, the endings are -**amo**, -**emo**, -**imo**, according to conjugation.

The generalization of *-iamo* is part of a widely observable tendency in Italo-Romance for conjugational distinctions to be neutralized in the first person plural present. In Corsican and some northern dialects, thematic [**a**] has been replaced in the first person plural by [**e**]; in parts of Lazio, **-emo** has been extended to all conjugations. The basis for such generalizations is possibly the high frequency of forms such as *volemo* 'we want', *avemo* 'we have' and, above all, *semo* 'we are', from *essere*. In Piedmont and parts of Liguria and Lombardy, continuants of the Latin SUMUS (e.g., Piedmontese *suma*) are the source of the generalized first person plural inflection *-uma* (e.g., *venduma*; *parluma*).

The reasons for the spread of the inflection *-iamo* are obscure,[27] although it clearly originates in the Latin second and fourth conjugation subjunctives in -EAMUS and -IAMUS. Wanner (1975) observes that in mid-thirteenth century Florentine the *-iamo* ending was general in subjunctives of all conjugations (e.g., *portiamo* 'let us carry', *vendiamo* 'let us sell', *dormiamo* 'let us sleep'), and also consistently present in *indicatives* of the first conjugation (e.g., *portiamo* 'we carry'), but not yet firmly established in first person plural indicatives of other conjugations (we find indicative *vendemo* or *vendiamo*, and only *dormimo*). He reconstructs the following development: the ending *-iamo* (together with its second person plural counterpart *-iate*) was originally restricted to a small handful of (very frequent) verbs[28] which had retained the Latin subjunctive endings -EAMUS and -IAMUS (together with second person plural -EATIS and -IATIS): e.g., HABEAMUS 'let us have' > ***a'bjamo** > *abbiamo*; SAPIAMUS 'let us taste' > ***sa'pjamo** 'let us know' > *sappiamo*. On the model of such verbs, the endings *-iamo* (and *-iate*) spread to all first person plural subjunctive verbs. This generalization had occurred at an early date (although traces of the first conjugation subjunctive ending *-emo* are still found in thirteenth century Pistoiese). The fact that, by the mid thirteenth century, *-iamo* has also substituted indicative **-amo** in the first conjugation (***por'tamo** has given way to *portiamo*), can be ascribed to the identity of first conjugation indicative **-amo**, with **-amo** the inflection of second and third conjugation subjunctive forms (so subjunctive ***ven'damo** and ***dormamo** are replaced by *vendiamo* and *dormiamo*). Having established a bridgehead in the first conjugation, *-iamo* then extends to the first person plural indicative forms of the remaining conjugations. We may add that a possible contributory factor was the replacement of continuants of CL SUMUS 'we are', by **'seːmo** (still widely attested in many central Italian dialects), on the analogy of other first person plural forms such as **a'veːmo** 'we have'; **vo'leːmo** 'we want', etc. This new analogical indicative happens to be identical with the subjunctive **'seːmo**, from the CL subjunctive SIMUS (cf. Rohlfs (1968: 268)). The spread of *-iamo*, as described above, could then have led to simultaneous replacement of subjunctive and indicative **'seːmo** by *siamo*. Formal identity between indicative and subjunctive in such a frequent and important verb could, no doubt, have favoured the generalization of *-iamo* in other verbs.

A difficult, and unresolved, question is why parallel developments are not observed in the second person plural (why does the replacement of subjunctive *__ven'daːte__* by subjunctive *vendiate* not trigger replacement of indicative **por'taːte** by indicative ***portiate*? – given the identity of the inflection of the first conjugation indicative with that of the subjunctive elsewhere?). In the absence of a cogent explanation, we can only repeat the observation that the change in the first person plural corresponds to a wider tendency for first person plural markers to become identical across conjugations and moods.

8.3.2 The second person

The origin of the second person singular inflection *-i* has already been discussed at length in Ch.2: 12, where the view was expressed that *-i* (and the OTuscan first conjugation inflection *-e*) are due to phonetic raising of the vowels before original final -s. The second person singular subjunctive ending *-a* (e.g., *tu venda* 'you sell' < *__'vendas__*), seems to be modelled on the first and third persons singular, reinforced by the formal identity of the first, second and third person singular subjunctive inflections in the first conjugation. The subjunctive inflection *-i* survives in the small class of verbs which form their imperative from the subjunctive: *avere*: *abbi* 'have'; *sapere*: *sappi* 'know'; *volere*: *vogli* 'want'; *essere*: *sii* 'be'. The final *-i* of the passato remoto second person singular (*amasti* 'you loved') is derived directly from the CL final -I (AMA(UI)STI).

The CL second person singular imperatives AMA and DORMI are directly continued in Italian *ama* 'love' and *dormi* 'sleep'. The final -E of UENDE has been replaced by *-i* (*vendi* 'sell'), probably under the analogical influence of the indicative *vendi* and indicative and imperative *dormi*. The imperatives *sta'* 'stand/be'; *da'* 'give'; *di'* 'say'; *fa'* 'do', continue CL STA; DA; DIC; FAC. The alternative imperative forms *dai*, *stai*, seem to be modelled on the indicative, possibly on the analogy of those non-first conjugation verbs, where imperative and indicative are morphologically identical.

In the negative, the second person singular imperative is identical to the infinitive: *non cantare* 'don't sing'; *non venire* 'don't come', etc. The origins of this structure lie in the CL negative imperative contruction NOLI UENIRE; NOLITE UENIRE (literally 'refuse to come'). Its subsequent restriction in Italo-Romance to the second person *singular* remains to be explained.

The CL second person plural inflection, -TIS, yields **-te** (apparently after loss of the final **-s**): AMATIS > *amate* 'you love'; HABETIS > *avete* 'you have'; AMA(UI)STIS > *amaste* 'you loved'; HABUISTIS > *aveste* 'you had'. The imperfect subjunctive second person plural (which is always identical to the second person plural passato remoto) continues a syncopated form of AMA(UI)S(SE)TIS; HABUIS(SE)TIS: *amaste*; *aveste*. The second person plural imperative is identical to the present indicative, and directly continues the CL imperative ending -TE: AMATE > *amate* 'love'; UENITE > *venite* 'come'.

For the origins of the second person plural subjunctive in *-iate*, originally restricted to verbs which had preserved reflexes of the Latin subjunctive endings -EATIS or -IATIS, and later extended to all present tense subjunctives, cf. 8.3.1 above.

8.3.3 The third person

The CL third person singular inflection -T is lost throughout Italo-Romance, with the exception of Sardinian and of a cluster of dialects in the far south of Basilicata (cf. Lausberg (1939)). Thus CL DAT; AMAT; UIDET; DICIT > *dà* 'he gives'; *ama* 'he loves'; *vede* 'he sees'; *dice* 'he says'.

The third person singular passato remoto endings of *amò* 'she loved'; *batté* 'she beat'; *finí* 'she finished', require special comment. The source of *amò* is CL AMAU(I)T (there is evidence for loss of the [**i**] from this tense form in many Vulgar Latin inscriptions). The Sicilian *cantau* 'she sang' preserves the original diphthong, which is subject to regular monophthongization (Ch.2: 4.4) in Tuscan. The form FINIUIT gave *finio* (cf. Sicilian *finiu*), which subsequently lost final *-o* (> *finì*). On the analogy of *finire finì*, we have *credere credé* 'she believed'; *battere batté* 'she beat', etc. (cf. Rohlfs (1968: 319f.)). Forms such as *amao*, *finio*, with *credeo*, which is probably analogically modelled on the other two conjugations, are attested in early lyric poetry and in some Tuscan writers, such as Latini. They are generally assumed to reflect southern Italian, and particularly Sicilian, literary influence.

The *-no* inflection which characterizes most Italian third person plural forms (*vengono* 'they come'; *faranno* 'they'll do'; *chiamarono* 'they called' etc.) cannot be derived directly from CL -NT. Rohlfs (1968: 255) seeks to explain its emergence as follows:

(i) With loss of final -T, -NT is continued by **-n** (***'kantan**; ***'vendon**, etc.).
(ii) Third person plural SUNT becomes identical to first person singular ***son** (< SUM 'I am').
(iii) The first person singular inflection **-o** (*canto* 'I sing', etc.), is introduced to first person singular ***son**, whence *sono* 'I am'.

(iv) The formal identity of third person plural ***son** with first person singular ***son**, means that the third person plural, as well, becomes *sono*;

(v) On the model of *sono*, other third person plural verbs acquire final *-o* (*cantano* 'they sing'; *vendono* 'they sell'; *cantavano* 'they were singing'; *vendevano* 'they were selling', etc.).

In fact, the evidence suggests a slightly modified scenario (proposed, and corroborated from eighth and ninth century Latin texts, by Politzer (1958), and supported by the evidence of dialects of Lazio and Umbria[29]), in which final -NT is deleted, and later replaced by **-no**. A remnant of deletion of -NT may be seen in Italian third person plural passato remoto forms such as *vollero* 'they wanted'; *ebbero* 'they had' < UOLUERUNT; HABUERUNT. Significantly, Politzer observes that the nasal seems to have been continued only in the third person plural of ESSE (as SUN or SUM). Once first person singular ***son** had become ***sono**, the third person plural followed suit (in the manner described above), and from the third person plural of *essere*, **-no** appears to have been reanalysed as a semi-autonomous clitic marker of third person plural, which is analogically extended to other third person plural verb forms (cf. the spread of *-iamo* from *siamo* 'we are' – 8.3.1). Not only does it extend to verbs, but to pronouns, giving rise in OTuscan to the plurals *eglino* and *elleno*. Like other clitics, it is subject to *rafforzamento sintattico* (Ch.2: 8.2) when attached to monosyllabic third person plural. forms (e.g. ***da** < DANT; ***sta** < STANT): ***da** + ***no** > *danno* 'they give'; ***sta** + ***no** > *stanno* 'they stand/are' – cf. the cliticized imperative **da** + **lo** > *dallo* 'give it'). The same development is observable in those Tuscan dialects where the passato remoto third person singular form has been extended into the third person plural (cf. Rohlfs (1968: 313f; 318; 320)): *cantò cantonno*; *sparì sparinno*. Like the clitic pronouns, **-no** is disregarded for the purposes of stress placement (Ch.2: 1.2): just as we have antepropar oxytonic stress in *màndamelo* 'send it to me'; *prendètecelo* 'take it from us', etc., so we have antepropar oxytonic third person plurals *pìzzicano* 'they sting'; *telèfonano* 'they telephone', etc.

The ending *-ro* (< Latin -RUNT) of the passato remoto presents an obstacle for the spread of *-no*, since the former already constitutes a distinctive marker of third person plural. The outcome in modern Italian is that *-no* has penetrated passato remoto verb forms which were originally paroxytonic, being suffixed to the right of *-ro* (e.g., *cantaro* 'they sang'; *finiro* 'they finished' > *cantarono*; *finirono*). But *-no* has not established itself in the third person plural of originally proparoxytonic forms (e.g. *presero* 'they took'; *seppero* 'they knew'; *ebbero* 'they had'), and consequently not in the third person plural of the conditional, which is based on *ebbero* (*canterebbero*, see 8.8.5). The old imperfect subjunctive third person plural forms *amasseno*; *dovesseno* < AMAUISSENT; DEBUISSENT become *amassero*; *dovessero*, etc., apparently under the analogical influence of the third person plural conditionals. In the thirteenth and fourteenth centuries we witness a tussle between *-no* and *-ro* in Tuscany, documented by Nencioni (1953), in which *-no* is sometimes suffixed to *-ro*, even in proparoxytonic passato remoto forms (*preserono*; *sepperono*; *canterebberono* etc., are attested), and sometimes *replaces -ro*, producing a variety of formal variants, including deletion of the first [**o**], e.g., *cantarno*. But in the proparoxytonic passato remoto forms the trend is overwhelmingly towards *replacement*, rather than suffixation.

The pattern which survives in modern Italian, and survived in many varieties of fourteenth- and fifteenth-century Tuscan, is *presero*, etc. This is in the face of an alternative tendency, also widespread in those centuries, but particularly firmly established by the mid fourteenth century in the speech of Florence, for replacement of *-ro* by *-no*: *dissono/disseno* 'they said'; *feciono/feceno* 'they did', etc. Why the proparoxytonic third person plural rhizotonic preterites should favour replacement, rather than suffixation, is difficult to say. A result of the attachment of *-no* in other tenses, such as the present and imperfect indicative, is that the characteristic shape of the third person plural is a proparoxytone, the final syllable of which, *-no*, is the person and number marker (e.g., *parlano* 'they say'; *amavano* 'they loved'). In this light, *-ro* of the proparoxytonic third person plural passato remoto (e.g., *seppero*; *presero*) may have been interpreted as equivalent in function to *-no* of the other tense forms. Therefore, it could either be retained unmodified, as has generally occurred, or could be supplanted by *-no*, as occurred in Florentine.

8.4 The present tense

The present tense stem remains close to its CL structure. The rhizotonic third conjugation first and second persons plural (**PER**DIMUS; **PER**DITIS), become arhizotonic ((OTuscan *perdèmo* 'we lose'; *perdète* 'you lose'). The second conjugation third person plural ending -ENT is replaced by -EUNT (TENENT; UALENT > TENEUNT; UALEUNT, which utimately yield *tengono* 'they hold'; *valgono* 'they are worth' (see 8.4.1 for further details of this change)).

In the present subjunctive, the stem-final [**e**] characteristic of the first conjugation, and the [**a**] of the remaining conjugations, are continued as *-i* and *-a* (1Sg. CANTE(M), 2Sg. CANTES, 3Sg. CANTET, 3Pl. CANTENT > *canti* 'I sing', *canti* , *canti, cantino*; 1Sg. UENDA(M), 2Sg. UENDAS 3Sg. UENDAT, 3Pl. UENDANT > *venda* 'I sell', *venda, venda*, *vendano*; 1Sg. UENIA(M), 2Sg. UENIAS, 3Sg. UENIAT, 3Pl. UENIANT > *venga* 'I come', *venga, venga, vengano*. In the first and second persons plural, *-iamo* and *-iate* (from second and fourth conjugation -EAMUS, -EATIS; -IAMUS, -IATIS) have been generalized to all conjugations. The replacement of inflectional *-i* by *-e* has yet to be satisfactorily explained. In OTuscan (and modern Tuscan dialects), this *-i* is frequently extended into other conjugations (*dichi* 'say'; *venghi* 'come'; *facci* 'do'; *abbi* 'have').

8.4.1 Present stem allomorphy

Stem allomorphy is rare in the present tense of the CL verb, being confined to a few highly irregular verbs such as POSSE 'to be able', UELLE 'to want' and ESSE 'to be'. The principal allomorphic cleavage is between perfective and imperfective stems in second and third conjugation verbs. A major morphological innovation of the Romance languages is the introduction of patterns of stem allomorphy into the present tense, with considerable disruption of the previous one-to-one relationship between form and meaning. In the subsequent reorganizations of these patterns of allomorphy, a new factor, *conjugation*, plays an important role: allomorphy tends to be eliminated from the first conjugation; elsewhere, it tends to be augmented.

Most varieties of present tense stem allomorphy are the result of regular phonetic change, which have been discussed in Ch.2. With the loss of rhizotonic stress in the third conjugation, a pattern of stress is established throughout the present such that stress falls on the root, except in the first and second persons plural. This means that the present displays the vocalic alternation resulting from the divergent evolution of stressed and unstressed vowels: 'stressed' variants appear in the first, second, third persons singular, and in the third person plural, and 'unstressed' variants in the first and second persons plural. Here belong the alternations illustrated in Ch.2: 4.1, of which we give here just the singular and plural of the second person: *siedi* 'sit', *sedete*; *vieni* 'come', *venite*; *muori* 'die', *morite*; *vuoi* 'want', *volete*; *odi* 'hear', *udite*; *devi* 'owe', *dovete*; *getti* 'throw', (archaic) *gittate*. Palatalization by yod, produced by the first person singular indicative endings -IO and -EO, third person plural indicative -IUNT, -EUNT, and subjunctive -IA(M), -EA(M), -IAS, -EAS, -IAT, -EAT, -IAMUS, -EAMUS, -IANT, -EANT, gives rise to palatal alternation of the root-final consonant in these parts of the verb: e.g., (from ***ˈvɔljo**, etc.) *voglio* 'I want' *vuoi vuole vogliamo volete vogliono; voglia voglia voglia vogliamo vogliate vogliano*. Most verbs undergoing palatalization by yod have, in recent centuries, been subject to certain adjustments (to be considered below). The original pattern of palatal alternation is better preserved in the medieval language: *seggio* 'I sit' (< ***ˈsɛdjo** < SEDEO) *siedi siede seggiamo sedete seggiono*; *seggia seggia seggia seggiamo seggiate seggiano*; *tegno* 'I hold' (< ***ˈtɛnjo** < TENEO) *tieni tiene tegnamo tenete tegnono*; *tegna*

tegna tegna tegnamo tegnate tegnano; *muoio* 'I die' (<*ˈ**mɔrjo** < MORIOR) *muori muore moiamo morite muoiono*; *muoia muoia muoia moiamo moiate muoiano*. The effects of palatalization of velars triggered by front vowels (Ch.2: 6) are still audible in the verb, where palatalization occurs in all persons except the first person singular and third plural indicative, and the first, second and third persons singular, and third person plural, of the subjunctive:[30] **ˈviŋko** 'I win' **ˈviɲtʃi ˈviɲtʃe viɲˈtʃaːmo viɲˈtʃeːte ˈviŋkono**; **ˈviŋka ˈviŋka ˈviŋka vinˈtʃaːmo vinˈtʃaːte ˈviŋkano**; **ˈlɛggo** 'I read' **ˈlɛddʒi ˈlɛddʒe ledˈdʒaːmo ledˈdʒeːte ˈlɛggono**; **ˈlɛgga ˈlɛgga ˈlɛgga ledˈdʒaːmo ledˈdʒaːte ˈlɛggano**.

An interesting exception to velar palatalization is the first conjugation present subjunctive: although characterized by stem-final [**e**] in CL, this [**e**] (and its modern Tuscan continuant [**i**]) never triggers palatalization: e.g., *paghi* 'I pay' *paghi paghi paghiamo paghiate paghino*, etc. There is no indication, either in Tuscan or in other Italo-Romance dialects nor, for that matter, in Ibero-Romance dialects, that palatalization ever took place in the present subjunctive of the first conjugation. It appears that the analogical pressure of the otherwise invariant root-final consonants of this conjugation either ousted, at a very early date, the palatal alternants of the subjunctive, or possibly resisted such palatalization altogether. At any rate, the result is that Italo-Romance inherits a first conjugation root which is consonantally invariant, and whose only form of allomorphy is vocalic.

8.4.1.1 Morphological and lexical replication of present stem allomorphy

The pattern of stem-allomorphy distinguishing the singular persons and the third person plural, on the one hand, from the first and second persons plural, on the other, is replicated by the emergence in the present tense, of other suppletive stem-shapes. This is manifested in at least three separate cases: the integration into the present tense of the originally inchoative suffix -**isk**- (*inchoative* forms express the commencement or unfolding of an action); the combination of the stems *and*- and *vad*- in the verb 'to go'; the introduction of stems based on *uscio* 'door' into the present tense of the verb derived from CL EXIRE 'to go out'.

CL possesses a so-called inchoative infix -SC- which is attached to the thematic vowel (principally [**e**] and [**i**]) of certain verb stems: OBDORMIO or OBDORMISCO 'I fall asleep'; FLOREO or FLORESCO 'I flourish'). In Italo-Romance, -**isk**- (and in some central dialects -**esk**-) is introduced into the majority of verbs in thematic [**i**], notably those denoting a change of state or the inception or cessation of an action, such as *finire* 'to finish'; *fiorire* 'to flower'; *ingiallire* 'to turn yellow'; *annerire* 'to blacken'; *guarire* 'to cure'; *appassire* 'to wilt', etc.; but the suffix is restricted just to the present tense, and is absent from the first and second persons plural: e.g., *finisco* 'I finish' *finisci finisce finiamo finite finiscono*. In a few verbs it remains optional: *mento/mentisco* 'I lie', *tosso/tossisco* 'I cough', etc. The suffix is not introduced into a number of highly frequent verbs (including all those that have other kinds of stem allomorphy, such as *venire* 'to come', *morire* 'to die', *udire* 'to hear'). See Rohlfs (1968: 243f.).

The CL verb 'to go', IRE, nowhere survives fully intact in the Romance languages. The CL present indicative and present subjunctive EO, IS, IT, IMUS, ITIS, EUNT and EAM, EAS, EAT, EAMUS, EATIS, EANT are replaced in the Proto-Romance singular and third person plural forms by roots in **vad**- (< CL UADERE 'to go', 'to make one's way'). The resulting pattern of present tense alternation survived in OTuscan (and in modern southern dialects – cf. Rohlfs (1968: 280f.): *vado vai va gimo gite vanno*; *vada vada vada giamo giate vadano* (also, infinitive *gire;* imperfect *giva* etc.). The reason for this pattern of replacement is unclear; it is possible that the relative 'insubstantiality' of the phonetically regular outcomes of the relevant forms of IRE (indicative *?**jo** *?**is** *?**i** *?**jo**; subjunctive *?**ja** *?**jas** *?**ja** *?**ja**) might have favoured replacement by a phonetically more 'substantial' form. But monosyllabic roots are not inherently intolerable, as is shown by Italian *ho* 'I have', *hai*, *ha*, *è* 'he is', *dà* 'he gives', etc.

Tuscany lies on the periphery of a zone, principally comprising Gallo-Romance dialects, in which this pattern of suppletion has been replaced by yet another variety of suppletion. The continuants of IRE have been wholly ousted by another verb (of uncertain etymology – cf. Rohlfs (1968: 281)) *andare*. But speakers have not seized the opportunity of replacing the whole paradigm with this morphologically invariant first conjugation verb stem (a development which does occur, for example, in Sardinian). The effect of this replacement is to change the *phonetic substance* of the allomorphy, while leaving intact the earlier suppletive *pattern* of alternation, so that we have *vado vai va andiamo andate vanno*; *vada vada vada andiamo andiate vadano*.

The unique vocalic alternation, [**ɛ**] vs. [**u**], observed in the reflex of CL EXIRE (*uscire* 'to go out': *esco esci esce usciamo uscite escono* and *usciva* etc.) has arisen in Tuscan as a result of contamination from the semantically (but not etymologically) related *uscio* (< CL OSTIU(M) 'doorway'). It is striking that the merger of these two forms has occurred in such a way that it exactly replicates the familiar pattern of present stem allomorphy.[31] Something similar can be observed with *sapere* 'to know'and *avere* 'to have'. There are a number of very common verbs whose present indicative (but not their subjunctive) has been subject to the analogical influence of *dare* and *stare*. Forms such as *fo*, an optional variant of *faccio* 'I do', *fai*, *fa*, *fate* and *fanno* and *vo* (beside *vado*) *vai va* and *vanno* are modelled on *sto* 'I stand/am' *stai sta* (*stiamo*) *state stanno* and *do* 'I give' *dai dà* (*diamo*) *date danno*. In the case of *sapere* and *avere* this analogy has worked differentially, reproducing the usual pattern of present stem allomorphy: *so sai sa sappiamo sapete sanno*; *ho hai ha abbiamo avete hanno*.

8.4.1.2 Expansion of present stem consonant allomorphy
The same allomorphic pattern appears from yet another quarter. Palatalization (and lengthening) of stem-final consonants by yod (Ch.2: 5) originally occurred throughout the present subjunctive of verbs, e.g., *vegna* 'I come' *vegna vegna vegnamo vegnate vegnano*; *saglia* 'I go up' *saglia saglia sagliamo sagliate sagliano*; *muoia* 'I die' *muoia muoia moiamo moiate muoiano*. In some verbs, the stem allomorph produced by yod has survived: *facciamo* 'we do'; *piacciamo* 'we are pleasing'; *vogliamo* 'we want'; *sappiamo*; *abbiamo* 'we have'. In the modern language, the subjunctive stem of certain verbs has been reorganized in such a way that the palatalized alternants have been evicted from the first and second persons plural, so that these alternate with other persons of the verb according to the familiar pattern: *venga venga venga veniamo veniate vengano*; *muoia muoia muoia moriamo moriate muoiano*; *salga salga salga saliamo saliate salgano*.

The allomorphic differences which, as a result of regular sound change, make first person singular and third person plural forms of the indicative, together with the singular and third person plural forms of the subjunctive, distinct from the remaining persons of the verb, have been *expanded*. Such expansion has taken two forms:

– Analogical introduction of such allomorphy into previously invariant verb stems.
– Increase in the degree of phonological difference between existing alternants, due to substitution of velar alternants for palatal alternants.

In the medieval language, the alternation pattern [**ddʒ**] vs. [**d**] was occasionally extended into verbs with previously invariant root-final [**d**]: *chiuggio* or *chiudo* 'I close' vs. *chiudi*; *caggio* or *cado* vs. *cadi*; *chieggio* or *chiedo* 'I ask' vs. *chiedi*. On the analogy of regular palatal alternation in verbs such as *leggere*, the verb *fuggire* 'to flee', which in OTuscan had root-final [**ddʒ**] throughout the paradigm (*fuggio fuggi*; *fuggia fuggiano*, etc), acquires[32] a velar alternant [**gg**] in the indicative first person singular and third person plural, and into all singular persons and the third person plural of the subjunctive: **'fuggo 'fuddʒi 'fuddʒe fud'dʒaːmo fud'dʒiːte 'fuggono**; **'fugga 'fugga 'fugga fud'dʒaːmo fud'dʒaːte 'fuggano**.

Generalization of the velar alternant does not stop at the replication of existing patterns of alternation in verbs not previously subject to such alternation. Often, the velar alternants replace older palatal alternants, and thereby create patterns of alternation without precedent in the language: the palatal alternants [ʎʎ], [ɲɲ] and [ddʒ] have been extensively replaced, respectively, by the velar alternants [lg], [ŋg] and [gg]. Thus the alternations [ʎʎ] vs. [l], [ɲɲ] vs. [n] and [ddʒ] vs. [d] found in OTuscan *vegno vieni*; *rimagno rimani*; *saglio sali*; *vaglio vali*; *veggio* 'I see' *vedi*; *seggio siedi*, etc., give way to [lg] vs. [l], [ŋg] vs. [n] and [gg] vs. [d] (e.g., *vengo vieni*; *salgo sali*; *valgo vali*; *seggo siedi*). The analogical *chiuggio* and *chieggio* etc., (see above), are sometimes subject to the same change, yielding *chiuggo chiudi*; *chieggo chiedi* etc. A unique and unprecedented alternation pattern arises in *trarre* 'to draw': from CL TRAHO, TRAHIS, etc., we would expect **ˈ**trao**, ˈ**trai**; the actually occurring *traggo*, *trai*, etc., possibly result from the conflation of two Proto-Romance verbs *ˈ**traere** and *ˈ**tragere** (see Malkiel (1974: 335)).

The Italian verb system displays a historical tension between the reinforcement and amplification of existing, largely idiosyncratic, alternation patterns, and a tendency for one meaning to be represented by one morphological form – a tendency manifested through the mechanism of analogical levelling (elimination) of allomorphy. Both these elements, mediated by 'hypercorrection', have been at work in velar substitution. In the medieval language the verbs with velar-palatal alternations show a *tendency* to oust the velar alternant in favour of the (majority) palatal alternant: *colgo/coglio* 'I pluck', *cogli*, *coglie*; *colga/coglia*, etc.; *leggio/leggo* 'I read', *leggi*, *legge*, *leggia/legga* etc.; *spegno/spengo* 'I extinguish', *spegni*, *spegne*; *spegna/spenga*, etc. This tendency is ultimately resisted in favour of the etymologically 'correct' velar alternants. But correction appears to have led to hypercorrection, in that even etymologically correct [ɲɲ], [ʎʎ] and [d(d)ʒ] have given way to [ŋg], [lg] and [(g)g]. Thus *tegno tegna*; *saglio saglia*; *rimagno rimagna*; *sceglio sceglia*, etc. are supplanted by the hypercorrect, and entirely novel, alternants *tengo tenga*; *salgo salga*; *rimango rimanga*; *scelgo scelga*, etc.

8.4.1.3 Analogical levelling of vocalic allomorphy, and conjugation

Analogical levelling operates, more or less sporadically, in all verbs. What is striking is that it has operated to a greater degree in the first conjugation , which was always characterized by a high degree of stem regularity. In contrast to the regularity of the first conjugation, of some 140 verbs in thematic [e], modern Italian has only about 12 with invariant roots (e.g., *godere* 'to enjoy'; *splendere* 'to shine'; *vedere* 'to see'; *battere* 'to beat'). We have observed that consonantal allomorphy has always been absent from the first conjugation; and that it was never[33] penetrated by the analogical replacement of palatals by velars observable in other conjugations. The only type of allomorphy found in the first conjugation is vocalic alternation due to stress. Such alternation has been subject to some levelling in all conjugations: in *mièterе* 'to reap' and *chièdere* 'to ask' the diphthong has been extended to unstressed syllables (*mietète*, *mietèva*; *chiedète*, *chiedèva*) and even to a closed syllable (*chiesto*). In verbs such as *scuòtere* 'to shake', *cuòcere* 'to bake' and *muòvere* 'to move', since about the eighteenth century, the diphthong has optionally appeared in all open syllable stems (*scuotèva*; *muovèva*). However, there persist a significant number of non-first conjugation verbs in which no such levelling has occurred: *commuòvere* 'to move (emotionally)'; *dolère* 'to ache'; *solère* 'to be accustomed'; *volère* 'to want'; *potère* 'to be able'; *sedère* 'to sit'; *tenère* 'to hold'; *venìre* 'to come'; *morìre* 'to die', etc.[34] Matters are quite different in the first conjugation. *All* first conjugation verbs have undergone levelling of vocalic alternation. In some of them it remains optional, although most speakers seem to prefer the invariant root with the generalized diphthong: *suonàte/sonàte* 'you play'. In most first conjugation verbs, the root is now wholly invariant: e.g., *nuotàte* 'you swim'; *vietàte* 'you forbid'. A feature of vocalic levelling in the first conjugation, unmatched in the other conjugations, is that levelling of the diphthong sometimes favours the *unstressed*, undiphthongized, alternant (*nègo negàte*; *vòlo volàte*). Even more remarkable is the fact that, in the first conjugation, the diphthong in stressed open syllables is occasionally replaced by the historically underlying, undiphthongized, stressed vowel: e.g., **rin'nɔːva rin'nɔːvano** 'renew'; **'lɛːva 'lɛːvano** 'lift' (cf. the related adjectives *nuovo* 'new' and *lieve* 'light', with the diphthong). The only interpretation available here is that the characteristic regularity of the first conjugation actually favoured *resistance* to the process of diphthongization. Generalization of the vowel [ɔ] is also encountered in one third conjugation verb, *coprire* 'to cover', levelled in favour of the non-diphthongized stress vowel [ɔ] (**'kɔːpre**). It is perhaps significant that this verb has an otherwise invariant stem (except for past participle *coperto*).[35]

In the case of the (occasional) raising of unstressed [**e**] and [**o**], all such alternations have given way in the first conjugation to invariant stems. By the late middle ages, original [**o**] vs. [**u**] alternations had been eliminated from *fiutàre* 'to smell'; *rubàre* 'to steal'; *lodàre* 'to praise'; *giocàre* 'to play', etc. The syncopation of [**u**] between *aiùto* and *aitiàmo* etc., is also lost. The [**i**] vs. [**e**] alternation in *gettàre* 'to throw' (Ch.2: 4.6.1) disappears from the literary language during the nineteenth century.

In the levelling of vocalic alternation, we see not so much a tension between language-specific and universal morphological principles, as an interaction between them, such that levelling is most consistent in that morphological class, the first conjugation, which is already characteristically invariant.

8.4.2 The present of essere

The CL verb ESSE, 'to be', is conjugated as follows in the present (9):

(9)

	Indicative	Subjunctive
1Sg.	SUM	SIM
2Sg.	ES	SIS
3Sg.	EST	SIT
1Pl.	SUMUS	SIMUS
2Pl.	ESTIS	SITIS
3Pl.	SUNT	SINT

The present indicative has been subjected to two major regularizing influences. Initial [**s**] is extended analogically into the second person forms, giving *sei* and *siete*. The vowel [**ɛ**] of the third person singular *è* (< EST) is generalized into the second person forms, and into the OTuscan first person plural (*siemo*). The absence of diphthongization in *sei* may be due to the influence of third person singular *è*. In some Tuscan dialects we find both *sete* (with [**ɛ**]) and diphthongized *siei* (cf. Rohlfs (1968: 267f.)). First person singular SUM and third person plural SUNT would both have yielded ***son** in Proto-Italo-Romance. For the evolution of both to *sono*, see 8.3.3. The root ***sjɛ-**, appears also to have been introduced into the subjunctive, where it combines with the subjunctive inflection -**a**, which has been analogically introduced from other non-first conjugation verbs. As a result of regular sound change (Ch.2: 4.3), the form ***sjɛa** gives *sia*, etc., on which have been modelled *dia* and *stia*, the present subjunctive forms of *dare* 'to give' and *stare* 'to stand/be'.

8.5 The passato remoto

The Italian passato remoto continues the CL past perfective tense form. In northern Italo-Romance dialects it has been in retreat in favour of the passato prossimo since at least the fourteenth century, dying out in Piedmont, Lombardy and the Veneto during the eighteenth and nineteenth century; it survives to this day in rural dialects of Emilia and Romagna.

All Italian passato remoto forms are arhizotonic in singular and plural forms of the second person (as they are in Latin). In the first person plural, in conformity with the arhizotonic pattern of other tenses, stress has been shifted off the root (MISIMUS > *mettemmo* 'we put'). The remaining persons, both of CL and Italian, can be split into two major groups, the *arhizotonic*, and the *rhizotonic*. Arhizotonic verbs generally continue Latin arhizotonics (note that in the second persons and in the third person plural, stress has been shifted from the 'UI' or 'UE' of CL onto the thematic vowel, with subsequent deletion of the newly unstressed syllable):

(10)

AMAUI	AMAUISTI	AMAUIT	AMAUIMUS	AMAUISTIS	AMAUERUNT
amài 'I loved'	*amàsti*	*amò*	*amàmmo*	*amàste*	*amàrono*

FINIUI	FINIUISTI	FINIUIT	FINIUIMUS	FINIUISTIS	FINIUERUNT
finìi 'I finished'	*finìsti*	*finì*	*finìmmo*	*finìste*	*finìrono*

Latin verbs in thematic [**e**] had partially rhizotonic perfects (see below). The handful of Italian arhizotonic passato remoto forms in [**e**] arose on the analogy of the other two conjugations having the pattern thematic vowel + ending: *battei* 'I beat' *battesti*, etc.; *mietei* 'I reaped' *mietesti*, etc. (CL BATTUI BATTUISTI; METUI METUISTI). There exists a second type of arhizotonic passato remoto in *-etti* (*vendetti* 'I sold' *vendesti vendette vendemmo vendeste vendettero*), which appears to have arisen by the following series of changes:

(i) CL UENDERE (perfect UENDIDI) was, originally, a derivative of DARE 'to give', and -DIDI is a variant of the perfect tense form of DARE, DEDI.

(ii) The perfect of DARE, namely DEDI, is continued as Italian *diedi*. But an analogical form, *detti* arises on the model of *stetti* 'I stood' < ***stetwi**.

(iii) The *-detti* ending extends to *vendere* (*vendetti*), alongside *vendei*.[36]

(iv) From *vendere*, the *-etti* ending is generalized to some other second conjugation verbs (*credetti* 'I believed'; *sedetti* 'I sat'; *perdetti* 'I lost', etc.).

8.5.1 The rhizotonic passato remoto

Latin perfect tense verbs with thematic [**e**] (and some of those with [**i**]) are, as in Italian, partially rhizotonic. In CL, stress falls on the root in the first person singular and plural, and the third person singular. In addition, the root is characterized throughout the perfect by often idiosyncratic vocalic and consonantal allomorphy. In the evolution of

Italian, root allomorphy has been well preserved (albeit with extensive adjustments), but only in the rhizotonic forms. Into the arhizotonic forms, the non-perfect root has been introduced, a development which has also occurred in the first person plural, where stress has been shifted from the root to the ending. The originally arhizotonic third person plural forms (e.g., FECERUNT) become rhizotonic in Italo-Romance (e.g., *fècero* 'they did'). The characteristics of the Italian 'rhizotonic' passato remoto, illustrated in (11), are:

(i) It is rhizotonic in the first person singular, and third person singular and plural only.
(ii) The roots of these rhizotones have highly idiosyncratic patterns of vocalic and consonantal allomorphy.
(iii) The rhizotonic forms have the characteristic inflections *-i* (first person singular), *-e*, (third person singular), *-ero* (third person plural), and they have the structure ROOT + PERSON MARKER.

(11)

CL	Italian	CL	Italian	CL	Italian
FECI	*fèci* 'I did'	U**I**DI	*vìdi* 'I saw'	**MI**SI	*mìsi* 'I put'
FEC**I**STI	*facèsti*	UI**DI**STI	*vedèsti*	MI**SI**STI	*mettèsti*
FECIT	*fèce*	U**I**DIT	*vìde*	**MI**SIT	*mìse*
FECIMUS	*facèmmo*	U**I**DIMUS	*vedèmmo*	**MI**SIMUS	*mettèmmo*
FEC**I**STIS	*facèste*	UI**DI**STIS	*vedèste*	MI**SI**STIS	*mettèste*
FEC**E**RUNT	*fècero*	UI**DE**RUNT	*vìdero*	MI**SE**RUNT	*mìsero*

How are we to explain the fact that just the arhizotonic forms of the passato remoto have the *non-perfective* root? The coincidence between the non-perfective root and lack of stress is striking but, from a historical point of view, probably accidental. The phenomenon is explicable in morphological, not phonological, terms. With the decline of the CL future perfect, pluperfect indicative, and perfective infinitive, the perfective root becomes restricted to the pluperfect subjunctive (MISISSE(M), etc.) (continued as the Italo-Romance imperfect subjunctive – see 8.6.2), and to the passato remoto (MISI, etc.). At this point, the perfect root is ousted, under the analogical pressure of the majority non-perfect root, from the whole of the imperfect subjunctive (MISISSE(M) gives way to *mettessi* 'I put', etc.), and from the arhizotonic forms of the passato remoto (*mettesti*, etc.). The rhizotonic forms are islands of resistance to this analogical change, and a reason for such resistance suggests itself if we consider the possible outcome of introduction of the non-perfective root into the rhizotones. We would have **ˈ**veːdi**,

'veːde and **'veːdero; **'metti, **'mette, and **'mettero; in short, the resulting first and third person singular forms of the passato remoto would be identical to the present tense. As for the third person plural, it is significant that in OTuscan, and especially in OFlorentine (see 8.3.3), alongside the type *misero* 'they put', *vollero* 'they wanted', the alternative *misono*, *vollono*, etc., is very common (cf. Rohlfs (1968: 310)), so that substitution of the non-perfect root could have resulted in a form ('mettono) identical to the third person plural present. That the rhizotonic forms had not given way earlier to the arhizotonic pattern (say ***mettei* ***metté* ***metterono*, instead of **misi*, etc.) is probably due to the fact that the pattern of rhizotonic first and third person singular, and third person plural, was supported by the model of the present tense, where the same pattern was well established.

There is only a handful of verbs in which the perfective root survives (with some modifications) in all persons: *dare* 'to give': *diedi desti diede demmo deste diedero*; *stare* 'to stand': *stetti stesti stette stemmo steste stettero*; *essere* 'to be': *fui fosti fu fummo foste furono*. These are verbs in which the perfective root also survives in the imperfect subjunctive: *dessi dessi desse dessimo deste dessero*; *stessi stessi stesse stessimo steste stessero; fossi fossi fosse fossimo foste fossero*.

Most of the CL vocalic alternations in the perfective root are continued in Italian (DO DEDI > *do* 'I give' *diedi*; FACIO FECI > *faccio* 'I do' *feci*; UIDEO UI:DI > *vedo* 'I see' *vidi*; FUNDO FU:DI > *fondo* 'I melt' *fusi*; MITTO MI:SI *metto* 'I put' *misi*; RUMPO RU:PI *rompo* 'I break' *ruppi*; UENUI UE:NI > 'vɛŋgo 'I come' 'venni; DIRIGO DIREXI > *dirigo* 'I direct' *diressi*. The vocalic allomorphs of FECI, STETI and DEDI have been extended to reflexes of HABUI and SAPUI, yielding Italian *ebbi* 'I had' and *seppi* 'I knew'.

A large number of CL verbs (especially those with root-final dentals or velars) had 'sigmatic' perfective roots in -s-. This pattern is not only retained in Italian (12a), but is expanded to embrace a wide range of verbs which previously formed their perfects in other ways, notably those in root-final dentals and velars (12b):

(12a)

CL 3Sg.Pres.	CL 3Sg.Perfect	It.3Sg.Pres.	It.3Sg.PR
RIDIT	RISIT	*ride* 'he laughs'	*rise*
RADIT	RASIT	*rade* 'he shaves'	*rase*
SCRIBIT	SCRIPSIT	*scrive* 'he writes'	*scrisse*
REMANET	REMANSIT	*rimane* 'he stays'	*rimase*
ARDET	ARSIT	*arde* 'it burns'	*arse*
DIRIGIT	DIREXIT	*dirige* 'he directs'	*diresse*

(12b)

PREHENDIT	PREHENDIT	*prende* 'he takes'	*prese*
OFFENDIT	OFFENDIT	*offende* 'he offends'	*offese*
PERDIT	PERDIDIT	*perde* 'he loses'	*perse*
FUNDIT	FUDIT	*fonde* 'it melts'	*fuse*
MORDET	MOMORDIT	*morde* 'he bites'	*morse*
SPONDET	SPOPONDIT	*(ri)sponde* 'he answers'	*(ri)spose*

CURRIT	CUCURRIT	*corre* 'he runs'	*corse*
MOUET	MOUIT	*muove* 'he moves'	*mosse*
UALET	UALUIT	*vale* 'it is worth'	*valse*
APERIT	APERUIT	*apre* 'he opens'	*aperse*
COLLIGIT	COLLEGIT	*coglie* 'he plucks'	*colse*
LEGIT	LEGIT	*legge* 'he reads'	*lesse*
UOLUIT	UOLUIT	*volge* 'he turns'	*volse*

New kinds of rhizotonic allomorphy were created in Proto-Romance as a consequence of the inflection *-**wi** (< CL -UI), with attendant, phonetically regular, lengthening of the root-final consonant (see Ch.2: 5). This -***wi** spread to a number of verbs which originally had formed their perfect differently in CL (13):

(13)

CL	Proto-Romance	Italian
UOLUI	***'volwi**	*volli* 'I wanted'
SAPUI	***'sapwi**	*seppi* 'I knew'
TENUI	***'tenwi**	*tenni* 'I held'
HABUI	***'abwi**	*ebbi* 'I had'
PLUUIT	***'plovwe**	*piovve* 'it rained'
PLACUI	***'plakwi**	*piacqui* 'I pleased'
PARUI	***'parwi**	*parvi* 'I seemed'
(CECIDI)	***'kadwi**	*caddi* 'I fell'
(BIBI)	***'bebwi**	*bevvi* 'I drank'
(STETI)	***'stetwi**	*stetti* 'I stood'
(RUPI)	***'rupwi**	*ruppi* 'I broke'
(UENI)	***'venwi**	*venni* 'I came'

The origins of *crebbi* 'I grew' and *conobbi* 'I knew' (CL CREUI and COGNOUI) are unclear; they may have been modelled on *ebbi* 'I had'.

8.6 The imperfect tense

8.6.1 The imperfect indicative

The modern Italian imperfect tense forms have the structure:

ROOT + THEMATIC VOWEL + IMPERFECT INDICATIVE/SUBJUNCTIVE MARKER + PERSON MARKER

The imperfect indicative keeps the Latin imperfect indicative form substantially intact:

(14)

AM**A**BAM	AM**A**BAS	AM**A**BAT	AMA**B**AMUS	AMA**B**ATIS	AM**A**BANT
*am**à**vo* 'I loved'	*am**à**vi*	*am**à**va*	*amav**à**mo*	*amav**à**te*	*am**à**vano*

UEN**DE**BAM	UEN**DE**BAS	UEN**DE**BAT	UENDE**BA**MUS	UENDE**BA**TIS	UEN**DE**BANT
*vend**è**vo* 'I sold'	*vend**è**vi*	*vend**è**va*	*vendev**à**mo*	*vendev**à**te*	*vend**è**vano*

AUDI**E**BAM	AUDI**E**BAS	AUDI**E**BAT	AUDIE**BA**MUS	AUDIE**BA**TIS	AUDI**E**BANT
*ud**ì**vo* 'I heard'	*ud**ì**vi*	*ud**ì**va*	*udiv**à**mo*	*udiv**à**te*	*ud**ì**vano*

CL verbs in thematic [**i**] form their imperfect in -IE- (AUDIEBA(M); DORMIEBA(M)). In Italo-Romance, -IE- has been replaced by the thematic vowel [**i**]: e.g., *udivo* 'I heard'; *dormivo* 'I slept', etc. In the medieval language the imperfect indicative endings *-ea* and *-ia* coexisted, respectively, with *-eva* and *-iva* (and persist in some modern Tuscan varieties). The use of *-ia* in place of *-eva* in medieval poetry (cf. Rohlfs (1968: 288)) is almost certainly an imitation of Sicilian models.

8.6.2 The imperfect subjunctive

The evolution of the imperfect subjunctive is rather more complex. It does not continue the Latin imperfect subjunctive, which is formed from the infinitive + person/number markers[37] (e.g., first person singular AMAREM; ESSEM); rather, it continues the CL *pluperfect subjunctive*, originally formed from the perfective stem:

(15)

AMAUISSE(M)	AMAUISSES	AMAUISSET	AMAUIS-SEMUS	AMAUIS-SETIS	AMAUIS-SENT
amassi 'I loved'	*amassi*	*amasse*	*amassimo*	*amaste*	*amassero*
DIXISSE(M)	DIXISSES	DIXISSET	DIXISSEMUS	DIXISSETIS	DIXISSENT
dicessi 'I said'	*dicessi*	*dicesse*	*dicessimo*	*diceste*	*dicessero*
FECISSE(M)	FECISSES	FECISSET	FECISSEMUS	FECISSETIS	FECISSENT
facessi 'I did'	*facessi*	*facesse*	*facessimo*	*faceste*	*facessero*

In Italo-Romance, the (arhizotonic) perfective stem is replaced by the imperfective stem: DIXISSE(M) gives way to *dicèssi*, and FECISSE(M) to *facèssi*.

8.6.3 The imperfect tense of essere

The verb 'to be' constitutes a special case: the CL indicative ERA(M), ERAS, ERAT ERAMUS, ERATIS, ERANT is continued (*ero eri era eravamo eravate erano*), except that the first and second persons plural are differentiated from the rest of the paradigm by the addition to the stem, in Florentine, of the [**v**] characteristic of the imperfect indicative: *ero* (OTuscan *era*) *eri era eravamo eravate erano*. In the subjunctive, an original pluperfect subjunctive form (showing the perfective stem) survives: FUISSE(M) FUISSES FUISSET FUISSEMUS FUISSETIS FUISSENT > *fossi fossi fosse fossimo foste fossero*. A modified form of the perfective stem DEDISSE(M), etc., is found in *dessi* 'I gave', which has analogically attracted the subjunctive of *stare* 'to stand', *stessi*.

8.7 The conditional *fora*

A remnant of the CL pluperfect indicative also persists into OTuscan, namely *fora* 'he would be' < FUERAT (also, occasionally, *amara* 'he would love' (< AMA(UE)RA(M)); *convenera* 'it would be useful' (< CONUENERAT), etc. – cf. Rohlfs (1968: 346f.)). These forms function as conditionals and may have been an importation into Tuscan from southern mainland Italy. They are still found in parts of the Abruzzi, Campania, Basilicata and upper Calabria.

8.8 The 'analytic' verb forms

8.8.1 essere/avere + *the past participle*

Analytic structures of the type AUXILIARY + PAST PARTICIPLE (e.g., Italian *ho amato* 'I have loved'; *sono venuti* 'they came', and the passive *è visto* 'he is seen') are restricted in CL to perfective forms of passive (see below). These analytic structures supplant CL synthetic perfective verb forms in the future perfect and pluperfect (AMAUERO >

avrò amato 'I will have loved'; UENERO > *sarò venuto* 'I will have come'; AMAUERAM > *avevo amato* or *ebbi amato* 'I had loved'; UENERAM > *ero venuto* 'I had come'); the passive structure *è visto* replaces the CL synthetic imperfective passive form UIDETUR.

The emergence of the analytic structures like *ho cantato* and *sono venuti* (i.e., the 'passato prossimo'), alongside the synthetic type *cantai*, *vennero* (i.e., the 'passato remoto'), has the effect of making explicit a distinction which had not been encoded in the CL verb: that between a completed (perfective) event in the present, and a completed event in the past (cf. Harris (1978: 134)). In modern Italian the distinction may be broadly described[38] as that between completed actions and events seen as having present reality, or retaining direct relevance to the present (a category which naturally tends to include recent events, whence the conventional, but misleading, label *passato prossimo*) and past perfective verbs, continuing the CL past perfect, whose actions are not viewed in this way (labelled in Italian *passato remoto*, although remoteness in time is not the determinant factor). On the model of the 'present perfective' analytic structure, the synthetic structures of the CL future perfect and pluperfect are replaced by the structure FUTURE/PAST AUXILIARY + PAST PARTICIPLE.

A CL structure similar to the modern complex-verb form with *avere* appears in phrases such as CENAM PARATAM HABEO 'I have the dinner prepared', but the similarity with Italian *ho preparato la cena* 'I have prepared the dinner' is superficial. In fact, this Latin phrase is equivalent to modern Italian *ho la cena preparata* 'I have the dinner prepared' or *ho la cena che è stata preparata* 'I have the dinner which has been prepared'. The Latin phrase contains two autonomous lexical verbs, HABERE 'to have/possess', and PARARE 'to prepare'. HABERE is a transitive verb, and the form HABEO in our example is a present imperfective form, taking CENAM PARATAM as its direct object noun phrase. PARATAM is the feminine singular (accusative) past participle of PARARE, modifying the object noun CENAM . The CL past participle is a kind of perfective verbal adjective, meaning roughly 'in the state resulting from the performance of the action expressed by the verb'. The underlying subject of the verb represented by the past participle is unspecified, and is not necessarily coreferential with that of HABEO: the dinner which I have may have been prepared by anybody, not necessarily by me.

The structures *è nato* 'he has been born' (passato prossimo) and *è visto* 'he is seen' (present passive), in contrast, *do* have a direct antecedent in a CL analytical construction. However, unlike Italian *è visto*, the CL complex-verb structure EST UISUS means not 'he is seen', but 'he has been seen' or 'he was seen': it is a *perfective* passive form corresponding to the active UIDIT 'he saw'. In CL, *imperfective* passives are expressed by means of a special set of inflectional affixes (e.g., UIDERI 'to be seen', present indicative UIDEOR UIDERIS UIDETUR UIDEMUR UIDEMINI UIDENTUR). These synthetic passives become wholly extinct in Proto-Romance. In their place appears the originally past perfective structure EST UISUS – reanalysed as a *present* tense form *è visto*. Correspondingly, the CL pluperfect ERAT UISUS 'he had been seen' is reanalysed as a past imperfective passive form, so that *era visto* is 'he was being seen'. The perfective tense forms of the new passive structure are derived by combining the perfective forms of the verb 'to be' with the past participle: *è stato visto* 'he has been seen', *era stato visto* 'he had been seen', etc.[39]

What of *è nato* 'he has been born' and *è morto* 'he has died', structurally identical to the passives, yet functionally passato prossimo forms? CL has a large number of so-called 'deponent' verbs: these are morphologically identical, and semantically similar, to the passive, but differ in that their grammatical subject does not originate as the object of a transitive verb. Many deponents are semantically 'middle'. That is to say that, unlike ordinary passives, they signal not an action carried out on the subject by some external agency, but an action originating, as it were, from within the subject, and in which the grammatical subject participates without being agent or instigator. Many middle deponents, such as NASCITUR 'he is born', perfect NATUS EST; IRASCITUR 'he gets angry', perfect IRATUS EST; PROGREDITUR 'he advances', perfect PROGRESSUS EST; MORITUR 'he dies', perfect MORTUUS EST; have no transitive counterparts. Already in CL there existed 'semi-deponent' verbs whose perfective forms *alone* had passive morphology (e.g., GAUDET 'he rejoices' vs. perfect GAUISUS EST). And the imperfective forms of deponent verbs also begin to shed their passive inflectional morphology, while retaining the structure ESSE + PAST PARTICIPLE in perfective forms. This state of affairs persists in Italian *muore* vs. *è morto*, and *nasce* vs. *è nato*, and characterizes many other semantically middle verbs in OTuscan: *sono levato* 'I arose'; *è bagnato* 'he bathed', etc.

8.8.2 Grammaticalization of the structure essere/avere + *past participle*

In what follows we shall examine the extent to which syntagms of the type *essere* + PP (already present in the verbal system of CL), and CL structures of the type HABERE + PAST PARTICIPLE have become grammaticalized. How far have the resultant complex-verbs become structurally and semantically equivalent to synthetic, inflectional verb forms?[40]

The AUXILIARY + PAST PARTICIPLE structures display properties of synthetic verb forms in that:

– They supplant synthetic STEM + INFLECTION forms (*ho visto* 'I have seen' = UIDI; *sono venuto* 'I have come' = UENI; *l'uomo è visto* 'the man is seen' = HOMO UIDETUR) and synchronically they correspond to other tense forms having the synthetic structure STEM + INFLECTION (first person singular present *vedo*, subjunctive *veda*, future *vedrò*, imperfect *vedevo*, imperfect subjunctive *vedessi*, passato remoto *vidi* and passato prossimo *ho visto*; first person singular present *vengo,* subjunctive *venga,* future *verrò,* imperfect indicative *venivo,* imperfect subjunctive *venissi,* passato remoto *venni*, and passato prossimo *sono venuto*).

– Like the inflections, the position of *avere* and *essere* in relation to the verb root is rigidly fixed, albeit to the left, rather than the right, of the verb stem; they precede the past participle, and auxiliary and participle cannot normally be inverted – although this was possible in the medieval language – cf. Rohlfs (1969: 331; 334f.)), and remains so today in the spoken language: *trovati non li abbiamo* 'found them we haven't'; *arrivata non è* 'arrived she hasn't' (cf. also Ch.4: 8.4.1).

– Auxiliary and past participle share a single grammatical subject, which is not necessarily true of the CL structure HABERE + PAST PARTICIPLE (see below): compare the distinction in modern Italian between the complex-verb in *ho perso il cappello* 'I've lost the hat', and *ho il cappello perso* 'I have the lost hat'. In the latter, the subject of *perso* is not necessarily identical with that of *ho.*

– The past participle cannot be removed from the complex-verb with *avere* without producing ungrammaticality or a semantically different reading. *Ho perso il cappello*, to take an extreme example, means almost the opposite of *ho il cappello.* CL HABEO LITTERAS 'I have the letters', in contrast, has the same truth value as HABEO SCRIPTAS LITTERAS 'I have the written letters'. In both cases, I *have* the letters.

– Romance verbs agree in number and gender with their grammatical subjects, but not with their grammatical objects. In the CL construction HABEO LITTERAS SCRIPTAS 'I have the written letters', as in modern Italian *ho le lettere scritte*, the noun is the grammatical object of HABEO (*ho*), and is modified by the verbal adjective SCRIPTAS (*scritte*), which, like all adjectives, agrees in number and gender with the noun it modifies. In the Italian construction, the noun is the direct object of a verb form comprising *avere* and past participle. Consequently, the participle does not agree with the noun: *ho scritto le lettere*, not *ho scritte le lettere.* However, we shall see that remnants of participial agreement with the object noun survived into the medieval language, and vestigially into modern Italian.

– The auxiliary verbs, unlike their lexical counterparts, do not possess a full array of tense forms: we have passato prossimo *ho fatto* 'I have done'; pluperfect *avevo fatto* 'I had done'; trapassato remoto *ebbi fatto*

'I had done'; future perfect *avrò fatto* 'I shall have done', but not ***ho avuto fatto* 'I have had done'; ***avevo avuto fatto* 'I had had done'; ***avrò avuto fatto* 'I shall have had done', etc.
– Auxiliary *avere* has lost any connotation of possession. Phrases such as *ho abbandonato il cappello* 'I have abandoned the hat' would otherwise be practically uninterpretable: you cannot (normally) possess something which you have abandoned.
– The lexical verb *avere* requires a direct object. Yet auxiliary *avere* can occur with intransitive verbs, lacking an object noun: *ho viaggiato* 'I have travelled'; *ho parlato* 'I have spoken'. This structure will be discussed further, below.
– The lexical verb forms *ho* 'I have' and *sono* 'I am' are present tense forms. The complex-verb structures emerged in Proto-Romance as perfective past forms distinct from the perfects UIDI 'I saw' and UENI 'I came' in that they signalled actions close to or relevant to present time. This distinctive present-time association persists in central and southern Italy (*ho visto* vs. *vidi*); but it is an indicator of the grammaticalization of the auxiliaries that in northern dialects, and in the standard Italian of northern Italy, the analytic structures have lost any necessary association with present time, having wholly supplanted the passato remoto forms *vidi*; *venni*, etc.

Various phonological, syntactic and semantic properties of the AUXILIARY + PAST PARTICIPLE structures continue to reflect vestigial properties of the lexical verbs HABERE and ESSE, and of the past participle as an independent verbal adjective:

– Phonologically, the auxiliaries carry independent word stress, and correspondingly (cf. Ch.2: 2.3) are able to manifest the vowels [ɛ] *è* and [ɔ] *ho*: e.g., *ho perso* 'I've lost' **'ɔ p'pɛrso**; *è venuto* 'he's come' **'ɛ vve'nu:to**.
– The auxiliaries retain a measure of syntactic autonomy from the past participle, in that some material can be intercalated between them, particularly time adverbials: *ho ormai detto tutto* 'I've now said everything'; *aveva, già nel 1936, stabilito le leggi* 'it had, already in 1936, laid down the laws'; *abbiamo sempre amato i fiori* 'we have always loved flowers'. In OTuscan this autonomy was even greater, in that other adverbials, and object noun phrases could be intercalated between auxiliary and past participle (cf. Rohlfs (1969: 331)).
– The past participle retains traces of its adjectival origin in that it continues to agree in number and gender with its object, if that object is a clitic pronoun. With third person clitics such agreement is obligatory, with others it is now optional (cf. Lepschy and Lepschy (1988: 209–11)): e.g., *mi ha visto* or *vista* 'he has seen me (feminine)', *ci ha visto* or *visti* 'he has seen us', but *la ha vista* 'he has seen her', *li ha*

visti 'he has seen them (masculine)', *le ha viste* 'he has seen them (feminine)'. Very occasionally (more frequently in the last century than today), the literary language also makes the past participle agree with a preceding relative pronoun: e.g., *i libri che ho letti* 'the books which I have read', but *i libri che ho letto* is the normal structure.[41] Otherwise, the modern language does not make agreement between past participle and object: e.g., *abbiamo sempre amato i fiori* 'we have always loved flowers' not *abbiamo sempre amati i fiori*. The modern examples of participial agreement are all that remains of the situation predominant in OTuscan, and prevailing to this day in some southern dialects, particularly of Lazio, Campania and Puglia, in which the past participle agreed in number and gender with its object (cf. Lucchesi (1963); Smith (1991)): e.g., Novellino (thirteenth century) *a rifiutata la nobile cittade* 'he has refused the noble city'; Boccaccio *aveva la luna, essendo nel mezzo del cielo, perduti li raggi suoi* 'the moon, being in the middle of the sky, had lost its rays'. Vestiges of such agreement persist in the literary language into the nineteenth century, but the retreat of participial agreement, a clear sign that the participle had ceased to be analysed as an adjective, commences in earnest in OTuscan from the latter part of the twelfth century onwards, particularly where the past participle preceded its object.

– The principles governing the selection of *avere* or *essere* as auxiliaries are rooted in the semantic and structural properties of the CL lexical verbs HABERE and ESSE and their continuants, and in the nature of the semantic relationship between the subject of the verb, and the action or state expressed by it. It is these principles which we shall discuss in detail in the following section.

8.8.2.1 Selection of the auxiliaries *avere* and *essere*, and their origins

The distribution of the auxiliaries *avere* and *essere* is subject to the following general principles in modern Italian:

– All transitive verbs (those taking a direct object noun complement) select *avere*: *ho cambiato le lenzuola* 'I've changed the sheets'; *hanno migliorato il sistema* 'they've improved the system'; *hai alzato il volume* 'you've raised the volume', etc.

– All reflexive verbs (including the impersonal reflexive structures) select *essere*: *mi sono alzato* 'I've got up'; *si è dormito* 'one has slept'; *ti sei fatto male* 'you've hurt yourself', etc.

– The auxiliary selected for the passive is *essere*: *la carne è mangiata* 'the meat is eaten'; *il gatto è visto* 'the cat is seen', etc.

– Some intransitive verbs select *essere*, others *avere*. The ongoing debate about the determinants of auxiliary selection in modern Italian intransitives is a complex one, with major theoretical ramifications, and cannot be reviewed in detail here (cf. Rosen (1984); Burzio (1986); Blake (1990: 32–40); Perlmutter (1989); Van Valin (1987; 1990)). The fundamental perception is that selection of auxiliaries is not arbitrary; rather, verbs selecting *avere* have grammatical subjects[42] which share properties with the grammatical subjects of transitive verbs, while the subjects of verbs selecting *essere* have common properties with the grammatical objects of transitive verbs, and are thereby akin to the grammatical subjects of passives (in which the grammatical subject originates as the object of a transitive verb, and where the auxiliary verb employed is also *essere*).

The hypothesis that such grammatical subjects are, in some sense, also 'objects' receives support from an unexpected quarter, namely the syntactic behaviour of the partitive object pronoun *ne*. In transitive sentences *ne* can only be interpreted as an *object* of the verb. *Ne hanno cantato* can mean only 'they sang some of them', never 'some of them sang'. But with certain intransitive verbs, *ne* can function as a grammatical *subject* (e.g., *ne arrivano/vengono* 'some arrive/come'; *ne sono arrivati/venuti* 'some have arrived/come'. With other intransitive verbs (including verbs like *cantare*, which can be used either transitively or intransitively) *ne* cannot function as grammatical subject: e.g., ***ne cantano/telefonano* in the sense 'some of them sing/telephone', ***ne hanno cantato/telefonato* in the sense 'some of them have sung/telephoned', are impossible sentences. So the subject of these intransitive verbs is a grammatical form which is characteristically an *object* of transitive verbs. And it is striking, for our hypothesis, that the subjects of verbs taking auxiliary *essere* are in some sense 'objects', that the intransitive verbs which admits *ne* as a subject complement can be shown to be precisely the same verbs that select *essere* as its auxiliary (*arrivare* 'to arrive', *partire* 'to leave', *nascere* 'to be born', and so forth).

A central point of contention in the debate about auxiliary selection is whether the shared properties are inherently syntactic, in that the grammatical subjects of verbs taking *essere* originate as objects of the verb, those of verbs taking *avere* originate as subjects, or semantic. It is certainly the case that broad semantic generalizations can be made: intransitives whose grammatical subjects are inherently *agents* of the action expressed by the verb take *avere* (*ha viaggiato* 'he has travelled'; *ha parlato* 'he has talked'; *ha nuotato* he has swum'; *ha camminato* 'he has walked'); those whose subjects share with grammatical objects the property of 'inertness' or 'patienthood',[43] in that they do not effect or actively participate in the state or action expressed by the verb, select *essere*. They may 'undergo' the action expressed by the verb, or simply be nouns about which the verb expresses some state or condition, or simple existence. Among these latter are verbs of existence, condition or state (*è esistito* 'he has existed'; *è stato* 'he has been'), and change of existence, condition or state (*è cambiato* 'he has changed'; *è diventato* 'he has become'; *è migliorato* 'it has improved'; *è arrivata* 'she has arrived'; *è caduto* 'he has fallen'; *è svanito* 'he has vanished'; *è nata* 'she has been born'; *è morto* 'he has died'; *è rimasta* 'she has remained'; *è restato* 'he has stayed'; *è risultato* 'he has turned out', etc.). Under 'state' or 'condition' we may also classify verbs expressing value or quantity (*è valso mille lire* 'it was worth a thousand lire'; *è pesato tre chili* 'it weighed three kilos'; *è costato due sterline* 'it cost two pounds', etc.). Verbs of spatial displacement whose grammatical subjects are not *inherently* agents – in that the subject can equally be animate or inanimate (e.g., *la ragazza è tornata* 'the girl has returned' and *la palla è tornata* 'the ball has returned') also select *essere*. Such verbs are *andare* 'to go'; *venire* 'to come'; *salire* 'to go up'; *scendere* 'to go down'; *uscire* 'to go out'; *entrare* 'to go in'; *partire* 'to leave'; *tornare* 'to return'. Problematic for a semantically based account are verbs which admit both auxiliaries, such as *è/ha corso* 'he has run'; *è/ha volato* 'he has flown'; *è/ha emigrato* 'he has emigrated'; *è/ha durato* 'he has lasted' and inherently subjectless 'weather' verbs (*è/ha piovuto* 'it has rained', *è/ha nevicato* 'it has snowed', *è/ha tuonato* 'it has thundered', etc.). Also problematic is the choice of auxiliary with *deviare* 'to deviate' (*il colpo ha deviato* 'the blow missed') and with verbs, such as *sudare* 'to sweat', expressing involuntary bodily functions, in which the 'neutral' role of the subject might lead us to expect *essere*, rather than the occurring *avere*. In contrast, we might expect *riuscire* 'to succeed', in so far as the grammatical subject is usually the agent and instigator of the action, to select *avere*, rather than its actual auxiliary *essere* (e.g., *sono riuscito con grande astuzia ad ingannare il nemico* 'I succeeded with great cunning in deceiving the enemy').

Recent work by Van Valin favours a semantically based approach, but shifts the focus away from the relation between verb and subject, to the semantics of the verb itself, proposing that the auxiliary is selected according to whether the verb expresses *activity* (taking *avere*) or predicates some *state* (including verbs of *accomplishment* or *achievement*— which might be interpreted as 'arrival in a state'), in which case the verb takes *essere*. The 'state' anlysis can clearly be extended to passive verbs as well. It is significant that time adverbials with *per* (indicating duration of an activity) are only admitted with verbs selecting *avere*, and *in* (indicating time taken for the realization of some action) only with verbs selecting *essere* (cf. Bertinetto (1986: 274–85)). This principle helps to account for the selection of alternative auxiliaries in those verbs which admit either: *è corso a casa in un'ora* 'he ran home in an hour' vs. *ha corso a casa per un'ora* 'he ran at home for an hour'; *ha piovuto per due ore* 'it rained for an hour' but not ***è piovuto per due ore*.[44] What emerges clearly from the debate about auxiliary selection is that it is governed, in very large measure, by the same principles which govern selection of *avere* in transitives, and of *essere* in passives, although an abiding problem for semantically based approaches is, perhaps, the selection of *avere* in verbs of involuntary emanation (*l'uomo ha sudato* 'the man sweated'; *il vaso ha traboccato di vino* 'the glass overflowed with wine') and with *mancare* 'to lack' (*gli italiani non hanno mai mancato di'ispirazione* 'the Italians have never lacked inspiration').

Returning to the diachronic origins of *avere* and *essere*, we can show that the modern distribution of auxiliaries reflects in part the semantics and syntax of the original lexical verbs HABERE and ESSE . CL HABERE is a transitive verb, and consequently selects two 'arguments' or associated nouns, a grammatical subject, and grammatical object. With transitive verbs the subject may be agent (*Giovanni accende la radio* 'Giovanni turns on the radio'), experiencer (*Giovanni sente il freddo* 'Giovanni feels the cold'; *Giovanni conosce Mario* 'Giovanni knows Mario'), or even a *locative*, and it is the locative function which is particularly characteristic of verbs of possession, like HABERE whose subject represents the thing or person at or with which the thing possessed (scil. the grammatical object) is located. Indeed, in some languages 'to have' is expressed by a locative phrase, e.g., Irish *tá leabhar ag an mbean* '(there) is a book at the woman/the woman has a book'. For the close connection between transitive subjects and locativity, consider also the use of originally locative expressions *da* (and in OTuscan *per*) to express the agent in passive constructions: *Giovanni legge il libro* 'Giovanni reads the book' = *il libro è letto* da *Giovanni*[45] 'the book is read by Giovanni'. The object of a transitive verb, in contrast, is semantically 'inert' or a 'patient', in that it takes its interpretation from the meaning of the verb, rather than from any independently definable function, such as agentivity or locativity.

The argument structure of HABERE helps explain its original deployment with transitive (two-argument) verbs. A crucial stage in the emergence of the analytic structure is identification of the grammatical subject of the participle with the grammatical subject of HABERE. Such analysis of the subject of both verbs as one and the same seems to have emerged first in Late Latin (cf. Lucot (1940: 249)) with verbs whose subject is an 'experiencer'. This has a clear pragmatic motivation, in that experiencer verbs predicate internal mental states which cannot readily be 'possessed' by another subject. On the syntactic analogy of such structures, the HABERE + PAST PARTICIPLE structure spreads to transitive verbs in general. Subsequent generalization of HABERE to intransitive verbs is a major structural innovation, and a clear indicator of the advancing grammaticalization of HABERE, since it involves abandonment of the two-argument structure of the lexical verb. Such generalization is clearly analogical, although it remains moot (see the review of the modern situation above) whether the basis of such analogy is syntactic (HABERE becomes the auxiliary associated with intransitive verbs having inherent subjects), or semantic (HABERE is the auxiliary associated with agent subjects). The selection of *avere* in structures such as *il vaso ha traboccato di vino*; *l'uomo ha sudato*; *gli italiani non hanno mai mancato d'ispirazione* reflects the locative role of the subject of HABERE, since the grammatical subjects in these cases represent the location, origin or source of the action. Compare the use of *avere* in semantically similar locutions: *ha la febbre* 'he has fever'; *ha il singhiozzo* 'he has hiccups'. *Mancare* (*di*) 'to lack' is practically a negative of *avere*.

CL ESSE is an intransitive verb, in that it selects only one argument noun phrase – which appears as its grammatical subject. The subject of ESSE is usually its 'theme', that of which a *state* or *condition* is predicated by the verb (e.g., MARCUS EST ROMANUS 'Marcus is Roman'; PUELLA LÆTA EST 'the girl is happy'), and it is semantically 'inert' with respect to the meaning of the verb, in that it does not have the role of an 'agent' or 'causer'. The motivation for generalization of ESSE as the auxiliary of single argument verbs, whose subjects are 'inert', and which predicate a state or condition of their subject, is very clear. We have seen that, in late CL, the use of auxiliary ESSE is already established in passives: we shall see below that certain morphologically passive (and semantically 'middle' – see 8.9) verbs, the so-called 'deponents', retain *essere* in their perfective tense forms (e.g., NATA EST > *è nata* 'she has been born'). The association between *essere* and 'middle' meaning facilitates the deployment of *essere* as the auxiliary of other other semantically 'middle' verbs (e.g., OTuscan *è bagnato* 'he bathed'). Since ESSE is, *par excellence*, the verb of predication, its use as auxiliary of lexical verbs predicating state, motion, change of state, etc. of their grammatical subjects is clearly motivated.

Whether or not auxiliary selection in modern Italian intransitives is wholly determined semantically remains a moot point. But there is both internal and external (comparative) evidence to suggest that auxiliaries can and do abandon their semantic motivation. The grammaticalization of auxiliary *essere* is apparent in reflexive verbs, all of which select *essere*. On semantic grounds this is odd, since true reflexives are basically transitive verbs, whose objects happen to be referentially identical to their subjects: cf. auxiliary *avere* with the stressed reflexive pronoun (*Mario ha ucciso se stesso* 'Mario has killed himself') but *essere* with the clitic pronoun (*Mario si è ucciso*).[46] In the language of the thirteenth century, *avere* is indeed employed as a reflexive auxiliary: e.g., Novellino *questi due cavalieri longamente s'aveano amato* 'these two knights had long loved each other', where the reflexive structure is reciprocal and, with an indirect reflexive object, *Bito s'avea messa la più ricca roba di vaio* 'Bito had put on the finest fur robe'; Macinghi Strozzi *quello che mi ho veduto* 'what I have seen for myself', *i' m'ho fatto pensiero* 'I have thought to myself'; Bandello *Non me l'ho smenticata* 'I haven't forgotten it'; *io ti vo' dir ciò che tacciuto m'averei* 'I will tell you what I would have kept to myself'; *aversi l'un l'altro posto il cimiero in capo* 'each to have put the helmet on the other's head'; Cellini *m'avevo fatto amicizie* 'I had made myself friendships'; Michele Benvenga (late seventeenth century) *l'autorità che s'hanno acquistata* 'the authority that they have acquired'; *s'ha fatta anch'egli una cappella a casa* 'he too has made himself a chapel at home'.

The generalization of *essere* to all reflexive verbs seems to have its origin in analogical pressure exerted by semantically 'middle' verbs (cf. Vincent (1982: 96)), which already took *essere* as their auxiliary: middle verbs come increasingly to be expressed by reflexive structures (*bagna* 'he bathes' and *alza* 'he gets up' give way to *si bagna* and *si alza)*, but initially (in the thirteenth century), the reflexive forms did not penetrate the analytic forms of the verb (cf. Brambilla Ageno (1964: 200–5)). In the thirteenth century Florentine chronicles we find *il re di Scozia si rubellò* 'the king of Scotland rebelled', but *le terre che lli erano rubellate* 'the territories which had rebelled against him'. The subsequent generalization of the reflexive pronoun from the synthetic into the analytic forms of middle verbs, such that *è bagnato* and *è alzato* become *si è bagnato* and *si è alzato*, on the model of *si bagna* and *si alza*) seems to have triggered a syntactic analogy, such that all reflexive verbs have been made to conform to this pattern.

The grammaticalization of auxiliary selection, and with it the final abandonment of the semantic and structural properties of HABERE and ESSE, is far more advanced outside Italian. In Castilian *haber* has become the sole auxiliary; in French, *être* has been generalized to all reflexives, but otherwise abandoned in favour of *avoir* (with a handful of exceptions); in Romanian the distribution of auxiliary *a fi* 'to be', and *a avea* 'to have' has been grammaticalized along lines of tense and finiteness (*am telefonat* 'I have telephoned' but *a fi telefonat* 'to have telephoned' – literally 'to be telephoned'). In an illuminating scrutiny of auxiliary selection in Italo-Romance dialects, Tuttle (1986) shows that in parts of the Veneto HABERE has been generalized to all verbs except those expressing motion, while elsewhere either HABERE (e.g., Valle d'Orte (Lazio) and Valle del Pescara (Abruzzo)), or ESSE (e.g.,

Terracina (Lazio)) have been generalized to all verbs. Sometimes such generalization depends on the person of the verb; for example, in Roiate and Zagarolo (Lazio) ESSE has not established itself in third person forms.

8.8.3 The 'progressive' structures stare/andare/venire + *gerund*

In the earliest Italo-Romance attestation of the construction *sta facendo* 'she is doing', *stare* has all the attributes of an autonomous lexical verb, meaning 'to stand' or 'remain'. It can occur in all tense forms and in the imperative, and is readily separable from the gerund: e.g., Aretino *sono stato un poco pensando meco* 'I stood/was a while thinking to myself'; Brusoni *stette buona pezza il cavaliere pensando su questa lettera* 'the knight stood a good while thinking about this letter' (cf. Durante (1981: 180)). This complex-verb structure is still rare in northern Italian dialects,[47] but very frequent in the south and centre (Rohlfs (1969: 108f.)). It begins to gain ground in Tuscan from the sixteenth century, but its basic meaning remains, until relatively recently, stative, rather than progressive (cf. Durante (1981: 180; 268f.); Bertinetto (1986: 137 n7)). The 'immobility' inherent in the lexical verb *stare* (meaning 'stand', 'remain in place'), debarred combination of *stare* with dynamic or 'transformative' verbs (e.g., those expressing motion or change of state), so that *sto leggendo* 'I'm reading' has always been admitted, but not *sto andando* 'I'm going' nor *sto diventando* 'I'm becoming'. It is only from the middle of the twentieth century, and possibly under the influence of English *be . . . ing* constructions (Durante (1981: 269)), that this structure begins to appear regularly with verbs expressing the progressive development or unfolding of any action: *sta andando* 'she's going'; *sta venendo* 'she's coming', etc. According to Durante, even at the beginning of the 1980s the type *sta piovendo* 'it's raining' was still little used by the older generation. A detailed account of the expanding use of the *stare* + gerund structure is given in Squartini (1990).

In the structure *venire* 'to come' or *andare* 'to go' + gerund, the auxiliary verbs remain close to their lexical meaning. *Venire* in this construction indicates movement towards some goal, hence 'gradual achievement of an action', (cf. Lepschy and Lepschy (1981: 135f.)), just as the lexical verb indicates movement towards a goal located with or near the speaker; *andare* expresses movement or progression, without any necessary aim. Both auxiliaries retain the full morphological paradigm of the corresponding lexical verbs: *è andato cercando* 'he has gone looking'; *è venuto costruendosi* 'it has been getting built', etc. The auxiliaries are also separable from the gerund, e.g., *va ogni due o tre giorni cercando funghi* 'she goes every two or three days looking for mushrooms'. The structure with *andare* is already established in the seventeenth century (e.g., Galileo *va continuamente scuoprendo* 'he's continually discovering'), but Squartini observes that in the first half of the nineteenth century, it is the verb forms with *andare* (and the much less frequent *venire*) which serve to express the gradual, incremental progression of an event or action, while *stare* + gerund indicates principally imperfectivity and durativity. Yet over the past two hundred years, *stare* has tended to take over the functions originally expressed by *andare* in combination with the gerund, with a corresponding major decline in the frequency of the latter.

8.8.4 The passive with andare *and* venire

The verbs of motion, *andare* and *venire* have also been pressed into service as passive auxiliaries. The origins of the *venire* construction are uncertain, and is not attested in texts before the thirteenth century at the earliest. Rohlfs (1969: 128f.) regards it as a direct development of an old construction comprising a third person form of *venire* and a PAST PARTICIPLE + INDIRECT PERSONAL OBJECT, expressing the involuntary or fortuitous occurrence of an action to somebody. Thus from Boccaccio (Decameron): *gli venne pensato* 'it occurred to him'; *gli venne questo spago trovato* 'he happened across this string'; *gli venne veduta una giovanetta* 'he chanced to see a maiden'; Cellini: *le gran cose che mi venne fatto insino a quest'età* 'the great things which happened to me until that age'; Michele Benvenga (late seventeenth century) *mi venne veduta una maravigliosa statua* 'I chanced to see a wonderful statue'. But it is equally plausible that the modern structure, which is not restricted to the third person and has no connotation of fortuitousness, has simply evolved by grammaticalization of the lexical verb *venire*, so that the meaning 'change of position' recedes in favour of the more general 'change of state', 'becoming' (or 'ending up'). It is this 'dynamic' sense of 'entry into some state' which characterizes the modern passive auxiliary *venire*. The sentence *i libri sono distribuiti tra gli studenti* is ambiguous between a dynamic and a stative interpretation: 'the books get distributed among the students' or 'the students have the books (which have been distributed among them)'. But the structure *venire* + gerund is unambiguously dynamic: *i libri vengono distribuiti* 'the books get distributed'. A property of auxiliary *venire* which distinguishes it from the passive auxiliary *essere*, but is reminiscent of the perfective auxiliaries *essere* and *avere*, is that it has no 'analytic' tense forms. We have *i libri erano stati distribuiti* 'the books had been distributed', but not ***i libri erano venuti distribuiti*.[48]

The earliest textual attestations of the passive with *andare* date from the sixteenth century (notably in the writings of Cellini). Attestations remain rare until the late nineteenth century. Fornaciari's observation

(1881) that this usage characterized the 'parlar familiare' ('familiar speech'), rather than 'nobili scritture' ('noble writings'), may help account for the scarcity of literary examples. The structure has two distinct meanings. One of them, still transparently retaining the sense of 'going (away)', involves loss or destruction (*la città andò distrutta* 'the city was destroyed'; *i guanti sono andati persi* 'the gloves have been lost'). The *andare* passive expressing obligation (*questo vino va bevuto fresco* 'this wine should be drunk chilled') is inherently imperfective, and correspondingly does not occur in perfective forms of the auxiliary. It is unlike both the lexical verb *andare*, and other passive auxiliaries, in that its grammatical subject is always inanimate and third person. But like *andare*, it does not admit agent structures with *da* (***quel manoscritto andò perso da un mio amico* 'that manuscript was lost by a friend of mine'), although many speakers now seem to accept agent phrases when the *andare* structure expresses obligation (e.g., *questo manoscritto va esaminato da un esperto* 'this manuscript should be examined by an expert').

Other verbs found in combination with the past participle, such as *finire* 'finish'; *rimanere* 'remain' and *restare* 'stay' have remained semantically transparent, and occur in all tense forms. The relevant structures (attested, with *rimanere*, since at least the fourteenth century) are not complex-verbs but rather have the structure VERB + ADJECTIVE: compare *rimase ferito* 'he was wounded'; *rimase respinta* 'she was rejected' with *rimase scontento* 'he was unhappy'; *rimase incinta* 'she got pregnant'; *rimarrà offeso* 'he will be offended'; *rimane escluso* 'he is excluded', etc.

8.8.5 The future

One of the most striking morphological discontinuities between CL and Romance is the formation of the future tense. The CL future is extinct in Romance.[49] Among the possible reasons for its demise are: (i) Suppletion (the marker of future is -B- in the first and second conjugations, but a vowel, -E-, (-A- in the first person singular) in other conjugations, cf. AMABIT 'he will love'; TENEBIT 'he will hold' vs. PERDET 'he will lose'; DORMIET 'he will sleep'); (ii) Loss of phonological distinctness due to merger of unstressed short [**i**] and [**e**] (cf. Ch.2: 2.3), third person singular present PERDIT and future PERDET would have become homophonous. Tuscany lies on the geographical fringe of that area of the Romance world (comprising principally Gaul and Iberia), in which there has emerged a Romance 'analytical' future tense composed of the INFINITIVE + HABERE (DARE + HABET > *darà* 'he'll give'; SAPERE + HABEMUS > *sapremo* 'we'll know', etc.).[50] In dialects south of a line between Viterbo and Ancona, the morphological future tense is lost, and future time is usually expressed by present tense forms, although an analytical construction, usually of the form *avere* + *a* + INFINITIVE, is also deployed to express future time, often with an overtone of obligation or necessity.[51]

Few traces of the original analytical structure with the auxiliary postposed to the infinitive survive in Italo-Romance,[52] for the original constituent elements, infinitive and auxiliary, have become morphologically fused, and tightly bound, in a single, synthetic word form. In Italian, the original auxiliary verb HABERE now functions as an inflectional marker of person and number, although it maintains a partial phonological identity with the present tense of the verb *avere*:[53] *parlerò* 'I shall speak' (*ho* 'I have'), *parlerai* (*hai*) *parlerà* (*ha*), and, *parleranno* (*hanno*). But in the first and second persons plural we find the shortened forms *-emo* and *-ete*, (*parleremo*, *parlerete*) not ***parleravemo*, ***parleravete*. The juxtaposition of infinitive and auxiliary creates the phonological environment for various word-internal phonetic changes, which in some verbs obscure the relationship between future stem and infinitive, by giving rise to allomorphy in the future stem. One of the simplest manifestations of this is that rhizotonic infinitives in stressed [**ɛ**] or [**ɔ**] have future stems in [**e**] and [**o**], since the verb root does not bear word stress in the future: e.g., **ˈpɛrdere** 'to lose' but **perdeˈrɔ**, *avere* 'to have' *avrò*; *dovere* 'to owe' *dovrò*, etc.) or, in the case of unstressed thematic [**a**], to regular raising to [**e**] before [**r**] (see Ch.2: 4.6.3): *parlare parlerò*, etc. The futures of *stare* 'to stand', *dare* 'to give' and *fare* 'to do' retain [**a**] (*starò*, etc.);[54] it is likely that *sarò*, the future of *essere*, is modelled on these verbs. Occasional syncope of the thematic vowel gives rise to consonant clusters which are subject to assimilation (Ch.2: 8.2), thereby creating new kinds of consonantal root allomorphy: ***veniˈrɔ** > ***venˈrɔ** > *verrò* 'I shall come'; ***voleˈrɔ** > ***volˈrɔ** > *vorrò* 'I shall want'; ***remaneˈrɔ** > ***remanˈrɔ** > *rimarrò* 'I shall remain'.

An even more significant innovation, in that it creates a tense form without antecedent in CL,[55] is the so-called conditional, or 'future-in-the past'. Just as time subsequent to the present can be signalled by combining the infinitive and the present tense of HABERE, so time subsequent to a moment in the past can be signalled by combining the infinitive with a *past* tense form of HABERE. In many Romance varieties (e.g., Gallo-Romance and Ibero-Romance) a phonologically reduced form of the imperfect tense of HABERE is used. The type *darea* 'I would give'; *portarea* 'I would carry' is attested in medieval Aretine. More common in the medieval literary language, and widely diffused in many modern dialects (cf. Rohlfs (1968: 339f.)), is the ending *-ia* (*daria*; *saria*, etc.), ultimately from ***aˈveva**, although its phonological form shows that it cannot be of Tuscan origin. It is wholly absent, for example, from the early fifteenth century Florentine Macinghi Strozzi letters, although it frequently occurs in later texts alongside the indigenous form in *-ebbe* (discussed below); Bandello has *promettendole che mai non l'abbandonaria e che l'aiutaria a maritare, di modo che starebbe bene* 'promising her that he would never abandon her and that he would help her marry, so that she would be all right'. Rohlfs (1968: 339) discusses the possibility that its ultimate source is literary Provençal.

A peculiarly Italo-Romance (specifically, northern Italian and Tuscan) development is the formation of the 'conditional' by combining the infinitive with the passato remoto, rather than the imperfect, of *avere*. This is particularly apparent in the third person forms, singular *canterebbe* 'he would sing'; *verrebbe* 'he would come' and plural *canterebbero*; *verrebbero*. Phonologically reduced forms of *avesti*, *avemmo*, *aveste* appear in *canteresti*, *canteremmo*, *cantereste*, etc. OTuscan first person singular *canterebbi* has given way to *canterei*, possibly on the analogy of second conjugation first person singular passato remoto forms in *-ei*. The syntactic and semantic evolution of the conditional, which in the modern language no longer signals futurity, will be discussed in Ch.4: 8.4.1.

8.8.6 Syntactic periphrases

A number of VERB + INFINITIVE structures are only *syntactically* restructured, while their component verbs retain a high degree of lexical and morphological autonomy. In syntactic restructuring, noun phrases and clitics which are, semantically, arguments of the infinitive, behave syntactically as if they were arguments of the complex structure VERB + INFINITIVE. Restructuring may be obligatory (as in the case of causative verbs), or optional (as with the structures MODAL + INFINITIVE, and VERB OF PERCEPTION + INFINITIVE).

8.8.6.1 The causative structure *fare/lasciare* + infinitive

The causative structure *fare/lasciare* + INFINITIVE (e.g., *lo faccio cantare* 'I make him sing'; *le lascio entrare* 'I let them come in'; *te lo fanno mandare* 'they have it sent to you', etc.) is a Romance innovation, amply attested in the medieval language (cf. Robustelli (1992: 88f.)). In CL, causatives are expressed by means of a *biclausal* structure consisting of a verb of causation (FACIO/EFFICIO), followed by the particle UT and a subordinate verb in the subjunctive: FACIO UT CANANT 'I make them sing'; FACIUNT UT TIBI ID MITTANT 'they make them send it to you', etc. Biclausal structures of a similar kind are also found in Italian: *fanno che/fanno sì che/fanno in modo che te lo mandino*.

Various aspects of the syntax of causative structures testify to their reanalysis as monoclausal structures having properties of synthetic verb forms. The position of *fare* is fixed to the left of the subordinate verb, and no syntactic material can be intercalated, so that the grammatical objects of *fare* are collocated to the right of the whole syntagm: *faccio cantare Maria* 'I make Mary sing', not ***faccio Maria cantare*. This is to say that *Maria*, although it is the grammatical *subject* of *cantare*, is treated syntactically as the grammatical object of the whole complex-verb. In the medieval language, traces of an original biclausal structure are still, occasionally, visible, in that the subject of the infinitive, and other material, can still be intercalated (cf. Robustelli (1992: 83; 90)) between *fare* and the infinitive: e.g., Guido Fava *e faremmo l'auxelli supra le ramelle cantare versi de fino amore* 'and we would make the birds on the branches sing songs of gentle love'. Another indication of the analysis in the modern language of the causative structure as monoclausal is that clitics which are arguments of the subordinate verb treat it as a complex whole, rather than as comprising two lexical verbs, and are thereby attached to *fare* (*la faccio cantare* 'I make her sing'; *te ne faccio parlare* 'I make you talk about it'– where *la* and *ne* are grammatical objects of *cantare* and *parlare*, not of *fare*). It is a feature of Italian clause structure that the verb can occur with only one direct object argument. Any other object noun phrase arguments must not be direct objects (and are usually indirect objects): *do il libro* [direct object] *a Maria* [indirect object] 'I give Maria the book'. The behaviour of subordinate clauses in causative structures is consistent with the monoclausal analysis. If the subordinate clause contains no object, then the subject of the subordinate clause simply becomes the direct object of the causative verb *fare* (*faccio cantare Maria* [direct object] 'I make Maria sing', *la faccio cantare* 'I make her sing'). But if the subordinate clause also contains a direct object (e.g., *Maria* [subject] *canta la canzone* [direct object] 'Mary sings the song'), then in the corresponding causative construction we find that the subject of the subordinate clause becomes the *indirect* object (*faccio cantare <u>a Maria</u>* [indirect object] *la canzone* [direct object] 'I make Mary sing the song', *<u>le</u>* [indirect object] *faccio cantare la canzone* [direct object] 'I make her sing the song'). This modification comes about because *faccio cantare* is analysed as a single verb, and a structure such as **faccio cantare Maria* [direct object] *la canzone* [direct object] would violate the constraint against two direct objects appearing in the same clause. Robustelli (1992: 90) observes that there were still a few, rare, examples in medieval Italo-Romance of a 'double direct object' in causatives, presumably reflecting an original biclausal structure: e.g., Guittone d'Arezzo *fanno me, lasso, la mia terra odiare e l'altrui forte amare* 'they make me, alas, hate my own country, and love greatly that of another'; Dante *che fé Nettuno ammirar l'ombra d'Argo* 'which made Neptune wonder at the shade of Argos'. The double direct object disappears from Boccaccio onwards.[56]

A feature of the other structures we have examined is that the lexical verbs, rather like the roots of synthetic verb forms, are morphologically invariant (apart from past participial agreement for number and gender), and that the auxiliary alone signals person, tense and mood. In causative structures, the infinitive is also wholly invariant: only the present infinitive is admitted, regardless of the tense of *fare*, and reflexive or passive infinitives are debarred: *lo faccio alzare* 'I make him get up' not ***lo faccio alzarsi*, and *faccio costruire il palazzo dai lavoratori* 'I have the palace built by the workers' not ***faccio essere costruito il palazzo dai lavoratori*. Nor can the infinitive be negated: ***lo faccio non cantare*. The auxiliary *fare*, in contrast, retains a full range of tense, mood, voice and person forms: *lo aveva fatto entrare* 'she had let him come in'; *furono fatti uscire* 'they were made to go out', etc. The use of the preposition *da* to mark the agent of the infinitive (as in *faccio costruire il palazzo dai lavoratori*) is attested only from the fourteenth century (cf. Robustelli (1992: 92)). It seems that *da* became liberated from its close association with morphologically and syntactically 'passive' verbs (see also 8.9). In passive constructions the agent – introduced by *da* – is 'demoted' or 'backgrounded' (*il palazzo è costruito dai lavoratori* 'the palace is built by the workers') and the underlying object of the verb is 'promoted' to become its grammatical subject. Given that causative verbs were already characterized by a structure in which the agent of the verb was introduced by a preposition (*a*) (*faccio costruire il palazzo ai lavoratori* 'I make the workers build the palace'), it was a simple structural change for this preposition to be replaced by another, *da*, as the marker of a semantically 'backgrounded' or 'demoted' agent.[57]

Modal and 'aspectual' verbs (e.g., *potere* 'to be able'; *volere* 'to want'; *dovere* 'to owe'/'to have to'; *sapere* 'to know' and *cominciare a* 'to begin to'; *finire di* 'to finish'; *tornare a* 'to . . . again'; *stare a*; 'to be . . . ing'; *venire a* 'to come to') with infinitives, are susceptible to optional syntactic restructuring. Clitics which are arguments of the infinitive may be attached instead to the modal verb (*devo farlo* or *lo devo fare* 'I must do it'; *possono andarci* or *ci possono andare* 'they can go there'; *volete parlarne* or *ne volete parlare* 'you want to talk about it'; *vengo a trovarti* or *ti vengo a trovare* 'I'm coming to get you'; *cominciano a farlo* or *lo cominciano a fare* 'they are beginning to do it'. The usual auxiliary of the modal verbs is *avere*; but where the infinitive complement selects *essere* as its auxiliary, *essere* may also be selected as auxiliary of the entire modal structure: *hanno dovuto partire* 'they had to leave'; *hanno potuto entrare* 'they managed to get in'; *ha cominciato a cadere la pioggia* 'the rain has begun to fall' or *sono dovuti partire*; *sono potuti entrare; è cominciata a cadere la pioggia*. If the clitic is attached to the modal, then the auxiliary of the infinitive is obligatorily selected. *ci sono voluti andare* 'they wanted to go there', but not ***ci hanno voluto andare*.[58] Restructuring is discrete, not a matter of degree: in other words, it is not possible to produce a 'semi-restructured' syntagm such as ***ti devo darlo*; one says either *devo dartelo* or *te lo devo dare* 'I must give it to you'. These optional restructurings are no recent innovation: they are well attested already in the thirteeenth century Novellino: *noi vi ti volemo al postutto menare* 'we want to take you there after all'.

The structure VERB OF PERCEPTION + INFINITIVE is also optionally restructured, as the syntactic behaviour of object nouns and clitics shows: *sento il ragazzo cantare la canzone* or *sento cantare la canzone al ragazzo* 'I hear the boy sing the song'; *lo sento cantarla* or *gliela sento cantare* 'I hear him sing it'. For further discussions of the modern syntax of these structures, see Lepschy (1976) and Skytte and Salvi (1991: 509–13).

8.9 Reflexive verbs

CL reflexive verbs are primarily transitives whose subject and object are identical (coreferential): the subject executes some action upon itself. In the first and second persons, the reflexive pronominal objects are, correspondingly, morphologically identical to other object pronouns; only the third person possessed a morphologically distinct reflexive pronoun (SE): UOS UIDEO 'I see you', NOS UIDENT 'they see us', UOS UIDETIS 'you see yourselves', NOS UIDEMUS 'we see ourselves', MULIER SE UIDET 'the woman sees herself', MULIERES SE UIDENT 'the women see themselves' (e.g., in a reflection). These structures are continued into Italian (*vi vedo*, *ci vedono*, *vi vedete*, *ci vediamo*; *la donna si vede*, *le donne si vedono*). But the reflexive structures have accumulated new functions, such that their subject can also be 'patient' of the verb, and the reflexive construction is thereby able to function also as a passive. The resultant 'passive' reflexive structures of the type *si vedono le donne* 'the women are seen', where *si* occupies the canonical position for transitive subjects, and *le donne* that of transitive objects, have favoured the reanalysis of third person *si* as a 'non-specific personal' *subject* pronoun. How did this come about?

The CL transitive reflexives are continued into Italian, but other morphologically reflexive structures arise which are not transitive, but 'middle': they signal not an action carried out by the subject on itself, but an event originating, as it were, from within the subject, and in which the subject plays a more or less active role. Certain verbs which are inherently middle (e.g., *accorgersi* 'to realize'; *ammalarsi* 'to fall ill'; *arrabbiarsi* 'to get angry'; *vergognarsi* 'to be ashamed'; *rammaricarsi* 'to regret'; *pentirsi* 'to repent'; *arrampicarsi* 'to climb';

rompersi 'to break') cannot appear without the reflexive clitic (you cannot say ***accorgo*),[59] and the fact that the reflexive clitic is not a direct object is reflected in the impossibility of substituting it by a stressed reflexive object (e.g., ***accorgo me stesso*). A number of basically transitive verbs also have 'middle' forms of this kind (e.g., *alzarsi* 'to get up'; *addormentarsi* 'to fall asleep'; *annoiarsi* 'to get bored'; *svegliarsi* 'to wake up'; *fermarsi* 'to stop'; *lavarsi* 'to wash'; *seccarsi* 'to get annoyed'; *stancarsi* 'to get tired'; *scaldarsi* 'to get hot'; *irritarsi* 'to get irritated'). To take the example of *mi annoio*, it is not normally the case that I bore myself (i.e., this is not a reflexive equivalent of 'he bores me'), but rather that I become or get bored, so *mi annoio* is not synonymous with *annoio me stesso*.

The use of reflexives with middle function occurs occasionally in CL, and becomes widespread in early Romance. The fact that, in middle verbs, the subject is only secondarily involved in the action, facilitates the extension of the 'middle' reflexive *si* structure to verbs whose grammatical subjects are inert or 'patients'. In other words, the reflexive comes to function rather like the passive. This development, a Romance innovation, is represented in modern Italian structures of the type: *si vendono i libri* 'the books are sold'; *si beve il vino* 'the wine is drunk'. Indeed, one occasionally finds the agent marker *da*, generally associated with true passive constructions (e.g., *il vino è bevuto dai ragazzi* 'the wine is drunk by the boys'), used with 'passive' reflexives (e.g., *il vino si beve dai ragazzi*). The reflexive structure is also occasionally extended, in OTuscan, to certain other verbs which, like 'passives' and 'middles' have 'inert', object-like subjects, namely those verbs, selecting *essere* as their auxiliary, which predicate states or conditions of their subject (see 8.8.2.1). Thus we encounter in OTuscan *andarsi* 'to go', *venirsi* 'to come' and even *essersi* 'to be'. This structure has largely disappeared, not without leaving traces in verbs such as *andarsene* 'to go away', *tornarsene* 'to come back', etc., and in the lexicalized expression *qualsiasi* 'any', literally, 'whichever it be'.

It is important to note, for our understanding of the subsequent evolution of the reflexives (see below), that in the medieval language *si* has yet to be generalized into the analytic forms of middle verbs in *essere* + past participle. The probable reason for this is that the reflexive structure with *si* is dynamic, focusing on the performance or execution of the action expressed by the verb. The forms with *essere* (*è bagnato* 'he has bathed', *era alzato* 'he had got up') focus rather on the *state* resultant from the action. It is only from the fourteenth century that, on the analogy of the synthetic forms (*si bagna si alzava,* etc.), *si* begins to penetrate the analytic forms as well (*si è bagnato*, *si era alzato,* etc.).

It is in the nature of passive structures that the identity of the transitive subject is not obligatorily specified, and that the grammatical subject is interpretable as semantic object. On this basis, passive reflexive structures of the type *si legge il libro* 'the book is read' are reanalysed as a *transitive structure*, where *il libro* is object, and *si* is interpretable as a non-specific personal (i.e. [+human]) subject. Non-specific personal *si* in modern Italian retains the traces of its reflexive origins, in that the verb usually agrees with the object noun (*si leggono i libri*), although *si legge i libri*, where such agreement does not occur, is not impossible. Absence of agreement is widespread in earlier centuries: e.g., Macinghi Strozzi *con tutti e sagramenti che si richiede al buono e fedele cristiano* 'with all the oaths which are required of a good and faithful Christian'; Cellini *si destò tutti quei mia nemici* 'all those enemies of mine were awakened'. The analysis of *si* as a non-specific personal *subject* pronoun is also evident in the fact that it can occur in transitive constructions taking direct object pronouns (e.g., *si può vederli* 'one can see them'), where *si* cannot itself be the direct object, and in single-argument verbs (such as *si balla* 'one dances'; *si parla* 'one talks') which lack a grammatical object, and require *agentive* grammatical subjects (i.e., the class of intransitives which normally selects auxiliary *avere*).

The possibility of using non-specific personal *si* with intransitive verbs is also a relative innovation. In the thirteenth century (cf. Cennamo (1991: 253)), the use of *si* with intransitive verbs is still circumscribed[60] to 'bivalent' intransitives, i.e., to those with latent but unexpressed objects (e.g., *si dice* from *dire* 'to say'; *si legge* from *leggere* 'to read'). That *si* has abandoned its transitive object status in structures such as *si può vederli* is apparent in the fact that it does not behave like an object clitic, since it escapes the restructuring constraint which debars separation of object clitics governed by analytic verbs. It is a characteristic of verbs having human, but unspecified, grammatical subjects, that they take predicate adjectives in the plural (e.g., *bisogna essere prudenti* 'one must be careful' – cf. the use of plural structures in an unspecified subject construction like *dicono* 'people say', 'it is said'): the past participle in compound forms of the non-specific personal *si* construction correspondingly shows plural agreement with its subject: *si è arrivati* 'one has arrived'. The impersonal *si* still resembles its reflexive, middle and passive counterparts, in that it selects *essere* as its auxiliary.

A further development, particularly characteristic of modern Tuscan, and emerging no earlier than the fourteenth century (cf. Cennamo (1991: 255)) is the extension of the referential domain of the reflexive *si* (+ third person verb) as a first person plural subject pronoun: e.g., *si canta* = *cantiamo* 'we sing'; *si è arrivati* = *siamo arrivati* 'we have arrived').

9 The pronouns

9.1 Morphology of the pronouns

The pronominal system occupies a special place in the historical morphology of Italian. It straddles the noun/adjective and the verbal system, in that it expresses not only number and gender, but also person. In addition, it preserves a rudimentary case system, distinguishing nominative (subject) from oblique (non-subject) forms and, in the third person, differentiating direct and indirect object functions. Some third person non-clitic forms also encode humanness and animacy. A further formal division, among object pronouns, separates clitic and non-clitic (or 'disjunctive') pronouns. It is characteristic of clitic forms that they are morphologically attached to some 'host' (chiefly the verb), cannot stand in isolation from their verb, are monosyllabic, and cannot carry contrastive stress.

(16)

Person	1Sg.	2Sg.	3Sg.		1Pl.	2Pl.	3Pl.	
Gender			M	F			M	F
Subject	*io*	*tu*	*egli* *esso* *lui*	*ella* *essa* *lei*	*noi*	*voi*	*loro* *essi*	*loro* *esse*
Object	*me*	*te*	*esso* *lui*	*essa* *lei*	*noi*	*voi*	*loro* *essi*	*loro* *essi*
Refl.	*me*	*te*	*sé*	*sé*	*noi*	*voi*	*sé*	*sé*

Clitics:

Subject				(none)				
DO	*mi*	*ti*	*lo*	*la*	*ci*	*vi*	*li*	*le*
IO	*mi*	*ti*	*gli*	*le*	*ci*	*vi*	*loro* *gli*	*loro* *loro*
Refl.	*mi*	*ti*	*si*	*si*	*ci*	*vi*	*si*	*si*

9.1.1 The first and second person forms

The forms *io*, *me*, and *tu*, *te*, directly continue Latin EGO, ME, and TU, TE. They retain a case distinction between the subject forms *io* and *tu* and the non-subject forms (employed as objects of verbs, and after prepositions) *me* and *te*. But in the modern language the subject *tu* shows signs of becoming restricted to a 'semi-clitic' status, in that if it is conjoined with a preceding pronoun, it is replaced by the oblique *te*: *io e te cantiamo* 'me and you sing'. In popular usage, *tu* tends to be replaced by *te* when the pronoun is emphatically stressed (e.g., *canti te?* 'are *you* singing?'). *Noi* and *voi* are generally assumed to continue CL NOS and UOS, although Sornicola (1991) has examined the possibility that, at least in some dialects, these may be reflexes of the CL dative/ablative forms NOBIS and UOBIS.

The clitic continuants of NOS and UOS appear in early Tuscan texts as *no* or *nu*, and *vo* or *vu*. These forms, now extinct, are found in the earliest texts alongside the alternative forms *ne*/*ni*, and *ve*/*vi*. *Ne*, widely used in the medieval language and employed by some writers as late as the seventeenth century, has given way to *ce*/*ci*. The earliest surviving Florentine text, the bankers' book of 1211, contains all three first person plural clitics (with *ci* functioning exclusively as a dative). The consensus (cf. Tekavčić (1980 II: 189)) is that *ne*, *vi*, and *ci* originate respectively in the CL locative particles INDE,[61] IBI and (ECCE) HIC. These etymologies raise problems. INDE is the most likely source of the partitive clitic *ne*, in the sense 'of/from him/her/it/them/there', and of the Calabrian and Salentino first person plural pronouns **nde** or **ndi**. It is therefore reasonable to assume that it underlies Tuscan first person plural *ne*. But why should INDE be associated with the first person plural? After all, the partitive *ne* actually excludes first person reference (*ne parlate* = 'you talk about him', etc., but not 'you talk about us').

Two additional factors may have provided the motivation for replacement of *no* by *ne*: *no* is dysfunctional, because it sounds almost identical to the negative particle *non*; *ne* or *nde* are suitable replacements because, quite accidentally, they display the initial nasal segment also characteristic of the first person plural pronoun. The analogy of other clitics containing the vowel [**e**] (*me*, *te*) has probably played a role here, too. First person plural *ne* and congeners, once widespread in central Italy, is now restricted to some northern dialects and to dialects of lower southern Italy. In its place has appeared *ci*, identical with the locative particle *ci*. This form is widely assumed to continue Latin ECCE HIC, but this is questionable, because reflexes of HIC otherwise survive only in stressed forms (e.g., survival of the neuter HOC in *ciò* 'that' < ECCE HOC). Perhaps more plausible is derivation from HINCE ('hence'), the semantic counterpart of INDE ('thence'). It is significant that many upper southern Italian dialects have the first person plural pronoun **ntʃi** or **ntʃe**. Although it is true that CL HINCE (or ECCE HIC) encodes nearness to the speaker, it retains no such connotation in old or modern Italian (cf. the use of *ci* in existential *ci sono* 'there are', or *ci vado* 'I go there', which suggests motion *away* from the self). If IBI is the source of the pronoun *vi*, this is unlikely to be because IBI has retained its original sense of distance from the speaker: in Italo-Romance it is neutral as to proximity.[62] Indeed, Italian locative *vi* and *ci* are semantically interchangeable (although stylistically differentiated, the former being characteristic of more formal styles). As with *ne*, the dominant influence in the incorporation of these forms into the pronominal system must be the phonetic similarity with other forms of the pronoun, in the case of *vi* (cf. *voi*), and the analogical influence of other pronominal forms in [**i**] and [**e**], such as *te*/*ti* and *me*/*mi*.

The forms *ne*, *ci*, and *vi* have, then, no original correlation with person. Rather, they might be seen as manifestations of a tendency, widely observable in Italo-Romance, for locative particles to assume the functions of clitic personal pronouns. *Ci* also functions as a third person IO clitic: *ci parlo* is 'I speak to him/her/them' in Tuscan and many other dialects (and is often identified as a feature of popular Italian). Even in the standard language, *ci* may function as a third person IO form where the object is inanimate. The frequent, and extremely widespread, use of an originally locative pronoun *ci* as an indirect object form in very informal registers is foreshadowed in the many dialects (including Tuscan) in which *ci*, or other locative forms, fulfil this function – although Cortelazzo (1972: 90f.) points out that the geographical distribution of this phenomenon is not entirely coextensive with its dialectal distribution. In the spoken language, *ci* is particularly common as a pronominal substitute for *con* + noun: *non ci esco mai* = *non esco mai con lui* 'I never go out with him'. In the dialect of Paliano (Lazio) **ʧi** even serves as a second person clitic; reflexes of HINCE are widely employed as third person forms in Umbria, Abruzzo, Lazio, Calabria and Campania. Elsewhere (southern Basilicata, northern Calabria and parts of Salento) INDE often furnishes the third person IO clitic (cf. Lausberg (1939: 142)).

A development particularly associated with the spoken language is the attachment of *ci* to certain verbs where its locative association is severely attenuated, or nil. While the existential verb *esserci* 'there to be' (cf. *c'è* 'there is') has been admitted in written/elevated registers, the use of *averci*, *volerci* or *farcela* (equivalent to *avere* 'to have', *occorrere* 'to be necessary', *riuscire* 'to succeed') is principally characteristic of spoken and informal registers. D'Achille's survey (1991: 267–75) of the emergence of *averci* for *avere*, reveals examples of *ci* with weakened locative value as early as the fifteenth century, and clear examples of *ci* devoid of locative force from the seventeenth and eighteenth centuries onwards.

9.1.2 Third person forms

The modern third person pronouns *egli ella lui lei* and *loro* have in common that their referents are, as a rule, persons,[63] and that their source is the CL demonstrative pronoun ILLUM, ILLAM, etc. The forms *egli*, *lui* and *lei* reflect the analogical influence of the relative pronoun: the CL masculine singular relative, QUI:, appears to have given rise to a masculine nominative singular demonstrative form *ILLI:, yielding OTuscan *elli*. Modern *egli* originates as a palatalized variant (cf. Ch.2: 6.2) of *elli* and gradually supplanted the latter between the thirteenth and the fifteenth centuries; a now extinct variant of *elli* is *ei* (later *e'*). *Lui*, originally a non-nominative ('oblique') form, reflects late Latin genitive and dative singular forms *ILLUIUS (for CL ILLIUS) and ILLUI (for CL ILLI), modelled in turn on the corresponding forms of the relative pronoun, CUIUS and CUI (the source, also, of modern relative *cui*). On the analogy of ILLUI, the feminine singular genitive and dative form *ILLÆ (itself replacing CL ILLIUS and ILLI), becomes *ILLÆI, whence *lei*.[64] OTuscan has plural forms *egli* and *elle*. But these rapidly fall into desuetude, and are rivalled by the masculine plural *eglino* and, less commonly, feminine *elleno* (cf. 8.3.3). The plural oblique form *loro* (for both genders) originates in the masculine genitive plural form ILLORUM.

We observed in 1.2 that nouns denoting persons tend to preserve nominative case forms in nouns; it is consistent with this observation that precisely those pronouns denoting persons, *egli* and *ella*, should have preserved distinct nominative forms (rather than the non-nominative *lui* and *lei*). But these, too, have tended to recede in favour of oblique forms, beginning, in the thirteenth century, with the masculine singular. By the late fourteenth century, the third person subject forms give way to the originally oblique forms *lui, lei* and *loro*. The prescriptivism of the sixteenth century firmly locates *egli* and *ella* in literary usage, but these wither away in spoken language. For a detailed account of the introduction of the oblique forms, see D'Achille (1991: Ch.6).

The third person pronouns *esso essi essa esse* originate in CL IPSU(M), IPSA(M), etc. (meaning 'self same'), and have never distinguished case morphologically. They may have both human and non-human referents, although the modern language tends to differentiate [+human] *lui* and [–human] *esso*. In modern Italian, all these forms are rare, and largely restricted to elevated and literary registers. In familiar speech, [+human] referents are expressed by *lui* and *lei*, whilst [–human] referents are often represented by the demonstratives *questo*, *questa*, etc, although *lui* and *lei* are sometimes used in the modern spoken language with [–human] reference as well (cf. Berruto (1990: 74f.)). In southern dialects **'essu**, etc. provides the principal third person pronoun form.

Egli, *ella* and *esso* are semi-clitic in that, while they can be syntactically separated from their verb, they cannot stand in isolation (for example, as answers to questions), nor can they be conjoined with other noun phrases (e.g., ***Egli e Maria si parlano* 'He and Maria talk to each other').[65] They are further differentiated syntactically from *lui* and *lei* by the fact that they are purely anaphoric, never deictic.

The third person direct object clitic forms *lo, la, li, le* continue the final syllable of the Latin accusative demonstratives ILLU(M), ILLA(M), ILLOS, ILLAS. The OTuscan masculine singular forms *'l, 'el, il* derive from ILLU(M), stressed on the initial syllable. The Latin datives ILLI (masculine and feminine singular) and ILLIS (masculine and feminine plural) are the source of the indirect object form *gli* (also *li* and *i* in OTuscan) which signals feminine, as well as masculine, singular and plural dative (cf. Rohlfs (1968: 154–7; 163f.)). The feminine form *le*, which has asserted itself in the literary language over earlier *gli* or *li*, probably arises from an alternative feminine singular dative form *ILLÆ. *Gli* (< ILLIS) is the normal and indigenous plural form in Tuscan dialects; the third person plural IO pronoun *loro* (from the Latin genitive ILLORU(M)) is not an indigenous Italo-Romance dative form, but is probably of Gallo-Romance origin (cf. Rohlfs (1968:164)). It is restricted to formal registers, and its exotic origins are reflected in its still imperfect integration into the clitic system: unlike other clitics it is bisyllabic; syntactically, it is invariably positioned to the right of the verb, although it is sometimes positioned to the left in OTuscan; in AUXILIARY + PAST PARTICIPLE structures, it may follow either the past participle, or the auxiliary (*ho parlato loro, ho loro parlato* 'I have spoken to them' – see also Cardinaletti (1991)). The masculine plural direct object form *li*, and the indirect object *gli*, are originally identical: both are *li*, with the positional variant *gli* occurring before a vowel. Later, the two allomorphs occur in either phonological environment both in their direct and indirect object functions; this and functional formal ambiguity has played a role in the reordering of some clitic sequences (see below). Their modern specialization as direct object form (*li*) and indirect object form (*gli*) becomes firmly established only in the nineteenth century.

It is a feature of the spoken, as opposed to the written, language that *gli* also functions as a third person plural indirect object form, instead of *loro*. In very informal registers *gli* also replaces feminine singular indirect object *le*. Generalized use of indirect object *gli*, particularly as a feminine singular pronoun, is usually identified as a feature of 'italiano popolare' (cf. Cortelazzo (1972: 86–8)).

9.2 Comitative pronouns

Old Tuscan had a further series of 'comitative' pronouns, continuing Latin pronouns followed by the particle CUM 'with' (e.g., MECU(M), NOBISCU(M)), meaning 'with me', 'with you', etc.: *meco*; *teco*; *seco*; *nosco*; *vosco*; *seco*. The singular forms are still occasionally found in the literary language as late as the nineteenth century.[66] However, the third person forms, from CL reflexive SECU(M), lose their reflexive association: Cellini *stetti seco* 'I stayed with him', Bandello *aveva voluto venir a visitarla e starsi un pezzo a ragionar seco* 'he had wanted to come and visit her and stay a while to talk to her'.

9.3 Clitic subject pronouns

A striking deviation between Italian and Florentine, which was probably developing by the beginning of the sixteenth century, is the use of obligatory subject clitic pronouns; Renzi (1991) gives a historical account. Northern Italy, including much of northern Tuscany (and Florence) displays clitic subject, as well as object, pronouns (cf. Rohlfs (1968: 140–7)); these subject pronouns are usually obligatory. Modern Italian follows central and southern dialects in possessing only non-subject clitics; but modern Florentine makes extensive use of the obligatory clitic subject pronouns *i* or *e* (first person singular), second person singular *tu* or *t* (before a vowel), first person plural *nu*, second person plural *vu*. The subject clitic is used most consistently in the third person: masculine singular *e* or, before a vowel, *gli*, feminine singular *la*; masculine plural *e*; feminine plural *le*: e.g., *gli è vero* 'it is true'; *la viene* 'she's coming', etc.

9.4 The syntax of clitics

Part of the definition of clitics is that they are obligatorily adjacent to some 'host', which in Italian is the verb. Unlike inflectional morphemes, however, their position is variable, in that they must be either proclitic (positioned to the left of the verb) or enclitic (positioned to its right). In early Italo-Romance, the collocation of clitics in relation to their hosts is relatively free, the major constraint on their position being a matter of clause structure. According to a principle of syntactic distribution of clitics in Romance languages discerned by Tobler (for OFrench) and by Mussafia for Italian (hereafter the 'Tobler–Mussafia Law'), clitics are debarred in clause-initial position,[67] with the effect that enclisis is obligatory at the beginning of the clause. Thus, from the Novellino (thirteenth century), *menolvi* (= *ve lo menò* 'he led him there'); *el greco la prese, e miselasi in pugno e puoselasi all'orecchie* 'the Greek took it, and placed it in his fist and put it to his ears'; *e pure alzasi e mostrolli il culo* 'and also he gets up and showed him his arse' (note that *e*; *ma*; *e pure* are clause conjoiners and, being *external* to the clause, do not count as clause-initial elements); from the Divine Comedy, *dicerolti* (= *te lo dirò*) *molto breve* 'I'll tell you it very briefly'; *guardommi un poco* 'he looked at me a while'; *e menommi al cespuglio* 'and he led me to the bush'; Macinghi Strozzi (late fifteenth century) *Concedacene Iddio la grazia, e di male ci guardi Iddio* 'may God give us grace of it, and may God save us from evil'. When the verb is not at the beginning of the clause, proclisis is the norm in the medieval language: Novellino *e poi lo fece chiamare* 'and then he had him summoned'; *non mi rispondere* 'don't answer me'; *or mi di'* (= *dimmi*) *donna* 'now tell me lady'; Divine Comedy *mal volontier lo dico, ma sforzami la tua chiara favella* 'I say it unwillingly, but your clear speech forces me'; Decameron *io il ti prometto e farollo* 'I promise you it, and I'll do it'; *tanto mi tocca che io mi sveglio* 'he touches me so much that I wake up', and so forth.

Outside clause-initial position, proclisis is general after relative pronouns, subordinating conjunctions, interrogative particles, predicate complements, negative particles (such as *non*), and preceding direct and indirect objects. Proclisis is predominant after most adverbs and adverbial or prepositional phrases, and after subject nouns or pronouns. However, enclisis is already obligatory in the thirteenth century with infinitives preceded by a preposition (*per farlo* 'in order to do it' not ***per lo fare*). In this respect OTuscan differs from southern dialects, where proclisis is the norm with infinitives governed by prepositions, e.g., Neapolitan *pe la vedere* 'in order to see her'. The reason for this constraint in OTuscan is probably that positioning a clitic directly after a preposition would come into conflict with the principle that prepositions are followed by disjunctive pronouns (cf. Rohlfs (1968: 185)).

9.4.1 The origins of verbal clitics, and the Tobler–Mussafia Law

A detailed account of the origins of the Romance verbal clitics is provided in Wanner (1987). In broad terms, its is usually assumed that they emerged as follows: CL tended to conform to a principle widespread in early Indo-European languages (and beyond – cf. Spencer (1991: 355)) such that unstressed elements (including unstressed pronouns) appeared in the position immediately following the first element of the clause, the so-called 'Wackernagel Position'.[68] In addition, the change from a predominant OV word order to VO (cf. Ch.4: 1.1), and various other factors favouring movement of the verb towards the beginning of the clause – particularly in imperative and presentative structures – entails a massive increase in the incidence of verbs at or near the beginning of the clause. The resulting frequent juxtaposition of verbs with pronouns, with the unstressed pronoun either preceding or following the verb, together with the fact that the object pronouns are, after all, arguments of the verb, contributes to the reanalysis of the unstressed pronouns as clitic forms which have a verb as their host. The clitics may also take the presentative particle *ecco* 'lo/behold', as a host.[69]

The major change in the more recent history of Italian has been the liberation of clitic placement from dependency on clause structure, and the emergence of an ever increasing sensitivity to morphosyntactic properties of the host verb. In modern Italian clitic pronouns precede all finite verb forms (i.e., those forms encoding tense and person): *te lo prometto* 'I promise you it'; *lo farò* 'I'll do it'; *ne parlavo* 'I talked of it', etc. All non-finite verb foms (past participles, gerunds, infinitives) and all imperatives (save those formed from the third person present forms of the subjunctive) select enclitic pronouns: *fattolo, uscì* 'having done it, she left'; *non avendolo visto, ce ne andammo* 'not having seen him, we went'; *debbo parlartene* 'I must talk to you about it'; *adesso facciamolo* 'now let's do it', etc.

By the thirteenth century conformity to the Tobler–Mussafia Law is already being undermined in clauses occupying second position in the sentence, for example after preceding subordinate clauses and after the protases (see Ch.4: 9.4) of 'IF'-clauses: Novellino *Papirio veggendo la volontà della madre, si pensò una bella bugia* 'Papirio seeing his mother's wish, thought up a fine lie'; Dante *se tanto scendi, gli potrai vedere* 'if you descend so far, you will be able to see them'; Macinghi Strozzi *se n'avete bisogno, lo dite e ve ne manderò* 'if you need some, say so and I'll send you some'. There is a tendency for encliticization to non-finite forms of the verb from the time of the earliest texts (cf. Wanner (1987: 266f.)), probably favoured by the fact that gerunds and infinitives are, themselves, clausal constituents, and frequently occurred at the beginning of their clause, selecting enclitic pronouns. By the fifteenth century, a major reanalysis is under way, whereby clitic position is reinterpreted as a function of the morphosyntactic category of the host verb. But this is a change in which, according to Weinapple (1983), Florence is in the rearguard. In Florence in the early sixteenth century the Tobler–Mussafia Law still prevails, while proclisis has become general in the literary language outside Florence. Encliticization becomes the rule with gerunds, infinitives and participles. After *non*, proclisis is generally found with these non-finite verb forms in the sixteenth and seventeenth centuries: Cellini *non gli dato altro che una ceffata. . .* 'not having given him more than a slap'; Carletti *non si potendo conservare* 'not being able to be kept'; *il non ti vedere ogni dì* 'not seeing you every day'; *egli disse di non mi cognoscere* 'he said he didn't know me', etc. But Weinapple has demonstrated that this is a development peculiar to Florence, which failed to establish itself in the face of literary Italian as used in the rest of Italy, where enclisis in these constructions was already established.

It is in the nature of imperatives that they tend to occur clause-initially, and that consequently they select enclitic pronouns. The reanalysis of enclisis as an inherent property of imperatives establishes itself much more slowly than with non-finite forms (cf. Wanner (1987: 277)). Proclisis with negative imperatives remains the norm in the literary language until the nineteenth century (cf. Weinapple (1983:

51)), and is optionally possible to this day: *non facciamolo* or *non lo facciamo* 'let's not do it'; *non parlarmi* or *non mi parlare* 'don't talk to me'; *non ditelo* or *non lo dite* 'don't say it', etc. Remnants of proclisis with positive imperatives are observable in Tuscany and some southern dialects (cf. Rohlfs (1968: 172)).

Enclisis with finite verb forms becomes rare in the sixteenth century, although it survives to this day in the now lexicalized expression *qualsiasi* 'any', in deliberately archaizing or didactic styles, (*aggiungasi* 'let it be added'; *dicasi* 'let it be said'; *come volevasi dimostrare* 'Q.E.D.'), and in the language of advertisements (*vendesi* 'for sale'; *affittasi* 'to let'; *comprasi* 'for purchase'). In the last case, enclisis probably has more to do with economies of space in advertising copy, than with retention of an archaism. Weinapple (1983) suggests that the didactic and archaizing connotations may have been present already in the sixteenth century. The probable cause of the reanalysis of proclisis as an inherent feature of finite verb forms is that they (unlike their non-finite counterparts) are frequently preceded by their grammatical subjects. The Tobler–Mussafia Law would have given rise, therefore, to a high incidence of preverbal clitics, where the grammatical subject is the first element in the clause.

9.4.2 Clitic concatenations

The morphology and ordering of concatenations of clitic pronouns constitutes one of the most intricate chapters in the history of Italian.[70] Such ordering is multiply opaque, in that it rarely mirrors the normal order of the corresponding phrasal constituents, and is not always consistently predictable from the function of the individual clitics. For thirteenth century Florentine, it is appropriate to distinguish between *case-sensitive* and *case-insensitive* clitics: the former differentiate direct object (DO) and indirect object (IO) functions, both morphologically (e.g., *lo* vs. *li*), and syntactically, in that IO clitics generally precede DO clitics, except that *third person* DO forms precede IO forms. The remaining clitics are morphologically invariant for case, and their syntactic position is generally invariant, regardless of case function: *mi* precedes clitic *ti*, *vi* and *ci* (as in modern Italian);[71] *vi* (personal or locative) usually precedes *ti* and *ci*, and *ti* usually precedes *ci*; *ne* is ordered after all other clitics (e.g., Libro dei sette savi *portarlone* 'they took it away'), and the reflexive pronoun *si* is ordered after all other clitics except *ne*. We may surmise that the ordering of *mi* and *ti* before *si* mirrors the greater prominence of discourse participants (speaker and addressee) over the purely anaphoric third person *si*, while the initial positioning of *mi* may reflect the greater psychological prominence of the first person pronoun to the speaker. Such principles do not apply, however, to the ordering of plural *ci* and *vi* – and it is perhaps significant that these, unlike *mi* and *ti*, were not originally personal pronouns. Collocation of *ne* at the end of the clitic chain may reflect the relatively late integration into the clitic system of continuants of the locative adverb INDE: some Romance languages (e.g., Romanian) apparently never developed a clitic from this source, and in others (e.g., Castilian) it failed to become established, and was abandoned at an early date; and the failure of the vowel **e** to undergo raising to [**i**] in Florentine (cf. ME > *mi*) suggests that *ne* may have originated as a *stressed* form. The case-sensitive third person forms have notably greater mobility in the clitic chain than do other clitics: however such mobility is to be explained, it may be significant that the relevant forms also originated as demonstrative, rather than as personal, pronouns.

The major changes in the organization of clitic concatenations since the thirteenth century are:

– Reordering of third person IO clitics (including *si*) before third person DO clitics.
– Reordering of *ne* before third person DO clitics.
– Appearance of the allomorphs *me*; *te*; *ce*; *ve*; *glie*, which were originally restricted to the environment of a following *ne* (*me ne*, etc.), before third persons DO clitic (*me lo*; *te la*, etc.).

The ordering in thirteenth- and fourteenth-century Florentine of third person DO clitics before IO clitics (e.g., Novellino *e miselasi in pugno e puoselasi all'orecchie* 'and he put it in his fist and placed it to his ears'; Divine Comedy *dicerolti molto breve* 'I'll tell you it very briefly') is doubly aberrant, in that all other IO clitics precede DO clitics, and that in nearly all other Italo-Romance dialects (including Sienese) the order is exclusively IO–DO. Examples of *me lo*; *te lo*, etc., begin to appear from the late thirteenth century (they are slightly predominant in the Decameron), and this order is fully established by the fifteenth century. The reversal of ordering in such sequences seems to have gone hand in hand with the replacement of *mi*; *ti*; *si*, etc., by *me*; *te*; *se*. Melander (1929) argues that the forms *me*; *te*, etc., rather than *mi*; *ti*, reveal that the re-ordered sequences have their origins in dialects in which, unlike Florentine, atonic [**e**] had not been raised to [**i**] (cf. Ch.2: 4.6.1). *Me ne* and *gliene* are also held to reflect a non-Florentine source, although Castellani (1952: 103) suggests that these forms are the result of an assimilation of [**i**] to [**e**] before the [**e**] of *ne*, and that this development in turn contributed to the substitution of *mi*, etc., by *me*, etc., in other combinations of pronouns. It seems, at any rate, that the allomorphy of *me*/*mi*; *te*/*ti*, etc. is at least in part due to borrowing, perhaps from some other prestigious variety, such as Sienese.[72] Significantly, those clitic sequences which have remained stable throughout the history of Florentine (e.g., *mi ti*; *mi ci*; *vi ti*) show no sign of replacing [**i**] by [**e**]. However, the sequences *me ne*; *te ne*, etc., which are present from the earliest records of Tuscan, and possibly reflect an early ***m ene** (< ME INDE), prosecute a wholly indigenous development (see Rohlfs (1968: 167)). Lombard's suggestion (1934: 40f.) that a contributory factor in the establishment of the *me lo* pattern may have been the very high incidence of words ending in the sequence of sounds VOWEL + [**l**] + VOWEL (e.g., *cavolo* 'cabbage'; *angelo* 'angel'; *utile* 'useful'; *possibile* 'possible', etc.) is far from implausible, if we bear in mind Tuttle's observations (1974 and Ch.2: 4.6.4.1) that endings of this kind might also have contributed to a major reorganization of the Tuscan atonic vowel system.

From the late thirteenth century *ne*, ordered after all other clitics in OFlorentine begins to migrate to the left of the DO clitics *lo*, *la*, *li*, *le*, and occurs there regularly by the fifteenth century. The order *ne lo*, etc., is already the predominant pattern in other Italo-Romance dialects, including some Tuscan ones, such as Sienese, so that Florentine may also have imitated external models. But the facts are not wholly consistent with the hypothesis of borrowing since, unlike Florentine, most dialects place *ne* before the third person IO form as well.[73] The *ne lo* pattern begins to appear about a quarter of a century later than *me lo* etc., a fact which leads Lombard (1934: 44) to propose, in effect, that *ne lo* is introduced on the model of *me lo*. Similarly, the rise of the reordered sequence INDIRECT OBJECT REFLEXIVE CLITIC + DIRECT OBJECT CLITIC, seen in *se gli porta* or *se li porta*, meaning 'she carries them to/for herself' is argued by Lombard (1934: 42f.) to be the source of a tendency, which persisted into the nineteenth century (Lombard (1934: 51–4)) for the *direct* object reflexive clitic as well, to be placed before the *indirect* object clitics *gli* or *li*: e.g., Manzoni (Promessi Sposi) *il vecchio se gli accostò* 'the old man approached him'.[74]

The reasons for reordering third person DO clitic pronouns after other clitics are uncertain, but it may be more than a matter of simple dialect borrowing. Reordering of the DO after IO clitics might be a response to the rise of predominant *proclisis* in finite verbs, and to the fact that the DO is a less 'peripheral' argument of the verb, in that it, unlike the IO, directly undergoes the action expressed by the verb. The greater 'centrality' of the DO may tend to be reflected in its collocation in a position immediately adjacent to the verb. For as long as enclisis is predominant, the order DO–IO (*mandalomi* 'he sends it me') allows the DO to appear next to the verb. In proclisis, however, the DO is *separated* from the verb by the IO clitic (e.g., *lo mi manda* 'he sends me it'). It may be the case that, with the rise of predominant proclisis, the discrepancy between syntactic 'peripheralness' and semantic 'centrality', resulting from proclitic positioning of the DO, was corrected by a general reordering of the DO to the right of the IO, so that the DO was again immediately adjacent to the verb. This hypothesis seems to be borne out by the evidence of thirteenth-century texts (see Pearce (1991: 260–2)), in which the reordered sequences appear earliest in preverbal, rather than postverbal, position, with postposition of the DO becoming general only during the fourteenth century.

By the late thirteenth century sequences of third person DO and IO clitics are subject to neutralization of number and gender distinctions. The combinations *lili*, *lile*, *glile*, *lele*, *gliele*, *gliene*, *gnene* each represent all the possible permutations of gender and number in DO–IO sequences: e.g., Novellino *lile donò* "he gave it to him'; Cellini *gliene faceva dire quel galant' huomo* 'that gentleman had them said to him' (scil. 'the words', etc.). The origins of these grammatically neutralized fused forms await explanation;[75] what is certain is that, after the inversion of DO–IO order, the second element *le* came to be identified with the feminine plural DO clitic *le*. Accordingly, such sequences were reanalysed as comprising an IO clitic, *glie*,[76] followed by a DO clitic, (whence masculine *glielo do*, plural *glieli do*; *gliele do*, etc.). Similarly *gliene* is reinterpreted as IO + *ne*.

The clitic concatenations are also subject to constraints debarring successive phonologically identical clitics. Sequences such as **ci ci* or **vi vi* have never been attested (we find *vi ci* instead).[77] The sequence **ne ne* is not allowed. Similarly, reflexive *si* and 'impersonal' *si* can never be conjoined: in such cases, the reflexive clitic appears as *ci* (*ci si fa male* 'one hurts oneself', etc.).[78] The 'neutralized' DO–IO sequences *lili lile* etc., discussed above, were rapidly replaced during the fifteenth century by *gliele*, *glile* etc., in which we may discern yet another example of phonological dissimilation of successive clitics.

9.5 The demonstrative pronouns

The demonstrative pronouns *questo*, *questa*, etc., are formally identical to the demonstrative adjectives. However, like the third person pronouns, they have a masculine singular personal form in **-i** (*questi* and *quegli* (also *cotesti*)), and like the pronouns they developed oblique case forms in *-ui*, *-ei* and *-oro* (*costui costei costoro* and *colui colei coloro*) (see 9.1.2) although, as early as the fourteenth century, these were being employed as subject forms. *Costui*, etc., corresponds to the adjective *codesto*, and like it carries pejorative connotations. The form *colui*, etc. has acquired the specialized function of pronominal antecedents of relative pronouns (*colui/colei/coloro* + *che* = 'he/she/they who'). *Questi*, and especially *quegli*, are restricted to literary usage, and often have the anaphoric function of indicating, respectively, 'the latter' and 'the former'. Of similar origin to *questi* and *costui* are *altri* 'somebody else', and its oblique form *altrui*.

Ciò is an invariant, non-personal anaphoric pronoun whose referent is usually a whole clause, or a proposition: *ciò che dice è falso* 'what he says is false'; *cioè* 'that is to say'; *ciò di cui abbiamo parlato* 'that about which we have spoken'. Its origin is reconstructable as CL ECCE HOC, literally 'behold this'. Rather like *colui* (see above), *ciò* shows signs of becoming restricted to the environment of the relative pronoun *che*, while elsewhere it gives way to *questo* or *quello*. Indeed, *questo mi piace* 'I like this' is considered by many speakers more natural than *ciò mi piace* (cf. Berruto (1990: 78)). A survivor of the CL neuter pronoun HOC also appears in *però* 'however', (< PER HOC), whose original meaning is 'therefore' (cf. modern *perciò*). For the transition to the modern adversative meaning of *però* (already present in Dante), compare the use of *per* in the sense of 'despite' in expressions such as *per quanto* meaning 'even though', 'for however much'.

9.6 Pronouns of address

The CL second person pronouns distinguished singular (TU) and plural (UOS). This system is continued in many southern Italian dialects (e.g., in Abruzzo, southern Marche, southern Puglia and parts of Campania and Calabria), but in the history of Italian (together with many other Romance dialects, among them the Italo-Romance varieties of Naples, southern Calabria, northern Puglia, Rome, Canton Ticino and Corsica), a morphological distinction has arisen, originally encoding deference towards, or respect for, the addressee, but acquiring, in more recent times, the additional function of indicating politeness, distance, or membership of a distinct social group from the speaker.[79] In about the third century, second person plural forms begin to be used for singular polite or deferential address, with corresponding verb forms (but singular adjectives): the same development is observable across many of the world's languages.[80] Of later date, and more restricted in its geographical extent (among Romance languages it is limited to Ibero-Romance and Italian, and is not well established in the Italo-Romance dialects, particularly those of the centre and south[81]), is the use of a third person pronoun, singular *Lei* and plural *Loro*. These originate in the use as forms of address of honorific nouns, rather like English 'your honour', 'your worship', 'your ladyship' – cf. Brown and Levinson (1987: 276f.); the language of the sixteenth century developed a profusion of honorifics such as *vostra signoria*; *vossignoria*;[82] *vostra eccellenza*, etc. It seems that the use of such devices received a considerable impetus from Spanish models, such as *Vuestra Merced* (> *usted*) in the sixteenth century, although the employment of third person forms is detectable as early as the thirteenth (cf. Brunet (1987: 12)). These (usually feminine) nouns are replaced by feminine third person pronouns, which are the source of modern *Ella, Lei* and plural

Loro. For the use of capital letters with these forms, see Brunet (1987: 43–7). The perception that third person address forms are a product of foreign influence prompted the Fascist authorities, in the 1930s, to denounce *Lei* in favour of the supposedly more 'Italian' polite *voi* (see Brunet (1987: 69–78)). Such denunciation served only to promote a reaction in favour of *Lei* in the post-Fascist period.

The stylistic differentiation between (originally nominative) *Ella* and (originally oblique) *Lei* permits a further differentiation in modern Italian, in the singular, between *Lei* and the strictly formal and elevated *Ella*. While the distinction between *tu* and *Lei* is firmly established in the singular, it is less so in the plural, where *voi* is still regularly directed to individuals who, singly, would be addressed as *Lei*. For many Italians, the use of polite *Loro* connotes a higher degree of formality, than does *Lei* (see Brunet (1987: 21f.)). The clitic forms of these pronouns are *La* and *Le*, although it is not uncommon to hear *lo*/*gli* where the addressee is male. The plural form corresponding to *Loro* is commonly *li* with male addressees. Adjectives qualifying *Lei* normally take the gender form corresponding to the sex of the addressee, except that the past participle usually has feminine agreement with preceding direct object clitic *La*, particularly where the vowel is elided: e.g., *L'ho vista* 'I've seen you (masculine)', etc. For contemporary usage of the pronouns, see Brunet (1987), and Berruto (1990: 93f.).

9.7 Relative and interrogative pronouns (and adjectives)

CL possessed the following relative and interrogative pronouns, of which the singular forms are given below (17):

(17)

	Relative			Interrogative		
	M	F	N	M	F	N
Nom.	QUI	QUÆ	QUOD	QUIS	QUIS	QUID
Acc.	QUEM	QUAM	QUOD	QUEM	QUEM	QUID
Gen.	CUIUS			CUIUS		
Dat.	CUI			CUI		
Abl.	QUO	QUA	QUO	QUO	QUA	QUO

The feminine and plural forms are extinct in Italo-Romance. QUOD survives as a complementizer, in some dialects (see Ch.4: 7). The genitive and dative forms survive in OTuscan as oblique (non-nominative) forms of the *relative* pronoun (*cui*), which is preserved in modern usage only after prepositions (*la donna di cui ti parlo* 'the woman about whom I am speaking to you'; *la professoressa a cui dovevo dare il libro* 'the teacher to whom I was supposed to give the book'); dative *cui* tends not to occur in modern popular usage, *a cui* being preferred. A remnant of the genitive function appears in the modern possessive relative *il* (*la*, *i*, *le*) *cui* (e.g., *un professore i cui studenti non studiano mai* 'a teacher whose students never study'). The most widely used relative pronoun, *che*, appears to be a historical amalgam of accusatives QUEM and QUID. QUID is the source of the final [**d**] observable before vowels in OTuscan, which also accounts for the fact that *che* triggers *rafforzamento sintattico* (Ch.2: 8.2): e.g., OTuscan *queste parole ched io parlo* 'these words which I speak'; modern Italian **le ˈkɔːse ke pˈpɛnsi** 'the things which you think', etc. The masculine nominative relative pronoun persists as an independent relative, equivalent to 'he/she/they anyone who' (*chi non lo sa è un ignorante* 'anyone who doesn't know it is an ignoramus'; *puoi parlare con chi vuoi* 'you can talk to whom you like'). However, *chi* (from QUI) supplants all the interrogative forms having [+human] reference (e.g., *chi canta?* 'who's singing?'; *con chi parli?* 'whom are you talking to?'; *chi hai visto?* 'whom did you see?'; *di chi è questa penna* 'whose is this pen?'; *a chi pensavi?* 'of whom were you thinking?'), leaving *che* (< QUID) for [–human] referents.

The syntactic ambiguity of relative *che*, which distinguishes neither gender nor number, can be circumvented by use of *il/la quale*, *i/le quali*, from Latin QUALIS, originally an interrogative adjective meaning 'of what kind?' In some northern dialects (e.g., of the Veneto) the [–human] interrogative *che* has been replaced by *cosa*, literally 'thing?'. In Tuscan *cosa* or *che cosa* coexists with *che*.

Latin interrogative QUIS (etc.) also functioned as an interrogative adjective, and is continued by *che*: e.g., *che libro leggi?* 'which/what book are you reading?'. *Quale* (< QUALE(M) 'of what kind?'), also performs this function: e.g., *quale libro leggi?*.

The use of so called 'polyvalent *che*' (especially in the spoken language and in the usage of less educated speakers) as an all-purpose relative marker, performing the multiple functions of subject, direct object, indirect object, locative,[83] partitive, possessive and temporal relative, is shown by D'Achille (1991: 205–60) to be present at least from the time of the earliest surviving texts. The non-subject forms appear in two syntactic types, both of which seem also to be of great antiquity (cf. Berruto (1990: 131)): one in which the function of the relative is not signalled at all (e.g., *fare una guerra che* (= *di cui*) *nemmeno capiamo lo scopo* 'to fight a war whose purpose we don't even understand'; *un barbiere borghese che* (= *da cui*) *m'andavo a tosarmi prima* 'a civilian barber I went to to get my hair cut before'), and another, sometimes labelled an 'analytic' relative, in which the relative marker is accompanied by an appropriate clitic form (or a possessive adjective, in the case of possessive relatives), expressing its function:[84] e.g., *in questa zona che ci* (= *dove*) *siamo* 'in this zone we're in'; *Mario B. che l'hanno portato l'altro giorno* 'Mario B. who they carried the other day'; *un soldato affianco a me che gli* (= *a cui*) *dissi io* 'a soldier beside me who I told'; *una donna che suo* (= *il cui*) *marito era morto* 'a woman whose husband had died'. While 'polyvalent *che*' characterizes the usage (spoken and written) of less educated speakers, it is also to be encountered in the speech even of educated Italians. It is at its rarest in formal written language. Berruto's observation (1990: 125f.), that in modern 'italiano popolare' the construction *che* + clitic case marker is especially common with non-restrictive, and [+animate], object relatives, is also confirmed by D'Achille's survey (1991: 259) of texts from earlier centuries.

9.8 Indefinite, negative and distributive pronouns

The indefinite pronouns *qualcuno* 'someone' ([+human]) and *qual(che)cosa* 'something' ([−human]) are transparently derivable from *qualche* 'some'[85] and *uno* 'one' or *cosa* 'thing'. *Uno* is also available as an indefinite [+human] pronoun. *Qualcosa* is rather less transparent in its structure since it selects masculine agreement, despite the feminine gender of *cosa*. The negative *nulla* 'nothing', particularly characteristic of northern Tuscany, continues a Latin feminine NULLA(M) (RE(M)) 'no thing'; *niente* 'nothing' is of disputed origin, but its most widely accepted source (cf. Rohlfs (1968: 218)) is *NE GENTE, although the semantic development whereby GENS 'race', 'people' loses its [+human] reference is obscure. The [+human] *nessuno* 'nobody' derives from NEC + IPSE + UNU(M) 'not even one' (also OTuscan *niuno* < NEC UNU(M)). The OTuscan *veruno* ('somebody', or 'nobody' in negative contexts – e.g., *non viene veruno* 'nobody comes') reflects a combination of Latin UNU(M) 'one' with UERUM 'real', 'true', employed as an intensifying prefix. The distributive *ognuno* 'everyone' is transparently *ogni* 'each' (< OMNE(M)) + *uno* 'one'; cf. the [−human] *ogni cosa*. Tuscan *catuno* 'each one' (usually *cadauno* in the literary language) reflects Greek distributive KATA + Latin UNU(M); *ciascuno* 'each one' is of Gallo-Romance origin (cf. French *chacun*, from a fusion of KATA with Latin QUEMQUE 'each').

10 The prepositions

Italian prepositions can be subdivided into those consisting of bare roots, and originally 'analytic' structures, composed of historically independent words. The former generally continue CL prepositions (e.g., *a* < AD; *con* < CUM; *di* < DE, *in* < IN), often having little intrinsic semantic content. Their function, especially that of *a* and *di* – cf. Rizzi (1988: 511) – is determined largely by the context in which they occur. The low semantic autonomy of certain synthetic prepositions is also apparent in the ease with which phonological similarities between etymologically distinct prepositions can favour, diachronically, their functional, and sometimes formal, fusion: INFRA 'below' and INTRA 'within, between' yield the now functionally identical *fra* and *tra*; the continuant of PER 'through' has absorbed the functions of CL PRO 'for', 'in place of' (*l'ho fatto per lui* 'I did it for him'; *l'ho scambiato per un altro* 'I mistook him for someone else'); *entro* 'by', 'within' arises from a confusion between INTER 'between' and INTRO 'in'; *sino*, exactly equivalent to *fino* (< CL FINE(M) 'end'), represents confusion of the latter and OTuscan *sì* 'until'. A number of original nouns and adjectives (cf. 1.2) are the source of Italian prepositions: *durante* 'during'; *nonostante* 'despite'; *senza* 'without'; *tramite* 'by means of'; *lungo* 'along'; *rasente* (*a*) 'hard against'. *Su* 'on', and *sotto* 'under', derive from the adverbs SURSU(M) 'upwards' and SUBTUS 'beneath'.

A common Romance device for the formation of temporal or locative adverbial expressions is prefixation of **de** to a noun, adjective or preposition (cf. Italian *di sopra* 'upstairs'; *di sotto* 'downstairs', etc.). The modern prepositions *dietro* 'behind' (< DE RETRO), *dentro* 'inside'(< DE INTRO); *davanti* 'in front of' (< DE AB ANTE); *dopo* 'after' (< DE POST) originate in such structures. The preposition *da* probably derives from combination of DE and AB, both meaning 'from'. The use of *da* to mean 'at' (location in or toward), a function expressed in CL by AD, suggests a coalescence of DE AB with DE AD[86] (see also Robustelli (1992: 100f.)).

Italian has acquired new analytic prepositions having the structure *di/a/in* + NOUN + *di/a*: *accanto a* 'beside'; *allato a* 'beside'; *affianco a* 'beside'; *appiede di* 'at the foot of'; *dirimpetto a* 'opposite'; *in mezzo a* 'in the middle of'; *in cima a* 'at the top of'; *in fondo a* 'at the bottom of'; *in faccia a* 'in the face of'; *di fronte a* 'in front of'. These transparently originate in locative noun phrases of the type 'by the side of', where initial *di/a/in* indicates locative function, and following *di* or *a* are complementizers linking the prepositional noun with the modified noun. The use of *a* as a complementizer linking prepositions with nouns has been generalized to other prepositions (e.g., *sopra* < SUPER AD; *davanti a*), and optionally (especially where motion is implicit – cf. Rizzi (1988: 522)) to *attraverso a* 'across'; *dentro a* 'inside'; *dietro a* 'behind'; *lungo a* 'along'; *rasente a* 'hard against'; *sotto a* 'under', and even *sopra a* 'above'.

A problem awaiting historical elucidation is the use of *di* when prepositions precede a definite personal pronoun: *verso di lui* 'towards him'; *dopo di te* 'after you'; *fra di loro* 'between them'; *senza di lei* 'without her'; *contro di te* 'against you'.

11 Derivational word formation

Certain grammatical structures serve both to derive new words from existing words, and to relate words to each other. Although lengthy and detailed lists of the methods of derivational word formation acquired by Italian have been drawn up (notably Rohlfs (1969); and Tekavčić (1980 III)), a study of their semantic and structural evolution remains one of the major desiderata of Italian historical linguistics. We shall make no attempt here even to cover the ground already covered by Rohlfs and Tekavčić, and shall restrict ourselves instead to a few general remarks about the evolution of such structures.

11.1 Compounding

Compounding involves the fusion into a single word (usually a noun or adjective) of previously autonomous words. Its hallmark is a fixed order of the compounded elements, and the impossibility of separating them. The transparency of compounds (the possibility of analysing them into component elements) is a matter of degree. At one extreme are semantically opaque ('exocentric') compounds, whose referential meaning cannot be derived from any of its components parts. For example, *pungitopo* means the plant 'holly', but the literal meaning of its components is 'prick mouse', from *pungi* 'prick' and *topo* 'mouse', presumably because its leaves are thought to 'prick mice'? A method of compounding which has become particularly common over the last century, is juxtaposition of nouns. Compounds thus formed remain highly transparent, and are sometimes separated orthographically: *formato tessera* 'passport sized (photograph)'; *senzatetto* 'homeless', 'having no roof'; *rosso fuoco* 'flame (lit. 'fire') red'; *treno merci* 'goods train'. But the semantic relationship between components is often not exhaustively derivable from its elements. *Pescespada* 'swordfish' and *grillotalpa* 'mole cricket' contain clearly recognizable autonomous words, and have identical internal structures, but the former means 'fish, part of whose anatomy looks like a sword – a swordfish', and the latter 'cricket which (because it lives underground) is like a mole'.

The first element of a compound frequently deviates morphologically from the corresponding autonomous word. Many CL compounds displayed an element [**i**] – of uncertain origin – following the stem of the first part of the compound: CAPRIMULGUS 'goatsucker', UINIUIORAX 'wine guzzling', and an unexplained feature of some Italian compounds, possibly a matter of semi-learnèd imitation of CL models, is the appearance of a linking [**i**] in forms which are not inherited from

CL: e.g., *capinera* 'blackcap'; *pettirosso* 'robin redbreast'. A Romance innovation (see Tekavčić (1980 III: 206f.)), not foreshadowed in CL, is the formation of compound nouns and adjectives of the form VERB + NOUN. Italian has also acquired compound nouns having the structure VERB + VERB. A structurally and semantically peculiar characteristic of these compounded verb forms is that they are always morphologically identical to the second person singular imperative of the verb: e.g., *battiscopa* 'skirting board' (literally 'beat broom'); *baciamano* 'hand kissing' (literally 'kiss hand'); *coprifuoco* 'curfew' (literally 'cover fire'); *girasole* 'sunflower' (literally 'turn sun'); *portamoneta* 'purse' (literally 'carry change'); *spartiacque* 'watershed' (literally 'separate waters'); *dormiveglia* 'doze' (literally 'sleep wake'); *fuggi fuggi* 'rush' (literally 'flee flee'), etc. The motivation for the use in such cases of a form identical to the imperative is obscure, and the presence of an imperative would be very hard to understand in forms such as *girasole* (one would hardly be likely to order the flowers to turn to the sun). Whatever the origins of this structure, it constitutes in the modern language a morphological peculiarity of the verbal elements of compound nouns and adjectives which reduces their morphological autonomy. Some compounds are also morphologically opaque to the extent that grammatical categories are signalled only by word-final inflection. The first element is morphologically invariant: the (now rare) plural *pomidoro* 'tomatoes' (literally, 'fruits of gold'),[87] and *capicuochi* 'head chefs'; *casseforti* 'strong boxes', are structurally transparent, reflecting their source as the syntagms *pomi d'oro*; *capi cuochi*; *casse forti*; while *pomodori*; *capocuochi*, with internal structural invariance, have clearly been reanalysed as words, thereby losing the structural autonomy of their components. In many compounds, such morphological opacification is complete: we have only *i capolavori* 'the masterpieces', not ***i capilavori*. Others inflect only the first element (where that element is the 'head' of the compound): *i pescispada* 'the swordfishes'; *i grillitalpa* 'the mole crickets'. Compounds comprising two adjectives inflect only the second element: *i sordomuti* 'the deaf and dumb'.

The elements of Italian compounds remain autonomous to the extent that:

(i) They *tend* to reflect the syntactic order of verb phrases, noun phrases, or adjective phrases to which they correspond in meaning[88]: NOUN + ADJECTIVE *camposanto* 'cemetery' (literally 'holy field'); *pettirosso* '(robin) redbreast'; *terraferma* 'mainland' (literally 'firm land'); VERB + OBJECT NOUN: *portacenere* 'ashtray' (literally 'carry ash'); *passamontagna* 'balaclava' (literally 'pass mountain'); *lanciamissili* 'missile launcher' (literally 'launch missiles'); *apriscatole* 'tin opener' (literally 'open boxes'); PREPOSITION + NOUN: *senzatetto* 'homeless person' (literally 'without root'). Combinations of ADJECTIVE + NOUN possibly reflect the order of syntagms such as ADJECTIVE + *come* 'like' + NOUN: *nerofumo* 'lampblack' (literally 'smoke black' *perhaps* reflecting *nero come il fumo* 'black like smoke'). Some compounds of the structure NOUN + NOUN seem to reflect the order of structures of the type NOUN + PREPOSITION + NOUN, or NOUN + RELATIVE CLAUSE: *capostazione* 'station master' (literally, 'station head', perhaps reflecting *capo della stazione* 'head of the station'), *cassapanca* 'box seat' (literally, 'chest bench', perhaps reflecting *una cassa che è (anche) una panca* 'a chest which is (also) a bench'), etc. But this syntactic resemblance to other structures of the same meaning is by no means universally valid: a *batticuore* 'palpitations' is not an implement that 'beats the heart' (cf. *batti il cuore* 'you beat the heart'); rather, it corresponds to *il cuore batte* 'the heart beats'.

(ii) They possess certain phonological properties of independent words. Although *terra-* 'earth' and *porta-* 'door', do not carry primary stress, they are optionally pronounced with the low mid vowels which occur in the stressed syllables of the corresponding independent words, in **tɛrra'ferma** *terraferma*, **pɔrta'tʃenere** *portacenere*. The presence of the low mid vowels is accompanied by a 'secondary' stress, reflecting the stress pattern of the corresponding word (see Lepschy (1992a)). In regional varieties of Italian which voice word-internal intervocalic [**s**] (cf. Ch.5: 3.1.3.4), voicing is absent within compounds. Thus northern Italian **kampo'santo**, not ****kampo'zanto** *camposanto*.

(iii) They sometimes inflect like independent words (see above). Another indicator of autonomy is that masculine compounds whose final element is a feminine ending *-a* do not inflect their final element. We have (optional) plural *i portaceneri* (*cenere* 'ash' is feminine), but *i cavalcavia* 'the flyovers' (literally 'straddle road'). In principle, one might expect a regular masculine plural: ***i cavalcavii*. That such forms are debarred seems to reflect a residual morphological autonomy of the feminine noun, since feminines in *-a* do not normally form their plurals in *-i*. The other possibility, that the second element *via* should inflect like an ordinary feminine plural (***i cavalcavie*) is not admitted, because masculine plural words never terminate in *-e*.

11.2 Affixation

A common method of word formation in Italo-Romance, as in Latin, is the attachment of affixes to the roots of existing words. There is a vast range of such affixes (whose history is documented in detail in Rohlfs (1969: 347–471)),[89] and we must limit ourselves here to a few general observations. As a rule, prefixes display greater structural and semantic autonomy than do suffixes. Many original suffixes are no longer analysable as independent elements of word structure. Most of the generalizations made below appear to have held throughout the history of Italian.

Prefixation is rarer than suffixation. Many of the prefixes found in Italian are of learnèd origin, and are borrowed from Latin or Greek (e.g., *anti-* 'against', 'anti-'; *retro-* 'backwards'; *inter-* 'between'; *para-* 'alongside'). One originally learnèd prefix which has acquired a novel meaning in the modern language is *auto-*, 'self-' (e.g., *autocritica* 'self criticism'; *autoritratto* 'self-portrait'). Because of *automobile* 'automobile', *auto* has acquired the additional sense of 'pertaining to motor cars' (e.g., *autostrada* 'motorway'; *autolavaggio* 'car wash', etc.), as well as becoming an autonomous noun *l'auto* 'the car'. Another example of a learnèd prefix which has become an independent word is *ex-*, as in *l'ex-Presidente degli Stati uniti* 'the former President of the United States', which may also be used as a noun (*il mio ex non lo posso vedere* 'I can't stand my ex-husband').

Many non-learnèd prefixes also show a high degree of semantic and formal autonomy from the word to which they are affixed: *ri-* (< Latin RE-) normally denotes repetition of an action (e.g., *rivenire* 'to come back'; *rimangiare* 'to eat again', but also *riposare* 'to rest', not 'to place again'); *contra-* denotes resistance (e.g., *contrattacco* 'counterattack'; *contravveleno* 'antidote to poison'); semantically even more autonomous, and productive, is *contro-*, identical to the modern Italian preposition meaning 'against', e.g., *controdecreto* 'counter decree'. Certain prefixes exist also as independent words: *sotto-*, like the corresponding preposition *sotto*, generally indicates 'under', in a literal or figurative sense: e.g., *sottostare* 'to stand/be underneath'; *sottoscrivere* 'to undersign', 'underwrite'; *sottotitoli* 'subtitles', etc.; *fra-*, like the preposition *fra*, generally[90] indicates 'between', 'among': e.g., *frapporre* 'to place between'; *frammischiare* 'to mix in/among', etc. An extremely important prefix, usually having a negative or privative sense, is *s-*, which continues both Latin EX- 'out', whose learnèd form was mentioned above, and, sometimes, the negative prefix DIS-; it is often difficult to determine which of these is the source of the modern prefix (cf. Rohlfs (1969: 350)). Some examples are *sbarcare* 'to get out of a boat', 'disembark'; *spiacere* or *dispiacere* 'to displease', 'to cause regret'; *scortese* 'discourteous'. For other, pejorative and intensifying, senses, see Rohlfs (1969: 352f.).

Prefixes are phonologically like independent words, in that certain phonological changes that characteristically occur *inside* words, but not across word boundaries, are blocked across the boundary between the prefix and the word to which it is attached.

In those varieties of Italian (Ch.2: 7.2), where intervocalic sibilants are voiced word-internally, such voicing does not occur after a prefix: compare *presenti* **pre'sɛnti** 'you have presentiment', analysable as consisting of *pre* – 'before' and *sentire* 'feel', with *presenti* **pre'zɛnti** 'you present' (< CL PRÆSENTAS 'you place before', derived in turn from PRÆSENS 'being in front of'), which has long ceased to be analysed as comprising a separate suffix and root. It is a concomitant of their structural and formal autonomy that prefixes are usually highly productive, in that they can be freely affixed to any verb, adjective or noun. It is a phonological property of most prefixes that they comprise at least one syllable (*s*- is an exception), and generally, like full words, end in a vowel. It is noteworthy, in this connection, that when the reflex of the 'repetitive' prefix (RE-) appears as *r*- (non-syllabic), rather than the syllable *ri*-, it is often not analysed as a meaningful element of word structure: *rallentare* 'to slow down', is not analysed as 'repetitive prefix' + *allentare*, the basic meaning of which is 'to loosen'; *raggirare* is 'to swindle', not to 'surround (*aggirare*) again'. In both cases a repetitive form could be produced by prefixing *ri*-: *riallentare* 'to loosen again'; *riaggirare* 'to go round again'.

Suffixes, in contrast to most prefixes, have relatively low structural and semantic autonomy. Few words containing suffixes are semantically transparent. There is already a measure of structural opacity inherent in the fact that the suffix is attached not to the whole word (i.e., root or stem + inflection), but to the root of the word: we have *ragazzino*, with the suffix immediately following *ragazz*-, and not ***ragazzoin*, with the suffix attached to the whole word. This means that forms containing suffixes cannot be simply broken down into the structure 'word + affix' (unlike forms containing prefixes, usually analysable as 'affix + word').[91] Phonologically, they rarely constitute syllables, and so could not stand as independent words (most suffixes have the structure 'vowel + consonant'). Occasional, jocular, uses as independent words of some of the more semantically transparent and productive suffixes, such as the pejorative *-accio* (e.g., *È proprio accio!* 'It's really nasty' – cf. Lepschy and Lepschy (1988: 179)) in fact comprise not just the suffix, but also the inflectional ending (here *-o*). Another phonological indicator of the tighter cohesion between roots and suffixes than between prefixes and roots, is that the suffixes usually carry primary word stress, stress being removed from the root (e.g., *ragàzza* but *ragazzìna*); prefixes never involve stress shifts.

Among the most transparent suffixes in the modern language are the diminutives *-in-* (e.g., *treno* 'train', *trenino* 'little train'; *ragazza* 'girl' *ragazzina* 'little[92] girl') and *-ett-* (e.g., *carro* 'cart', *carretto* 'little cart'). A noun, or adjective, 'X', bearing these suffixes can be interpreted as 'small X'; *-ino* in particular (cf. Brunet (1990: 137f.)) also has strong connotations of endearment.. But even *-ino* cannot be indiscriminately affixed to any word: *poverino* (from *povero* 'poor') means 'poor fellow' (deserving of sympathy), but *poveretto* (employing another diminutive suffix common in the modern language) means 'wretch', 'beggar'. As for *cucchiaino* (from *cucchiaio* 'spoon'), it is not any 'small spoon' but specifically a 'teaspoon'. A *scarpetta* is a woman's or child's shoe, but not necessarily a small shoe. The suffix *-ett-* appears to be rather less productive and transparent than *-in-*. There is also a lack of morphological autonomy since some (but not all) roots in final [**n**] add [**ʧ**] when combined with *-in-* (e.g., *milione* 'million' *milioncino* 'a mere million'; *camion* 'lorry', *camioncino* 'little lorry'; *boccone* 'mouthful', *bocconcino* 'morsel'). Other changes are also attested, such as *cane* 'dog', but *cagnolino*, *città* 'city' but *cittadina*. Suffixation of *-in-* is also sometimes associated with change of gender: e.g., *la finestra* 'the window', but *il finestrino* 'the window (of a train, etc.)' (cf. 4.1). The augmentative suffix *-one* has a similar effect, save that it confers masculine gender: e.g., *la bocca* 'the mouth', but *il boccone* 'the mouthful'.

The diminutive suffix *-ello*, once very productive, is now little used for the formation of new diminutives. In many words its suffixal status is no longer apparent. We have *agnello* 'lamb', but no ***agno* (except in southern dialects, where diminutive suffixes are, overall, much rarer than in Tuscany or northern Italy), *uccello* 'bird' but no ***uccio*. We have *fratello* 'brother' and *sorella* 'sister', originally diminutives of *frate* and *suora*, both of which survive in central and southern dialects; but in Tuscan *frate* and *suora* have acquired the specialized religious meanings of 'monk' and 'nun'. As for *cappella* 'chapel', this is not the diminutive of *cappa*, which means 'cloak', 'cape'. Even where it retains a diminutive (or pejorative) value, there may be unpredictable modifications or additions to the stem: e.g., *asino* 'donkey', *asinello* but *fuoco* 'fire', *fuocherello*; *ramo* 'branch', *ramoscello* 'twig'; *busta* 'envelope', *bustarella* 'bribe' (because given in a little envelope), etc. Other diminutive suffixes are no longer recognizable as such in Italian. The Latin diminutive suffix -(U)LU(M)[93] (which usually yields [**jo**] in Italian – cf. Ch.2: 4.6.4) is no longer perceived as a suffix of any kind: *occhio* 'eye' < OC(U)LU(M); *fibbia* 'brooch' < FIB(U)LA(M); *orecchia* 'ear' < AURIC(U)LA(M); *ginocchio* 'knee' < GENUC(U)LU(M); *guglia* 'spire' < *ACUC(U)LA(M) 'little needle'; *lenticchia* 'lentil' < LENTIC(U)LA(M), etc.

A suffix important particularly in the formation of agentive nouns and adjectives, and derived from Latin -ARIU(M), appears in no less than four different forms: *-ai-* (e.g., *macellaio* 'butcher'; *cavallaio* 'horse trader'), is the normal Tuscan development (Ch.2: 5.2); *-ar-* (e.g., *campanaro* 'rustic'; *zampognaro* 'bagpipe player') is the commonest Italo-Romance form of the suffix outside Tuscany, and usually an indicator of non-Tuscan origin; *-ier-* (e.g, *barbiere* 'barber'; *cavaliere* 'knight', 'horseman'; *guerriere* or *guerriero* 'warrior') is of French origin, and *-ari-* (e.g., *funzionario* 'civil servant'; *rivoluzionario* 'revolutionary') is a learnèd continuation of the Latin suffix.

Suffixes modifying lexical meaning are rarer in verbs, although some which can be affixed to nouns and adjectives can also be affixed to verbs, e.g., *salterellare* 'to jump about'; *sghignazzare* 'to sneer'; *sgambettare* 'to scamper'. It is noteworthy that *-azz-* (-**atts**-), rather than its etymological cognate *-acci-* (-**attʃ**-) (Ch.2: 5.2), generally occurs in the verb.

Some suffixes (but not prefixes) have the specific function of relating words of different morphosyntactic classes (e.g., verbs and nouns, nouns and verbs, adjectives and nouns, etc.). Among the suffixes which relate nouns to verbs are the feminines *-azione*[94] (highly productive), *-anza* and *-enza* (much less productive): e.g., *creare* 'to create', *creazione* 'creation'; *credere* 'to believe', *credenza* 'belief'. Still moderately productive is the masculine *-aggio*, suffixed to the roots of first conjugation verbs, of Gallo-Romance origin (see Rohlfs (1969: 384f.)): e.g., *lavaggio* 'washing'; *atterraggio* 'landing'. Characteristic of informal registers is the affixation of augmentative or diminutive suffixes to adverbs: *tardino* 'a bit late', 'latish'. Adjectives are often related to nouns by means of the suffix *-oso* (e.g., *paura* 'fear', *pauroso* 'fearful'). A device common to a number of Romance languages (with precedents already in CL, such as DEFENSA 'defence' > *difesa*) is the formation of nouns, often with the meaning 'accomplishment of the action expressed by the verb', by using the feminine past participle of the verb. For example, *corsa* 'race', 'running' (from *correre* 'to run'); *letta* 'quick read' (from *leggere* 'to read'); *fermata* 'act of stopping' and also 'place of stopping' (from *fermare* 'to stop'); *caduta* 'fall', 'act of falling' (from *cadere* 'to fall'); *salita* 'place/action of going up' (from *salire* 'to go up'). The participial ending *-ata* has been reanalysed as a derivational suffix, and has been extended also to nouns: e.g., *giornata* 'whole day'; *risata* 'laughter', 'act of laughing'; *boccata* 'mouthful'; *carrettata* 'cartload'. A major group of suffixes which relate verbs to nouns have their origin in *-**i'djare**, derived in turn from the Greek verb suffix -IZEIN. Among these are *-eggiare* (e.g., *guerreggiare* 'to wage war', based on *guerra* 'war'; *amoreggiare* 'to philander', based on *amore* 'love'), *-ezzare* (Ch.2: 5.2) (e.g., *battezzare* 'to baptize' from the Greek verb BAPTIZEIN, and related to *battesimo* 'baptism'; *spetezzare* 'to break wind', based on *peto* 'fart', etc.). The still extremely productive *-izzare* (*centralizzare* 'to centralize'; *socializzare* 'to socialize', etc.) is a learnèd imitation of the Greek suffix -IZ . Forms in *-izzare* and *-eggiare* sometimes coexist, but the former is often transitive (e.g., *toscanizzare* 'to Tuscanize'), and the latter intransitive (e.g., *toscaneggiare* 'to act in a Tuscan way', 'to affect a Tuscan manner or style', etc.). On this, see Dardano (1978: 34f.).

11.3 Acronyms

A method of word formation which presupposes literacy and which has flourished in the twentieth century, in Italian as in other European languages, is the creation of acronyms (*sigle*). This technique of word formation is peculiar to the standard language, and has no counterpart in any other Italo-Romance dialect. The titles of major organizations are particularly susceptible to such treatment. Some, like *FIAT* (*F̲abbrica i̲taliana a̲utomobili T̲orino*) form words which are readily pronounceable in Italian. Others, containing combinations of letters which violate native phonotactic constraints, are pronounced using the names of some or all of the components letters: *DNA* **di'ɛnne'a**, *PC* **pit'tʃi** (*Partito comunista*), *CGIL* **tʃi'ddʒil** (*Confederazione italiana generale del lavoro*). In these cases the constituent letters are treated phonologically as independent words (note the [ɛ] of **'ɛnne** (Ch.2: 2.3), and *rafforzamento sintattico* after **pi** (Ch.2: 8.2)). In other cases *sigle* behave phonologically as single words, even allowing some violations of normal phonological constraints (e.g., the final consonant cluster in *CISL* **tʃizl** *Confederazione italiana sindacati lavoratori*). *Sigle* are often semantically opaque: many Italians would be hard pressed to say what, exactly, *FIAT* stands for, and opacity is complete in loans of acronyms from other languages, such as English *NATO*, *CIA*. A kindred phenomenon consists in the creation of new words by combining some or all of the initial syllables of a title: *POLFER* (*Polizia ferroviaria* 'railway police'), *CONFESERCENTI* (the full form of which is *Confederazione italiana esercenti attività commerciali turistiche e dei servizi*) or the *MINCULPOP* (*Ministero della cultura popolare*) of Fascist Italy;[95] also *colf* for *collaboratrice familiare* 'home help'.

Notes

1. For a further description of the Latin inflectional system, see Vincent (1988b: 40–4).
2. See also Rohlfs (1968: 6).
3. The reasons for the invariance of *il boia i boia* 'executioner' are unclear, but it is perhaps because the word originally denoted not the person, but rather an instrument (the pillory) used by executioners.
4. See Rohlfs (1968: 40f.). In this respect, the relevant southern dialects resemble Romanian, in which language a reflex of this ending (namely

-uri) is used to form the (feminine) plural of a large class of masculine singular nouns denoting inanimates (e.g., *timp timpuri* 'time'; *lift lifturi* 'lift, elevator').

5. The plural reflects an earlier *-**arii**, where [**ii**] has become [**i**].
6. Both singular *orecchia* and plural *orecchi* exist in the modern language, but are much rarer than *orecchio orecchie*. Singular *orecchia* is used in some regions, usually with the meaning 'hearing' rather than 'ear'.
7. Such words are also the locus for irregularities of plural morphology in English (e.g., *louse lice*; *tooth teeth*; *ox oxen*, etc.).
8. We use this term, rather than 'inanimate', since the relevant semantic factor seems to be that the referent has no *prominent* sexual characteristics.
9. See also Malkiel (1983: 155–78).
10. In some northern dialects the names of the fruits are masculine, while the tree names are formed by addition of reflexes of the suffix -ARIUM. See Rohlfs (1969: 394).
11. *Fica* has become a taboo word meaning 'female pudenda', so that modern Italian uses the masculine both for tree and fruit.
12. For a detailed account of the situation in modern Italian see Nespor (1988); also Vincent (1986).
13. *Stesso* is preposed when it means 'the same', postposed when it means 'that one, and no other': *ho visto lo stesso cane* 'I saw the same dog' vs. *ho visto il cane stesso* 'I saw that very dog.'
14. There are exceptions: some dialects of Puglia (around Taranto, Bari and Brindisi) have a two term system; some varieties of Piedmontese retain a vestigial three term system.
15. See Harris (1978: 67–77) for a detailed account in pan-Romance perspective.
16. The voicing of [**t**] leads Rohlfs (1968: 210) to propose a French origin (but cf. Ch.2: 7.2).
17. But see Berruto (1990: 120) for further generalization of *i* in *italiano popolare*.
18. See Rohlfs (1968: 103f.; 105f); Agostiniani (1982).
19. Only speakers who are carefully trying to imitate the original pronunciation of these names pronounce the [**h**]. But *lo* may be employed, even where the [**h**] is not pronounced.
20. For some observations on possible functional differentiation in Proto-Romance between ILLE and IPSE, see Renzi (1976: 28–30).
21. For some possible stylistic constraints against omission of the article, see Renzi (1988: 375).
22. But see Renzi (1988: 374).
23. For the type of construction *Di magnifiche rose, ne ho comprate*, see Renzi (1988: 381).
24. Medieval constructions (cf. Rohlfs (1968: 33)) such as *le palle dell'oro* 'balls of gold' (Dante); *le colonne del porfido* 'pillars of porphyry' (Boccaccio) seem to represent a combination of the preposition *di* 'made of', 'of', with the definite article before generic nouns. It is striking that this use of the partitive article (which falls into decline from the fourteenth century) seems to be dependent on the presence of a preceding definite

article: we tend to find *le palle dell' oro* but *una palla d' oro*, etc.

25. The past participle occasionally has active value, as in *fattolo, se ne andò*, 'having done it, he went'. But this structure may have originated as a learnèd borrowing from Latin.
26. Some first conjugation verbs which formed their past participle in -ITU(M), such as SONARE 'to sound', acquired new participle forms in -ATU(M): *sonato*.
27. See Wanner (1975: 156–88) and Tekavčić (1980 II: 281–4) for a review of some other attempted explanations.
28. In most verbs the thematic yod had been abandoned, yielding -**amo** and -**ate**.
29. See Merlo (1909). In these dialects -**no** appears in the first conjugation only: e.g., **'peːsa 'peːsanu** 'weigh' vs. **'parte 'partu** 'leave'
30. The palatal consonant of the first and second persons plural subjunctive is problematic. The introduction of the endings -**jamo** and -**jate** into these verbs (cf. 8.3.1) long postdates palatalization due to yod. The presence of [**ʧ**] in these roots is probably due to the analogical influence of the first and second persons indicative. If so, this analogy is yet another example of the pervasive and self-replicating pattern of present tense root allomorphy described in 8.4.1.1.
31. Tekavčić (1980 I: 75; 1983) assumes that the [**u**] is a phonetic development of unstressed [**e**] before [**ʃ**]. But his reason for assuming this is precisely the supposed implausibility of a 'semantic contamination' from OSTIUM affecting only certain persons of the verb, and not others. In reality, the notion of a rounding effect of [**ʃ**] on a preceding unstressed vowel is not well motivated in general phonetic terms, and one of the main supporting examples he adduces, the Tuscan dialect form *usciolo* for the *assiuolo* 'scops owl', is plausibly attributable to semantic contamination from a derivative of *uscio*, namely the verb *usciolare* 'to eavesdrop', 'to listen at doorways', because the bird, which has prominent ear-like headfeathers, is considered to be an 'eavesdropper'.
32. The Macinghi Strozzi letters show that forms such as *veggo* 'I see'; *rimango* 'I remain', etc., were becoming established by the fifteenth century.
33. Some penetration of this kind has occurred, however, in Corsican. See Maiden (1992: 304f.).
34. The role of frequency in determining the preservation of alternation should not be overestimated: some infrequent verbs keep alternation (e.g., *solère* 'to be wont'), and some highly frequent ones lose it (e.g., *chièdere* 'to ask'). See Maiden (1992: 300f.).
35. Disappearance of the diphthong in *piòvere* (OTuscan *piuovere*) is phonologically motivated. See Ch.2: 4.2.
36. Also *vendiedi* 'I sold' in OTuscan, extended in Florentine, and some other dialects, to other verbs such as *battiedi* 'I beat' etc.
37. Remnants of this structure probably survive in the so-called personal infinitive of Sardinian (cf. Jones (1988: 332f.)). See also Rohlfs (1968: 306–8) for some other apparent remnants.
38. See Bertinetto (1986: 436) for a detailed account.

39. For a more detailed account of the emergence of the Romance analytic passive, see Harris (1978: Ch.8).
40. For an analysis of the interaction of periphrasis and inflection, with particular reference to Italian, see Vincent (1987).
41. The maintenance of agreement in these cases may have a perceptual motivation. The modern language allows deletion of the vowel of the masculine and feminine third person singular clitic pronouns; in earlier centuries (and to this day, in the spoken language), the vowel could be deleted in the plural forms, as well (e.g., *l'ho visti* 'I've seen them'). Participial agreement therefore serves to signal the number and gender of the third person pronoun *l'*. It also performed the same function with the relative pronoun *che*, which is morphologically invariant. See Lucchesi (1963: 220f.).
42. The grammatical subject, from a *syntactic* point of view, is simply that noun phrase with which the verb agrees in number and gender; but it may enter into a variety of *semantic* relationships with the verb.
43. In the theoretical literature such verbs are often labelled 'unaccusative'. Their counterparts with participant subjects, but lacking grammatical objects, are labelled 'unergative'. For an account of the notion of (un)accusativity, and its antecedents (e.g., the label 'ergative' in Burzio (1986)) see, for example, Blake (1989: 29–40).
44. Not all speakers find this unacceptable, however.
45. On *da* and *per*, see Statha-Halikas (1977).
46. But Van Valin (1990: 256–8) discerns a semantic distinction between the stressed and clitic variants, such that the clitic reflexive structures may be said to conform to the exclusively semantic principles which he proposes for selection of *essere*. It is not clear that the distinction he discerns *always* differentiates clitic vs. stressed reflexive structures. In non-specific personal reflexive structures, such as *si è giocato* 'one played', where the subject is unambiguously agent, we are forced to say that the selection of the auxiliary is grammaticalized. The problem also arises of explaining why the reflexive clitic constructions were ever able to select *avere*. It may be that there is a plausible semantic motivation for either pattern of auxiliary selection, but that there is also a degree of grammatical determination in deciding which of these alternative principles shall prevail.
47. OTuscan also had a construction *essere* + PRESENT PARTICIPLE (cf. Bertinetto (1986: 136)).
48. See also Vincent (1987: 248f.).
49. Apart from some fragments of the future of ESSE 'to be': OFrench *ert* (< ERIT) and Castilian second person singular present *eres* (< ERIS) .
50. For the early history of this construction, see Fleischman (1982).
51. See Rohlfs (1968: 335f.); also Loporcaro (1988b: 286–8) and Gioscio (1985: 81) for fuller details on the expression of time and modality in the southern analytical constructions.
52. Some examples of futures with a separate auxiliary, placed in front of the verb, occur in medieval northern dialects. See Rohlfs (1968: 334).
53. OTuscan has an optional first person singular *aggio* 'I have', and correspondingly an optional future *faraggio* 'I shall do'.

54. They do not show the raising to [**e**] characteristic of unstressed [**a**] followed by [**r**] (Ch.2: 4.6.3). This is probably due to the analogical influence of the stressed singular forms *dà*; *sta*; *fa*.
55. Apart from the marginal CL periphrastic construction AMATURUS ERAM, 'I was about to love', combining the (extinct) future participle and the verb 'to be'.
56. For an analysis of the occasional 'double indirect object' structure, found in the medieval language (notably Boccaccio), but now extinct, see Robustelli (1992: 94–7).
57. An alternative view (cf. Ageno (1964: 240) and the discussion in Robustelli (1992: 102–4)) is that the appearance of *da* in causatives marks a 'reanalysis' of the infinitive as 'passive'. But the definition of 'passive' is as much morphological and syntactic, as semantic, and the infinitive shows no sign whatever of adopting 'passive' morphology or syntax.
58. For further analysis of the syntax of 'restructured' verbs in modern Italian, see Skytte and Salvi (1991).
59. Except that, in causative structures with *fare* the reflexive clitic must be omitted: *Paolo fa vergognare Giovanni* 'Paolo makes Giovanni be ashamed'. Transitive reflexives, in contrast, are wholly debarred in such structures, with or without the reflexive clitics: ***Paolo fa vedere/vedersi Giovanni* 'Paolo makes Giovanni see himself'.
60. Cennamo (1991) points out that the construction with *si* was already present in the monovalent verb *convenire*.
61. Dissenting views with regard to INDE are expressed in Lausberg (1966: 186f.), Negri (1977) and Loporcaro (1988b: 243).
62. This *pace* Tekavčić (1980 II: 417).
63. OTuscan also had *ello* < CL ILLUM or ILLUD. Boström (1972: 11f.; 31) observes that, at least in Florentine, the morphological animate-inanimate distinction in third person forms is not detectable before the present century.
64. For an account of the evolution of these forms, see Barnett (1965).
65. See Cordin (1988: 536). Boström (1972) gives a detailed account of the evolution of the Florentine third person pronominal system.
66. The first and second persons singular forms persist in parts of Tuscany (e.g., Florentine) and cognate forms recur in many southern dialects (Lazio **ko t'tiku** 'with you'; **ko n'nosko** 'with us').
67. This principle is still well preserved in some Romance varieties, such as European Portuguese (cf. Spencer (1991: 362–5) and, vestigially, in some Italian dialects (cf. Rohlfs (1968: 174f.)) .
68. Recent and as yet unpublished work by J. Adams suggests that, in Latin at least, unstressed pronominal elements were *enclitic* to focalized (or 'emphasized') elements. Focalized elements tended to occupy clause-initial position, whence the characteristic second-position collocation of clitic elements in the clause.
69. Prepositions and certain adverbial phrases could also act as hosts to clitics: *dietrogli* 'behind him'; *allatogli* 'beside him'; *dentrovi* 'in it', etc.
70. Many of the following data on the syntax of clitics are given in Melander (1929) and Lombard (1934). For further extensive documentation of the

situation in thirteenth century Florentine (and elsewhere), see Castellani (1952: 79–105).

71. Not all speakers accept *mi*/*ti*/*ci*/*vi* + *gli*, but *gli* + *mi* is generally rejected as wholly ungrammatical – see Wanner (1977: 109f.).
72. For a convincing rebuttal of the views of D'Ovidio, Parodi and others, who see the *me*/*mi* alternation as a purely internal morphological or phonological evolution, see Melander (1929: 169–79). Rohlfs (1968: 166f.) proposes that the vowel [**e**] conserves the secondarily stressed initial vowel of a following pronoun ***ello** (***m ello da** 'he gives it to me'). But this ignores the fact that, by the time third person DO forms came to be ordered after IO forms, they had lost their etymological initial vowel.
73. See Lombard (1934: 27), but also the comments in Castellani (1952: 87), for a discussion of occasional *ne gli* sequences in OFlorentine, and especially in the writings of Boccaccio.
74. For the history of (relatively rare) sequences of three or more clitics, see Lombard (1934: 71f.) and Rohlfs (1968: 180f.). Also Lepschy and Lepschy (1988: 213) for the modern rules. The fundamental ordering principles are those stated for two-clitic sequences.
75. See Rohlfs (1968: 168) for some suggestions.
76. It is perhaps this reanalysis of *glie-* as an IO that favoured the general reanalysis of *gli*, originally in free variation with *li* (see above), as an indirect object form. See also Lombard (134: 53f.).
77. Wanner (1977: 121) also observes that locative *ci* and *vi* tend to be avoided, respectively, before host verbs beginning with [**ʧ**] and [**v**].
78. Rohlfs (1968: 234) identifies this *ci* with the first person plural clitic pronoun, invoking a close semantic link between impersonal constructions and the category first person plural: this overlooks the fact that it is the reflexive, not the impersonal, clitic which is replaced by *ci* (the impersonal clitic is the rightmost one in clitic sequences: *lo si canta* 'one sings it'). We have here yet another case of the multivalence of *ci* as a clitic personal pronoun, discussed above. Rohlfs (1968: 185; 186) also shows that *ci* functions as a reflexive pronoun in parts of Puglia, Abruzzo and in Tuscany on the Isola del Giglio.
79. For an account of the changing functions of the address forms in Romance (and elsewhere) see Brown and Gilman (1960).
80. For some reflections on its origins see Brown and Levinson (1987: 198–204).
81. It is best established among northern dialects, notably of Piedmont and the Veneto, but often with a masculine pronoun (corresponding to Italian *lui*), where the addressee is male. See Rohlfs (1968: 183).
82. Forms such as *vussignuría, vussía* continue to be available as reverential or polite forms of address in many areas of southern Italy (and also in parts of Liguria and Piedmont), although usually accompanied by a *second person singular* verb form.
83. Berruto (1990: 124f.) also notes a trend in the modern popular language to generalize *dove* in place of *in cui* 'in which', *per cui* 'for which'.
84. Clitic function-marking is rare with temporal relatives. See D'Achille (1991: 258f.).

85. The origin of *qualche* in this sense seems to be locutions of the type *una cosa qual che sia* 'a thing which ever it may be'.
86. The evolution of *da* in expressions of value (*un biglietto da mille lire* 'a thousand lire note') and manner (*comportati da persona seria* 'behave like a serious person') remains problematic.
87. The (rare) third type of plural of this word, *i pomidori,* illustrates a curious phase in which the word has been analysed as comprising two independent elements. An example of reanalysis, of the phrase *d'oro* as an adjective (*doro*), is the Milanese *carta dora* 'gold paper' (see Rohlfs (1968: 79)).
88. We do not mean to suggest that, synchronically or diachronically, such compounds are necessarily *derived* from such syntagms.
89. For a comprehensive account of modern suffixes, and the allomorphy which sometimes accompanies them see, for example, Brunet (1991). For affixation generally, and other techniques of word-formation, see Dardano (1978). Also Lepschy and Lepschy (1988: 176–82).
90. But it can also have a pejorative or privative sense, not shared by the preposition: e.g., *fraintendere* 'to misunderstand', *frastuono* 'hubbub'.
91. A concomitant of suffixal autonomy is that those suffixes which are semantically more transparent (and more productive) tend to be 'outermost' in the word. That is to say that they are collocated to the right of any other suffixes. Thus we might have *fuocherellino* 'tiny little fire' or *fuocherellaccio* 'nasty little fire', but not ***fuocherinello* or ***fuocheraccello*. And (with the exception of *tavolinetto* 'little side table' – cf. Brunet (1991: 161)), *-in-* is always ordered to the right of *-ett-*: e.g., *un pochettino* 'a tiny little bit'.
92. Even here, of course, there is a certain semantic idiosyncrasy. A *ragazzina* is a girl who is very young but not, necessarily, one who is physically small, or endearing.
93. It survives in the learnèd *-colo*: e.g., *libercolo* 'booklet'; *opuscolo* 'small work', 'pamphlet', both Italianizations of Latin LIBERCULUM, OPUSCULUM.
94. A variant of this suffix, which derives from Latin -ATIONE(M), is *-agione* (e.g., *cacciagione* 'game', 'hunter's catch'). See also Ch.2: 5.2.
95. The adoption of acronyms and similar formations may, of course, be reinforced by existing words. FIAT has positive and authoritative associations in the Latin phrase FIAT LUX 'let there be light', and *MINCULPOP* rather ribald ones (clearly not intended by its originators!) in *minchia* 'prick', *culo* 'arse' and *poppe* 'tits'.

Chapter 4

History of Sentence Structure

1 Clause word order

1.1 Dominant word order

The *dominant* order of elements in the Latin clause is S(ubject) + O(bject) + V(erb), e.g., LUPUS MARCUM UORAT 'The wolf devours Marcus'. In Italian, as in other Romance varieties, the dominant order of object and verb has been reversed, so that the verb generally precedes its object: *Il lupo divora Marco.*[1] In neither language is such ordering rigid: examples of (S)VO ordering are not infrequent in classical, and especially popular, Latin, while in OTuscan (in literary and non-literary texts alike) SOV ordering is common – to the extent that one doubts whether it is purely attributable to imitation of Latin models. Remnants of it survive in some modern proverbial expressions (e.g., *Cosa fatta capo ha*, literally, '(a) thing done (a) head has').[2] Inversion of verb and subject (VS) is also common with verbs introducing their grammatical subjects as 'new' information in the discourse: e.g., *È successo un incidente* 'An accident has happened'; *È arrivata la polizia* 'The police have arrived', etc.[3]

1.2 Dislocation

Dislocation is a device particularly common in the spoken language, involving systematic deviation from the SVO word order, whereby a noun phrase may be extracted from its normal position in the clause, and collocated to the right or to the left of the clause. The evolution and function of left and right dislocation is a much debated issue, a detailed study of which is available in D'Achille (1991). Broadly speaking, however, we may say that it serves to identify and throw into relief the topic or 'theme' of the sentence, that about which something (the 'rheme') is being asserted. There is also a close relation between the dislocated element and the property of 'givenness', or being already known, as opposed to 'newness', which characterizes the remaining elements of the sentence. The syntactic function of dislocated nouns (other than subjects), is usually indicated within the clause by a clitic pronoun, acting as a kind of syntactic trace of the dislocated element (*Il gatto, l'ho visto* or *L'ho visto, il gatto* 'I've seen the cat'). The syntactic function of indirect object, locative (and sometimes partitive) dislocated elements is usually, but not always, signalled by an appropriate preposition (e.g., *A Mario, gli ho parlato* or *Mario, gli ho parlato* 'I've talked to Mario'). Dislocation is certainly not a recent innovation,[4] and is already present in the earliest surviving Italo-Romance texts (for example, the tenth century *Placiti Cassinesi*). We give some examples here from the late fifteenth-century Macinghi Strozzi letters, and from the writings of Benvenuto Cellini in the following century: Macinghi Strozzi *Assai ne muore di questi forestieri* 'A lot of these foreigners are dying'; *il cavallo, Giovanni l'ha governato* 'Giovanni has fed the horse'; *Iscriverrogli una lettera a Matteo, e dirogli. . .* 'I'll write Matteo a letter, and I'll tell him.'; Cellini *Ulivieri mio maestro gli venne occasione di venire a Firenze* 'My master Ulivieri had occasion to come to Florence'; *Intorno a ditto specchio vi fece un verso latino* 'Around the said mirror he put a Latin verse'.

There emerges over time an increasingly sharp differentiation between written and spoken language with respect to dislocation, due at least in part to the fact that the phenomenon appears (see D'Achille (1991: 202f.)) to be especially typical of allocutionary (face-to-face) discourse, and hence of spoken language. D'Achille's exploration of the history of the phenomenon reveals that left dislocation begins to recede during the sixteenth century from more elevated, literary, texts (hence those furthest removed from spoken language). Such retreat is clearly due, at least in part, to the influence of prescriptive grammarians (cf. D'Achille (1991: 98–113)). As for right dislocation, it becomes increasingly restricted to those texts closest in character to the spoken language, from the fourteenth century. In such texts the incidence of left dislocation shows a steady increase from the thirteenth century onward (with a period of relative stability during the fifteenth and sixteenth), with an increasing predominance of the direct object as dislocated element. Right dislocation, actually more frequent than left dislocation in the fourteenth century, goes into rapid decline thereafter.

2 Verb–subject agreement

In Italian, as in Latin, verbs agree in number (and gender) with one of their associated (or 'argument') nouns, the 'subject'; verbs having a single argument noun take that noun as their grammatical subject: MORTUAE (femine plural) SUNT (plural) ROMANAE (feminine plural); *sono* (plural) *morte* (feminine plural) *le romane* (feminine plural) 'the Roman women have died'. However, Italian has occasionally deviated from this principle, in that a third person *singular* (and masculine) verb sometimes appears with a single argument noun which is *plural* (and may be feminine). This absence of agreement (cf. Brambilla Ageno (1964: 159–76); Rohlfs (1969: 20); Salvi (1991: 231f.)) becomes rare in the written language after the sixteenth century, but still occurs in modern Tuscan dialects.[5] In the majority of such cases, we find that the argument noun is collocated to the *right* of the verb: e.g., from Sercambi's Novelle (thirteenth century): *Andatosene* ***le donne*** *a casa* ...'The women having gone home...'; *Partitosi* ***le persone***... 'The people having left...'; Macinghi Strozzi *e giovedì mi* ***venne*** *a vicitare* ***due gentiluomini*** 'and on Thursday there came to visit me two gentlemen'; *che ci* ***è stato*** *molto* ***spiacevoli tempi*** *di neve e vento* 'for there have been very unpleasant (sorts of) weather with snow and wind'; *Dicestimi che t'era capitato costì* ***una schiava*** 'You told me that a slave girl had turned up there'; *Poi furono presi, e fu tagliato* ***la testa*** *a tre* 'Then they were captured, and the heads of three of them were cut off', etc.; Bandello (fifteenth century) *che se forse non era mosso* ***guerra*** *a Carlo, sortiva un altro fine* 'for perhaps if war had not been made against Charles, things would have turned out differently'; Cellini (sixteenth century) ***Venne*** *alquanti* ***soldati*** 'There came some soldiers'. The subject noun is seen in these examples to occupy the canonical *object* position, that following the verb, and the verbs in question are typically those which select *essere* as their auxiliary.[6] It is significant that these are verbs which we identified in Ch.3: 8.8.2.1 as having grammatical subjects possessing properties associated with *objects*. Since the Italian verb does not usually agree with its object, we may see lack of agreement, and collocation to the right of the verb, as manifesting syntactic properties of objecthood.

A clear case of reanalysis of an original subject noun as an object, both semantically and syntactically, is observable in occasional modern reflexive constructions of the type *si compra due penne* 'one buys two pens'; *si scrive libri* 'one writes books' for *si comprano due penne*; *si scrivono libri* (cf. Ch.3: 8.9). Here *si* has been reanalysed as an 'indefinite' or 'non-specific' personal subject pronoun, which selects singular verbal agreement. The phenomenon is attested already in OTuscan,[7] but remains marginal, even in the modern language (cf. Lepschy (1986: 146f.)).

A major variety of deviation from verb–subject agreement, especially common in spoken and informal registers Italian, is plural agreement determined by the plural reference of nouns which are grammatically singular: *La gente cantano* 'People sing'; *La maggior parte sono d'accordo* 'Most agree'; *L'esercito hanno ricevuto gli ordini* 'The army have received the orders', etc. D'Achille (1991: Ch. 4) shows that such so-called '*ad sensum*' agreement is attested from the earliest texts, but recedes markedly from the literary language as a consequence of the grammatical prescriptivism of the sixteenth century, requiring that grammatically singular nouns should have singular verb agreement.

3 Interrogation

In 'polar' questions (those requiring an answer 'yes' or 'no'), the most common mode of interrogation involves a simple modification in intonation, without change of morphological or syntactic structure: *Maria mangia la mela* 'Mary eats the apple', and *Maria mangia la mela?* 'Does Mary eat the apple?'. The same device appears to have been available in spoken Latin. Since orthography has never represented intonation, the historical evolution of this device is a chapter of Italian linguistic history which remains to be written. In the absence of a general theory of intonational change, the regionally variant patterns of interrogative intonation observable in modern Italian serve only to complicate the picture. The commonest pattern of intonation associated with interrogation involves a rising tone (often accompanied by lengthening of the vowel) in the final stressed syllable of the phrase (cf. Fava (1984: 155)). Italian usually inverts verb and a subject pronoun in interrogative constructions (Dante (*Commedia*) *Sei tu già costì ritto, Bonifazio?* 'Art thou standing there already, Boniface?'; Boccaccio (*Decameron*) *Credete voi che egli vi manuchi?* 'Do you think he'll eat you?'; modern Italian *Puoi farlo tu?* (where *tu* carries emphatic stress) rather than *Tu puoi farlo?* 'Can you do it?' (cf. Fava (1984: 161f.)). Until the sixteenth century, the situation was rather different: in Florentine, and in northern Italian dialects, interrogative sentences lacking overt noun subjects were *normally* formed by positioning a subject pronoun to the right of the verb, even where no subject pronoun would have been employed in the corresponding declarative sentences. Thus, the interrogative corresponding to declarative *Viene*, 'He comes', would be *Viene egli?* 'Is he coming': e.g., Novellino (thirteenth century) *S'io li le cheggio, darebbelm'egli?* 'If I ask him for it, would he give it to me?'; *Messere, che domanda mi fate voi?*, 'Sir, what question do you ask me?'. Patota (1990) shows that this state of affairs persists in the literary language into the second half of the nineteenth century, but that postposition of the subject pronoun is in decline in spoken Florentine from the sixteenth century. In the latter part of the nineteenth century the device of interrogative inversion disappears entirely from the literary language apparently, according to

Patota, in response to Manzoni's proposal (cf. Ch.1: 2.3) that contemporary spoken Florentine, from which this interrogative structure had long disappeared, should form the basis of Italian.

The array of Latin interrogative particles NE, NUM (anticipating a negative reply) and NONNE (anticipating an affirmative reply) is wholly extinct. However, Italian occasionally makes use of *forse* in anticipation of a negative response (roughly equivalent to English 'surely not?'): *Lei mi chiama forse bugiardo?* 'Would you be calling me a liar?'). For the use of *che* and *o* as interrogative markers in Tuscan and other dialects see Rohlfs (1969: 157–9). The word *no*, and the phrase *non è vero?* or *vero?*, have a similar function: *Partite domani, no* / (*non è*) *vero?* 'You're leaving tomorrow, aren't you?'. In indirect questions, the Latin particles NUM, AN, 'whether', have been replaced by *se*: e.g., *voleva sapere se fossero partiti* 'he wanted to know whether they'd left'.

The fate of the Latin interrogative pronouns has been discussed in Ch.3: 9.7. The various other interrogative forms develop as follows: QUANDO > Italian *quando* 'when'; QUOMODO > *come* 'how'; QUANTUS 'how great?' > *quanto* 'how much'; QUALIS 'of what kind?' > *quale* 'which?'; UBI > *ove* 'where?' or, combined with DE, *dove*. The forms CUR 'why?' and the dual UTER 'which of two?' are extinct, having been replaced respectively by the more transparent *perché* (literally 'for what?') and *quale dei due?* (literally 'which of the two?'). QUOT 'how many?' has been replaced by the plural of *quanto*, namely *quanti*.

4 Negation

Italian inherits directly from Latin the device of sentential negation by means of preverbal *non* : NON UENIT > *non viene*[8] 'he is not coming'. *Non* also replaces HAUD (the negator of adverbial and adjectival phrases), NOLI/NOLITE (used in negative imperatives) and NE (employed with subjunctive verbs). For example, HAUD MALE; NOLI DICERE; NE UENIAT > *non male* 'not badly'; *non dire* 'do not say'; *non venga* 'let him not come'. The negators *né . . . né* 'neither . . . nor' continue Latin NEC . . . NEC. In common with other Romance languages, Italian has also made use of NON (> *no*) as a negative pro-sentence, meaning 'no', in opposition to *sì* (< CL SIC 'thus', '(it is) so'): *Hai fame? No/Sì.* 'Are you hungry? No/Yes.'.

A major syntactic innovation with respect to CL, originally common to all Romance languages, is the device of double negative marking, such that verbs in clauses containing negative pronouns or adverbs are additionally preceded by a reflex of NON. In Italian (unlike French or Romanian) *non* is employed only when the negative pronoun or adverb *follows* the verb: cf. Italian *Nessuno ha cantato*; *Non ha cantato nessuno* 'Nobody has sung' vs. French *Personne n'a chanté*; *Il n'a chanté personne*; Romanian *Nimeni n-a cîntat*; *N-a cîntat nimeni*).[9] For omission of preverbal *non* in some modern spoken varieties, see Ch.5: 2.3.2.1.

Most of the negative pronouns and adjectives (*niente* 'nothing'; *nessuno* 'nobody'; *nulla* 'nothing'; *né* 'nor'; *nullo* 'none') are traceable to Latin negative forms characterized by initial [**n**]. An exception is *mai* 'never', which supplants Latin NUMQUAM, but originates as positive MAGIS 'more': its frequent occurrence in negative contexts (*non . . . mai* 'never more') seems to have conferred upon it a negative value. In OTuscan it was always accompanied by *non*, even when it preceded the verb (cf. Rohlfs (1969: 278)); subsequently, on the model of *nessuno viene* 'nobody is coming', etc., *non* could be omitted where *mai* preceded the verb.

5 Conjunctions

Conjunctions may be subdivided into those which conjoin main clauses (paratactic conjunctions), and those which conjoin subordinate clauses to main clauses (hypotactic conjunctions). The principal paratactic conjunction is *e* (< CL ET), which, in the medieval language could conjoin preceding subordinate as well as main clauses, often expressing a rapid succession of events (cf. Rohlfs (1969: 164)): e.g., Dante (*Commedia*) *com'ei parlava, e Sordello a sé il trasse* 'as he spoke, Sordello pulled him towards himself'; Boccaccio (*Decameron*) *quando colui verrà per li danari, e io il menerò dentro* 'when he comes for the money, I'll lead him in'. *Sì* (< CL SIC) also functions as a paratactic conjunction in the medieval language (cf. Rohlfs (1969: 165f.)). *O* (< CL AUT), with its derivatives *oppure*, *ovvero*, *ossia* , is the conjunction of alternativity; its negative *né* derives from CL NEC. The adversative *ma* arises from Latin MAGIS 'more', 'rather'; *anzi* 'rather', may have originated as an originally prevocalic variant (cf. Ch.2: 5.2) of ANTE 'before', 'sooner', 'rather'. The modern adversative *però* originally signified 'therefore' (< PER HOC 'for/by this'); its adversative function ('despite this', 'but') is acquired by a semantic development comparable with that which has occurred also in French *pourtant* ('however', but originally 'therefore').

Among the subordinating conjunctions, we find the temporal *quando* 'when', continuing the Latin *interrogative* QUANDO, replacing Latin UBI and CUM; *mentre* 'while', from *DUM + INTERIM (cf. OLombard *domentre che*); *appena* 'as soon as', which is a Romance innovation combining *a* and *pena* (literally 'with difficulty' – cf. English '*hardly* had she arrived . . .'). Many Italo-Romance temporal conjunctions employ the subordination marker *che*. Thus *subito che* 'as soon as';

tosto che 'as soon as'; *dopo che* 'after' (also OTuscan *poscia che* 'after' < POSTEA); *prima che* 'before' (also OTuscan *pria che*); *avanti che* 'before'; *innanzi che* 'before'; *finché* 'until'; *sinché* 'until'. *Quando che*, *mentre che* and *appena che* are also attested in the history of Italian (cf. Rohlfs (1969: 172–8)), and in modern 'italiano popolare', although not in the standard language.

The commonest causal conjunction is *che* (< QUID, substituting QUOD, in its meaning of 'because' – see section 7). In the spoken modern language, *che* frequently functions as a paratactic conjunction, indicating a (loose) causal connection between clauses: *me ne vado, che* (= *perché*) *non c'è più niente da vedere* 'I'm off, 'cos there's nothing left to see'. Both purpose and cause are articulated by *perché*, differentiated respectively by subordinate verbs in the indicative and the subjunctive: *glielo dico perché capisce* 'I'm telling her because she understands' and *glielo dico perché capisca* 'I'm telling her in order that she should understand'.

None of the Latin concessive conjunctions (QUAMUIS; QUAMQUAM; QUAMLIBET; LICET, etc., all meaning 'although') are directly continued in Italo-Romance. The function of a concessive may be defined as '*conceding* the truth of some proposition Y in a subordinate clause, which appears to contradict a main proposition X, because, in fact, Y does not contradict X'. For example, *Sebbene stia piovendo* (Y), *non sono bagnato* (X) 'Although it's raining (Y), I'm not wet (X)'. The function of concessives is reflected in the fact that the source of most of the Italian concessive conjunctions is adverbial expressions of the type 'it is *well* that Y/ you may *well* say Y' (cf. *sebbene*, *benché*); 'you may not like Y/whether you like Y or not . . .' (cf. *malgrado (che)*); 'Y is *all* true/*albeit* . . .' (cf. OTuscan *(con) tutto che*); 'to whatever extent Y is true . . .' (*per quanto* . . .); 'let Y happen . . .' (cf. OTuscan *avvegnaché*); and 'it is still the case that Y, (but . . .)' (cf. *ancorché*).[10] *Nonostante* 'notwithstanding' is probably a learnèd borrowing from the Latin phrase NON OBSTANTE (literally, 'not standing in the way').

6 Comparison

Comparisons of equality are expressed in Latin by TOT . . . QUOT (UENERUNT TOT HOMINES QUOT FEMINAE 'There came as many men as women'), adverbial TAM . . . QUAM or TANTO . . . QUANTO. Of these, Italian continues only the last, in the form of *(altret)tanto . . . quanto*, both in adjectival and adverbial functions: e.g., *Vennero (altret)tanti uomini quante femmine* 'As many men came as women'; *Scrive tanto quanto legge* or *Scrive quanto legge* 'She writes as much as she reads'. The adverbial function may also be expressed by *così . . . come*: *È così intelligente come voi* or *È intelligente come voi* 'She's as intelligent as you'.

Comparisons of inequality are expressed in Italian by *più* 'more' or *meno* 'less' (see Ch.3: 5.1 for the morphology of the comparative adjective and adverb). In CL, the term of comparison (that against which some entity or property is compared) can be introduced by the particle QUAM (ALTIUS EST QUAM LATUM; 'It is higher than it is broad'; ALTIOR EST QUAM MARCUS 'She is taller than Marcus'). Where the term of comparison is a noun phrase, it can also be expressed by the ablative case: ALTIOR EST MARCO. CL QUAM has been replaced by *che* (although some dialects retain a form **ka**), while the structure employing an ablative noun phrase is succeeded, already in Late Latin, by DE (> *di*) + noun phrase: *È più alto che largo* 'It is more high than broad'; *È più alta di Marco* 'She's taller than Marcus'. The structure *che* + noun phrase (*È più alta che Marco*), more common in OTuscan, and characteristic of most Romance languages, remains in use in modern northern varieties of Italian (cf. Belletti (1991: 838; 839)); it is also regularly employed in comparison of two noun phrases having the same grammatical function (as subject or object): e.g., *Conosco lo sposo* (object) *meglio che la sposa* (object) 'I know the groom better than (I know) the bride'.

Terms of comparison which are verb phrases may be introduced by *che*, or may be expressed as relativized noun phrases introduced by *quanto* or *quello che*: *Gianni è più intelligente di quello che credevo*, literally, 'Gianni is more intelligent than that which I believed'.

Where the term of comparision is a verb phrase introduced by *che*, it is preceded by so-called 'expletive *non*'. Where this *non* is employed, the following verb is invariably in the subjunctive: e.g., *È più intelligente che non credessi* 'He's more intelligent than I thought'; *Faceva più freddo che non mi aspettassi* 'It was colder than I expected'. The source of this semantically redundant *non* may lie (see Price (1990: 106–31)) in speakers' perception that 'X is more intelligent than Y' is practically equivalent to 'Y is *not* as intelligent as X'. However, if *modern* Italian expletive *non* were still motivated by the perception that the term of comparison is somehow 'negative', one would expect this *non* to be absent in comparisons involving the opposite of *più*, namely *meno* 'less', where the term of comparison is implicitly 'positive'. In fact, it is regularly present: *Carlo è meno intelligente che tu non creda* 'Carlo is more intelligent than you think'. Price (1990: 146–91), observing the mutually implicational relationship between the comparator *che,* expletive *non*, and the subjunctive mood of the verb, proposes that the motivation both for the presence of *non* and for the subjunctive mood is the essentially formal one of syntactic disambiguation: the subjunctive mood after *non* serves to show that this particular *non* does not have the normal function of simply negating the truth of the verb (cf. . . . *che tu non credi* '. . . that you don't believe' vs . . . *che tu non creda* ' . . . than you believe'), while the presence of *non*, in turn, serves to disambiguate the comparator *che* ('than') from the sentential complementizer *che* ('that'). The use of *non* after *che* in comparative structures has been analogically (and only optionally) extended to comparisons introduced by *di quanto*, as well: e.g., *È più intelligente di quanto tu non creda*. The obligatory combination of expletive *non* with the subjunctive verb seems to have occurred as recently as the seventeenth century. Before that time we find that *non* is always followed by an indicative verb, whilst in comparatives without *non* a subjunctive verb usually occurs.

7 Verb complementation

7.1 Types of complementation

A verb may take as its *complement* an object noun phrase (*Voglio acqua* 'I want water') or another verb phrase (*Voglio bere* 'I want to drink'). Modern Italian has two major kinds of verb complement structure: those consisting of an infinitive (or of an infinitive preceded by a preposition – notably *a* or *di*), and those consisting of the complementizer *che* followed by a finite verb: *Voglio cantare* 'I want to sing'; *Devono partire* 'They must leave'; *Comincio a cadere* 'I'm starting to fall'; *Decidesti di entrare* 'You decided to enter'; *Vedo partire la ragazza* 'I see the girl leave', and *Voglio che cantiate* 'I want you to sing'; *Dico che è vero* 'I say that it's true'; *So che verrete* 'I know that you'll come'; *Pare che piova* 'It seems that it's raining'; *Vedo che volete cantare* 'I see that you want to sing'.

The system of Latin verbal complementizers is, at first sight, similar. But the complement structure PREPOSITION + INFINITIVE is unknown; and in COMPLEMENTIZER + FINITE VERB structures there are *two* major classes of complementizer, UT (with its negative counterpart NE), and QUOD. The infinitival complement is found with modal and impersonal verbs, and with verbs of volition, perception and assertion. In such cases the grammatical subject of the complement clause appears in the object case form, namely the accusative (the so-called 'accusative and infinitive' construction): OPORTET PUEROS CANERE 'It is necessary that the boys sing'; UIDI EAM CANERE 'I saw her sing'; DIXIT ME LATRONEM ESSE 'He said I was a thief'; CREDO TE CÆSAREM ESSE 'I believe you to be Caesar', etc. In verbs of volition, the pronominal object does not appear when the subject of the main verb and the subordinate infinitive are coreferential: UOLO EOS CANERE 'I want them to sing'; UOLUNT ME ABIRE 'they want me to go', but UOLO CANERE 'I want to sing'; UOLUNT ABIRE 'they want to go'. The complementizer UT (or NE) occurs with verbs of ordering, causing, avoidance or prevention[11]. The complementizer QUOD was originally a relative pronoun having the sense 'the fact that', 'with regard to the fact that', and hence 'because', 'because of the fact that': GAUDEO QUOD UALES 'I'm pleased that/because you are well'; BENE EST QUOD ID FECIT 'It's good that he did it'; CREDO QUOD RECTE FECIT 'I think he did rightly'. In addition to QUOD, QUIA, 'because', is also employed as a complementizer. UT is extinct in Romance. Already in Late (and particularly Christian) Latin, UT is being supplanted by QUOD, which in turn is supplanted in most Romance varieties by reflexes of QUID (just as the relative pronoun QUOD was replaced by the originally interrogative QUID), whence Italian *che*, (and OTuscan *ched* before vowels), Castilian *que*, French *que*, etc.[12]

In the modern language, bare infinitive complements – those not preceded by a preposition – survive with a number of modal verbs, and in impersonal constructions: *Voglio cantare* 'I want to sing'; *Debbo partire* 'I have to leave'; *Posso entrare* 'I can come in'; *Bisogna cantare* 'It is necessary to sing'; *Occorre firmare* 'It is necessary to sign', etc. The accusative and infinitive structure has largely retreated in favour of the structure comprising complementizer *che* + FINITE VERB – its surprising frequency in the written language of the thirteenth, fourteenth and fifteenth centuries is perhaps attributable to imitation of Latin models. In the modern language, the infinitive with accusative subject of the complement verb survives in verbs of perception, i.e., precisely in those verbs where the subject of the complement verb (e.g., *Maria canta*; *Maria balla*) is also the object of the perception verb (e.g., *Sento Maria*; *Vedo Maria*): *Sentono Maria cantare* 'They hear Maria sing'; *Vedo Maria ballare* 'I see Maria dance', etc. The accusative and infinitive pattern is reinforced by the fact that in causative structures the Latin type EFFICIO UT CANAT ('I cause that she sing' = 'I make her sing') gives way to the Romance structure *fare* + INFINITIVAL VERB + NOUN PHRASE: e.g., *Faccio cantare Marco* 'I make Marco sing'; *Lascio entrare la ragazza* 'I let the girl come in'; *Li faccio cantare* 'I make them sing', etc. Here the noun phrase is simultaneously the subject of the complement sentence (e.g., *Marco canta*; *La ragazza entra*; *Essi cantano*) and the object of the causative verb *fare* where the subject noun phrase of the complement is also the object of the main verb. But when the object of the main verb, and the subject of the complement verb, are not identical, the accusative and infinitive structure has generally yielded to *che* + VERB: *Dice che sono ammalato* 'He says I'm ill'; *Voglio che cantino le ragazze* 'I want the girls to sing'; *So che cantano le ragazze* 'I know the girls are singing', etc.

An important Romance innovation is the introduction of the

complementizer structure PREPOSITION + INFINITIVE. As a rule of thumb, the preposition *a*, true to its original association with 'motion towards', is employed in certain inceptive, final or goal-oriented complements, thereby taking over some of the functions performed in Latin by UT + SUBJUNCTIVE: *Lo persuasi a venire* 'I persuaded him to come'; *Mando Marco a chiamare il medico* 'I send Marco to call the doctor'; *Si è risolto a comprare la macchina* 'He has made up his mind to buy the car'; *Sono stato costretto a vendere la macchina* 'I have been forced to sell the car'; *Comincio a cantare* 'I start to sing', etc. It is far more difficult to identify any semantic motivation for the complementizer preposition *di*, but the origins of *di* may throw some light on the problem. Like certain other structures associated with complementation (e.g., the Latin infinitive, which was, originally, a locative case form of a verbal noun) the original sense of DE was the more general 'about', 'concerning'. Unlike AD (> *a*), then, DE (> *di*) was, semantically neutral, a fact which has facilitated its use in a wide range of contexts, and its establishment as a polyvalent complementizer with the infinitive, equivalent to *che* with finite verb. It is especially common where the subject of the main verb and of the complement are coreferent: *Dice d'essere ammalato* 'He says he's ill'; *Vedo d'esser stato bocciato* 'I see I've been failed'; *Credevo d'avere chiuso la porta* 'I thought I'd closed the door'. It sometimes performs the functions of Latin UT + SUBJUNCTIVE constructions: *Gli ordino di ritornare* 'I order him to return'; *Gli hanno impedito di entrare* 'They prevented him entering'. Verbs with the complementizer *a* do not usually have finite counterparts in *che*, although *perché* + SUBJUNCTIVE is possible, so that we do not find ***Ho mandato Marco che chiami il medico*, but *Ho mandato Marco perché chiami il medico* 'I have sent Marco to call the doctor'.

A feature of OTuscan complementation is the appearance of an occasional redundant or 'expletive' *non* after verbs of prohibition, doubting or fearing: e.g., *Decameron* (fourteenth century) *io non dubito che voi non dobbiate vivere il più consolato signor del mondo* 'I have no doubt that you must live as the most contented gentleman in the world'; Macinghi Strozzi (late fifteenth century) *per paura che io non ammalassi e non avessi disagio* 'for fear that I might fall ill and suffer discomfort'; Bandello (sixteenth century) *non potete in alcun modo vitarmi ch'io non la pigli* 'there is no way that you can prevent me taking it'; *chi ti divieta che teco ne le spedizioni non la meni?* 'who is preventing you from taking her with you on the expeditions?'; Cellini (sixteenth century) *e tu impedisci il mio figliuolo che non facci la voglia mia* 'and you are preventing my son from doing my will'. The origin of this phenomenon is unclear: as with expletive *non* in comparisons (see section 6), it may be due to an inherent negative implication in such expressions: in preventing and fearing one wishes that the event should *not* happen; in expressing doubt one voices the view that some proposition is probably *not* true.[13]

7.2 Complementizer deletion

Modern Italian occasionally admits deletion of the complementizer *che*, particularly in clauses governed by the verbs *parere* 'to seem', *bisognare* 'to be necessary', *volere* 'to want', *pregare* 'to pray' and *credere* 'to believe',[14] and also in sentences where another *che* is present: e.g., *Pare lo facciano apposta* 'It seems they're doing it deliberately'; *Soggiunse che preferiva non si fosse mai parlato tra noi, di questo* 'He added that he preferred that we had never discussed this'; *Non credo sia distante più di un centinaio di chilometri* 'I don't think it's more than a hundred kilometres away'; *un albero che aveva dato ordine fosse serbato* 'a tree which he had ordered should be preserved'; *Telefonò al suo capo pregandolo gli confermasse l'incarico* 'He phoned his boss asking him to confirm his appointment'; *Non era necessario lo facesse* 'It was not necessary for him to do it'; *Simona capiva gli avrebbe fatto un piacere enorme, e lo invitò a pranzo* 'Simona realized it would give him great pleasure, and invited him to lunch'.[15] Such deletion, still rare in the language of the thirteenth and fourteenth centuries (cf. Wanner (1981: 56–8)), becomes extremely common in the fifteenth, when it affects not only the sentential complementizer *che* (regardless of the mood of the subordinate verb), but any *che* introducing a clause, including the comparator (see section 6). Thus, from Macinghi Strozzi: *ti prega gliele mandi presto* 'he asks you to send it to him soon'; *che Iddio il sa, il dispiacere ebbi quando intesi non potevi venire quando fusti a Livorno* 'for the Lord knows how sorry I was when I heard you couldn't come when you were in Livorno'; *chè sta peggio non ti credi* 'for he's worse than you think'; *Io ho scritto a Iacopo quello mi pare sia di bisogno* 'I wrote to Iacopo what I think is necessary'; *Vorrei m'avvisassi quanti furono e danari ti dissi mi serbassi per espese nella malattia di Lorenzo* 'I'd like you to let me know how much money I told you to keep for me for expenses during Lorenzo's illness', etc. By the seventeenth century, deletion becomes again extremely rare, although still more extensive than in the modern language. This retreat of complementizer deletion is probably the result, as Wanner (1981: 75f.) suggests, of Bembo's advocacy, in the previous century, of norms based on the language of two or three hundred years earlier (cf. Ch.1: 2.3) in which deletion had been much less common.

8 Aspect and tense

The CL verb expresses perfective and imperfective aspect (see 8.1), time relative to the time of utterance (the present, the past and the future), and time relative to some reference point in the past or future (the pluperfect FECERAM 'I had done' and the future perfect FECERO 'I shall have done' are perfective aspect forms which also denote anteriority to an event in the past or future). All of these distinctions persist in Italian, although their expression is, in some cases, radically modified. The major changes may be summarized as follows:[16]

(i) The perfective (and anterior) forms are substituted by analytic structures AUXILIARY VERB + PERFECTIVE (*or* 'PAST') PARTICIPLE: e.g., CL FECI/AMAUI > *ho fatto/ho amato* 'I have done/loved'; FECERAM/AMAUERAM > *avevo fatto/avevo amato* 'I had done/loved'; FECERO/AMAUERO > *avrò fatto/avrò amato* 'I shall have done/loved'. The morphological development of these forms has been surveyed in Ch.3: 8.8.1–2. In the case of the past perfective, both the analytic and synthetic structures coexist (see below), and express a distinction, not made in CL, between present perfectivity and past perfectivity.

(ii) The synthetic future tense forms are supplanted by originally analytic structures comprising INFINITIVE + PRESENT TENSE OF HABERE: e.g., FACIAM/AMABO is replaced by *FACERE/AMARE HABEO > *farò/amerò* 'I shall do'/'I shall love'. This development has been surveyed in Ch.3: 8.8.5.

(iii) On the model of (ii), a new[17] category is created indicating future time relative to a reference point in the past (the so-called 'future-in-the-past' or 'conditional'), expressed by means of the structure INFINITIVE + PAST TENSE FORM OF HABERE: e.g., Italian *farebbe* 'he would do'; *amerebbe* 'he would love'. The corresponding perfective and anterior form is modelled on the perfective structures in (i), and takes the form 'FUTURE-IN-THE-PAST' AUXILIARY + PERFECTIVE ('PAST') PARTICIPLE: e.g., *avrebbe fatto/amato* 'he would have done/loved'. The syntactic and semantic evolution of Italian conditionals will be surveyed in 8.4.1 and 9.4.

(iv) A peculiarity of OTuscan, to be surveyed in 8.4, is the use of analytic verb forms to distinguish punctual (or non-durative) from non-punctual (durative) action. Such structures were subsequently deployed to signal *successivity*.

8.1 Perfective and imperfective aspect

In imperfective aspect, the action or state expressed by the verb is viewed from the perspective of its internal constituency (focusing on, for example, progression, continuity, repetition), and without regard for its temporal limits; in the perfective, the action or state is viewed from an external perspective, with the focus on its temporal limits. Perfective forms are particularly used where the event is viewed as complete or punctual (non-durative). Broadly speaking, this aspectual distinction has survived intact into modern Italian. It is particularly clear in the opposition between Italian imperfect and perfect tense forms (the latter being the only remnants of the CL perfective forms – cf. Ch.3: 8.1 and Ch.3: 8.5). For example:

– *Luigi dormiva* [progressive] *placidamente nel suo letto quando (all'improvviso) scoppiò* [punctual/completed] *un tuono formidabile.* 'Luigi was sleeping quietly in his bed when (suddenly) a terrible thunder clap was heard'.
– *In quel periodo Marco si alzava* [repetitive]/*si alzò* [punctual] *alle sette.* 'At that time Marco used to get up/got up at seven.'
– *Durante l'incontro, Marco guardava* [continuous/durative] *davanti a sé con aria desolata.* 'Throughout the meeting, Marco was looking in front of himself with a desolate air'.
– *Gianni accendeva* [continuous/iterative]/*accese* [completed/punctual] *la pipa, che gli si spegneva* [continuous/iterative]/ *spense* [completed/punctual] *per la pioggia.* 'Gianni kept lighting/lit his pipe, which kept going out/went out because of the rain'.

It is the essential 'open-endedness' of the imperfect – its failure to specify the completion of some event – which facilitates its employment, notably in the spoken language, with the additional function of a 'future-in-the-past', indicating some event which had yet to occur: e.g., *Ha promesso che tornava lo stesso giorno* 'She promised she was coming back the same day' or 'She promised she would come back the same day'.[18]

There have been two major innovations in the history of the Italian aspectual system. One is the creation of perfective forms by means of the analytic structure AUXILIARY + PAST PARTICIPLE. The second involves the expression of durativity in the verb, and the deployment of the periphrastic structure to mark non-durativity (punctuality), a development which, in turn, appears to have had major repercussions on the tense system, especially with regard to the signalling of future time.

8.2 The analytic perfective structures

All Romance varieties developed a perfective form (cf. Ch.3: 8.8.1) of the present tense by means of an analytic structure comprising a present tense auxiliary (from CL HABERE 'to have' or ESSE 'to be') and a perfective participle of the verb. In CL, the 'perfect' verb form (FECI 'I did', AMAUI 'I loved', etc.) functions both as a past perfective verb form, and as a present perfective. The introduction of the present perfective analytic structure (the source of the modern Italian 'passato prossimo') differentiates the two functions. This distinction is continued in Tuscan and in most dialects of central and southern Italy, but in Salento, Calabria and Sicily the periphrastic structure is rarely used – cf. Rohlfs (1969: 45f.). Because an event which is *completed* (perfective) at a given point in time must necessarily be anterior to that point (cf. Harris (1978: 137f.)), the periphrastic present form must express an event anterior to the present (i.e., *past* time): indeed, in northern Italian dialects the PPr. has largely supplanted the PR as the exponent of past perfectivity,[19] so that the distinction between present and past perfectivity has again become neutralized. Where both forms persist, the PPr. retains its association with present time, in that the effects of the event expressed by the verb are viewed as persisting at the moment of utterance (cf. Bertinetto (1991: 89–95)): e.g., *Ho trovato questo libro che vedi sul tavolo una quarantina di anni fa* 'I found this book you see on the table about forty years ago'; *È nato il 20 maggio 1957* ('He was born on the 20th May 1957' – the subject is implied to be still alive) vs. *Nacque il 20 maggio 1457* ('He was born on the 20th May 1457' – the subject is implied to be dead). It is in the nature of things that events whose effects thus persist into the present tend to have occurred in the recent past (whence the name 'passato prossimo'),[20] but proximity in time is not an essential condition for its use, any more than distance in time is a condition for the use of the 'passato remoto'. If there is no particular link with the moment of utterance, the PR may be employed, even for very recent events (cf. Bertinetto (1991: 95)). The PPr. also shares with the present tense certain 'atemporal'[21] and 'habitual' uses not shared by the PR: *Una persona che ha studiato/**studiò non deve comportarsi così* 'Somebody who has studied should not behave like that'; *Tutte le volte che lo incontro, lui mi parla dell'ultimo libro che ha letto/**lesse* 'Every time I meet him, he talks to me about the latest book he has read'. Like the present tense forms, and unlike the PR, it may also refer to future time: e.g., *Ti raggiungerò quando ho finito/**finii* 'I'll join you when I've finished'. And it alone can be used with adverbial expressions indicating present time: e.g., *Adesso finalmente ho appagato/**appagai ogni mio desiderio* 'Now at last I have quenched my every desire'.

It remains difficult, however, to generalize about the relationship between the use of PPr. and PR in the literary language, and in modern Tuscan. Overall, it seems (see Lepschy and Lepschy (1992)) that the literary language shows an ever increasing propensity to use the PPr., where modern Tuscan dialects, and the regional Italian, of Tuscans, might employ the PR.

The other perfective forms of the Latin verb are wholly replaced by periphrastic structures (but see Ch.3: 8.7). The pluperfect (expressing a completed event anterior to some reference point in the past – e.g., FECERAM 'I had done', AMAUERAM 'I had loved'), the future perfect (expressing a completed event anterior to some reference point in the future – e.g., FECERO 'I shall have done', AMAUERO 'I shall have loved') and the perfective infinitive (FECISSE 'to have done', AMAUISSE 'to have loved'), are replaced respectively by the analytic structures *avevo fatto* 'I had done', *avevo amato* 'I had loved'; *avrò fatto* 'I shall have done'; *avrò amato* 'I shall have loved'; *aver fatto* 'to have done'; *aver amato* 'to have loved', etc.[22]

8.3 Durativity

Durativity is not, strictly speaking, a matter of verbal aspect. Rather, it concerns the nature of the action expressed by the verb, focusing on the temporal continuity of that action (cf. Bertinetto (1991: 27–32)). Although perfective and imperfective aspect tend to be closely linked with durative and non-durative action, respectively, they are in principle neutral with regard to durativity. This is broadly true of the imperfect vs. PR distinction in OTuscan and modern Italian, but the association between PR and *reduced* durativity, or absence of durativity, is stronger in the modern language than it was in the Middle Ages. In the modern language, the PR is usually interpreted as expressing a *lesser* duration than an accompanying imperfect; often, the PR is *punctual*, whilst the imperfect is *durative*: *Uscì mentre pioveva* 'He went out while it was raining'; *Si nascose dentro una grotta, perché la polizia lo inseguiva* 'He hid inside a cave, because the police were pursuing him'. It appears that in the medieval language, and as late as the sixteenth century, the PR – unlike the imperfect which positively specified durativity – was neutral as regards the specification of durativity. That is to say that the PR did not *necessarily* express a state or event whose duration was lesser than that of an accompanying verb in the imperfect. Rather, it could be employed to express a past state in its *totality* (cf. Ambrosini (1960: 115)), whose temporal duration might be coextensive with, or greater than, that of an accompanying verb in the imperfect. This use of the PR is especially prominent in the introduction of narratives, where it serves to provide a factual 'frame' for the entire narrative. Thereafter, PR or imperfect may be selected according to the aspectual principles already described: e.g., Novellino (thirteenth century) *uno re **fu** nele parti di Egitto, lo quale **avea** uno suo figliuolo primogenito* . . . 'there was a king in the region of Egypt, who had a firstborn son . . .'; Bandello (mid sixteenth century) *Non sono ancora molti anni, che in una città di Lombardia **fu** una onorata gentildonna* . . . 'Not so many years ago, there was an honourable gentlewoman in a city of Lombardy . . . ', etc.

The distinction is apparent in other contexts as well. In the following examples the verbs in the imperfect and those in the PR are temporally coextensive, and in some cases denote one and the same action or state; but the imperfect forms focus on the internal consistency of the action, such as habituality, repetition, incompleteness, etc., and the PR forms focus on the totality of the action, as evidenced by their occurrence with adverbial expressions like *continuo a tutti* 'continually to everyone', *mai* 'never', *in tutta questa guerra* 'throughout this war': Sacchetti (fourteenth century) *Chi* ***domandava*** *in un modo e chi in un altro. A tutti* ***rispondea*** *ch'e' pesci grandi si* ***mangiavano*** *i piccolini; e così continuo a tutti* ***rispose****, e mai non* ***disse*** *altro* 'Some asked in one way, and some in another. To all he answered that big fishes ate little ones; and thus he continually answered everyone, and he never said anything else.'; Compagni (thirteenth century) *Siena* ***puttaneggiava****: ché in tutta questa guerra non* ***tenne*** *il passo a' nemici né dalla volontà dei Fiorentini in tutto si* ***diparti****. I Bolognesi si* ***tennono*** *forte co' Fiorentini contro lo imperadore, perché* ***temeano*** *forte di lui* 'Siena was playing the whore; for throughout this war she did not bar her enemies' passage, nor did she wholly depart from the will of the Florentines. The Bolognese stood firm with the Florentines against the emperor, because they were greatly afraid of him'.

In the modern language it is the imperfect tense which is employed in framing past actions. Indeed, the association of the imperfect with 'scene-setting' in narratives may well be at the root of a peculiarity of the 'ludic' use of the imperfect in the preparatory phases of children's games: *Facciamo che tu eri il medico e io ero l'infermiera* 'Let's pretend that you're the doctor and I'm the nurse'; *Adesso volavo, e cadevo. Tu mi aiutavi e mi soccorrevi* 'Now I'm flying along and I crash. You help me and rescue me', etc.

8.4 Punctuality and analytic verb forms

In the modern language, a PR is normally interpreted as expressing a more restricted duration than that of a verb in the imperfect. How the durational 'neutrality' of the PR ultimately came to be lost is unclear, but it is probably this original neutrality (cf. Ambrosini (1960: 117; 118)) which favoured or, at any rate, did not impede, the creation in the medieval language of a form which, unlike the PR, was *distinctively* non-durative, namely the 'trapassato remoto' (TR). The TR consists of the passato remoto form of the auxiliary verb, and the past participle (*ebbi fatto* 'I had done'; *fui partito* 'I had left'), and originally functioned as a distinctive marker of punctual, immediate, non-durative events or actions in the past. In the modern language,[23] the TR has become grammaticalized, and is little more than a contextually conditioned variant of the pluperfect, which is selected after certain temporal conjunctions (and in the construction PAST PARTICIPLE + *che* + PR AUXILIARY): e.g., *Appena fu tornata, mi telefonò* 'I soon as she had come back, she phoned me'; *Quando l'ebbi vista ritornai a casa* 'When I had seen her I went home'; *Dopo che furono partiti, mi addormentai* 'After they'd left, I fell asleep'; *Fatto che ebbe questo discorso, tacque* 'When she'd made this speech, she fell silent', etc.

Bertinetto (1991: 111; 113f.) observes that the TR is now employed only where the event *immediately precedes*, and is concluded prior to, a reference point in the past. It could not be used, for example, in a context such as *Da quando aveva/**ebbe terminato la scuola, Luciano non aveva mai trascorso/trascorse mai tante ore al tavolino come quel giorno* 'From the time he had finished school, Luciano had never spent so long at his desk as that day'. The modern state of affairs – which appears to have established itself in the literary language in the fifteenth century (cf. Stussi (1960: 127f.)) – is a remnant of a once more widespread function of the TR, that of signalling *immediate successivity*, but not necessarily anteriority, with respect to some reference point in the past. Brambilla Ageno (1964: 299) (also Ambrosini (1960)), identifies an aspectual distinction between PR and TR in OTuscan such that the latter indicates the immediate accomplishment or the final point of an action, and is strongly 'punctual' and hence *non-durative*: (*Decameron*) *questo diavolo di questa femina maladetta mi si parò dinanzi ed ebbemi veduto* 'this devilish accursed woman stopped in front of me and saw me'; *Né poté ella, poi che veduto l'ebbe, appena dire Domaine, che il lupo le si fu avventato alla gola, e, presala forte, la cominciò a portare via* 'And once she had seen it, she could hardly say 'Domaine', before the wolf had sprung at her throat and, grasping her, started to carry her off'; Macinghi Strozzi *che a dì 6, cioè domenica passata, la notte a ore 5, e prigioni ebbono rotto, e usciti fuori nella corte* . . . 'for on the 6th, that is last Sunday, at 5 in the morning, they broke out of jail, and having gone out into the courtyard . . .'; Sercambi Novelle *E subito calzatosi tornò in Siena et in Campo fu venuto, dicendo a chi trovava se avea veduto Besso mercadante d'oghe* 'And having put on his shoes immediately, he went back to Siena and went straight back to the Campo, asking any he met if they had seen Besso the goose seller'; *E subito presolo, in ispalla sel puose e in Arno l'ebbe gittato* 'And having taken him straight away, he put him over his shoulder and threw him in the Arno'. What remains to be explained is why the TR was subsequently eliminated from usage, save from the environment of certain temporal expressions explicitly marking immediate anteriority. But we may surmise that its 'punctual' function was gradually ousted as the PR became increasingly associated, itself, with punctuality.

Analytic structures have also been employed to mark punctuality (rather than anteriority) in other tense forms. In the medieval language, the structure FUTURE AUXILIARY + PAST PARTICIPLE often indicates immediate completion of an event in the future, although this construction does not appear to have survived into modern Italian. Thus, in the late thirteenth century writings of the Umbrian Iacopone da Todi we find *Or ecco lo stare c'ha l'omo 'n sto mondo . . . Recolto el biado e vendegnato, arò semenato per tempo futuro. Mai non si compie questo mercato.* 'Now this is man's condition in this world . . . (As soon as) the wheat is harvested and the vintage gathered, I shall (immediately) sow for the future. This routine never ends.'; from Boccaccio (fourteenth century) *Sarà dunque Sofronia tua [. . .], e io, il mio amore leggiermente ad un'altra volgendo, avrò te e me contentato* 'So Sofronia shall be yours [. . .] and I, easily turning my love towards another, will satisfy you and myself'; Macinghi Strozzi (late fifteenth century) *pure da dua di en qua è migliorato: se seguirà, sarà iscampato* 'even over the last two days he has got better: if he continues in this way, he will pull through'); *A questo piglierò consiglio da Tommaso, che duo dì fa tornò d'ufficio: e tu arai veduto dipoi come stanno e suo' fatti, e avisera'mi* 'To this end I shall take the advice of Thomas, who came back from his duty two days ago; and then you'll see how his business is, and you'll let me know'. Brambilla Ageno (1964: 310) also adduces examples of the punctual analytic form in imperative and final clauses, where the emphasis appears to be on the fact that the action must be completed, and completed within a certain time limit.

8.4.1 Punctuality, successivity and the future-in-the past

Substitution of an analytic for a synthetic structure occurs even where there is no obvious correlation with punctuality. As Brambilla Ageno (1964: 314) shows, in many southern Italian dialects a pluperfect (analytic) past subjunctive substitutes an imperfect subjunctive, in final, consecutive and indirect imperative clauses. This phenomenon is still rare in OTuscan, but appears in final clauses with some frequency in literary usage from the nineteenth century onwards (cf. also Rohlfs (1969: 63f.)): Imbriani, *gli diede tre palle e li portò sur una piazza e gli disse che l'avessero buttate per aria* 'he gave them three balls and he took them into a square and told them to throw them into the air'; Pitrè, *scrisse: Che li avessero ammazzato i figli e la moglie, e alla moglie prima le avessero tagliate le mani* 'he wrote that they should kill his children and his wife, and cut off his wife's hands first'; *quando fu in fin di morte, chiamò la sua figliola e gli disse che avesse seguitato a far la limosina come faceva lei* 'when she was at death's door, she called her daughter and told her that she should continue to give alms as she did', etc.

Brambilla Ageno is sceptical about the possibility of assigning a particular aspectual value to these uses of the pluperfect subjunctive (1964: 320), even though she allows that they probably originate with a perfective function; rather, she views the phenomenon (1964: 324f.) as providing a distinctively *past* tense counterpart to the imperfect subjunctive which, in some southern dialects, also functions as a *present* subjunctive (cf. Ch.5: 2.3.2.8). But this analysis will not work for Tuscan, where the imperfect subjunctive is not used with reference to the present. What is striking about the examples Brambilla Ageno cites[24] is that the innovatory use of the pluperfect subjunctive form signals events *subsequent* to a main reference point in the past; in other words, the analytic form functions as a kind of 'future-in-the-past'. It is inherent in punctual verb forms that they do not express simultaneity with other perfective verb forms, and it follows that such forms express serialization or *successivity* of events. Given this, and bearing in mind the association between punctuality and analytic verb forms, we perhaps have an explanation of why an analytic past subjunctive came to be used as a marker of events subsequent to some point in the past.

It is an idiosyncrasy of modern Italian that an event in the future viewed from the perspective of some point in the past is signalled by means of an analytic conditional form, rather than the synthetic conditional form employed by some other Romance tongues (e.g., *avrebbe fatto* rather than *farebbe*): compare Italian *Disse che* ***sarebbe venuta***; *Alle otto non c'era ancora, ma* ***sarebbe arrivata*** *più tardi* 'She said she would come; At eight she still wasn't there, but she would arrive later', with French *Elle a dit qu'elle* ***viendrait****; A huit heures elle n'y était pas encore, mais elle* ***arriverait*** *plus tard* and Spanish *Dijo que* ***vendría****; A las ocho ya no estaba, pero* ***llegaría*** *más tarde*. The analytic conditional future-in-the-past is wholly absent from the writings of Dante, Boccaccio and Sacchetti, while the analytical form functions exclusively to indicate unrealized action in the past (cf. Brambilla Ageno (1964: 351f.)), as in *se fosse venuta, l'avremmo vista* 'if she had come we would have seen her'. The analytic future-in-the-past begins to appear frequently only from the first half of the seventeenth century, often alongside the simple conditional form. The latter remains in common usage in the literary language well into the nineteenth century, for example in the writings of Manzoni and Fogazzaro.

Once the new structure becomes established, the synthetic conditional is relegated to modal functions, among them[25] particularly that of expressing the result of a presently unfulfilled condition (*Se venisse, la vedremmo* 'If she came, we would see her'). It is probably safe to assume, with Goggio (1922), that the analytical form has long existed in popular Tuscan speech, infiltrating the literary language only in recent times. The parallels with other substitutions of synthetic by analytic structures (and especially that of the imperfect subjunctive by the pluperfect subjunctive[26], discussed above) are suggestive. A hypothesis which, in the absence of a more thorough investigation of early texts and modern Tuscan dialects, must remain speculative, is that the analytic conditional future-in-the-past – although not now particularly linked with perfective aspect (cf. Bertinetto (1986: 515)) – originated in punctual perfective expressions,[27] and that the 'successivity' inherent in such uses promoted reanalysis of the analytic conditional as a future-in-the-past. It is noteworthy in this connection that in southern Italy the synthetic conditional, like the synthetic future, appears to have an exclusively modal function, and does not express future time (cf. Rohlfs (1969: 54; 57)). These southern conditionals probably originated as imitations of Tuscan or northern Italian models. That they should have a purely modal function perhaps indicates the historical predominance of modal over temporal uses in early Tuscan,[28] favouring the adoption of a distinctively temporal analytic form. It is striking that, while the synthetic conditional future-in-the-past is the prevalent form in the first eighteen Novelle of Bandello, from the sixteenth century, (e.g., *[dicendo] che eternamente le sarebbe servidore e che mai altra donna non ameria* 'saying that he would be her eternal servant and that he would never love another woman'), an analytic form occurs precisely in a context (Novella 16, where the subject's presence is about to be unmasked by the lighting of a candle in a darkened room) in which a sudden, rapid, succession of future actions is expressed: *facendo buon animo si preparava a dir la sua ragione a la meglio che sapeva, portando ferma openione che come la donna veduto l'avesse, che sarebbero incontinente venuti a le mani* 'gathering his courage he prepared to explain himself as best he could, being quite convinced that when the woman saw him, they would immediately come to blows'.[29]

9 Mood

9.1 Uses and functions of the subjunctive

The subjunctive mood, in Latin and in Italian, is closely associated with the expression of states or events viewed as 'internal', mental, concepts, whose 'external', objective, reality is not asserted. The subjunctive may be employed because the event or state is contrary to fact, because the factual reality of what is asserted is uncertain, or because its reality is simply 'backgrounded', or viewed as 'immaterial'. The subjunctive appears particularly in the following cases:

(i) In clauses whose proposition is presented as false: e.g., *Non voglio dire che l'italiano sia una lingua difficile, ma non è neanche facile*

'I don't mean to say that Italian is a difficult language, but it's not easy either'; *Entrò senza che nessuno lo vedesse* 'He came in without anybody seeing him'; *Lo accettò non perché gli piacesse ma perché aveva fretta* 'He accepted it not because he liked it, but because he was in a hurry'; *Nego che mio marito sia stato coinvolto in attività criminali.* 'I deny that my husband has been involved in criminal activities';[30] *Non c'è nessuno che sappia il francese* 'There's nobody who knows French'; *Se io fossi ricco, sarei contento* 'If I were rich, I'd be happy'.

(ii) Where the reality of an event, action or state expressed by the verb is uncertain because the identity of the verb's subject is indeterminate or unspecified:[31] e.g., *Chiunque venga, io non mi sposterò* 'Whoever comes, I shall not move'; *Gli studenti che non superino l'esame verranno bocciati* '(Any) students who don't pass the exam will be failed'.

(iii) Where the truth of the proposition is regarded as immaterial: e.g., *Facesse anche bel tempo, non uscirei* 'Even if the weather were nice, I wouldn't go out'; *Sia bello o no, non mi piace* 'Whether it's beautiful or not, I don't like it'; *Per quanto sia bello, non mi piace* which can mean either 'However beautiful it may be, I don't like it', or 'Although it is beautiful, I don't like it'.

(iv) In clauses (main or subordinate) in which there is expressed some, usually unrealized, condition, ideal or concept. This category includes expressions of volition, ordering, prohibition, or purpose, where the event or state desired, ordered, intended, permitted or forbidden is unfulfilled: e.g., *Accettiamo la proposta a condizione che/a patto che/sempre che il prezzo venga ridotto* 'We accept the proposal on condition that the price be lowered'; *Dice che non tornerà finché non si senta meglio* 'She says he won't be back until she feels better';[32] *È necessario che i treni rispettino l'orario* 'It is necessary that trains keep to the timetable'; *Bisogna che ubbidiate alla legge* 'You must obey the law'; *Voglio che vengano* 'I want them to come'; *Impedirò che cantino* 'I shall prevent them singing'; *Parla lentamente perché lo capiscano* 'He talks slowly so that they will understand him'. In main clauses, the subjunctive generally expresses a wish or exhortation: *Venga domani!* 'let him/may he come tomorrow!', *Fosse vero!* 'if only it were true',[33] *Non cantino* 'Let them not sing'.

A syntactic innovation of Italian and other Romance languages is the use in *main* clauses of the complementizer *che*, in the expression of wishes or orders (e.g., *Che vengano domani!* 'Let them come tomorrow'; *Che non cantino!* 'Let them not sing'). Presumably this development originates in the close association between *che* and the subjunctive in subordinate clauses. For some observations on the use of this device in OTuscan, see Stefinlongo (1977: 273–6). *Che* + SUBJUNCTIVE is also sometimes used in Italian in interrogation (*Che sia lui?* '(I wonder) could it be him?', *Che sia un bel libro?* 'Is this a good book, (do you think)?'), which probably reflects the use of the subjunctive in subordinate interrogative clauses (see 9.2).

The semantic conditions for the selection of the subjunctive may be *implicit* (in main clauses, where the subjunctive form of the verb alone expresses the 'internal' perspective), or *explicit* (in subordinate clauses, where the content of the governing clause, or a conjunction determines the selection of the subjunctive mood). The extent to which semantic factors play a role in the selection of the subjunctive in subordinate clauses is variable. It ranges from 'strong' semantic determination, in which the governing clause, or a conjunction, makes explicit the semantic determination of the subjunctive (e.g., *volere che* 'to want that'; *ordinare che* 'to order that'; *evitare che* 'to avoid'; *senza che* 'without'; *a condizione che* 'on condition that'), through 'weak' semantic determination, in cases where the governing clause may introduce either assertions of opinion or assertions of fact (e.g., *credere che* 'to believe that'; *pensare che* 'to think that'; *non sapere che* 'not to know that'; *non dire che* 'not to say that'), to 'arbitrary' ('grammaticalized' or 'lexicalized') determination.

The verb is always in the subjunctive in subordinate clauses which are placed to the left of their governing clause, even where that governing verb asserts an incontestable truth: *È vero che Mario è un ladro*, 'It's true that Mario is a thief', but *Che Mario sia un ladro è vero*, 'That Mario is a thief is true'. But this is *not* an example of grammaticalization of the subjunctive: rather, the anteposition of the subordinate clause focuses attention on the idea or notion that Mario might be a thief, whose veracity is subsequently confirmed.

A detailed diachronic study of the evolution of the subjunctive remains a major desideratum of Italian historical linguistics. Here we can only outline certain trends in its development:

(i) A tendency for the indicative to prevail over the subjunctive in subordinate clauses having relatively 'weak' semantic determination.
(ii) Changes in the semantically arbitrary selection of the subjunctive.
(iii) Substitution of the subjunctive by the conditional (or the indicative), in certain kinds of hypothetical sentence.

It is by no means certain that the subjunctive is significantly more or less commonly used in modern Italian than at earlier stages in the history of the language. If there is truth in the suspicion (cf. Berruto (1990: 70–2)) that there has been some recession of the subjunctive in modern times, this may be due, in part, to the acquisition of Italian by native speakers of central and southern dialects in whose speech the (present) subjunctive is little used, and to the relative morphological complexity of the Tuscan subjunctive for speakers of non-Tuscan dialects (cf. Mioni (1983)).

9.2 Indicative and subjunctive in subordinate clauses

The subjunctive is usually selected in subordinate clauses governed by expressions of mental impression, such as belief, opinion, doubt, uncertainty, evaluation, emotional reaction, etc. (*Credo che sia vero* 'I think it's true'; *Mi sorprende che siate arrabbiati* 'I'm surprised you're angry'; *Ritengo che abbiate sbagliato* 'I reckon you've made a mistake'; *Dubito che sia vero* 'I doubt that it's true'; *Non so se siano arrivati* 'I don't know whether they've arrived'; *Sono contento che lo facciate* 'I'm pleased you're doing it'). It should be borne in mind that the incidence of such clauses increases greatly in Romance with the retreat of the Latin accusative and infinitive construction (see section 7), in favour of the structure COMPLEMENTIZER + FINITE VERB. Expressions equivalent to 'the idea/notion that'[34] (e.g., *L'idea che Giovanni sia un ladro è assurda* 'The idea that Giovanni is (could be) a thief is absurd'; *Che Giovanni sia un ladro è assurdo* 'That Giovanni is (could be) a thief is absurd') may also govern a subordinate verb in the subjunctive. In all these cases, the selection of the subjunctive is only weakly determined by semantic factors, in that the verb in the subordinate clause may also be conceived as an expression of 'external' factual reality.

While it is true that in spoken and informal registers of modern Italian there is a tendency for the indicative to encroach on the subjunctive in subordinate clauses, what emerges clearly from Wandruszka's survey (1991)[35] is that the subjunctive is most resistant in those clauses where there is a strong, explicit semantic motivation for its selection. Thus clauses introduced by inherent expressions of unrealized, ideal, states or events, such as *volere che*, generally retain the subjunctive (*voglio che venga* 'I want him to come'). Other verbs, such as *credere che* 'to believe that'; *pensare che* 'to think that'; *sperare che* 'to hope that'; *sembrare che* 'to seem that'; *non sapere che* 'not to know that', etc., may govern clauses whose content is, or is conceived as, factually real. With such verbs, the semantic determination of subjunctive selection is weak, and indicatives frequently occur, particularly in spoken language and informal registers: *non credo che viene* 'I don't think he's coming'; *sembra che è vero* 'it seems it's true'; *speriamo che viene* 'let's hope she comes', etc. Among such verbs, however, those which express a higher degree of inherent uncertainty than do *credere* and *pensare*, such as *supporre* 'to suppose'; *sospettare* 'to suspect'; *presumere* 'to presume'; *ammettere* 'to grant', appear more resistant to the indicative. The vacillation between subjunctive and indicative which is particularly characteristic of 'weakly determined' subordinate clauses is of some antiquity. A strikingly similar picture to that painted by Wandruszka emerges from Stefinlongo's survey (1977) of the subjunctive in subordinate clauses in the thirteenth and fourteenth centuries. Here there is no attestation of the use of an indicative in subordinate verbs governed by *volere*, which confers strong semantic determination but, in the case of *credere* (1977: 481f.), selection of the indicative seems to be particularly favoured if *certainty* is expressed by some accompanying adverb, or after first person forms of the verb (the speaker is more likely to be certain with respect to what he or she believes than with regard to that which is believed by others). Stefinlongo also notes that *credere* is more likely to govern the subjunctive when it appears in a subordinate clause, than when *credere* appears in a main clause. Similar observations apply to *pensare che*.

9.3 Semantically arbitrary selection of the subjunctive

Some occurrences of the subjunctive in subordinate clauses, in Latin as in Italian, are semantically arbitrary, but there is relatively little historical continuity in this respect. CL ANTEQUAM and PRIUSQUAM 'before' almost always select the subjunctive (cf. Hofmann and Szantyr (1965: 600)). Their successors in Italian, *prima che* 'before'; *innanzi che* 'before', etc., do likewise. While there is a possible semantic motivation for the choice of mood in the context of successfully forestalling some possible, but unrealized, event (e.g., *Fuggì prima che la polizia lo arrestasse, e rimase in libertà fino alla sua morte* 'He fled before the police (could) arrest him, and remained free until his death'), this structure is clearly grammaticalized in contexts where the subsequent event incontestably occurred, and where there is no suggestion of avoidance, such as *Il paziente morì tre minuti prima che arrivasse l'ambulanza* 'The patient died three minutes before the ambulance arrived'. The Latin complementizer UT originally governed the indicative in resultative clauses, and the subjunctive in purposive or causative clauses; but in the classical language the subjunctive had made considerable inroads on resultative clauses as well (cf. Hofmann and Szantyr (1965: 329)).

The Italian successors of such constructions, in contrast, regularly differentiate mood in purposive clauses (which express an unrealized ideal) and resultative clauses (which are statements of factual events): *Il naufrago accese un fuoco, in modo che lo vedessero chiaramente* 'The shipwrecked man lit a fire, in order that they should see him clearly' vs. *Esce la luna, in modo che la vedete chiaramente* 'The moon comes out, so that you can see it clearly'. There has been, none the less, a measure of grammaticalization in the causative expression *fare sì che*, which governs a subordinate subjunctive even in resultative uses: e.g., *Il sole ha fatto sì che appassiscano i fiori* 'The sun has caused the flowers to wilt', where, obviously, there is no implication of purpose. The CL particle CUM 'when' or 'since/as' also selected a subjunctive in circumstances where what is asserted is a fact (a usage which possibly originated in certain adversative uses – cf. Handford (1947: 166–72)). The particle CUM is not directly continued in Italian, but its various successors *quando*; *siccome*; *come*; *perché* select the indicative. The Latin subjunctive is also grammaticalized to the extent that it is employed in indirect questions (most consistently in the classical authors, less so in popular usage – cf. Hofmann and Szantyr (1965: 538)). Selection of mood in Italian indirect questions is, by and large, semantically conditioned. Where the factual content of the question is at issue, the indicative is used: *Mi domandavo/Non sapevo se volevano del pane* = 'The question I was asking myself was whether they wanted bread'; when the questioner's uncertainty is to the fore, the subjunctive may be used instead: *Mi domandavo/Non sapevo se volessero del pane* = 'I was wondering whether they wanted bread' (cf. Wandruszka (1991: 468f.)). The selection of mood in subordinate clauses after the Latin complementizers QUOD and QUIA seems to have been far less systematically dependent on the meaning of the main clause than was the case in modern Italian (see Hofmann and Szantyr (1965: 577–9)). After expressions of evaluation and emotional reaction, QUOD was frequently followed by an indicative: GAUDEO QUOD UALES 'I am glad you're well'.

With the concessive conjunctions[36] *benché*; *sebbene*; *nonostante*; *ancorché*; *quantunque*; *malgrado*; *con tutto che*; all meaning 'although'; selection of the subjunctive is the norm[37] in the modern language, even though the verb may express an incontestable fact: e.g., *Benché la Calabria sia una regione mediterranea, il suo clima può essere severissimo* 'Although Calabria is a Mediterranean region, its climate can be very harsh'. It is possible that the use of the subjunctive with these conjunctions originated in those cases where the reality of the proposition contained in the concessive cause is 'backgrounded', or presented as immaterial (i.e., 'this may or may not be true, but anyway . . .'). At least until the seventeenth century, *benché*, *sebbene*, *con tutto che* select either the subjunctive or the indicative, and we have been unable to discern any systematic principle of mood selection: e.g., Cellini *se bene io continuo avevo la febbre* 'although I continually had fever'; *con tutto che io ne fussi malissimo pagato* 'even though I was extremely poorly paid for it'; *ancora che questo fussi la verità* 'even if this were the truth'; *con tutto che io ne sapevo qualche cosa* 'even though I knew something about it'; *se bene e' ci fussi quel gran Michelagnolo Buonarroti* 'even though the great Michelangelo Buonarroti was there'; *Con tutto che questa opera ci paia molto bella* . . . 'Even though this work seems very beautiful to us . . .', etc.

The subjunctive has also become grammaticalized in comparative structures of the type *È più intelligente che non crediate* 'He's more intelligent than you think', whose emergence from the originally alternative structures *che non* + INDICATIVE and *che* + SUBJUNCTIVE has been discussed in section 6. The presence of the subjunctive in such structures is difficult to explain, but it might be associated with the use of the subjunctive in constructions of the type *Per quanto lui sia intelligente, loro sono ancora più intelligenti* 'However intelligent he may be, they are yet more intelligent', where the factual reality of the event or action represented by the first verb is 'backgrounded' or 'immaterial'.

9.4 Mood in hypothetical ('conditional') sentences

Hypothetical (or conditional) sentences generally comprise a *protasis* (in which some hypothesis is postulated), and an *apodosis* (in which the result of the fulfilment of that hypothesis is asserted). In CL, conditional sentences fall into three major types, according to whether the propositions contained in their protases are (a) real, (b) improbable or (c) false. In 'real' hypotheticals the fulfilment of the condition is a fact, or is viewed as certain or likely to come about, and the full range of possible indicative tense forms can, in principle, be deployed both in the protasis and the apodosis; the most common pattern in CL is a future indicative form in both clauses. In type (b) the fulfilment of the condition is considered improbable, whilst in (c) the condition has either failed to be fulfilled or is known to be impossible. Types (b) and (c) are characterized by a subjunctive verb in protasis and apodosis:

Real
(FUTURE) INDICATIVE + (FUTURE) INDICATIVE
SI UENIET, UIDEBIT
'if he comes, he'll see'

Present improbable
PRESENT SUBJUNCTIVE + PRESENT SUBJUNCTIVE
SI UENIAT UIDEAT
'if he were to come [he may or may not], he would see'

Past improbable
IMPERFECT SUBJUNCTIVE + IMPERFECT SUBJUNCTIVE
SI UENIRET UIDERET
'if he had come [he may or may not have done], he would have seen.'

Present false
IMPERFECT SUBJUNCTIVE + IMPERFECT SUBJUNCTIVE
SI UENIRET UIDERET
'if he came [which he hasn't/won't] he would see'

Past false
PLUPERFECT SUBJUNCTIVE + PLUPERFECT SUBJUNCTIVE
SI UENISSET UIDISSET
'if he had come [but he didn't] he would have seen'

The system of 'real' conditionals is preserved more or less intact in Italian, retaining indicative verbs in protasis and apodosis, although the verb in the protasis is usually in the present tense, rather than in the future: *Se viene vedrà* 'If he comes he'll see'. But the morphological distinction between present improbable and present false disappears in Tuscan (and other Romance varieties – cf. Harris (1978: 237f.)),[38] and the imperfect subjunctive (derived from the Latin pluperfect subjunctive – Ch.3: 8.6.2) comes to function as a present 'false' *or* 'improbable' hypothetical (at least in the protasis – the apodosis is discussed below): *Se venisse vedrebbe* 'If he were coming/ if he came he'd see'. The *past* 'false' or 'improbable' conditional comes to be signalled by means of the pluperfect (analytical) subjunctive in the apodosis: *Se fosse venuto vedrebbe* 'If he had come he would see'. The distinction between false and improbable[39] conditions is effaced, so that in the modern language a morphological distinction is made between hypotheses which are presented as true, or at any rate probable (*Se viene vedrà* 'If he comes he will see'), and those which are considered false, or at least improbable (*Se venisse vedrebbe* 'If he came he would see'; *Se fosse venuto avrebbe visto* 'If he had come he would have seen').

9.4.1 Replacement of the subjunctive by other forms in apodoses
The CL pattern of identical mood and tense forms in protasis and apodosis (*se venisse, vedesse* 'if she came she would see') survives marginally in northern Italy, and is widespread in Campania, Abruzzo, Puglia and parts of Calabria, as well as being predominant in Sicily – see Rohlfs (1969: 141f.) for examples. This pattern does not survive in OTuscan, where from the earliest surviving texts the conditional appears to have supplanted the subjunctive in apodoses (cf. Brambilla Ageno (1964: 362f.)). However, where an apodosis contains a syntactic context normally requiring a subjunctive, OTuscan tends to employ an imperfect or pluperfect subjunctive rather than a synthetic or analytic conditional. Among such contexts are clauses subordinate to verbs like *credere* and *pensare*, and certain kinds of indirect question – cf.

Brambilla Ageno (1964: 353–61; 368–74): e.g., Sacchetti *s'egli avesse voluto combattere, io non so se io mi vi fosse condotto* 'if he had wanted to fight, I don't know whether I would have gone there'; Macinghi Strozzi *che un altro non credo si trovassi di sua condizione* 'I don't think you would find another of her kind'; *E se Niccolò facessi la via di qua alla tornata sua a Napoli, non so s'io mel lasciassi uscire tralle mani* 'And if Niccolò travelled through here on his way back to Naples, I'm not sure if I would let him slip through my hands'; Boccaccio (*Decameron*) *Bernabò, io non so quello ch'io mi facessi del tuo sangue, se io vincessi* 'Bernabò, I don't know what I would do with your blood, if I won'. The modern language has substituted such uses of the subjunctive in the apodosis with conditional forms: *io non so cosa farei del tuo sangue, se io vincessi*, etc.

Various 'attenuative' uses of the conditional signalling, for example, politeness or deference (e.g., *vorrei un gelato per cortesia* 'I'd like an ice cream please') – a function often performed by the subjunctive in Latin – or in reporting statements whose veracity the speaker does not guarantee (e.g., *Secondo l'agenzia di stampa, sarebbe scoppiata una bomba a Londra* 'According to the press agency, a bomb has gone off in London'), probably originate as 'virtual' hypothetical structures, where some protasis is implicit (say, *. . . se mi fosse permesso* '. . . if I were allowed'; *. . . se dovessimo credere a quanto ci dicono* '. . . if we were to believe what they tell us', etc.).

Another method of indicating past 'false' hypotheticals, especially common in the spoken and informal varieties of the language, employs the imperfect indicative in protasis and apodosis: *Se veniva lo faceva* 'if she had come she would have done it'. This structure is common in dialects of Salento, eastern Basilicata and Calabria (cf. Rohlfs (1969: 145)) and is also observable in some dialects of Abruzzo, Sicily, Umbria and Piedmont (cf. Rohlfs (1969: 145–7), who detects precursors of it in Latin). It is already frequent in fifteenth- and sixteenth-century writers such as Macinghi Strozzi and Cellini, and is discussed by sixteenth-century grammarians (cf. D'Achille (1991: 297f.)). From D'Achille's investigations (1991: 310), it appears that in the earliest attestations the imperfect appears in the apodosis only. It is from the fourteenth century that the imperfect begins consistently to appear in protasis and apodosis. A prominent factor in the employment of the imperfect tense form in counterfactual utterances is the 'incompleteness' or 'lack of realization' which is inherent (cf. 8.1) in the imperfect tense (see also D'Achille (1991: 299f.)).

Notes

1. For an exploration of the change from Latin to Romance word order, and of the hypothesis that certain other changes, such as the reversal of a predominant adjective-noun order, in favour of the order adjective-noun, have a coherence within a typological framework, see Harris (1978, particularly chapters 1–3).
2. In early Italo-Romance, as in Latin, auxiliary and modal verbs frequently follow main verbs (cf. Rohlfs (1969: 323)). This order is observed predominantly at the beginnings of clauses in OTuscan, and probably reflects the same principles which debar clause-initial clitics in OTuscan (Ch.3: 9.4.1).
3. See Benincà, Salvi and Frison (1988: 123–5) for further discussion.
4. The modern spoken language also evinces what may be a type of left dislocation of the verb, in an infinitival or participial form: e.g., *dormire, dormo* 'I do *sleep*'. In this construction, however, the verb is also retained in its original position. This device is of unknown antiquity. D'Achille (1991: 127) finds no trace of it in the texts he surveys.
5. We have seen (Ch.3: 8.8.2.1) that in OTuscan the *participle* often agrees in number and gender with a following direct object noun. It is notable that in OTuscan participial gender and number agreement is sometimes maintained even where the preceding verb does not agree: Macinghi Strozzi *ne venne presi tre* 'three of them were caught'; *n'è morti otto di pesta* 'eight of them died of plague', etc. See also Brambilla Ageno (1964: 162).
6. The examples cited, for example, by Brambilla Ageno (1964) involve verbs (including passives) which take *essere* as their auxiliary. The sole exceptions involve what are probably active past participle constructions (see Brambilla Ageno (1964: 161–8)).
7. See also Brambilla Ageno (1964: 168–70).
8. For the dialectal use of words such as *mica* 'crumb', *punto* 'stitch', *goccia* 'drop', as negators, see Rohlfs (1969: 304f.); Harris (1978: 25).
9. For some reflections on the origins of this syntactic feature, see Posner (1984).
10. See further Rohlfs (1969: 78f; 186f.) and Harris (1988). For the origins of OItalian *ma che* 'although', see Mazzoleni (1990: 151–7).
11. QUIN (extinct in Romance) was employed after certain verbs of preventing or doubting.
12. In Sicily, Calabria, Puglia and parts of the Abruzzo, reflexes of QUIA (usually **ka**) function as the general complementizer in verbs of perception and assertion, whilst in verbs of volition and ordering, reflexes of QUOD, QUID or MODO (= 'in (such) a way') are employed. See Rohlfs (1969: 188–90).
13. See also Rohlfs (1969: 306).
14. For an account of the tendency for deletion to occur with certain lexical verbs, and with certain grammatical persons of those verbs, see Wanner (1981: 51f.).
15. See Wandruszka (1991: 423; 426) for further details on the modern situation.

16. A detailed analysis of the Latin and Romance tense and aspect systems may be found in Harris (1978: 132–56).
17. To express future time viewed from the past, CL could make use of the periphrasis FUTURE PARTICIPLE (a category extinct in Romance) + ESSE: AMATURUS ERAM 'I was about to love' = 'I would love'.
18. See Bertinetto (1991: 41–62) for a detailed account of aspectual distinctions in modern language. For details of the opposition in OTuscan, see Ambrosini (1960) and Stussi (1960).
19. Some remnants persist in Emilia and Romagna. On the other hand, the PR is being abandoned in the dialects of Lunigiana. Rohlfs ascribes the lack of a PPr. in the far south to Greek adstrate influence. Even in these dialects, however, the PPr. may be employed, to emphasize the present state resulting from some past event: e.g., Calabrian *aju jutu* = '[I know the place because] I've been [there]'.
20. See Skubic (1967) and Fogarasi (1990: 214f.).
21. For so-called 'gnomic' uses of the PR in proverbial and other expressions (e.g., *Un bel tacer non fu mai scritto* 'A fine silence was never written down'), see Bertinetto (1991: 98).
22. Note that the analytical verb forms which do not indicate tense (e.g., the infinitive *aver fatto* or the gerund *avendo fatto*) indicate a purely aspectual distinction: *Spero di aver fumato il sigaro prima che tu torni* 'I'm hoping to smoke the cigar before you come back'.
23. Ambrosini (1960: 34) argues that it was originally characteristic of popular, rather than literary, usage.
24. The apparent exceptions, such as the quotations from Masuccio in Brambilla Ageno (1964: 325), are interpretable as, respectively, a true past anterior subjunctive, and an imperfect subjunctive + *adjectival* past participle.
25. For other functions of the simple conditional, see Bertinetto (1991: 128f.).
26. Occasionally one finds the analytic conditional and the pluperfect subjunctive employed with future-in-the-past reference. Thus De Amicis (*La Carrozza di Tutti*): *pensando sempre che sarebbe stato fortunato il cittadino d'Italia su cui ella avesse racchiuso le sue ali* 'ever thinking that the citizen of Italy over whom it folded its wings would always be fortunate'.
27. See also Bertinetto (1986: 214f.).
28. It is significant in this regard that Bertinetto (1986: 495f.) argues for a reversal of the traditionally assumed historical evolution of uses of the future tense form, such that 'epistemic' (modal) uses (e.g., *saranno le otto* 'it must be 8 o'clock') were historically prior to the use of the synthetic future as a tense form. Perhaps an originally modal use could be postulated for the morphologically parallel synthetic conditional?
29. Note that there is no question, here, of interpreting this as a 'counterfactual' past conditional, of the kind 'if she had seen him, they would have come to blows', because the subject anticipates that she definitely will see him.
30. Wandruszka (1991: 433) points to an incipient grammaticalization of the subjunctive with *negare* 'to deny', since it tends to occur also where this

verb is negated (and where the *truth* of the subordinate clause is thereby asserted): *non nego che sia vero* 'I don't deny that it's true' rather than *non nego che è vero*.

31. See Wandruszka (1991: 465) for the role of unspecified reference in relative clauses introduced by superlative constructions (including *solo* 'only'; *unico* 'only'; *ultimo* last; *primo* 'first' + *che*), such as: *Datemi il vaso più bello che avete/abbiate* 'Give me the nicest vase you have'.
32. The subjunctive is usually employed where *finché* refers to a future event, where the sense is akin to 'for however much time . . .'. With past events, where the duration is *known*, the indicative is normal: *Mi distesi sul letto finché non mi sentii meglio* 'I lay down on the bed until I felt better' (cf. Lepschy and Lepschy (1988: 106f.)).
33. It may also have concessive force: *Mi uccidano pure, non rivelerò il segreto!* 'Let them even kill me, I'll never reveal the secret!'.
34. See also Wandruszka (1991: 449–52).
35. See also Satta (1987: 151–3)
36. For vacillation between subjunctive and indicative uses after Latin QUAMUIS and QUAMQUAM 'although', see Handford (1947: 172).
37. A following *future* tense is sometimes found.
38. Such developments are anticipated already in CL: see Handford (1947: 122–4).
39. A possible remnant of the present improbable occurs in the occasional use, in protases, of a present subjunctive (especially where the protasis is introduced by *quando*, rather than *se* – cf. Rohlfs (1969: 139)). But in such cases *se* or *quando* are usually interpretable as introducing a provisional condition (cf. *purché*, *a condizione che*, etc.). In a conjoined protasis, introduced by *e*, OTuscan sometimes employs a subjunctive: Macinghi Strozzi *Che se Iddio mi presta vita qualc'anno, e la Lesandra m'esca di casa, vi fornirò sì di pannilini la casa.* 'If God lets me live a few more years, and Lesandra leaves home, I will furnish your house with linen'.

Chapter 5

Variation in Modern Italian

1 Types of variation

1.1 Contemporary sources of variation

We observed in Chapter 1 that no human language is structurally homogeneous. Different subgroups within a linguistic community use their common language in systematically different ways, and individual speakers know, and command, a repertoire of subvarieties of their language. If Italian was relatively invariant and homogeneous at the time of political unification, this was largely due to its having become almost exclusively a written language, ill-adapted to use in everyday discourse, and lacking much of the variegation that naturally evolves when a language is employed by a widespread speech community for a multiplicity of purposes. At the time of Unification, it is doubtful whether there were any who could be described as 'native speakers' of Italian, in the sense that they acquired the language naturally during childhood and habitually and spontaneously spoke it; and it is certain that, in the late nineteenth century, only a very small minority of Italians knew their national language. We have seen in the preceding chapters that Italian did not become an immutable monolith after the sixteenth century, but the emergence of extensive variation according to region, social group and context of discourse is largely a product of the recent acquisition of Italian by the Italian people, and of their use of that language for a range of purposes to which it had never been put before.

1.2 Dimensions of variation

Before we examine the dimensions of variation in the modern language, it is important to stress that our use of terms such as 'deviant', 'non-standard' or 'substandard' is purely descriptive, and not a value judgement. There is nothing intrinsically 'wrong' or 'inferior' about varieties different from the standard, and there is no compelling reason to take standard Italian as the yardstick in terms of which other varieties are described, save the purely practical one that the standard language is the variety most familiar to most readers. At the same time, we should not lose from sight the fact that many Italians regard the prescribed, literary standard as 'correct', 'superior' and as a kind of paragon in terms of which other varieties may be judged inferior.

Classifications of the various types of modern Italian have proliferated in recent years; Berruto (1990: 13–19) offers a survey of them. A useful schema is that provided by Berruto himself, who identifies three intersecting axes of variation, the diastratic (pertaining to linguistic differences between social strata), the diamesic (pertaining to linguistic differences according to the medium of expression, i.e., written vs. spoken) and diaphasic (pertaining to the range or repertoire of speech varieties at the disposition of speakers). A further, major, dimension of variation, generally reflecting features of the underlying dialects, is the regional, or 'diatopic'. Some elements of regional variation (notably pronunciation) carry no connotations of 'inferiority' on the diastratic axis; others, particularly where morphology is concerned, are markedly 'substandard'.

Towards one pole of the diaphasic axis are located elevated registers of standard Italian, such as bureaucratic Italian, technical-scientific Italian, and a variety of extremely formal and ornate language labelled by Berruto 'italiano formale aulico'; towards the opposite pole are 'casual Italian' ('italiano informale trascurato') and 'slang Italian' ('italiano gergale'). In terms of grammatical and phonological structure these diaphasic variants diverge little from the standard based on the literary language, although the syntax of varieties at the more elevated pole tends to be markedly elaborate, with a particular predilection for complex noun phrases, and that of the more casual extremity looser and more disconnected, with frequent hesitation, and use of semantically empty 'fillers', such as *non so . . .*, *ma . . .*, *insomma . . .*, *cioè . . .* These differences are also characteristic of those between written and spoken languages to which the respective poles are, evidently, closer. But what distinguishes diaphasic variants is, in large measure, a matter of lexicon and phraseology (see Berruto (1990: 187–9)). Bureaucratic Italian, for example, shows a predilection for the use of grandiloquent periphrases rather than simple, single words (e.g., *effettuare il pagamento* for *pagare* 'to pay'; *procedere all'arresto* for *arrestare* 'to arrest', etc.), use of generic rather than precise terminology (e.g., *domicilio* 'domicile' for *casa* 'house, home', *appartamento* 'flat', etc.), selection of otherwise rare and elevated synonyms in preference for everyday terms (e.g., *recarsi* and *effettuare*, instead of *andare* 'to go' and *fare* 'to do'), in addition to the employment of a variety of set phrases characteristic of bureaucratic usage. For an account of specialist, sectorial, varieties of Italian (such as those associated with particular professions), see Berruto (1990: 154–68)) and Beccaria (1973).

We have already encountered some of the features of spoken (as opposed to written) Italian. It is important to stress that variants typical of spoken language are not necessarily regarded by Italians as 'substandard', or lower on the diastratic axis. Among the characteristic features of spoken or colloquial Italian are the use of polyvalent *che* (Ch.3: 9.7), including *che* as a loose causal connector between sentences (e.g., *esco, che fa caldo* 'I'm going out, 'cos it's hot'; *un attimo, che me lo segno* 'just a moment, I'm writing it down', etc.), use of the imperfect indicative in the protasis and apodosis of counterfactual sentences (Ch.4: 9.4.1), *ad sensum* agreement, of the kind *la gente vengono* 'people come' (Ch.4: 2), failure of agreement where verbs precede their subject (Ch.4: 2), redundant use of clitics such as *a me mi piace*,[1] etc., (Ch.4: 1.2), extension of *gli* as plural, and feminine singular, indirect object pronoun, non-use of the pronouns *egli*, *ella* and *esso* (Ch.3: 9.1.2); also, marginally, a tendency to use certain analytic comparative structures in place of synthetic ones (e.g., *più buono* or *più migliore* instead of *migliore* 'better'), certain analogical changes in verbal morphology, such as *dissimo* instead of *dicemmo* 'we said' (Ch.3: 8.5), a tendency to omit the negator *non* in constructions such as *esco mai* 'I never go out', *ha fatto niente* 'he has done nothing' (2.3.2.1 below). There are also lexical differences between written and colloquial Italian, the latter being distinguished by a large number of phrases introduced by *fare* (e.g., *fare fuori* for *uccidere* 'kill', *fare il biglietto* for *acquistare il biglietto* 'get one's ticket'), or – in very informal speech – by words such as *fregare* 'rob', 'rip off'; *stronzo* 'bastard'; *pazzesco* 'crazy'; *fifa* 'funk'. Berruto (1990: 143–5) gives further examples. A further feature of colloquial Italian is the use of *forte* or *tutto* as intensifying particles (e.g., *è tutto bello* 'it's really lovely'). Use of the demonstratives *sto*, *sta*, *sti*, *ste* – directly continuing Proto-Romance ***'esto**, ***'esta** etc., (Ch.3: 6), rather than *questo*, *questa*, etc. – is also characteristic of the spoken language.

1.3 Popular and regional Italian

Our main focus in what follows will be on those types of variation in which the structural divergence from standard Italian is most prominent: *popular* and *regional* Italian. Popular Italian is 'lower' on the diastratic axis than literary Italian; as we have already observed, regional variation in morphology, and to a lesser extent syntax, is also diastratically 'lower', but the same is not necessarily so of phonological regionalisms. Popular and regional Italian display all the features of colloquial Italian, but they also display distinctive characteristics attributable to the influence of the dialects. They reflect, in short, the native linguistic habits – i.e., the dialectal speech – of the great majority of the Italian people. 'Popular' Italian can be understood as a kind of Italian which has emerged as a result of the acquisition of the language, over the past century, by the mass of the population who have an imperfect knowledge of the standard grammar and pronunciation of Italian and are – or were in the early part of the twentieth century – predominantly dialect speakers. We would adopt Cortelazzo's definition (1972: 11) of 'italiano popolare' as a 'type of Italian imperfectly acquired by someone who has dialect as their mother tongue', with the qualification that this definition, probably true for the early part of the twentieth century, is likely to be untrue of many modern users of 'italiano popolare', who may not know any dialect. It is also generally true that popular Italian is spoken and written by the uneducated ('incolti'), but lack of education is a matter of degree, and the 'incolti' are not a clearly defined class. The fact that virtually all Italians deviate from the prescribed, Tuscan-based standard pronunciation – Canepari (1986: 46f.) has estimated that only about 3% of the population manifests a non-regional pronunciation, and only about 1% manifests the exact phonemic distribution of the literary standard – is a reflection of the fact that, historically, even the most highly literate were *phonologically uneducated*, being dependent on the *written*, not the spoken, word for their knowledge of Italian pronunciation.[2] Indeed, in the late nineteenth and early twentieth centuries it would have been almost impossible to find a teacher of Italian whose pronunciation was not in some way regionally marked – even in Tuscany. Today there is still no part of Italy where Italian is generally spoken without detectable regional features – not even Florence, whose dialect none the less forms the historical basis of the standard (cf. Galli de' Paratesi (1984: 208)).

Some features of popular Italian – in addition to those characteristic of spoken Italian generally – are encountered throughout the country. Others may be more or less regionally limited: they are a matter of spatial, or 'diatopic', variation. The dialectal should not automatically be equated with the regional: if the other Italo-Romance dialects all happen to differ in some respect from standard Italian, then deviations from standard Italian may and do arise which are no less dialectal for being pan-Italian. The distinction sometimes made between 'italiano popolare' (to which the adjective *unitario*, in the sense of 'displaying features found throughout the state of Italy', is often applied – e.g., De Mauro (1970) and Cortelazzo (1972)), and 'italiano regionale', reflecting principally the local influence of dialects, should not be given too much weight from the point of view of structural analysis of the resulting deviation from the standard. There are simply structural differences between the standard and popular usage, which may be more or less geographically widespread, but virtually all of which have origins in the native speech habits of the Italians.

Above all, it must be stressed that so-called 'italiano popolare' is not a coherent, self-contained, linguistic system. It is not a kind of 'alternative language' to standard Italian, on a par with, say, French or German, or a local dialect. Rather, it represents the attempts of Italians to speak and write standard Italian, and in this respect, at least, is 'unitario' (cf. Lepschy (1983)), but also reflects the interference of the dialects which they (or their recent ancestors) speak. What scholars may term 'italiano popolare' is, for most Italians, simply 'italiano'.

We shall not review here the plethora of definitional problems associated with 'italiano popolare' (cf. Berruto (1983: 38f.); Lepschy (1983)), nor the issue of categorizing regional variants. De Mauro's taxonomy[3] (1976) of four *major* regional varieties (*northern*, *Tuscan*, *southern*, *Roman*) and various *minor* ones such as Sardinian is convenient, but should not conceal the fact that some variations have a smaller or greater extent than these geographical delimitations indicate (cf. Sobrero (1988: 732f.; 740)). We shall focus here on the much narrower, and essentially 'internal' issue of the linguistic structures commonly identified, for example by Cortelazzo (1972), Berruto (1983; 1990) and De Mauro (1970), as characterizing 'italiano popolare' and regional varieties of Italian.

2 The dialects

A structural outline of Italo-Romance dialects is essential to an understanding of the recent history of Italian. The Italo-Romance dialects have all evolved from the Latin spoken in Italy, and have diverged in varying degrees, and in different ways, both from Latin and from each other. The modern dialects form a geographical continuum, such that the speech varieties of geographically adjacent areas tend to differ only minimally, and structural differences (and mutual unintelligibility) increase only gradually, with distance. Linguistically abrupt boundaries are rare within Italo-Romance. The classification of the dialects using geographical labels can be misleading, since geographical boundaries do not necessarily correspond to linguistically significant boundaries. Indeed, even the label 'Italo-Romance' is essentially a geographical expression: Italo-Romance dialects have no common, uniquely defining, linguistic characteristic. The distinguishing feature of preservation of Latin consonant length (Ch.2: 1.3) is found only south of the 'La Spezia–Rimini Line' (see below), whilst the nearest candidate for a common, unique, defining feature – namely the change of [**l**] to [**j**] in postconsonantal position (Ch.2: 3.3) – is really an extreme form of a more widespread Romance phenomenon and is, in any case, partly absent from some Italo-Romance varieties of Abruzzo. Problems also arise with regard to the classification of Sardinian,[4] which many scholars regard as a separate branch of Romance, despite its many points of resemblance to southern Italian dialects, and the fact that at least one of its principal distinctive characteristics (the conservation of Latin inflection **-s** and **-t** Ch.3: 8.3.2–3) reappears in mainland Italo-Romance dialects of southern Basilicata and northern Calabria. For one view of these classificatory problems, see Pellegrini (1975b), who includes both Sardinian and Friulian[5] (the latter regarded by some as a Rhaeto-Romance variety) under 'Italo-Romance'. We do not intend to explore here the various debates concerning the most appropriate classification of the dialects (see for example Bruni (1987: 290f.) and Pellegrini (1975a)), but certain geographical divisions can be usefully made.

It is generally accepted that the Romance dialects of Italy are divisible into two sectors, whose mutual boundary is marked by the so-called 'La Spezia–Rimini Line'. This line, running along the Apennines approximately from Carrara to Fano, represents a bundle of isoglosses (an isogloss is a delineation of the geographical limit of some linguistic feature), separating the dialects of northern Italy from the rest.[6] Dialects to the south of the Line do display a small measure of linguistic cohesion; for example, they all (together with Sardinian) conserve the long consonants of Latin, a feature which makes them unique among Romance varieties. Dialects to the north of the Line share a great many of their structural properties, particularly shortening of Latin long consonants, with other Romance varieties such as French, Occitan, Spanish and Portuguese. The following subdivisions are usually recognized, but they all conceal an exuberance of local subdivisions, as well as some transitional zones which are not easily classifiable:[7]

NORTHERN DIALECTS:
– 'Gallo-Italian' (Piedmont, Lombardy, Liguria and Emilia-Romagna)
– Venetan

(FRIULIAN)

TUSCAN DIALECTS (including Corsican)

CENTRAL-AND-SOUTHERN DIALECTS (*dialetti centromeridionali*):
– Central dialects (Marche, Umbria, Lazio)

– Upper southern dialects (Abruzzo, northern Puglia, Molise, Campania, Basilicata)
– Extreme southern dialects (Salento, southern Calabria and Sicily)

(SARDINIAN)

The 'Gallo-Italian' dialects show particular affinities, especially in phonology – for example in the development of front rounded vowels, diphthongization in stressed open syllables, and the extensive deletion of unstressed vowels – with French and Occitan dialects, while 'Venetan' (we use this term to distinguish the dialects of the Veneto from Venetian, the dialect of Venice; in the literature the term 'Venetian' is often used for both), has had a more conservative evolution, and shows closer structural similarities to Tuscan. Tuscan dialects are structurally very conservative in comparison with most other Italo-Romance varieties (see 2.2). Within the territory of the 'central' dialects, some scholars (e.g., Rohlfs (1972a: 3–25)) recognize a further 'bundle' of isoglosses, much looser, and more transitional, than the sharply defined 'La Spezia–Rimini Line', and running roughly between Rome and Ancona, marking the limit of certain features of southern dialects, such as southern Italian metaphony, weakening of postnasal consonants, 'mass' gender, enclitic possessive adjectives, which shall be discussed below.

The following structural sketch of the dialects of Italy attempts to draw attention to *some* of the major features which distinguish the modern dialects from Italian. Since many of these have already been discussed in foregoing chapters, frequent reference will be made to these earlier discussions.[8]

2.1 Terms of comparison

For comparison of the modern Italian dialects with standard Italian, and an understanding of the effect of the dialects on speakers' acquisition of Italian, it is useful to make certain distinctions at the outset. In phonology, dialects differ from the standard in respect of the range of speech sounds they possess. Of sounds which exist in the dialect, but not in standard Italian, only those which are the product of 'live' phonetic processes operating in the dialects are liable to be transferred into Italian.[9] Those which are the product of extinct phonetic processes are not transferred into Italian. The tendency of many southern dialects to lenite (Ch.2: 7.2), intervocalic voiceless consonants is a matter of 'live' phonetic modification, which automatically applies to any voiceless intervocalic consonant (for example, across word boundaries), and may be transferred into local pronunciations of Italian. In contrast, the front vowels [**y**] and [**œ**] of northern dialects are the product of now extinct processes of fronting of [**u**] and [**wɔ**]. For modern dialect speakers, these sounds are *lexicalized*: they have become part of the phonological representation of the words in which they appear, and there is no reason to derive them from underlying *[**u**] and *[**wɔ**]. Such sounds, which do not occur in standard Italian phonology are not, as a rule,[10] transferred into Italian. This leaves the third possibility that a sound which is the product of a now extinct phonetic process may be transferred into Italian if that sound is already part of the speech-sound inventory of Italian. Thus [**s**], which in many northern dialects arises from an earlier palatalization of velar consonants before front vowels (cf. 2.3.1.5), is readily transferred into northern pronunciations of Italian, because [**s**] is already present in that language: e.g., northern **si'ta** for standard Italian **ʧit'ta** 'city'.

As for morphology and syntax, it is useful to talk in terms of *exponence differences* (i.e., differences in the *means* by which a given grammatical category is expressed), and *category differences* (i.e., differences in the *kinds* of categories which are expressed in the grammar). That some dialects express verbal person and number principally by means of inflectional endings, and others by means of subject personal pronouns, is an exponence difference – the same grammatical categories are expressed by different means. But that some dialects divide the masculine into two subgenders 'mass' and 'count' (2.3.2.10) is a category difference, since in other dialects, and in Italian, no such gender distinction exists.

2.2 Italian vs. Tuscan and Tuscan vs. other dialects

The basis of Italian is Tuscan, and more specifically Florentine, and we shall commence our overview by contrasting, first, standard Italian with Tuscan, then Tuscan with other Italian dialects. Since all of the features listed have been discussed in detail in earlier chapters, we give here only brief references.

Standard Italian differs from most modern Tuscan dialects in the following *principal* distinctive respects (cf. Giannelli (1976)).

(i) Absence of spirantization (and of lenition) of intervocalic voiceless consonants (Ch.2: 7).
(ii) Presence of intervocalic [**ʤ**] (and [**ʧ**]), which in Tuscan are [**ʒ**] (and [**ʃ**]) (Ch.2: 6).
(iii) Presence of the diphthong [**wɔ**] in stressed open syllables, a feature absent in most Tuscan dialects (Ch.2: 4.2).
(iv) Maintenance of first person plural forms in *-iamo*, as opposed to Tuscan first person plural forms identical to third person singular reflexives: (*noi*) *si canta* (Ch.3: 8.9).
(v) Absence of clitic subject pronouns (Ch.3: 9.1.3).

As a very broad generalization, to which there are a number of exceptions, we may say that Tuscan (and therefore Italian) is *negatively* distinguished from other Italo-Romance dialects. The other dialects have acquired distinguishing features which have not emerged in Tuscan. But we list here the main features which *positively* characterize Italian with respect to other Italo-Romance dialects.

(i) Anaphonesis (Ch.2: 4.5) (e.g., **'liŋgwa**, rather than **'leŋgwa**).
(ii) Absence of morphological metaphonic alternation (Ch.2: 4.2) (e.g., M. *buono* 'good' vs. F. *buona*, but southern M. **'bwonu** vs. F. **'bɔna**).
(iii) Raising of unstressed [**a**] to [**e**] before [**r**] (Ch.2: 4.6.3) (e.g., **parle'rɔ**, not **parla'rɔ**).
(iv) The change of intervocalic [**rj**] to [**j**] (Ch.2: 5.2) (e.g., **'mwɔːjo** from ***'mɔrjo**, where most dialects have forms like **'mɔːro**).
(v) The existence of a distinction between intervocalic [**s**] and intervocalic [**z**], while other dialects have either intervocalic [**z**], or [**s**], but not both (Ch.2: 7.2).
(vi) The first person singular inflection in *-iamo* , as opposed to *-amo*, *-emo*, *-imo* elsewhere (Ch.3: 8.3.1).
(vii) The first person singular conditional ending *-ei* (*canterei*), rather than *-ebbi* or *-ia* (Ch.3: 8.8.5).

2.3 Dialects other than Tuscan

2.3.1 Major phonological features

2.3.1.1 Stressed vowels

Most of the major historical developments in the vowel systems of the Italian dialects, with the exception of unstressed vowel reduction in southern Italy (2.3.1.3), result from extinct historical processes. The system of seven stressed vowels ([**i**], [**e**], [**ɛ**], [**a**], [**ɔ**], [**o**], [**u**]), which underlies Tuscan, also historically underlies most Italo-Romance dialects. For the so-called 'Romanian' vowel system, encountered in a small area of Basilicata, near Potenza, the 'Sardinian' system, found in part of southern Basilicata and northern Calabria, and the 'Sicilian' system of the extreme south, see Ch.2: 2.1.

The stressed vowel system underlying Tuscan is conserved largely intact in most central Italian dialects. It is also relatively well maintained (albeit with certain divergences with respect to modern Tuscan) in many Venetan dialects. Elsewhere, there has been extensive modification in the quality of mid vowels, usually resulting in a system of five stressed vowels, such that the resulting mid vowel qualities do not correspond to those of modern standard Italian.[11] The details of such merger, which frequently involves lowering of the high mid vowels, are extremely complex (see Rohlfs (1966: 70–159)). It is particularly common in the dialects of south-eastern Italy between the southern Marche and Salento. An extreme example is the dialect of Teramo (Abruzzo), with just four stressed vowels, where [**e**] and [**ɛ**] have merged with [**a**], and [**o**] and [**ɔ**] have merged as [**o**]: *ˈ**mese**, *ˈ**mɛte**, *ˈ**nasu**, *ˈ**sole**, *ˈ**vɔle** > ˈ**masə** 'month', ˈ**matə** 'he reaps', ˈ**nasə** 'nose', ˈ**solə** 'sun', ˈ**volə** 'he wants'. There has also been extensive merger of the mid vowel heights among Gallo-Italian dialects, particularly in closed syllables. Among other features of Gallo-Italian dialects (other than those of Emilia-Romagna) are the existence of front rounded vowels (unknown in Italian), via a change [**u**] > [**y**] (e.g., ***muru** > Milanese **myr** 'wall'), and a change of the original diphthong [**wɔ**] (Ch.2: 4.2), to [**œ**], probably via *[**we**] (e.g., ***rɔta** > ***rwɔːda** > ***rweda** > Milanese **rœda** 'wheel'). In many dialects, the lengthening of stressed vowels in open syllables (Ch.2: 2.3) has favoured subsequent differentiation of vowel quality according to syllable structure: historical diphthongization of stressed [**e**] and [**o**] in open syllables is a feature of many Gallo-Italian varieties (e.g., *ˈ**teːla**, *ˈ**floːre** > Bolognese ˈ**tajla** 'canvas', **fjawr** 'flower'; Piedmontese ˈ**tɛjla**, **fjur**[12]). In Emilia and Romagna (and parts of the Marche, south-eastern Tuscany and northern Umbria), [**a**] has undergone raising and fronting in stressed open syllables (e.g., *ˈ**naːsu** 'nose' > Bolognese **nɛːz**). Open syllable diphthongization of all mid and high stressed vowels, and raising, sometimes combined with diphthongization, of [**a**], in paroxytones (the stressed vowels of proparoxytones behave like closed syllables), are also encountered in eastern Abruzzo, Molise and northern Puglia: e.g., Bitonto (Bari), *ˈ**spiːka**; *ˈ**peːra**; *ˈ**pɛːde**; *ˈ**fraːte**; *ˈ**nɔːva**; *ˈ**luːke** > ˈ**spɔikə** 'ear of corn'; ˈ**pairə** 'pear'; ˈ**pɛitə** 'foot'; ˈ**frɛutə** 'brother'; ˈ**nɔuvə** 'new'; ˈ**liutʃə** 'light', etc.

2.3.1.2 Metaphony

A major development affecting the Italo-Romance stressed vowel system is metaphony, the assimilatory raising of mid or low stressed vowels in the environment of a following unstressed high vowel [**i**] or [**u**]. It is sometimes claimed that in most northern dialects metaphony was not triggered by [**u**], but it is probably more accurate to say that final [**u**] had been lowered to [**o**] by the time when metaphony operated (cf. Maiden (1991: 124)). In most dialects only the mid vowels are subject to such metaphonic raising. According to locality, the low mid vowels are either raised to [**e**] and [**o**], or diphthongized as [**je**] and [**wo**]. Metaphonic raising of [**a**] (usually yielding [**ɛ**]) is much rarer: among modern dialects it is found in parts of Abruzzo and Molise, a small area to the north of Naples, in some parts of Romagna, and in the dialects of Canton Ticino. There are few regions of Italy where no trace of metaphony can be found: in the dialects of the Po Plain it is reduced to a few lexical remnants (cf. Maiden (1991: 197–9)), and its possible presence, at one time, in Tuscany has been discussed in Ch.2: 4.2. There are parts of southern Calabria and western Sicily in which there is no sign of metaphony, but the merger in these dialects of [**e**] and [**o**] respectively with [**i**] and [**u**] (Ch.2: 2.1) means that we cannot tell whether metaphony may, at one time, have applied to high mid vowels in these dialects (there are some southern Italian dialects where metaphony only operates on high mid vowels). The morphological consequences of metaphony, with examples of the resulting alternations, are considered below, in 2.3.2.2.

2.3.1.3 Unstressed vowels

The five unstressed vowels of proto-Romance are preserved largely intact (but see Ch.2: 4.6.1) in most central dialects, in Tuscan, and in the Veneto, except that in Tuscan and some adjacent central dialects, and in the Veneto, posttonic unstressed [**u**] is not found. Examples of conservation of the five final vowels in Lazio are *ˈ**mɔro**, *ˈ**mɔri**, *ˈ**mɔre**; *ˈ**mɔrtu**, *ˈ**mɔrta** > ˈ**mɔːro** 'I die', ˈ**moːri** 'you die', ˈ**mɔːre** 'he dies'; ˈ**mortu** 'dead' (M.), ˈ**mɔrta** 'dead' (F.). In Sicily, the south of Calabria, and Salento, we encounter a system of three unstressed vowels [**i**] [**a**] [**u**] resulting from general raising of [**e**] and [**o**] to [**i**] and [**u**] (see above), e.g., Sicilian ˈ**moːru**, ˈ**moːri**, ˈ**moːri**, ˈ**mortu**, ˈ**morta**. In the remaining dialects of southern Italy, and in Gallo-Italian dialects, there is a historical tendency towards a two vowel system, in which [**a**] is preserved, and the remaining vowels are deleted (in Gallo-Italian) or merge as [**ə**] (in the south). The details of such reduction of the unstressed vowel system are complex: as a general rule, vowels to the right of the stressed vowel (including final inflectional vowels) are more subject to reduction than those to the left. In the southern dialects, posttonic [**a**] is often also reduced to [**ə**], so that there is, in effect, one unstressed final vowel in this position: *ˈ**sposu**, *ˈ**sposi**, *ˈ**sposa**, *ˈ**spose** > Anzasca (Piedmont) **ʃpus** 'groom', **ʃpys**, ˈ**ʃpuza** 'bride', **ʃpus**; Casalincontrada (Abruzzo) ˈ**spausə**, ˈ**spəysə**, ˈ**spausə**, ˈ**spausə**. What principally differentiates north and south is that in the north deletion is no longer a 'live' process, while southern reduction to [**ə**] is still operative in the modern dialects: such reduction tends to operate most consistently in phrase-final position ([**a**], and sometimes [**u**] and [**i**], tend to persist when the vowel is not at the end of a phrase).

Since deletion in Gallo-Italian also affects the unstressed vowels of proparoxytones (Ch.2: 4.6.4.1), the occurrence of proparoxytones is much rarer in these dialects than in Tuscan, or in the dialects of the Veneto. The result in northern dialects is usually a paroxytone or a monosyllable. Compare Romagnol **gont** or Emilian ˈ**gumde**, 'elbow' with Tuscan ˈ**goːmito** or Venetan ˈ**gomedo**.

2.3.1.4 Consonant length and voicing

It was shown in Ch.2: 8 that Tuscan, central Italian, and southern dialects (including Sardinian) are distinguished from northern dialects by the presence of long consonants. The tendency to voice originally voiceless intervocalic consonants is, as we have seen in Ch.2: 7.2, found both in northern Italian dialects and in central and upper southern Italy. What principally differentiates the north from the rest of Italy, is that such processes are no longer 'live' in the north, whereas in Tuscany, and the south, lenition (of which both voicing and spirantization are varieties) remains an active phonetic process. Thus intervocalic voiceless consonants (e.g., those arising through earlier shortening of long consonants) in modern northern dialects are not further subject to voicing: **fi'niːða** 'finished' (F.) (or **fi'nia**) < *__fi'nita__, but **'meto** 'I put' < *__'metto__. A further difference is that intervocalic [**s**] is voiced in northern dialects but not, as a rule, in Tuscan and southern dialects: e.g., Tuscan **'kaːsa** 'house' vs. Lombard **'kaːza** 'house'.

A peculiarity of some southern dialects (including Sardinian, and also some dialects of Corsica) is that original long [**ll**] historically developed as a retroflex [**ɖɖ**] (which subsequently has become [**dd**] in some localities): e.g., *__'stella__ 'star' > **'steɖɖə** or **'steddə**. Similar developments occur in the Lunigiana and Garfagnana areas of Tuscany (cf. Savoia (1980: 266–88)).

Lengthening of consonants across word boundaries (*rafforzamento sintattico*) is, of course, absent from northern dialects. It is widespread in the south but, as we saw in Ch.2: 8.2, its distribution is quite different from that of Italian (it is not generally triggered, for example, by preceding word-final stressed vowels).

2.3.1.5 Labials and palatals

Many southern dialects are characterized by merger of proto-Romance labials [**v**] and [**b**]. In modern Neapolitan the result is usually [**v**] (e.g., **'vokkə** 'mouth'; **'varvə** 'beard' < *__'bokka__; *__'barba__), but sometimes [**bb**], as a result of syntactic doubling (provoked, for example, by the feminine plural definite article) or in certain loan words from Italian (e.g., **lə b'bokkə** 'the mouths'; **'abbələ** 'able' from Italian *abile*). For a discussion of the pronunciation [**b**] for [**v**] in southern Italian and other Romance dialects, see Tekavčić (1980 I: 107–13).

The palatal affricates [**ʤ**] and [**ʧ**] (from [**k**] and [**g**] followed by velar consonants – Ch.2: 6) have lost their palatal quality in the history of most of the northern dialects ([**ʤ**] remains in some parts of Lombardy and Piedmont) and, apparently via a stage [**dz**] and [**ts**] (still preserved in parts of Liguria), have developed to [**z**] and [**s**] (characteristic of most modern Gallo-Italian varieties), and even [**ð**] and [**θ**] (in parts of the Veneto, e.g., *__ʤe'lare__; *__'ʧeːna__ > Venetan **ðe'lar**; **'θeːna**).

Correspondingly, the sounds [**dz**] and [**ts**], derived from proto-Romance *[**dj**], *[**tj**] (Ch.2: 5.2), often became [**z**] and [**s**]: **'tɛrsa** < **'tɛrtja** 'third'; **'meza** 'half' < ***'mɛdja**. Rohlfs (1966: 392f.; 410f.) gives a more detailed account. We have seen (Ch.2: 6.1) that it is a feature of Tuscan dialects that single intervocalic [**ʧ**] and [**ʤ**] become fricatives [**ʃ**] and [**ʒ**]; the same treatment of [**ʧ**] is found in Lazio, parts of Umbria and the Marche, parts of northern Puglia and Campania, and extensively in Sicily (cf. Rohlfs (1966: 289f.)). Single [**ʤ**] does not normally occur in southern dialects, where the historical result of [**g**] followed by a front vowel is usually [**j**] (Ch.2: 6). Where [**ʤ**] has been introduced in loan words (from standard Italian), it is usually lengthened (e.g., **'adʤələ** 'agile' < Italian *agile*). In central and southern Italian (and in some northern varieties), [**ʎ**] (< *[**lj**]), yields either [**jj**] or the palatal occlusive [**ɟɟ**]: e.g., ***'fiʎu** > Lazio **'fijju** 'son', Abruzzo **'fiɟɟə**. In the majority of northern Italian dialects (cf. Rohlfs (1966: 397)), [**ʎ**] is not retained, yielding most commonly [**j**].

2.3.1.6 Consonantal clusters

In southern Italy, with the exception of southern Salento and southern Calabria, clusters consisting of nasal + occlusive show a weakening of the second element (cf. Rohlfs (1966: 356–61; 363f.)), such that [**nt**] and [**mp**] become [**nd**] and [**mb**] (***'dɛnte**; ***'kampu** > **'dɛndə** 'tooth'; **'kambə** 'field'), and [**ŋk**] becomes [**ŋg**] (***'blaŋku** > **'bjaŋgə** 'white'), while [**nd**] and [**mb**] become [**nn**] and [**mm**] (***'kwanto** > **'kwandə**; ***'kwando** > **'kwannə** 'how much'). The process remains 'live', in as much as it operates on loan words from Italian, and across word boundaries (e.g., Marchigiano **un** + **'diːtu** > **un 'niːtu** 'a finger'). A change of [**nd**] to [**nn**] is also attested in ancient Oscan. But whether postnasal weakening can be attributed to the original influence of an Italic substrate in southern Italy is impossible to determine. Similar phenomena are, after all, attested in other Romance varieties and beyond, for example in Gascon or Albanian.

In Gallo-Italian dialects, the historically underlying cluster [**kt**] has generally developed as [**ʧ**], via a stage [**jt**] preserved in parts of Piedmont: e.g., ***'lakte** > Piedmontese **lajt**, 'milk'; Lombard **laʧ** (Ch.2: 6.2). In Emilia-Romagna and the Veneto, however, the result is [**t**], presumably via *[**tt**] as in Tuscan. The clusters [**kl**] and [**gl**] yield [**ʧ**] and [**ʤ**] (or subsequent developments thereof) in modern northern dialects, e.g., ***'klama**; ***o'rekla** (> ***o'regla**) > Piedmontese **'ʧaːma** 'he asks', **u'rɛʤa** 'ear'. In some southern dialects, the cluster [**pl**], via [**pj**] (Ch.2: 3.3), has undergone a partial assimilation of the labial, resulting in [**kj**] and [**gj**] (e.g., ***'plombu** > Neapolitan **'kjummə** 'lead'); [**bl**] has undergone an even more extreme development, resulting in [**j**] or [**ʎ**] (e.g., ***'blaŋku** > Neapolitan **'jaŋgə** 'white'). The relevant process appears to be extinct. In dialects of the extreme south (Salento, Calabria and Sicily), clusters of dental + [**r**] acquire a retroflex pronunciation, e.g., **ʈɽe** 'three' < ***tre** (cf. Rohlfs (1966: 264)). The consonant [**s**] followed by an occlusive consonant tends to acquire a palatal articulation in various dialects, particularly of southern Italy, e.g., Sicilian **ˈfɛʃta** 'holiday' < ***ˈfɛsta**; **ˈmuʃka** 'fly' < ***ˈmoska**; **ˈvɛʃpa** 'wasp' < ***ˈvespa** (cf. Rohlfs (1966: 379f.)).

A widespread, and 'live', phonetic development occurring in southern Italian dialects, together with parts of Tuscany, (cf. Rohlfs (1966: 381)) is the epenthesis (insertion) of a [**t**] in sequences of sonorant ([**r**], [**l**], [**n**]) + [**s**]: e.g., Umbrian **ˈpɛntso** 'I think' < ***ˈpɛnso**; **ˈpartso** 'seemed' < ***ˈparsu**; **ˈfaltso** 'false' < ***ˈfalsu**, etc.

2.3.1.7 Initial [**r**], and final [**n**]

A further 'live' phonetic feature of many southern dialects, particularly Salento, Calabria, Sicily and Sardinia, is strengthening of initial [**r**] (cf. Rohlfs (1966: 223)): Sicilian **ˈr̠oːta** 'wheel' < ***ˈrɔta**. It is a feature of many northern dialects that word-final nasal consonants become velarized, e.g. Lombard **maŋ** 'hand' < ***man** < ***ˈmanu**; **boŋ** 'good' < ***bon** < ***ˈbɔnu**. However, in some localities, especially of Emilia-Romagna, the result is usually *nasalization* of a preceding stressed vowel. When a nasal precedes a consonant, the result is nasalization of a preceding vowel in most northern dialects (cf. Rohlfs (1966: 383; 428)).

2.3.2 Morphology and syntax

2.3.2.1 Negation

An exponence difference characteristic of the syntax of some northern dialects, which is reflected in northern regional varieties of Italian, is 'postverbal' negation, whereby all negation markers, including *non* (or its equivalent), are collocated to the right of the verb. This pattern is particularly characteristic of parts of Piedmont and Lombardy: e.g., Piedmontese *mi i parlo nen* 'I don't speak'; *mi i vnirai mai* 'I shall never come'. This pattern contrasts with central and southern dialects (and Italian) in which some negative element must occur to the left of the verb, as well as to the right (Ch.4: 4): *non verrò mai* 'I shall never come', etc.

2.3.2.2 Reduction of inflectional endings, and metaphony

A major exponence difference between Italian (together with Tuscan dialects) and other Italian dialects concerns word-final unstressed vowels. Italian makes extensive use of such vowels in its system of inflectional morphology: the four final vowels [**i**] [**e**] [**a**] [**o**] all perform multiple grammatical functions in the adjective, noun and verb. In dialects where final unstressed vowels have been preserved, these continue to perform their associated morphological functions. Indeed, in that area of central Italy where all five proto-Romance vowels, including **-u**, survive, inflectional **-u** functions as a marker of masculine 'count' singular (see below) and, in some localities, as a marker of third person plural in the verb (e.g., Cervara **'parto** 'I leave' vs. **'partu** 'they leave'). In the far south (southern Calabria, Salento, Sicily), where the five unstressed vowels of proto-Romance have been reduced to three through merger of the high and mid vowels, the inflectional distinction between historically underlying singular **-e** and plural **-i** (Italian Sg. *mese*; Pl. *mesi* 'month'), and between third person singular **-e** and second person singular **-i** (Italian *parte parti* 'he leaves/you leave') is neutralized: **'miːsi 'miːsi**; **'parti 'parti**, etc. In the Gallo-Italian and southern dialects where final unstressed vowels other than [**a**] have generally been lost or have merged, the consequences for inflectional morphology are drastic, since only [**a**] (the marker of feminine singular in some nouns and adjectives, and of third person singular indicative in the first conjugation) persists, the distinction between other final unstressed vowel inflections having been erased.

The morphological results of metaphony (2.3.1.2) have the effect of compensating, in part, for some of the obscuratory effects of phonetic erosion of inflectional desinences. It must be emphasized, however, that there is no reason to believe (as has been suggested by Devoto (1977: 183f.)) that metaphony developed *in order to* compensate for incipient erosion of inflections. Erosion and metaphony are historically independent phenomena; after all, metaphony has operated not only in dialects where the inflections have been eroded, but equally in those where they are perfectly well preserved. The combined morphological effects of metaphonic raising and merger of final unstressed vowels in a central Italian dialect may be illustrated (1b) by an example from the Lazio dialect of Castro dei Volsci (Vignoli (1911)), where metaphony of mid vowels[13] is triggered by final unstressed [**u**] and [**i**]. Metaphony therefore appears in masculine nouns and adjectives originally terminating in singular **-u** and plural **-i**, in the plurals of nouns and adjectives in singular **-e** and plural **-i**, in the second person singular of verbs with original inflectional **-i** and, apparently, before an original inflection **-u** (to which **-no** was later added – Ch.3: 8.3.3) in the third person plural of the verb; number alternations also occur between masculine singulars originally in **-u** and their corresponding plurals (Ch.3: 3.1) in **-a**. Similar patterns obtain in Gallo-Italian dialects, except that they normally only display metaphony triggered by [**i**], so that the metaphonic alternants in these dialects are usually to be found before original plural **-i**, and in the second person singular of the verb.

(1)
a. Proto-Romance
Noun/Adjective

	Sg.	Pl.
M.	'sordu	'sordi
F.	'sorda	'sorde

Sg.	Pl.
'nɛrvu	
	'nɛrva

'verde	'verdi
'vɛrme	'vɛrmi

Verb

1Sg.	2Sg.	3Sg.	1Pl.	2Pl.	3Pl.
'pɔrto	'pɔrti	'pɔrta	por'tamo	por'tate	'pɔrta
'vedo	'vedi	'vede	ve'demo	ve'dete	'vedu

b. Castro dei Volsci
Noun/Adjective

	Sg.	Pl.	
M.	'surdə	'surdə	'deaf'
F.	'sordə	'sordə	

Sg.	Pl.	
'njervə		'nerve'
	'nɛrvə	

'verdə	'virdə	'green'
'vɛrmə	'vjermə	'worm'

Verb

1Sg.	2Sg.	3Sg.	1Pl.	2Pl.	3Pl.	
'pɔrtə	'pwortə	'pɔrta	pur'taːmə	pur'taːtə	'pɔrtənə	'carry'
'vedə	'vidə	'vedə	və'daːmə	və'daːtə	'vidənə	'see'

Plural is inflectionally distinguished from the singular in many southern dialects in the class of masculine nouns having *feminine* plural -**a**; even more distinctive (because it is never phonetically eroded) is the feminine plural ending -**ora** – see Ch.3: 3.3 for examples. However, the feminine plural inflection in -**a** is extinct in much of northern Italy, having been replaced by -**i** (cf. Rohlfs (1968: 36)).

The number and gender of a noun may, of course, also be indicated by determiners (e.g., the definite or indefinite article, or demonstratives). But the 'partitive' article (Ch.3: 7.2) is absent from southern dialects, and its use is only optional in Tuscan and Italian. It is usually present, however, in Gallo-Italian dialects, with the result that the number (and gender) of nouns is clearly indicated: e.g., Milanese **mi a trøf dla mel** 'I find some honey'; **mi a trøf del formadʒ** 'I find some cheese'; **mi a trøf dij don** 'I find some women'. It is a striking feature of a number of northern dialects of the Po Plain, from which metaphonic number alternation has largely been eliminated, that such alternation is retained in the demonstrative adjectives and pronouns, with the result that singular **keʃt kaŋ** 'this dog', is distinguished from **kiʃt kaŋ** 'these dogs' (cf. Maiden (1991: 203f.)).

2.3.2.3 Person and number marking in the verb

Although the desinential expression of person and number is often effaced in the northern verb, these categories are usually expressed in the north by the *clitic subject pronouns*, a morphological class absent from Italian (although not from some Tuscan dialects – Ch.3: 9.3) and from central-southern dialects. These differences are illustrated from the verb 'to leave', in table 2. As these examples show, there is often more than one clitic subject element in northern dialects. For further discussion of the evolution of these forms, see Rohlfs (1968: 146f.).

(2) Expression of person and number on the verb

North (Ticinese)	Standard Italian	South
mi a part 'I leave'	parto	**ˈpartə**
ti a t part	parti	**ˈpartə**
ly al part	parte	**ˈpartə**
nœɲ a parˈtam	partiamo	**parˈtiːmə**
violtar a parˈti	partite	**parˈtiːtə**
lur i part	partono	**ˈpartənə**

2.3.2.4 Adjectives

A syntactic exponence difference characterizing southern dialects (and Sardinian) is that the order of noun and adjective is more rigid in the south than elsewhere. Adjectives (including possessives) are generally collocated to the right of the noun (cf. Rohlfs (1969: 330)). A peculiarity of mainland southern dialects is the existence of special, enclitic, possessive adjectives with singular names of close relatives: e.g. (from Lazio), **ˈmammata** 'your mother'; **ˈsɔːrata** 'your sister'; **mujˈjeːrama** 'my wife'; **ˈtsiːtu** 'your uncle', **ˈtsiːsu** 'his uncle' (cf. Ch.3: 5.2). Virtually all dialects diverge from standard Italian in that they do not make a distinction in the possessive adjectives between third person singular *suo* and third person plural *loro*, the local equivalent of *suo* being used in both cases.

2.3.2.5 Auxiliary selection

We saw in Ch.3: 8.8.2.1 that selection of the auxiliaries deriving from Latin ESSE and HABERE diverges widely in the dialects from that encountered in Italian, with widespread tendencies to generalize one at the expense of the other. A reflex of HABERE is usually employed with intransitive, as well as transitive verbs, in many parts of southern Italy, and in the Veneto (e.g., Sicilian **a statu** 'he has been'; **a murutu** 'he has died'; Venetan **m a parso** 'it seemed to me'). In contrast, some central Italian dialects of southern Lazio, southern Marche and Abruzzo, have generalized a reflex of ESSE into transitive verbs, except that HABERE frequently persists in the third person (cf. Tuttle (1986: 269f.)). Thus the dialect of Amaseno (Vignoli (1920)) forms the passato prossimo of **maˈɲa** 'to eat' as follows (where the auxiliary verbs in initial **s**- derive from ESSE, and those in **a**- from HABERE): 1Sg. **ai** or **so maˈɲaːtə**, 2Sg. **si mmaˈɲaːtə**, 3Sg. **a maˈɲaːtə**, 1Pl. **ˈseːmə maˈɲaːtə**, 2Pl. **ˈseːtə maˈɲaːtə**, 3Pl. **ˈau maˈɲaːtə**. The relevant dialects also generalize one or the other auxiliary into reflexive verbs.

2.3.2.6 Demonstratives

Broadly speaking, most northern Italian dialects make a morphological distinction in the demonstrative pronoun and adjective series between nearness to the speaker (**keʃt kaŋ** 'this dog') and distance from the speaker (**kel kaŋ** 'that dog'). We saw (Ch.3: 6) that in Tuscan, three terms are available, roughly corresponding to the three persons of the verb, so that 'distance from speaker' is subdivided into nearness to addressee, and distance both from speaker and from addressee; modern Italian, however, usually employs the two-term system (*questo* vs. *quello*) of the kind found in the north. In southern dialects, the three-term demonstrative system is consistently employed:

North	Tuscan and Italian	South (Puglia)
kest	questo	**ˈkiʃtə**
kel	quello/codesto	**ˈkissə**
kel	quello	**ˈkiddə**

2.3.2.7 Adverbs

The morphosyntactic category of adverbs is generally absent from southern dialects (cf. Rohlfs (1969: 243f.)), there being no formal distinction between adverbs and adjectives: e.g., Calabrian **faˈʧisti ˈbwoːnu** 'you did well', literally 'you did good'. Adjectives used in this way often agree in gender and number with the subject of the verb: e.g., Calabrian **faˈʧisti ˈboːna**, addressing a woman.

2.3.2.8 Tense and mood

The inflectional tense and mood system of central and southern dialects is less extensive than that of Tuscan, in that the morphological present subjunctive is virtually extinct in the south, the indicative often being used in its place. The morphological imperfect subjunctive is also sometimes employed, in Sicilian and other dialects of the far south, in expressions of wishing, ordering, or purpose, and in imperatives (Sicilian *venissi!* 'come!'). See Rohlfs (1968: 301; 1969: 61–3) for further details. The future tense derived from INFINITIVE + HABEO (Ch.3: 8.8.5) is rare in the south (cf. Rohlfs (1968: 333; 335f.)). Future time is usually signalled by devices equivalent to Italian *avere a* or *avere da*, often carrying strong modal overtones of obligation. In the far south (southern Calabria, Sicily, Salento), the passato remoto performs the functions both of the Tuscan passato remoto and the passato prossimo. In contrast, it is a feature of northern Italian dialects that the morphological passato prossimo corresponds both to the Italian passato prossimo, and to the passato remoto.

2.3.2.9 The infinitive

In the dialects of southern Calabria, Salento and Sicily, probably as a result of the influence of the Greek dialects once extensively spoken in the relevant areas, very little use is made of infinitival complements (cf. Rohlfs (1969: 102–6)). In their place appear finite present tense verb forms introduced by a special complementizer derived from Latin MODO or QUOD. In effect, one says not 'I want to eat', 'I came to see you', but 'I want that I eat', 'I came that I see you'. Thus Calabrian **'vojju mu 'mandʒu** 'I want to eat'; **'vinni mu ti 'viju** 'I came to see you'; Messina **pin'sau mi 'parti,** 'He thought to leave'; **ai rad'dʒuni mi ti 'laɲɲi** 'You're right to complain'; Salento **nun a'via ku'raddʒu ku 'kanta** 'He didn't have the courage to sing'. This syntactic feature differentiates the relevant dialects from the rest of Italo-Romance, but links them with various Balkan languages, such as modern Greek, Bulgarian, Romanian, Serbo-Croatian and Albanian, where very similar structures are encountered (cf. Rohlfs (1972c)).

2.3.2.10 'Mass' vs. 'count' gender

A major morphological characteristic of the dialects of central Italy, Campania, western Abruzzo and northern Puglia and Basilicata, is the existence of what is sometimes (and misleadingly) described as a 'neuter' gender. In reality, the relevant dialects have two grammatical genders, masculine and feminine, like standard Italian. But within the masculine gender, the semantic distinction between 'mass' nouns and 'count' nouns is morphologically signalled. 'Count' nouns are those which express individual, countable, entities, such as 'loaf', 'dog', 'finger', 'man', etc.; 'mass' nouns represent generic substances or abstract concepts, which are *uncountable*, and therefore only appear in the singular, such as 'bread', 'love', 'cheese', 'singing', etc. Determiners modifying masculine count nouns are, or were, originally, characterized by the inflectional vowel -**u** (e.g., **lu** (definite article), **kwistu** 'this'). The determiners of mass nouns have or had inflectional -**o** (e.g., **lo**, **kwesto**). A metaphonic alternation is regularly triggered in the demonstrative by the final -**u**. Additional markers of the count/mass distinction are final inflectional -**o** on the *noun* (never on the adjective) in some dialects of central Italy. This produces attendant metaphonic differences, since -**o** does not trigger metaphony. In parts of Campania, Basilicata and Puglia, there is a lengthening (a *rafforzamento sintattico*) of the initial consonant of a mass noun when it is preceded by a determiner. The -**o** vs. -**u** distinction also appears in the pronouns (e.g., object **lo** vs. **lu**) (3):

(3) 'Mass' and 'count' gender in southern Italy

	Count		Mass	
Umbria	**lu 'ferru**	'the iron tool'	**lo 'fɛrro**	'iron'
Marche	**lu 'peʃʃu**	'the (individual) fish'	**lo 'peʃʃo**	'fish'
	'viʃtu pa	'this loaf'	**'veʃto pa**	'this bread'
Lazio	**'kiʃtu 'kaːsu**	'this (individual) cheese'	**'keʃto 'kaːsu**	'this cheese'
S.Campania	**lu 'luːpu**	'the wolf'	**lu l'latti**	'milk'
Puglia	**u 'paːnə**	'the loaf'	**u p'paːnə**	'bread'

The debate about the origin of the mass/count distinction cannot be reviewed here. Suffice it to say that the most plausible account is that the distinction originated in the CL neuter determiners ILLUD and ISTUD, (the final [**d**] was probably the trigger of lengthening in the initial consonants of mass nouns). The selection of the neuter determiner may have its origins in the fact that neuter was the characteristic gender of many CL mass nouns: AURUM 'gold'; FERRUM 'iron'; MEL 'honey'; LAC 'milk'.

2.3.2.11 Prepositional marking of animate direct objects

A feature of the southern dialects (and Sardinian), extending as far north as Umbria and Lazio, is the syntactic marking of the distinction between animate and inanimate direct objects, by placing the preposition **a** before animates. Thus Lazio **si v'visto a f'fraːtimo** 'you've seen (to) my brother' vs. **si v'visto o 'sasso** 'you've seen the stone' (cf. Rohlfs (1969: 7f.)).

3 Structural influences of the dialects on popular Italian

In what ways may the dialects be said to have influenced popular Italian? As a general rule, that aspect of popular usage of Italian least deviant from the literary standard is morphology – the structure of *words*. Phonology is the area in which deviation is greatest. Speakers who deviate from Italian morphologically will almost certainly also do so phonologically and syntactically. Those who deviate phonologically (including relatively educated speakers) will not necessarily do so syntactically and morphologically. Speakers whose morphology is substantially dialectal, rather than Italian, will also display marked dialectal features in their phonology and syntax.[14] The relative stability of morphology is probably due to the fact that morphology is the domain of grammatical structure in which Italian is most conspicuously different from the dialects, and therefore constitutes that aspect of the grammar which speakers strive hardest to master in their acquisition of the national language. A contributory factor is, no doubt, that morphological differences are clearly perceptible in written language. Syntactic differences, precisely because they are less concrete and concern the relationships between sequences of words, are less readily grasped.

3.1 Phonology

3.1.1 The phonology of learned and exotic words

While deviation in pronunciation shows extensive regional variation, usually reflecting dialectal speech habits, there are respects in which popular pronunciation deviates from the standard all over Italy. This does not, of course, exclude a dialectal origin, for there are certain regards in which Italian phonology may differ from all, or virtually all, of the dialects. Throughout the history of Italian, and especially in learnèd and scientific language, words have been absorbed from foreign sources (notably Greek and Latin, and latterly English), which do not correspond to the general phonological structure of Italo-Romance dialects. The following, mainly learnèd, words contain consonant clusters alien to the phonotactic structure of Italo-Romance in general: *<u>bd</u>ellio* 'bdellium'; *<u>mn</u>emonico* 'mnemonic'; *a<u>tm</u>osfera* 'atmosphere'; *e<u>cz</u>ema*; *tu<u>ngst</u>eno* 'tungsten'; *a<u>mn</u>istia* 'amnesty'; *Vie<u>tn</u>am*; *eni<u>gm</u>a;* *te<u>cn</u>ica* 'technique'; *o<u>pt</u>are* 'to opt'; *e<u>tn</u>ico* 'ethnic'; *ga<u>ngst</u>er*; etc. In the mouths of Italians, sequences of sounds which were admitted in the *written* word have been adapted to native habits of pronunciation.

Certain types of consonantal cluster are alien to virtually all Italian dialects, including Tuscan, and tend, consequently, to be modified in spoken language. Such modification is more or less pan-Italian, although the fine details of its realization may be regionally variant. Southerners tend to insert a vowel ([ɩ] in the far south, [ə] elsewhere): **atəmo'sfɛːra**; **amәni'stiːa**; **e'nigәma**; **'tɛːkәnika**, etc. Central Italians, including Tuscans, tend to assimilate the first element of such clusters: **ammo'sfɛːra**; **anni'stiːa**; **e'nimma**; **'tɛnnika**, etc. The nature of such variation may also depend on the phonetic environment – cf. Troncon and Canepari (1989: 59). In the north, perhaps because the underlying dialects are rather more tolerant of consonant clusters, assimilation is sometimes only partial: **admo'sfɛːra**; **'tɛːgnika**; **'vjɛːdnam**, etc. *Gangster* and *smoking* are generally pronounced **'ganster**; **'zmɔːkin**.[15] Words ending in a consonant normally acquire a final vowel in the south and centre of Italy ([e] in the centre, [ɩ] or [ə] in the south): **'spɔrte** 'sport'; **'klubbe** 'club'; **'filme** 'film', etc. Northern varieties, because of the structure of the underlying dialects, which often delete final unstressed vowels, are more tolerant of word-final consonants, but tend to devoice final voiced consonants (**klup** 'club'; **nɔrt** 'north'; **zmɔk** 'smog', etc.).[16]

The sequences [lj] and [nj] are rare in the dialects, and in the standard language mainly characterize learnèd vocabulary (and first person plural verb forms, such as *voliamo* 'we fly'; *poniamo* 'we put'). In Lazio they are often realized as [ʎ] and [ɲ] (**vo'ʎaːmo**, **po'ɲaːmo**), in northern Italy (also in Abruzzo) as [ɲ-j] and [ʎ-j] (e.g., Lombard **kam'paɲ-ja** *Campania*, **i'taʎ-ja** *Italia*).

3.1.2 Regional pronunciation

3.1.2.1 Types of dialectal influence

Pronunciation is undoubtedly that area of the structure of Italian in which regional variation is strongest, and there is no one regional variety which has succeeded in asserting itself as a model universally imitated by Italians. Neither cultivated Florentine, nor the Roman variety which in the 1950s and 1960s prevailed in the language of the broadcast media and in the cinema – cf. De Mauro (1976: 121–6; 174–7). Virtually all regional variation in pronunciation is historically attributable to the speech habits of dialect speakers. Regional features of pronunciation need not, however, be exactly coextensive with the geographical distribution of the corresponding dialect features. Some features of pronunciation have become general over a region wider than the dialectal area in which they originate; this is the case, for example, with velarization of syllable-final nasals in northern Italy, spirantization in Tuscan Italian, or metaphony of stressed vowels in Sardinian, discussed below. We may divide our analysis into negative effects (those concerning differences between Italian and dialect which are the result of extinct phonetic processes in the dialect), and positive effects (the transference of 'live' phonetic processes from dialect into Italian). In some cases it seems likely that the phonological effects of dialects on Italian may have been mediated – given the importance of the *written* word in the acquisition of Italian – by ambiguities in the spelling system. These will be discussed in 3.1.3.

3.1.2.2 Negative phonological effects of the dialects

Distinctive dialectal sounds which are the result of extinct phonetic processes have not usually been transferred into Italian. Among these are: front rounded vowels arising from fronting of back vowels; falling diphthongs from diphthongization of stressed vowels in open syllables; diphthongs produced in closed syllables by metaphony; deletion of final unstressed vowels in northern dialects (which is no longer productive); voicing of intervocalic single consonants in northern dialects. That this last rule has long ceased to be productive is shown by the fact that it does not apply to voiceless intervocalic consonants arising from original long consonants: ***ˈmetto** > **ˈmeto**, not ****ˈmedo**. Other unproductive changes are [**ll**] > [**ɖɖ**]; palatalization of the clusters [**kl**] and [**kt**]. The results of extinct sound changes may, however, exercise a negative effect on the pronunciation of Italian. The absence of the diphthong [**wɔ**] from most Tuscan dialects (Ch.2: 4.2) is reflected in Tuscan (also Lazio) regional pronunciations such as **ˈfɔːho** *fuoco* 'fire' and **ˈbɔːno** *buono* 'good'. But hypercorrect pronunciations are not unknown, e.g., Lazio **le ˈfwɔːke** = *le foche* 'the seals' (cf. Troncon and Canepari (1989: 40)). The historical shortening of consonants in northern Italian dialects means that they lack the long consonants characteristic of central and southern Italo-Romance. The Italian of northern Italy correspondingly shows a tendency not to differentiate consonant length, particularly in rapid speech and in the utterances of less educated speakers. This fact can also give rise to hypercorrections, e.g., in Lombardy **deffinitˈtiːvo** for *definitivo* 'definitive', alongside **afiˈtaːre** for *affittare* 'to rent', or **baˈtutto** for *battuto* 'beaten'.

In Rome (and other parts of Lazio) Italian [**rr**] tends to be replaced by single [**r**], as it is in the underlying dialects (e.g., **ˈtɛra** for *terra* 'earth'). The affricates [**ʦ**] and [**ʣ**] are generally absent from northern dialects (Ch.2: 5.2), and tend to be avoided in northern Italian, being substituted by *sequences* of distinctly articulated consonants [**t-s**] and [**d-z**] (e.g., **ˈspat-sjo** for **ˈspatʦjo** 'space')[17]. The Italian sounds [**ʎ**] and [**ʃ**] are absent from many northern dialects, and tend to be realized as [**lj**] and sometimes [**sj**] in the north: e.g., **ˈfiːljo** *figlio* 'son'; **ˈsjaːme** *sciame* 'swarm'. The lack of intervocalic [**z**] in most southern Italian dialects means that the distinction between [**s**] and [**z**] is also absent from southern (and southern Tuscan) pronunciations: 'he asked' and 'churches', etc., are both **ˈkjɛːse**. This trait is probably reinforced by the fact that there is no orthographic distinction between the two pronunciations.

3.1.2.3 Positive phonological effects of the dialects

3.1.2.3.1 Vowels

An example of a feature of dialectal pronunciation which not only influences Italian, but spreads beyond its original geographical limits, is Sardinian metaphonic raising before [**i**] and [**u**]. This has percolated from central and southern Sardinian dialects into general Sardinian regional pronunciation of Italian (e.g., 'tempo *tempo* time' vs. **'tempi**), even in parts of northern Sardinia where metaphony is absent from the dialects – cf. Loi Corvetto (1983: 49f.). A similar effect is apparently to be observed in parts of eastern Lazio (cf. Troncon and Canepari (1989: 40f.)). Elsewhere, the phonetic process of metaphony is long extinct.

It is a conspicuous feature of dialects of southern Italy (excluding Salento, southern Calabria and Sicily) that unstressed vowels are weakly articulated, often involving deletion, or centralization as [**ə**]. In the Italian of a roughly corresponding area of southern Italy, such vowels are subject to various kinds of articulatory weakening through devoicing, centralization or even deletion (e.g., Pugliese **'prendənə** *prendono* 'they take'; **farmɐ'ʧist(ɐ)** *farmacista* 'pharmacist'; **'tutt(i)**, *tutti* 'all', etc.). In writing, such lack of distinction can sometimes lead to erroneous spellings of Italian final unstressed vowels.

3.1.2.3.2 Consonant length and voice

We discussed in Ch.2: 7 the 'weakening' of consonants in the history of Tuscan and other central and southern dialects, which takes the forms of spirantization and lenition (with voicing a frequent result of the latter): such 'weakening' is carried over into the corresponding regional varieties of Italian: e.g., Tuscan Italian (with spirantization and voicing) **la 'βiːβiθa** *la bibita* 'the drink'; **i 'ðaːði** *i dadi* 'the dice'; **le ɸa'θaːθe 'hɔtte** *le patate cotte* 'the cooked potatoes'; Umbrian Italian (with varying degrees of lenition, often resulting in voicing)[18] **le pa̬'ta̬ːte 'k̬ɔtte**, or **le ba'daːde 'gɔtte**, etc., characterizing the speech of virtually all of central and southern Italy except Salento and the far south of Calabria. A further feature of central Italian pronunciation (outside Tuscany) is lengthening of intervocalic [**j**] (**'nɔjja** *noia* 'boredom'; **da j'jɛːri** *da ieri* 'since yesterday', etc.).

3.1.2.3.3 Labials and palatals

Standard Italian intervocalic single [**b**] is pronounced as [**bb**] over virtually the whole of southern and central Italy, including parts of southern Tuscany; see 2.3.1.5 for similar phenomena in the dialects.

For example, Umbrian, **ˈabbile** *abile* 'able'; **ˈrɔbba**; *roba* 'stuff'; **la bˈbarka** *la barca* 'the boat', etc. Central and southern varieties of Italian tend to subsistute the fricatives [ʃ] and [ʒ] for the Italian intervocalic affricates [ʧ] and [ʤ]: in Tuscany, both consonants are affected (**la ˈʃeːna** *la cena* 'the dinner'; **ˈkaːʃo** *cacio* 'cheese'; **la ˈʒiːta** *la gita* 'the trip'; **ˈaːʒile** *agile* 'agile'). Elsewhere, this pronunciation affects only [ʧ], while [ʤ], in contrast, is susceptible to lengthening: **la ˈʃeːna**; **ˈkaːʃo**; **la dˈʤiːta**; **ˈadʤile**. The pronunciation [dʤ] is widespread all over the south (including parts of southern Tuscany); [ʃ] for [ʧ] is rare in the far south (Puglia, Basilicata, Calabria, Sicily). Italian intervocalic [ʎʎ] is usually rendered as [jj] (**ˈpajja** *paglia* 'straw') in Umbria, Marche, Lazio, and frequently also in Campania, Calabria and Sicily (cf. 2.3.1.5).

3.1.2.3.4 Clusters

A hallmark of central and southern Italian dialects, other than Tuscan and those of the extreme south of the mainland, is the weakening of labial and dental[19] stops after nasals (cf. 2.3.1.6). In the Italian of the relevant areas, there is corresponding weakening (with varying degrees of lenition) of postnasal voiceless consonants: e.g., **ˈkwant̬o** or **ˈkwando** *quanto* 'how much'; **ˈkamp̬o** or **ˈkambo** *campo* 'field', etc. Such pronunciation sometimes yields hypercorrections, such as **ˈlempo** for *lembo* 'scrap', **ˈvɛnto** for *vendo* 'I sell', etc. The pronunciation of the clusters [**tr**] and [**dr**] as [**ʈɽ**] and [**ɖɽ**] (or similar) characterizes Salento, Calabria and Sicily (e.g., **ˈʈɽɛːno** *treno* 'train'); realization as [ʃ] of [**s**] before a consonant (especially before [**t**] – e.g., **ˈʃtaŋko** *stanco* 'tired') is heard in parts of Abruzzo, Campania and western Sicily. Over most of central and southern Italy, including much of Tuscany (particularly the southern part), epenthesis of [**t**] in sequences of sonorant ([**l**], [**r**], [**n**]) + [**s**] (2.3.1.6) regularly occurs in Italian: e.g., **pertsaˈpernelˈtsɛntso** *per saperne il senso* 'to know the sense of it', etc. This occurs rather less consistently in the far south, where epenthesis often fails to occur in the clusters [**ls**] and [**rs**].

3.1.2.3.5 Final [**n**] and initial [**r**]

In northern Italy, and especially the Veneto, Italian syllable-final or word-final nasals tend to be realized as [ŋ]: Venezia Giulia **ˈgaŋba** *gamba* 'leg'; **ˈpeŋso** *penso* 'I think'; **noŋ a** *non ha* 'he hasn't'. The geographical extent of such realization of nasals in the underlying dialects is, however, smaller (cf. 2.3.1.7), and generally restricted to word-final nasals. It appears, then, that velarization is employed as a kind of 'supradialectal' realization of the syllable-final and word-final nasals of Italian. A more localized phenomenon, with clear origins in the relevant dialects (2.3.1.7), is 'strengthening' or intensification of initial [r] (e.g., Sicilian **la ˈɽaːdjo** *la radio* 'the radio') in Salento, Calabria, Sicily, Sardinia and parts of Abruzzo.

3.1.3 The influence of orthography

We suggested above that one of the reasons for variation in pronunciation, even among relatively educated speakers, was a lack of exposure to standard Italian in a spoken form, and dependence, at least in the earlier part of this century, on the *written* word as a guide to pronunciation. Some of the most striking areas of deviation from standard pronunciation occur precisely where orthography is ambiguous. In the complete absence of any standard orthographic representation of intonation, it is unsurprising that there is extensive regional variation in the intonation patterns of standard Italian (for an account of which, see Canepari (1986)). The ambiguity of the following letters of the alphabet favours variation in the pronunciation of the sounds they represent: 'e' ([**e**] *pesca* 'fishing' or [**ɛ**] *pesca* 'peach'); 'o' ([**o**] *botte* 'barrel' or [**ɔ**] *botte* 'blows'); 's' ([**s**] *chiese* 'asked' or [**z**] *chiese* 'churches'); 'z' ([**ddz**] *razza* 'ray' or [**tts**] *razza* 'race'). In addition, the distinction between single 'z' and double 'zz' is purely orthographic: both represent a long consonant in intervocalic position (*spazi* 'spaces' **ˈspattsi** vs. *spazzi* 'you sweep' **ˈspattsi**); 'i' and 'u' represent [**i**] and [**u**] but, when unstressed and followed by a vowel, [**j**] and [**w**] (*pieno* 'full' **ˈpjeːno**, *suono* 'sound' **ˈswɔːno**). The combinations of consonants in *gn*, *gli*, *sci/sce* represent phonetically long consonants in intervocalic position (*ragno* 'spider' **ˈraɲɲo**; *figlio* 'son' **ˈfiʎʎo**; *lascio* 'I leave' **ˈlaʃʃo**), although their orthography does not clearly represent length.

3.1.3.1 The mid vowels

It is in the central Italian dialects (Tuscany, Umbria, Marche, Lazio) that the proto-Italo-Romance distinction between open and closed mid vowels is best preserved. Even within this area, there exist notorious lexical differences in the aperture of mid vowels, about which orthography is silent. Where Florentine has **ˈlɛttera** *lettera* 'letter'; **bisˈtekka** *bistecca* 'steak'; **koˈlonna** *colonna* 'column'; **diˈmɔːra** *dimora* 'dwelling'; **ˈɛbbi** *ebbi* 'I had'; **faˈrɛbbe** *farebbe* 'he would make'; Roman has **ˈlettera**; **bisˈtɛkka**; **koˈlɔnna**; **diˈmoːra**; **ˈebbi**; **faˈrebbe**.[20] Venetian also distinguishes close and open mid vowels, albeit with a somewhat different distribution from Florentine. The distribution of mid vowel aperture in regional Italian sometimes reflects the dialectal distribution, and sometimes that of standard Italian. But it is indicative of the indeterminacy which is endemic in mid vowel aperture that some hypercorrect regional pronunciations (e.g., Venetian Italian **ˈpɔsto** *posto* 'placed'; **ˈveŋgo** *vengo* 'I come' for standard **ˈposto**; **ˈvɛŋgo** and dialectal

'posto; **'vɛɲo**) differ from the standard, even where standard and dialect happen to agree.[21] In the majority of Italian dialects, the distinction between high and mid vowels has disappeared. In the regional varieties of Italian (for example, southern Piedmont, Liguria, Emilia-Romagna), mid vowel aperture is often not systematically distinguished, and where aperture distinctions exist, they are usually determined by phonetic environment, and do not reflect standard pronunciation. In Lombardy [**ɛ**] tends to appear in stressed final syllables and in stressed closed syllables (e.g., in *pazzesco* 'crazy'; *certezza* 'certainty') but [**e**] in stressed, non-final open syllables, and before a syllable-final nasal (e.g., in *bene* 'well'; *dietro* 'behind'; *tempo* 'time'). The realizations of [**o**], at least in Milan, tend to be closer to that of the standard language (cf. Canepari (1986: 96f.)). Speakers from most of mainland southern Italy, with Sicily, do not systematically distinguish the apertures of the standard language, although in Abruzzo, Basilicata, and Puglia, there is a tendency to produce open mid vowels in stressed closed syllables, and closed mid vowels in stressed open syllables.

3.1.3.2 The glides [**j**] and [**w**], and the letters 'i' and 'u'
Of clearly orthographic origin is the pronunciation, in northern and more especially southern Italy, of yod after palatal consonants, whilst in standard pronunciation it is purely diacritic, or even redundant: e.g., **ba'tʃjaːre** for *baciare*; **'ʃjɛntsa** for **'ʃɛntsa** *scienza* 'science'; **'dʒjoːvane** for **'dʒoːvane** *giovane* 'young'. Pronunciations such as **'pieːde** *piede* 'foot'; **'uoːmo** *uomo* 'man' (for **'pjɛːde**; **'wɔːmo**), possibly reflecting the dialectal pronunciation of such diphthongs (cf. 2.3.1.1) are encountered in Basilicata, Puglia, and parts of Sicily.

3.1.3.3 Consonant length
Northern Italians often fail to distinguish long and short consonants, but are particularly prone to do so where the spelling does not unambiguously indicate length, as in *ragno* 'spider'; *figlio* 'son'; *lascio* 'I leave', all of which have long intervocalic consonants in Italian. *Rafforzamento sintattico* (cf. Ch.2: 8.2) is not represented in Italian orthography, except where adjacent words are, by convention, written as a single word (e.g., *oppure* 'or', *sebbene* 'although'). Consequently, even those northern Italians who might generally attempt to produce long consonants, may not do so in the case of lengthening across word boundaries (e.g., northern **a 'kaːza** rather than **a k'kaːsa** for *a casa* 'at home'). Since the incidence of *rafforzamento sintattico* in many central and southern dialects is different from that of Tuscan, it is unsurprising that there are many regional variations in the Italian of central and southern Italy. In Lazio, *da* 'from'; *dove* 'where' and interrogative *come?* 'how?', do not usually cause lengthening; the pronouns and

articles *lo la le li*, the pronoun *ne* and the negator *non* are usually not subject to *rafforzamento*, while *l'* tends to be lengthened if it is followed by a stressed vowel. The initial consonants of *più* 'more', *lì* 'there', *là* 'there', *così* 'thus', *chiesa* 'church', *merda* 'shit', *maschera* 'mask', *maledetto* 'accursed', *sedia* 'chair', tend to be lengthened whenever they are preceded by a vowel.[22] A similar state of affairs obtains in parts of Umbria and the Marche. In Abruzzo, *rafforzamento* often fails to occur after polysyllables ending in a stressed vowel, and after various monosyllables such as *dà* 'he gives' (and certain other third person singular verb forms), *da*, *già* 'already', *giù* 'down', *dove*, *come*; *qua* 'here', *chi* 'who', etc., while it is triggered by *mentre* 'while', *sempre* 'always', *ogni* 'each'. With certain lexical variations (see Canepari (1986: 70–80)), the situation is similar in much of mainland southern Italy, and in Sicily. Canepari (1986: 73; 231) reports a noteworthy dialectal interference in the Italian of parts of southern Basilicata and of Sardinia, where the underlying dialects preserve traces of the Latin third person singular inflection -T (Ch.3: 8.3.3), as a result of which third person singular verb forms may trigger *rafforzamento* (e.g., **bi'soɲɲa ppar'tiːre** *bisogna partire* 'it is necessary to leave').

3.1.3.4 The letters 's' and 'z'

In northern Italian dialects, both [**s**] and [**z**] occur between vowels, but their distribution is quite different from that of Tuscan, because [**s**] is a reflex of historically underlying *[**ss**] (*'**kassa** > '**kaːsa** 'chest') and [**z**] is a reflex of *[**s**] (*'**kaːsa** > '**kaːza** 'house'). It is probably the lack of orthographic distinction that favours the general northern pronunciation [**z**] ('**kjɛːze** *chiese* 'he asked'; '**kaːza** *casa* 'house'; '**naːzo** *naso* 'nose', etc.). The voiced pronunciation may be reinforced by the fact that in the underlying dialects the corresponding word is likely to contain [**z**], but it is noteworthy that even *cosa* 'thing', which in northern *dialects* usually has voiceless [**s**] (e.g., *'**kawsa** > Lombard '**koːsa**), is generally pronounced '**koːza** in northern regional Italian.

Even in Tuscany there is some hesitation over voiced and voiceless pronunciations of the sound written 'z' (cf. Canepari (1986: 58)). There is a widespread tendency, present even in Florentine, but encountered principally *outside* central Italy and Tuscany, to pronounce word-initial 'z' as [**dz**], even when the dialects themselves, like the standard language, have [**ts**]: e.g., '**dziːo** *zio* 'uncle'; '**dzukkero** *zucchero* 'sugar'; for '**tsiːo**, '**tsukkero**. The reason for this may lie in hypercorrection: voiced [**dz**] is characteristic of learnèd vocabulary (Ch.2: 7.2), and speakers consequently replace dialectal [**ts**] with the more prestigious [**dz**] (see Troncon and Canepari (1989: 50f.)). In intervocalic position, however, [**ddz**] is often realized as voiceless [**tts**], particularly in the south: e.g., **ˈrottso** *rozzo* 'rough'; **ˈmettso** *mezzo* 'half', etc. The orthographic distinction between 'z' and 'zz' induces some speakers to distinguish length in pronunciation (*spazi* 'spaces' **ˈspatsi** vs. *spazzi* 'you sweep' **ˈspattsi**), despite the fact that, in the standard language, both spellings are pronounced long in intervocalic position. Given that northern Italians often fail to observe consonantal length distinctions, in their speech the differentiation of the two 'z''s may arise from hypercorrection. In some southern varieties, however, 'z' is pronounced long in learnèd vocabulary when it continues original CONSONANT + [**tj**] (e.g., in *concezione* 'conception'; *azione* 'action' < CONCEPTIONEM; ACTIONEM), but short when it continues original VOWEL + [**tj**] (e.g., in *nazione* 'nation', *stazione* 'station' < NATIONEM, STATIONEM).

3.2 Grammatical features of 'italiano popolare'

Both 'category differences' and 'exponence differences' (see 2.1) impinge on regional varieties of Italian, but the domain of inflectional morphology is undoubtedly that in which the dialects affect Italian least. Distinctive inflectional features of the dialects for which there is no counterpart in Italian, are not, as a general rule, present in popular Italian. The special gender distinction between 'mass' and 'count' nouns encountered in parts of southern Italy is not usually transferred into regional Italian, probably because it depends crucially on inflectional distinctions such as that between unstressed inflectional -**u** and -**o**, and metaphonic alternation in roots, absent from Italian. The fact that final -**u** as a third person plural inflection in the verb does not penetrate regional Italian must be due both to the absence of final unstressed [**u**] in Italian, and to general resistance to inflectional influences. The relative absence of inflectional distinctions in the verb, adjective and noun in northern Italian dialects, the result of historical deletion of final unstressed vowels, is not carried over into northern varieties of Italian, where the Italian inflectional desinences are fairly faithfully represented. Nor is the Sicilian dialectal merger of the inflectional vowels [**i**] and [**e**] generally introduced into the regional Italian of Sicily. The proliferation of the feminine *plural* inflection -**a**, characteristic of many southern dialects, does not appear in southern regional Italian, even though it is marginally present in the standard language. We may include here the special enclitic possessive adjectives which in southern Italian dialects are attached to names of family members, but are never introduced into regional Italian. Save in those rare cases where it continues to be phonetically motivated, metaphonic alternation for gender, number and person never appears in the regional Italian of the relevant dialect areas.

3.2.1 The question of 'simplification'

It has sometimes been suggested, notably by Berruto (1983: 42; 1990: 116f.), that the syntactic and morphological features characteristic of 'italiano popolare' constitute a structural simplification of the standard language. But just as 'italiano popolare' cannot be forced in the procrustean bed of *unitarietà* (cf. Berruto (1990: 108f.)), so it is difficult to generalize about it in terms of the rather nebulous notion of 'structural simplification'. Berruto, keenly aware of the problems associated with 'simplification', nonetheless makes appeal to it in the various guises of 'having a smaller number of grammatical categories', 'involving a more transparent marking of grammatical and semantic categories', say, by the use of analytic rather than synthetic structures, or by loss of redundant distinctions – favouring a one-to-one relationship between form and meaning; use of a more generic and concrete lexicon for more specific and abstract equivalents in standard Italian (e.g., *carte* for *documenti* 'papers'); 'reinforcement of perception', say by by redundant repetition; 'economy', manifested by greater brevity of expression, or loss of syntactic agreement rules.[23]

Now it is very likely that simplification, assuming that it *can* be clearly defined, has played an important role in the formation of popular Italian, but there is very little that can be assigned primarily or exclusively to it. Virtually every distinguishing feature of popular Italian has identifiable roots in the dialects. If popular Italian is 'simplified' Italian, this is in the trivial sense of becoming more like what speakers are already used to – their native dialectal speech. From a structural point of view, this may just as well involve complication as simplification. The popular usage of southern Italy tends to lack a morphologically distinct future tense, and not to employ the morphological present subjunctive, and this is certainly a simplification in terms of the number of distinct morphosyntactic categories in the language, although it also involves a loss of semantic transparency – and therefore, arguably, a 'complication'. But its immediate motivation is the absence of a morphological synthetic future tense or subjunctive from the southern Italian dialects. In contrast, the introduction of a syntactic distinction between personal and non-personal direct objects (3.2.10) is a clear complication with respect to Italian! It is instructive in this connection to compare the supposed simplifications characteristic of 'italiano popolare', with the profound and genuine simplification of grammatical structure represented by Ethiopian Italian pidgin (5.1.2 below), where Italian has been acquired not by speakers of dialects of similar and roughly equal structural complexity, but by speakers of genetically unrelated and structurally dissimilar languages.

3.2.2 Features of spoken language in popular Italian grammar

We have seen that some features of 'italiano popolare' are features of the spoken or colloquial language in general. Among these are pronominal redundancy of the type associated with dislocation:[24] *a me mi piace* 'I like it'; *il ragazzo lo vedo* 'I see the boy', etc. (Ch.4: 1.2); the use of polyvalent *che*: *un ragazzo che gli do delle caramelle* literally 'a boy that I give to him some sweets'; *questo posto che ci siamo* literally 'this place that we are there', etc., (Ch.3: 9.7); the occurrence of grammatically singular subjects with plural verbs, where the subject is *semantically* plural (cf. Ch.4: 2), and failure of verbal agreement where verb precedes subject; use of the structure *se venivo, facevo* 'if I had come I would have done', in past counterfactual hypothetical sentences (Ch.4: 9.4); use of *gli* (and sometimes *ci*) for indirect object *loro* (Ch.3: 9.1.2) and, in very informal registers, even for feminine *le*. The redundant use of pronominal forms is hardly a simplification, unless we choose, with Berruto (1983: 46f.) to view the supposed increase in communicative efficiency offered by such forms as 'simplificatory'. In reality, the phenomenon may be interpretable as a tendency towards obligatory clitic signalling of objects – a tendency already observable in a number of Italo-Romance dialects (Neapolitan, Abruzzese, Tuscan, Piedmontese – cf. Cortelazzo (1972: 84f.), Berruto (1983: 46)), and which has become obligatory in certain Romance varieties, such as Romanian. As for polyvalent *che*, there is arguably some simplification of allomorphy (since *cui* disappears), but syntactic structure is evidently complicated by the use of an additional clitic to mark the case of the relative, and the emergent grammatical distinction which Berruto (1990: 126) discerns between animate direct object relatives marked by a clitic, and inanimates not so marked, is clearly a complication with respect to Italian. In purely structural terms, agreement *ad sensum* represents a complication, not a simplification (*pace* Berruto (1983: 45)), of the grammar. The arguments for and against regarding failure of verbal agreement as a structural simplification may be seen in Berruto (1983: 57f.). Generalization of *gli* and of the imperfect indicative in protasis and apodosis, are formal simplifications (cf. Berruto (1983: 48), but both also reflect structures widely attested in the dialects.

3.2.3 Filtering effects. Adjective position, partitives, clitic syntax

There are cases in which the structure of the dialects tends to invariance where the standard language admits variation. The southern Italian dialectal preference for postposed adjectives tends to be reflected in the corresponding regional varieties, as shown particularly by Loi Corvetto (1983: 131f.) for Sardinian Italian, while the standard language allows the adjective to be collocated to the left, as well as to the right, of the noun. The partitive article, optional in the standard language (Ch.3: 7.2), tends to be regularly used in northern Italy (e.g., *trovo del miele* 'I find some honey'), and omitted in the south (*trovo miele*), reflecting the dialectal substrate.

Standard Italian allows attachment of the clitic pronoun either (Ch.3: 9.4) to the infinitive or to the modal verb in MODAL + INFINITIVE constructions, *lo voglio vedere* or *voglio vederlo* 'I want to see it', and admits either enclisis or proclisis with negative imperatives, as in *Non lo dite* or *Non ditelo* 'Don't say it'. But central and southern Italy, reflecting underlying dialect usage, tend to prefer *Non lo dite*, *Lo voglio vedere*, etc. In Sicily, we encounter even *non lo trovando* 'not finding it' (cf. Leone (1982: 124)), which is not permitted in the standard. It hardly seems appropriate to appeal to 'simplification' here: regional popular usage may be simpler in admitting one structure where Italian allows two, but matters are complicated in that clitic collocation is different in negative and affirmative imperatives, and clitics are attached to verbs of which they are not, semantically, arguments. In a study of clitic placement in the Italian of Sardinia, Loi Corvetto (1983: 136f.) shows that in negative imperatives, and modals + infinitive, the Italian of that island closely corresponds to the patterns found in the underlying dialects, for example Logudorese Italian *non me lo dire*; *lo voglio vedere* vs. Gallurese Italian *non dirmelo*; *voglio vederlo*, etc.[25]

3.2.4 Negation

It is a feature particularly of modern northern regional varieties, which starts to appear from the beginning of this century, and is apparently gaining ground both diastratically, in that it is increasingly heard in the spoken language of educated people, and geographically, in that it is also to be encountered in southern Italy (cf. Molinelli (1984)), that preverbal *non* is sometimes omitted (e.g., *Si sente più nessuno* 'No-one can be heard any more', *Non sono ancora guarita del tutto, ma fa niente* 'I'm not completely better, but it doesn't matter', etc.). Its origins are probably to be sought in the postverbal negation characteristic (2.3.2.1) of northern dialects.

3.2.5 Differences in inflectional morphology

We have observed that there is relatively little deviation from standard Italian in respect of inflectional morphology, but there are some exceptions. Popular usage sometimes hypercharacterizes the inflectional marking of grammatical gender, so that *-a* is generalized to all feminine singulars, *-o* into all masculine singulars, and *-e* into feminine plurals: e.g., *il caporalo*; *il geometro*; *la moglia*; *le moglie*; *la guarigiona*, etc., for *il caporale* 'the corporal'; *il geometra* 'the surveyor'; *la moglie* 'the wife'; *le mogli* 'the wives'; *la guarigione* 'the cure', etc. But such developments must owe much to the fact that distinctions between final unstressed vowels have been phonetically obscured in many dialects. From one point of view we could say that we have here a simplification, since there is a more transparent, one-to-one, relationship between the grammatical category of gender and the inflectional desinences; but in reality what has happened serves to reinforce the largely arbitrary category of gender (cf. Ch.3: 4). It is striking that the even simpler alternative of generalizing ambigeneric singular *-e* and plural *-i* is not pursued in popular Italian (cf. Ernst (1981: 112)).

An inflectional number distinction is lost in the Veneto, Tuscany and Lazio, in that *-e* is sometimes generalized as a plural inflection of feminine nouns in singular **-e**, where the standard language requires plural **-i**: *le chiave* 'the keys'; *le voce* 'the voices'; *le noce* the nuts'; *le parte* 'the parts'. This has its origins in the underlying dialects, and in central Italy it may owe something to a phonetic tendency to lower final unstressed [**i**] to [**e**]. The feminine plural inflection *-a* is generally absent in northern dialects, and correspondingly tends to be replaced by inflectional *-i* in northern varieties of Italian (*i corni*; *i bracci* for *le corna* 'the horns'; *le braccia* 'the arms') – a development possibly favoured by the rarity and unpredictability of such plurals in Italian. A stronger candidate for description in terms of simplification might be the generalization of the first conjugation present subjunctive inflectional marker *-i* to all conjugations: *venghi*; *vadi*, etc., for standard *venga* 'come'; *vada* 'go' (cf. Cortelazzo (1972: 99f.)). But since this phenomenon has long been attested in Tuscan, and survives in modern Tuscan dialects and parts of Umbria (cf. Rohlfs (1968: 297–9; 301)), its presence in popular usage may equally be attributed to dialect influences. Formally simpler, but directly attributable to a dialectal origin, is the tendency to generalize *-etti* as a passato remoto inflection in upper southern Italy and Campania (cf. Troncon and Canepari (1987: 97)): e.g., *cerchetti*; *scrivetti*, for standard *cercai* 'I sought'; *scrissi* 'I wrote', cf. Ch.3: 8.5.

There is occasional deviation in thematic vowels (e.g., *credavamo*; *insistivo* for *credevamo* 'we believed'; *insistevo* 'I insisted').[26] One suspects that such loss of distinction may have more to do with the low perceptual salience of the thematic vowel when it is unstressed, and the tendency in many dialects for unstressed vowels to be neutralized, than with any general levelling of thematic vowel distinctions. A similar explanation may account for the occasionally observed confusion in popular usage between the third person plural present endings *-ano* and *-ono* (cf. Berruto (1983: 49)).

3.2.6 Differences in allomorphy

A tendency towards more explicit marking of grammatical categories does not necessarily imply simplification: the form *più* is often generalized in popular usage to all comparatives and superlatives, but not always with loss of inherently 'complex' suppletive (Ch.1: 5.3) allomorphy (cf. Cortelazzo (1972: 93)). Thus, *più migliore = migliore* 'better'; *più peggiore = peggiore* 'worse'; *più maggiore = maggiore* 'greater'. Similar developments are attested in Tuscan and southern Italian dialects (cf. Rohlfs (1968: 83)).

The subject/object case distinction in first and second person singular pronouns is sometimes abandoned – particularly in northern Italy – in favour of the object forms (*lo posso dire me* '*I* can say it'; *lo fai te* '*you* do it'). The loss of allomorphy reflects northern dialect morphology, where *mi* or *me* may function as subjects (cf. Rohlfs (1968: 131)). The occasional substitution of *si* for *ci* (*si siamo sposati* 'we got married') probably also has its roots in dialectal substrates (cf. Rohlfs (1968: 185f.)): and although it entails a reduction in the number of pronominal forms, it hardly entails 'simplification' (cf. Berruto (1983: 48)), in that it actually obscures person marking.

Loro, in its function both as an indirect object pronoun and as a third person plural possessive adjective, is probably not indigenous in Italy (Ch.3: 5.2 and Ch.3: 9.1.2); indeed, as a possessive it is frequently replaced in 'italiano popolare' by *suo*: e.g., *Sono venuti con i suoi amici* 'They came with their friends'.

In many regions, the masculine definite articles *lo* and *gli* are replaced by *il* and *i*. Thus Venetan *i zii* 'the uncles'; *un zaino* 'a haversack'; *i gnocchi* 'the dumplings'; *un scemo* 'a fool'; *i scatoloni* 'the boxes', etc. Troncon and Canepari (1989: 75f.) describe a similar situation in Lazio. This is undoubtedly formally simpler than Italian, but is is also attributable to the fact such allomorphy is absent from the great majority of dialects.

Differences in verbal allomorphy, such as generalization in central and southern Italy of the stressed allomorph (cf. Ch.3: 8.5) into first person plural passato remoto forms, (e.g., *dìssimo*; *vènnimo*; *potiamo* in place of *dicemmo* 'we said'; *venimmo* 'we came'; *possiamo* 'we may'), do not necessarily constitute simplification. The *range* of allomorphs has remained unchanged, since forms such as *dicesti* and *posso* persist; only their distribution has altered. In the case of *dire*, the number of occurrences of an otherwise 'irregular' allomorph has increased. For these changes a dialectal motivation is readily available: first person plural forms in stressed **diss**-, etc., and present tense forms in **pot**- are widespread in the dialects – cf. Rohlfs (1968: 311f.; 283). The use of imperfect subjunctive forms *dassi* and *stassi*, in place of *dessi* 'I gave' and *stessi* 'I stood', reflects the morphological structure of most of the

Italian dialects – including modern Tuscan. This is no doubt simpler than the standard Italian pattern of allomorphy, but it also has a clear motivation in the morphological structure of the dialects.

3.2.7 Adverbs

Where standard Italian has a distinctive adverbial ending *-mente*, popular usage often employs a form morphologically identical to the adjective (cf. Cortelazzo (1972: 111f.) and 2.3.2.7 above): *mangiare adatto* 'to eat properly'; *parte sicuro* 'it starts safely'; *devo andare urgente in Italia* 'I have to go to Italy urgently'; *canta buono* 'he sings well'; *mia figlia scrive chiara* 'my daughter writes clearly', etc. The last example manifests agreement of the adverbial adjective with the gender and number of the subject of the verb. The adverbial use of adjectives might be presented as a simplification if our criterion is that of reduction in the range of distinct morphosyntactic categories – although it should be noted that it is precisely the most idiosyncratic, suppletive, adverbs, such as *bene* 'well'; *male* 'badly'; *peggio* 'worse'; *meglio* 'better', that tend to persist. Hypercorrect adverb formation is occasionally encountered, such as *oppuramente* for *oppure* 'or rather', or *dinuovamente* for *di nuovo* 'again' (cf. Rovere (1977: 92)). In southern Italy, where the adverbial use of adjectives is particularly common, the morphological category of adverbs is also generally absent from the dialects.

3.2.8 Tense and mood

Reflecting the dialectal situation, the distinction maintained in the standard language (and in many central dialects) between the *passato prossimo* and the *passato remoto* is absent from northern varieties of Italian (e.g., northern *Quindici anni fa abbiamo fatto un bellissimo viaggio* = *Quindici anni fa facemmo un bellissimo viaggio* 'Fifteen years ago we made a lovely journey'). There is also a tendency to generalize the passato prossimo at the expense of the passato remoto in southern Italy, a fact which may (at least in the far south) be a matter of hypercorrection motivated by the perception that use of the passato remoto is excessively dialectal (cf. also Troncon and Canepari (1990: 95f.)). The absence of the morphological present subjunctive in southern Italian dialects particularly favours its substitution by the indicative in southern Italian (*Vuole che lo faccio* 'He wants me to do it'; *Ho paura che viene* 'I'm afraid he's coming'; *Disse che veniva* 'She said he should come').

3.2.9 Auxiliary selection

The selection of auxiliary verbs *avere* and *essere* is, as we saw in 2.3.2.5, subject to wide variation in the Italian dialects. Against the background of discrepancies between dialect and the standard, there is a widespread tendency throughout Italy to substitute *avere* for *essere*: e.g., Sicilian *ho caduto* 'I've fallen'; *mi avrebbe piaciuto* 'I'd have liked it'; *si ha alzato* 'he has got up'; etc.; Veneto *Si hanno fatto male* 'They've hurt themselves'; *Ha bisognato uscire* 'It was necessary to go out'. In some localities (e.g. parts of Lazio – see Troncon and Canepari (1989: 101; 102)), dialectal influence favours generalization of *essere*, in first and second person forms. For further examples and discussions of a popular tendency to generalize auxiliary *avere*, see Cortelazzo (1972: 117); Vanelli (1976: 302); Rovere (1977: 88); Berruto (1983: 49f.). For some uses of *essere* rather than *stare* as an auxiliary verb in Sardinia, see Loi Corvetto (1983: 157–60). In standard Italian, *avere* is both an auxiliary verb, and a lexical verb meaning 'to have', but in the Italian of southern Italy, *avere* is effectively restricted to the auxiliary function, since *tenere*, in standard Italian 'to hold', is the lexical verb 'to have': *tengo un giardino* = *ho un giardino* 'I have a garden'.

3.2.10 Marking of animate direct objects

A notable syntactic feature of southern Italian and Sardinian, which reflects usage in the underlying dialects (cf. particularly Loi Corvetto (1983: 114) for Sardinian Italian), is the employment of the preposition *a* to mark animate direct objects of the verb: Sardinian Italian *Chiama a Maria* 'Call Maria'; *Porta a Maria con te* 'Take Maria with you'; Sicilian Italian *Al mulo ora lo chiamano Bastiano* 'Now they call the mule Bastiano'; *Vuole a te* 'He wants you'; *Senti a me* 'Hear me'. The precise conditions for the selection of *a* are complex, and the definiteness of the object, as well as its animacy, seems to play a major role in determining its use in Sicily, and probably elsewhere – cf. Leone (1982: 141f.). This structure represents a major syntactic complication with respect to the standard language.

3.2.11 Further syntactic features of southern varieties

3.2.11.1 Word order

For discussion of a tendency in some southern Italian varieties to collocate finite verbs at the end of their clause, and therefore to the right of objects, gerunds, infinitives, etc. (e.g., *il giornale vuoi?*; *arrivato sono*; *parlando sto*), see Loi Corvetto (1983: 138–43), but also Leone (1982: 142f.).

3.2.11.2 Complementation

Southern varieties are distinguished by peculiarities of verb complementation. In the standard language, verbs of wishing, ordering, asserting or believing, select an infinitival complement only where the subjects of the main and the subordinate verb are coreferential. In the south, constructions such as *Voglio essere spiegata la lezione* 'I want the lesson (to be) explained'; *Voleva essere comprato il giornale* 'he wanted the newspaper (to be) bought', where the complement of *volere* is a passive clause, and *Crede di essere Carlo il colpevole* 'he thinks Carlo is the guilty one'; *Chiamò una serva per spazzare la stanza* 'he called a maid to sweep the room', are common, while the standard language would require *Voglio che sia spiegata la lezione*; *Crede che sia Carlo il colpevole*; *Chiamò una serva perché spazzasse la stanza.* The possible dialectal origins of these structures are unclear, although Rohlfs (1969: 131) discusses the type *volere* + PAST PARTICIPLE in far southern dialects.

3.2.12 A note on lexical variation

Regional variation is also present in the lexicon, and there are objects and concepts for which there exists no single, universally accepted, standard Italian word. Instead, we encounter a range of regionally variant synonyms, or 'geosynonyms'. An account of them may be found in De Mauro (1976) – who also draws extensively on a study by Rüegg (1956). Geosynonymy is particularly apparent in those domains of everyday life from which the literary Italian language was traditionally remote. Thus, the names for such referents as 'thimble', 'broom' and 'son' are *anello*; *granata* and *figliolo* in Tuscany, but *ditale*, *scopa* and *figlio* in most other regions, while the 'hatstand' is *ometto* in the north, *gruccia* in the central Italy, *stampella* in the south, and the 'watermelon' is *anguria* in the north and in Sardinia, *cocomero* in central Italy, including Tuscany, and *mellone d'acqua* or *mellone rosso* in the south. Even the word for 'now', and ways of telling the time, show regional variation, with southern *mo'* corresponding to Tuscan *ora*,[27] and *venti alle quattro* 'twenty to four' in Tuscany and a number of other provinces, versus the *quattro meno venti* found in most of Italy. Certain basic items of vocabulary may differ in meaning according to region: *trovare* 'to find' also has the sense of 'to look for' in southern Italy; *arrivare* 'to arrive' also means 'to happen' in northern varieties. Certain verbs of motion, which in the standard language are intransitive, such as *scendere* 'to descend'; *uscire* 'to go out'; *entrare* 'to enter'; *salire* 'to go up'; *restare* 'to stay'; *rimanere* 'to remain', may be transitive in southern Italian, and in the dialects – cf. Rohlfs (1969: 11): *ha sceso il pacco nello scantinato* 'he took the package down to the cellar'; *m'ha rimasto solo* 'he left me alone'.

3.2.13 Prepositions

There is occasional deviation from the standard in the employment of prepositions. The use of *su* 'on' in the sense of 'with regard to' (e.g., *abbiamo avuto dei problemi sui biglietti* 'we had problems about the tickets') appears to be supraregional (cf. Rovere 1977: 90f.)). The lack of distinction between *di* and *da* in certain dialects (cf. Rohlfs (1969: 208)) can lead to confusion between them: e.g., Ticinese[28] *amico da tuti*; *lo lasio fare di lei* for standard Italian *amico di tutti* cf. 'friend of everybody'; *lo lascio fare da lei* 'I let it be done by her'. For example, the type *posso a fare* 'I can do', used by persons from the Veneto, may be a hypercorrect reaction to the fact that where Venetan dialect has *vago fare*, Italian has *vado a fare* 'I'm going to do'. For further discussion of popular uses of prepositions, and the possible dialectal origins of some of them, see also Vanelli (1976: 303).

4 Emergence of 'neostandard' Italian?

The varieties of modern Italian are potentially capable of influencing each other, just as the dialects appear to have influenced the structure of Italian. Some scholars have discerned an emergent 'neostandard' Italian, reflecting the infiltration into standard Italian of forms and constructions until recently considered exclusively 'popular', 'regional' or principally characteristic of spoken, rather than of written, language, and occupying a place slightly lower on the diaphasic axis (cf. 1.2), than the standard based on the literary language. The nature and direction of such tendencies are still the subject of debate (cf. Berruto (1990: 62–5)). We list here some of the features given by Berruto (1990: 65–96): an increasing use of dislocation; use of the presentative relative structure *c'è . . . che*, once exclusively characteristic of spoken language, to focus some element of a clause (e.g., *C'è uno studente che piange nel cortile* 'There's a student who's crying in the courtyard' for *Uno studente piange nel cortile* 'A student is crying in the courtyard'), and of cleft sentences (e.g., *è Mario che piange* literally 'it's Mario who's crying') – a type of construction which Berruto sees as serving to articulate and simplify a complex block of information into two separate sentences; use of polyvalent *che*; use of imperfect indicative tense forms in protasis and apodosis of past counterfactuals; expanding use of the passato prossimo at the expense of the passato remoto; decline in the use of the subjunctive in subordinate clauses and after verbs of thinking (especially the present tense form); an increase in the use of the progressive construction in *stare* + gerund, and of the Tuscan use of *si va* instead of *andiamo* 'we go'; use of *gli* not only as a plural indirect object pronoun, but also as a feminine singular; retreat of locative *vi* in favour of *ci*; increased use of clitic *ci* as a semantically empty intensifying particle (particularly *averci* for *avere* 'to have', but also *vederci* 'to see', *sentirci* 'to hear', etc.); increasing acceptability of the pleonastic pronominal usage in *a me mi piace*; retreat of *ciò* in place of *questo* 'this' or *quello* 'that', of *che* or *che cosa* 'what' before *cosa* as interrogative pronoun, and of *il quale*, etc., in the face of *che* as direct object and *cui* as indirect object; agreement *ad sensum*; failure of agreement where the verb precedes the subject. The use of adjectives in an adverbial function also appears to be on the increase (e.g., *guidare veloce* 'to drive fast'; *mangiare sano* 'to eat healthily', etc.). Possibly due to English models (although Durante (1981: 256) invokes the influence of such structures in French) is the growth in syntagms of the type NOUN + NOUN (e.g., *uomo rana* 'frogman', *treno merci* 'goods train'); characteristic of Romance languages, rather than English, is the fact that the modifier follows the noun.

An interesting recapitulation of linguistic history (cf. Ch.3: 7.1) is a growing tendency to use *quello* not as a demonstrative, but as a kind of definite article, e.g., *Quello Shakespeare che ho scoperto è brutto, ma vero* 'The Shakespeare I have discovered is nasty, but real'. Berruto even foresees the possibility that the structure combining *qui* and *lì* with *quello* and *qui*, such as *quel libro lì* 'that book'; *quello lì è un bugiardo* 'that man is a liar' might eventually entirely substitute *questo* and *quello* in their demonstrative function. This pattern is, by the way, already common in the demonstrative system of northern Italian dialects and, correspondingly, in the Italian of northern Italy.

5 Italian Abroad

It is a paradox of the history of the Italian language that the massive emigration of the latter half of the last century and of most of the present one should have created incentives for the acquisition of Italian by dialect speakers (cf. De Mauro (1976: 53–63)). The perception that the ability to read and write was desirable as a means of bettering employment prospects, the need to communicate by letter – sometimes bearing gifts of money to pay for the teaching of reading and writing to children – with families left in Italy, and legal requirements in the USA that immigrants should be basically literate, all contributed to an increase in literacy, and hence in knowledge of Italian, among emigrants and their families. In addition, Italians from different dialect backgrounds tended to congregate in émigré communities, and attempted to overcome linguistic barriers between them by resorting, as best they were able, to some form of the standard language. In second and subsequent generations, knowledge of Italian began to become attenuated, or even disappear completely.

The Italian of the émigrés[29] – unlike the 'pidgin' varieties of the language (see 5.2) – displays the characteristics of 'popular' and regional varieties. In the emigrant communities, knowledge and use of standard Italian devoid of 'popular' features, tends to be limited to a cultured élite (cf. Berruto (1990: 180)), since standard Italian is not the language of public administration or the media. What differentiates émigré varieties from those of Italy is that dialectal influences originating in different regions of Italy, and which in Italy are associated solely with those regions, may become amalgamated, and that Italian may be structurally influenced by the language of the host country.[30] The major 'host' languages involved are English for Italophone communities in the USA, Canada, Australia and New Zealand – and to a much smaller extent Great Britain; Spanish for Italophones in South America, most notably Argentina and the River Plate; and German for Italophones in Germany, Austria and Switzerland.[31] The extent to which Italian abroad reflects the influence of the host language is variable, tending to be greater among second generation emigrants (cf. Bettoni (1986; 1991)).

A feature of the early stages of emigration, often subsequently attenuated as the distinctions between dialect, Italian and host language become more sharply defined (cf. Haller (1986)), is that there is extensive lexical influence from the language of the new country, especially in words for concepts or objects peculiar to that country. Such words are normally adapted entirely to the phonological principles of Italian, and receive Italian inflectional and derivational suffixes. Where these foreign words are really, or apparently, cognate with existing Italian words, they may substitute the latter (usually with phonological adaptation to the native pronunciation habits of the speakers).[32] We shall not examine lexical borrowings in detail here.[33] Phrases such as, from America, *Gli sciabolatori del Re Erode* (literally 'the sabre warriors of (the) King Herod' but meaning 'the *shovelers* of the *railroad*') or, from Australia, *incantesimo* (literally 'enchantment', but meaning 'income tax') or *devo lodare il trucco* (literally 'I must praise the makeup', but meaning 'I must *load* the *truck*'), are among the more extreme examples. Syntactic calquing, or translation into Italian of foreign phrases and expressions, keeping the original syntax more or less intact, is also common. Phrases such as *guardare bene* 'to be looking well', *prendere vantaggio* 'to take advantage' are reported for the Italian of San Francisco and, from Australia: *è una buona giobba che è finito* 'it's a good job it's finished'; *un aumento nello stipendio* 'an increase in wages' rather than *un aumento dello stipendio*; *essere chiamato* rather than *chiamarsi* for 'to be called', and *lavo le mie mani* 'I wash my hands', for *mi lavo le mani*, etc. Italian words may also undergo a shift in meaning under the influence of cognates in English. *Fattoria* 'farm' can mean 'factory' in Australia – where 'farm' is often *farma*; *allarme* 'alarm' also means 'alarm clock' (*sveglia*) in Canadian Italian. The inflectional and derivational morphological structure of Italian is generally much more resistant to foreign influence, and loans are often adapted to the morphological system of Italian (e.g., Sg. *la giobba* Pl. *le giobbe* 'job, -s'; *giobbista* 'pieceworker', from *job* and the Italian agent suffix *-ista*).

5.1 The case of cocoliche

In the River Plate region of South America, contact between Spanish and Italian speakers has led to the emergence, probably during the first half of this century, of a hybrid speech variety known as 'cocoliche' (pronounced **koko'liːtʃe**). Cocoliche constitutes an unstable linguistic *continuum* (but not a 'pidgin' – cf. Berruto (1990: 179)) which, according to the linguistic background of the speaker, may be more or less close to Italian or to Spanish. Spanish is a Romance language bearing strong structural resemblances to many Italo-Romance dialects, a fact which probably favours hybridization. Its influence on Italian is highly reminiscent of that exercised by the Italian dialects inside Italy. Indeed, cocoliche might in some respects be seen as another example of dialectal influence upon Italian – except that in this case the 'dialect' is another Romance 'language', and not an Italo-Romance variety. It is also likely that the influence of Spanish has reinforced tendencies present in the native dialects of Italian speakers. Many of the features listed by Meo Zilio (1955a,b,c; 1956) may be attributable to Spanish, but also to influences native to the speech of Italy. Among the characteristics of cocoliche are:

– Differences of gender, especially in inanimate nouns whose inflections are gender-neutral: *la latte* 'the milk'; *la miele* 'the honey', cf. Spanish *la leche*; *la miel*, but compare also the feminine gender of these words in northern Italian dialects (cf. Ch.3: 4.4).
– Abandonment of the allomorphs of the masculine article *uno* and *lo* (e.g., *il scolaro* 'the schoolboy' – Spanish has just *el* and *un*, but this feature is also widespread in popular Italian).
– Substitution of the possessive adjective *suo* for *loro* (cf. Spanish *su amigo* 'their friend'), which is also characteristic of most Italian dialects.
– Substitution of *li* for *loro* as clitic indirect object[34]; use of the demonstrative *esti*; *esso* for *questi*; *codesto* (cf. Spanish *estos*; *eso* but also **'isti**; **'issu** in southern Italian dialects).
– Structures of the type RELATIVE + CLITIC (*è uno che gli si può parlare* literally, 'he's a person that one can talk to him'), which are also characteristic of 'italiano popolare'.
– First person plurals in *-amo* (*andamo* 'we go') – cf. Spanish *andamos* 'we walk', but the thematic vowel [**a**] is also present in the first person plural in many Italian dialects (cf. Ch.3: 8.3.1).
– Use of *che* rather than *di* in comparative constructions (cf. Spanish *es más largo <u>que</u> el río* 'it's longer than the river', but also Ch.4: 6).

– Plurals such as *le legge* rather than *le leggi* (cf. Spanish *las leyes* pronounced, in Argentina, **lah 'leje**, but forms similar to *le legge* are also found in central and other Italian dialects).
– Generalization of the passato remoto at the expense of the passato prossimo: *Oggi venni a vederti* 'Today I have come to see you', and cf. Spanish *Hoy vine a verte*. Neutralization of the distinction between the tenses in favour of the PR is found in far southern Italian dialects.
– Use of the preposition *a* as a personal direct object marker (cf. Spanish *veo al chico* 'I see the boy'), a structure also widespread in southern Italian dialects (cf. 2.3.2.11).

Of unambiguously Spanish origin are:
– Pronominal enclisis in imperatives (*dìcami* 'tell me'; *vàdansi* 'go away' – cf. Italian *mi dica*; *se ne vadano* and Spanish *dígame*; *váyanse*).
– Use of *lo che* rather than *quello che* for 'that which' (*fai lo che vuoi* 'do what you want' = Spanish *haz lo que quieras*).
– *Tu eri* , meaning 'you were' in standard Italian, for *tu sei* 'you are' (cf. Spanish *tú eres*).
– Non-use of the clitic *ne* (for which there is no clitic equivalent in modern Spanish).
– Absence of definite articles with names of countries (*Italia è un bel paese* 'Italy is a beautiful country' – cf. Spanish *Italia es un país hermoso*).
– Use of *per* in passive constructions, instead of *da* (e.g., *è stato fatto per gli amici* 'it was done by the friends'), a clear imitation of Spanish *por* (*fue hecho por los amigos*).
– Adoption of plurals in **-s** (e.g. *i fuciles* for *i fucili* 'the rifles').
– The use of gerunds to qualify verbal *objects* (*Vidi all'uomo camminando* 'I saw the man walking') reflects a Spanish construction, *Vi al hombre andando*.
– *Tengo portato* for *ho portato* 'I've carried' possibly reflects (regional) Spanish auxiliary selection, in which *tener* is sometimes employed as an auxiliary verb. A similar development is detectable, however, in southern Italian dialects (cf. Rohlfs (1969: 126f.)). The correspondence between Spanish *tener*, the lexical verb 'to have/possess', and Italian *avere*, which is both lexical verb, and auxiliary (cf. Ch.3: 8.8.1), may also have played a role here.

A combination of hispanism and hypercorrection is found in the structure *èramo discutendo* 'we were discussing': *èramo* (for *eravamo*) is modelled on Spanish *éramos*, but the use of this verb as an auxiliary with the gerundive is alien to both languages (cf. Italian *stavamo discutendo* and Spanish *estábamos discutiendo*). Since Spanish regularly uses *estar* (cognate with Italian *stare*) in certain circumstances where Italian employs *essere* (cf. *è qui* 'he's here' vs.

Spanish *está aquí*) an assumed hispanism is corrected in favour of the supposedly more 'Italian' *essere*.

The phonological impact of Spanish on Italian is less striking, and some of it seems to be due to pronunciation of Italian words according to the rules of Spanish orthography (e.g., **'gerra** for *guerra* 'war'; [**s**] for the letters 'z', and 'c' before 'i' or 'e'; pronunciation of 'gn' and 'gli' as [**gn**] and [**gli**]). Other influences, attributable to live phonetic processes at work in River Plate Spanish, may serve to reinforce tendencies also present in some Italian dialects, such as intensification of initial [**r**] (**'ro:sa** *rosa* 'rose'), found also in Sicilian and Sardinian; consistently voiceless pronunciations of intervocalic [**s**], and merger of [**b**] and [**v**]. Of Spanish origin are a tendency to aspirate or delete syllable-final [**s**] (e.g. **ah'petto** for *aspetto* 'I wait'); the change [**sr**] > [**rr**] (**irrae'li:ta** for *israelita* 'Israelite'); prosthesis of [**e**] before word-initial [**s**] + consonant (e.g., *especiale*, but also hypercorrect *sclamare* for *esclamare* 'to exclaim').

Many of the features identified in River Plate Italian recur in other overseas varieties of the language. For example, Bettoni (1991) shows such traits as loss of allomorphy in the masculine article, generalization of the feminine plural inflection *-e*, use of plural for singular forms (e.g., *qualche volte* for standard *qualche volta* 'sometimes'), and deviation in the gender of inanimate nouns in inflectional -**e**, to be present also in Australian emigrant Italian, especially among second generation speakers. The influence of English on Italian morphology and syntax is, probably as a consequence of the major structural differences between the two languages, much inferior to that exercised by Spanish. But the effects of Australian English on Italian show some parallels to those of Spanish: the definite article may be omitted in contexts where it is also omitted in English, for example, with the names of countries, and the *entire* clitic pronominal system (cf. the disappearance of *ne*, reflecting its absence in Spanish) is tending to disappear – a development which may be due both to the absence of such a system in English, and to its inherent morphological complexity in Italian.

5.2 The Italian Pidgins

The colonial expansions of Romance speaking countries, (notably, France, Spain and Portugal) and the often enforced acquisition of the colonists' language by subject peoples sometimes having no native language in common, and speaking languages generally unrelated to Romance, have often been the source of radically restructured pidgin and creole varieties whose claim to being Romance languages often resides almost exclusively in their lexicon: the inflectional morphology, and the associated and sometimes arbitrary grammatical categories, of

Romance are often wholly absent; syntax is often characterized by a rigid word order, and the absence of subordination. In the process of creolization (acquisition by subsequent generations of an original pidgin as a native language) novel grammatical structures may arise which have no counterpart in Romance. Italy's brief colonial expansion into Africa has not given rise to an Italian creole, but a pidginized variety of Italian was to be found in Ethiopia at least as late as the 1970s, as witness Habte Mariam (1978), on whose data we are dependent for the following.

There is no obvious sense in which Ethiopian Italian is *phonologically* simpler than the source language. Rather, Ethiopian Italian retains phonological characteristics shared between Italian and the indigenous languages (such as consonant length), lacks features which are present in Italian but not in the indigenous languages (such as the sounds [**p**], [**v**], [**ʎ**], [**ʦ**], [**ʣ**] – replaced respectively by [**b**], [**b**] (or [**β**], intervocalically), [**lj**], [**s**], [**z**]), and reflects a number of, apparently, 'live' phonetic processes operating in the indigenous languages and potentially introducing sounds such as centralized [**ɨ**] (as an epenthetic vowel breaking up consonant clusters), or the voiceless palatal plosive [**c**] (as an occasional resolution of Italian [**kj**]).

It is in the domain of morphological structure that simplification is unmistakably present. Almost the entire inflectional apparatus of Italian is absent from Ethiopian Italian. Allomorphy in lexical stems is wholly lacking; nouns and adjectives are inflectionally invariant, and there is therefore no inflectional expression of grammatical gender, or of number; the inflectional system of the verb is reduced to a distinction between past perfective forms expressed by a form continuing the Italian past participle, and non-past perfectives expressed by a continuant of the Italian infinitive. Conjugational classes are not distinguished; person and number are expressed by obligatory subject pronouns; the case system in personal pronouns is lost (although the distinction persists between subject **ɨjo** and object **me**) – the indirect object being expressed by means of the proposition **ber** (< *per*). There is little formal marking of clause subordination: in addition to the relative marker **ki** (< *che*), clauses may simply be juxtaposed, and optionally linked by means of the anaphor **kwello**; *essere* 'to be' may be expressed by **stare** or **ʧe** (< *c'è* 'there is'), but often the copular verb is simply absent. The definite and indefinite articles are not used, even though the former has an equivalent in the substrate languages. These features are illustrated in the following examples:[35] **'kwesto 'due 'mɨjo so'rella**, *queste due sono le mie sorelle*, 'these two are my sisters'; **rɛ'gasi mɛn'jato**, *i ragazzi hanno mangiato* 'the boys have eaten'; **'ɨjo lɛw'rare 'sɛmbre** *io lavoro sempre* 'I always work'; **'ɨjo lɛw'rare do'mani** *io lavorerò domani* 'I'll work tomorrow'; **'ɨjo lɛw'rato** *ho/avevo lavorato* 'I have/had worked', **'kwesto 'cabe di 'βorta** *questa è la chiave della porta* 'this is the doorkey'; **'ijo ber'duto 'soldi ki/'kwello tu 'dato ber me** *ho perso i soldi che tu mi avevi dato* 'I lost the money you gave me'.

A device which has no exact counterpart in Italian, but is found in a number of the world's pidgin and creole languages (cf. Holm (1988: 89)), is the use of reduplication to express distribution or repetition: **bɛ'nire 'sera 'sera** *venire ogni sera* 'to come every evening'; **'dare 'due 'due 'bani ber 'tutti** *dare due pani a ciascuno* 'to give two loaves to each one'.

The picture painted by Habte Mariam for Ethiopian Italian is reflected in Berruto's sketch (1990: 175–7) of the Italian of (especially non-European) immigrants in modern Italy. According to Berruto (1991), a variety of pidgin Italian, which appears very similar in structure to that described for Ethiopia, also exists among foreign guest workers in German-speaking areas of Switzerland.

Notes

1. It should be noted that, while the structure *a me mi piace*, with redundant use of stressed and clitic pronominal forms, but usually spoken without audible pause between stressed and unstressed pronoun, is strongly associated with spoken language, and widely stigmatized as substandard, in other cases the 'redundant' clitic pronoun serves to point backwards or forwards to a noun phrase which dislocation has distanced from the verb of which it is an argument. Such redundant use of clitic pronouns serves to reinforce the connection between the verb and its argument noun, and is admitted even in the written language. See Lepschy (1992b).
2. It bears repetition that our terminology is purely descriptive. To say that speakers are uneducated is not to judge them as intellectually inferior to any other group of speakers. Our point is, rather, that even those who might themselves aspire to pronounce the literary standard according to canons of 'correctness' have not had sufficient exposure to that standard to be able to reproduce it perfectly, and this especially where phonology is concerned. Among the 'phonologically uneducated', in this sense, are many of the most 'educated' minds in Italy.
3. For a brief survey of accounts of regional variation in Italian before Unification, see De Mauro (1979: 369–75).
4. Since the usual reflex of postconsonantal [**l**] in Sardinian is [**r**] (e.g., **'praŋgere** < ***'plaŋgere**), its inclusion would further undermine claims that postconsonantal [**l**] becoming [**j**] is a typical Italo-Romance feature.
5. A brief structural sketch of Friulian is given in Pellegrini (1975b: 73–6).
6. The importance of this Line as the division between 'eastern' and 'western' Romance languages (cf. Wartburg (1967)) should not be overstated: it does *not* mark the boundary between 'western Romance' weakening of intervocalic voiceless consonants, and 'eastern Romance'

non-weakening (Ch.2: 7), nor between 'western' inflectional **-s** and 'eastern' inflectional **-i** or **-e** (Ch.2: 12).

7. For example, there are transitional dialects between Ligurian and Tuscan in Lunigiana, and, a little to the east, between Emilian and Tuscan, while the Trentino dialects are transitional between Lombard and Venetan.
8. For a succinct outline historical survey of the structure of the Italian dialects (especially of their phonology) see also Lepschy and Lepschy (1988, Chapter 3).
9. We must acknowledge a measure of circularity in this statement, since the diagnostic of whether a process is 'live' is often precisely the fact that it is transferred into the pronunciation of Italian words.
10. Such sounds may appear where whole dialectal words or phrases are intercalated into speech which is otherwise Italian, but they remain firmly linked with dialect, rather than Italian.
11. In some places, (e.g., much of Puglia, northern and eastern Basilicata, Cilento) the high and low mid vowels merge, yielding a five vowel system. Elsewhere, the distinctions remain, yet the qualities are radically altered. But the crucial point, from the perspective of comparison with Italian, is that mid vowel qualities no longer correspond to those of Italian.
12. The [**u**] probably arises via an earlier diphthong *[**ow**].
13. Castro is unusual among Lazio dialects in that it also has metaphony of [**a**], triggered only by historically underlying [**i**].
14. It should be borne in mind that, in addition to regional varieties of Italian influenced by dialect, there also exist Italianized varieties of dialect, from which some of the more idiosyncratic local features have been eliminated. See Pellegrini (1975a); Bruni (1987: 83–8).
15. For a further discussion of the phonological adaptation of loans from English, see Bruni (1987: 109f.) (also Klajn (1972) for other examples).
16. See Canepari (1986: 54f.).
17. For realizations such as [**tθ**] and [**dð**], see Canepari (1986: 93; 95; 103; 239).
18. See Troncon and Canepari (1989: 47f.) for variation between voicelessness, lenition and spirantization in Lazio Italian.
19. Velar consonants following nasals are also affected, in dialect and regional Italian alike: e.g., **uŋ gambo** *un campo*.
20. For lexical differences of aperture in the regional Italian of Campania, see Canepari (1986: 71).
21. See Lepschy and Lepschy (1988: 70f.); Canepari (1987: 45f.); also Lurati (1976: 133) for the Italian of Switzerland.
22. For details of *rafforzamento* in Lazio, see Troncon and Canepari (1989: 62–4).
23. Apparent lexical simplification is sometimes motivated by hypercorrection. Where the standard language possesses lexical synonyms (or near synonyms), there is a tendency to favour those alternatives which are most unlike the corresponding dialectal forms. Thus *faccia* 'face', *cascare* 'to fall', *pigliare* 'to take', all with near equivalents in many dialects, tend to be rejected in favour of the supposedly less 'vulgar' *viso*, *cadere*, *prendere*.
24. Popular usage also sometimes displays redundant *repetition* of clitics, such

as *ti voglio dirti* 'I want to say to you'. See Vanelli (1976: 303).

25. Another feature of southern Italian verb syntax is the formation of the negative second person imperative with *senza* + infinitive: *senza correre!* = *non correre!*. See Leone (1982: 144).
26. For some examples from Sicily and the Veneto, see Leone (1982: 126f.) and Canepari (1987: 101).
27. For *adesso*, of northern origin and originally characteristic of literary language only, see Rohlfs' account (1969: 268f.) of dialectal terms for 'now'.
28. Interestingly, these examples – taken from Bianconi (1989: 140f.) – date from the seventeenth or eighteenth centuries, and demonstrate that regional variation in Italian is by no means exclusively a product of this century.
29. The Italian spoken in the Swiss Canton Ticino has a rather special status, since it is not the result of emigration, and is one of the four official languages of Switzerland. It is rather archaic with respect to the Italian of Italy, and displays notable lexical differences. See Lurati (1976) and the references given in Berruto (1990: 180f.).
30. The Italian dialects spoken abroad are equally subject to the influence of the 'host' language. Returning emigrants have even introduced Anglicisms (especially lexical ones) into the dialects as spoken in Italy. See the bibliographical references in Bettoni (1986: 216).
31. For an account of a variety of Italian at one time spoken in Egypt, see Hull (1985).
32. Danesi (1985) gives a detailed account of the phonological (and morphological) adaptation of (Canadian) English words in Italian.
33. See, for example, Menarini (1947); Correa-Zoli (1974); Rando (1985); Danesi (1985), Clivio (1986).
34. Meo Zilio (1956) attributes this to Spanish influence. That the relevant form is *li* (cf Spanish Sg. *le*, Pl. *les*), suggests a possible Italian dialect origin.
35. We have no information on the length of vowels, and length is therefore not marked in our transcriptions, which attempt to render into the International Phonetic Alphabet those given by Habte Mariam.

Bibliography

AEBISCHER, P. (1960) La finale *-e* du féminin pluriel italien. *Studi linguistici italiani* **1**: 5–48.

AEBISCHER, P. (1961) La finale *-i* des pluriels italiens et ses origines. *Studi linguistici italiani* **2**: 73–111.

AGOSTINIANI, L. (1982) Sulla morfologia dell'articolo determinativo maschile singolare nei dialetti amiatini e fiorentino. *Quaderni dell'Atlante Lessicale Toscano*, pp. 65–91.

AGOSTINIANI, L. (1983) Aspirate etrusche e gorgia toscana: valenza delle condizioni fonologiche etrusche. In Agostiniani L. and Giannelli L. (eds), pp. 25–59.

AGOSTINIANI, L. and GIANNELLI, L. (eds) (1983) *Fonologia etrusca fonetica toscana: il problema del sostrato*. Florence: Olschki.

ALLEN, W. S. (1978) *Vox Latina*. Cambridge: Cambridge University Press.

AMBROSINI, R. (1960) L'uso dei tempi storici nell'italiano antico. *Italia dialettale* **24**: 13–124.

ASCOLI, G. (1873) Proemio. *Archivio glottologico italiano*. **1**: v–xli.

BANDELLO, F. (*see* F. Flora, ed.).

BARNETT, F. (1965) The origins of the *lui-lei* forms in Romance. *Transactions of the Philological Society* **64**: 97–104.

BECCARIA, G. (ed.) (1973) *I linguaggi settoriali*. Milan: Bompiani.

BELLETTI, A. (1991) Le frasi comparative. In L. Renzi and G. Salvi (eds), pp. 832–53.

BENINCÀ, P., SALVI, G. and FRISON, L. (1988) L'ordine degli elementi della frase e le costruzioni marcate. In L. Renzi (ed.), pp. 227–70.

BENVENGA, M. *Viaggio di Levante*. (*See* M. Guglielminetti (ed.)).

BERRUTO, G. (1983) L'italiano popolare e la semplificazione linguistica. *Vox Romanica* **42**: 38–79.

BERRUTO, G. (1990) *Sociolinguistica dell'italiano contemporaneo*. Rome: La Nuova Italia Scientifica.

BERRUTO, G. (1991) *Fremdarbeiteritalienisch:* fenomeni di pidginizzazione dell'italiano nella Svizzera tedesca. *Rivista di Linguistica* **3**: 333–67.

BERTINETTO, P. (1986) *Tempo, Aspetto e Azione nel verbo italiano. Il sistema dell'indicativo*. Florence: Accademia della Crusca.

BERTINETTO, P. (ed.) (1988) *Certamen Phonologicum*. Turin: Rosenberg & Sellier.

BERTINETTO, P. (1991) Il verbo. In L. Renzi and G. Salvi (eds), pp. 13–161.

BETTONI, C. (ed.) (1986) *Altro Polo. Italian Abroad: Studies in language-contact in English-speaking countries*. Sydney: Frederick May Foundation.

BETTONI, C. 1986a. Italian language attrition in Sydney: the role of birth order. In C. Bettoni (ed.), pp. 61–85.

BETTONI, C. (1991) Language shift and morphological attrition among second generation Italo-Australians. *Rivista di Linguistica* **3**: 369–87.

BIANCHI, B. (1888) *Il dialetto e la etnografia di Città di Castello*. Pisa: Lapi.

BIANCONI, S. (1980) *Lingua matrigna. Lingua e dialetto nella Svizzera italiana*. Bologna: Il Mulino.

BLAKE, B. (1990) *Relational Grammar*. London: Routledge.

BOLELLI, T. (1980) Nota sui rappresentanti di latino *-di-* nei dialetti toscani. In H. Izzo (ed.), *Italic and Romance. Linguistic studies in Honor of Ernst Pulgram*. Amsterdam: Benjamins, pp. 127–30.

BONGI, S. (1892) *Le croniche di Giovanni Sercambi lucchese pubblicate sui manoscritti originali. I*. Lucca: Giusti.

BOSTRÖM, I. (1972) *La morfosintassi dei pronomi personali soggetti della terza persona in italiano e in fiorentino. Contributo allo studio storico dei rapporti fra l'italiano standard e la varietà fiorentina*. Romanica Stockholmensia 5. Stockholm: Almqvist and Wiksell.

BRAMBILLA AGENO, F. (1964) *Il verbo nell'italiano antico*. Milan–Naples: Ricciardi.

BROWN, R. and GILMAN, A. (1960) The pronouns of power and solidarity. In T. Sebeok (ed.) *Style in Language*. Boston: MIT Press, pp. 253–6.

BROWN, P. and LEVINSON, S. (1987) *Politeness. Some universals in language usage*. Cambridge: Cambridge University Press.

BRUNET, J. (1979) *Grammaire critique de l'italien. 2*. Paris: Université de Paris VIII: Vincennes.

BRUNET, J. (1987) *Grammaire critique de l'italien. 9. Tu, voi, Lei*. Paris: Université de Paris VIII: Vincennes.

BRUNET, J. (1991) *Grammaire critique de l'italien 10–11. Les suffixes*. Paris: Université de Paris VIII: Vincennes.

BRUNI, F. (1987) *L'italiano. Elementi di storia della lingua e della cultura*. Turin: UTET.

BURKE, P. (1987) The uses of literacy in early modern Italy. In P. Burke and R. Porter (eds), *The Social History of Language*. Cambridge: Cambridge University Press, pp. 21–42.

BURZIO, L. (1986) *Italian Syntax. A Government Binding Approach*. Dordrecht: Reidel.

CAMASTRAL, P. (1959) Il vocalismo dei dialetti della Valle Mesolcina. *L'Italia dialettale* **23**: 72–191

CANEPARI, L. (1986) *Italiano standard e pronunce regionali*. Padua: CLEUP.

CANEPARI, L. (1987) *Lingua italiana nel Veneto*. Padua: CLESP.

CARDINALETTI, A. (1991) On pronoun movement: the Italian dative *loro*. *Probus* **3**: 127–53.

CARLETTI, F. *Ragionamenti del mio viaggio intorno al mondo* (*See* M. Guglielminetti (ed.)).

CASTELLANI, A. (1952) *Nuovi testi fiorentini del dugento*. I. Florence: Sansoni.

CASTELLANI, A. (1954) GL intervocalico in italiano. *Lingua nostra* **15**: 66–70.

CASTELLANI, A. (1960) Il nesso *si* in italiano. *Studi linguistici italiani*. **1**: 49–70.

CASTELLANI, A. (1962) Quelques remarques à propos de la diphtongaison romane. *Zeitschrift für romanische Philologie* **78**: 494–502.

CASTELLANI, A. (1967) Dittongamento senese e dittongamento aretino nei dialetti dell'Italia mediana. *Atti del V Convegno di studi umbri*, pp. 311–80.

CASTELLANI, A. (1970a) Note sul dittongamento toscano. In *Mille. I dibattiti del Circolo Linguistico Fiorentino 1945–1970*. Florence: Olschki, pp. 41–53.

CASTELLANI, A. (1970b) Ancora sul dittongamento italiano e romanzo. Seconda risposta a Friedrich Schürr. In *Cultura Neolatina* **30**: 117–30.

CASTELLANI, A. (1973) *I più antichi testi italiani*. Bologna: Patron.

CASTELLANI, A. (1980) Sulla formazione del tipo fonetico italiano. *Saggi di linguistica e filologia romanza (1946–1976) I*. Rome. Salerno, pp. 73–122.

CASTELLANI, A. (1982) Quanti erano gl'italofoni nel 1982? *Studi linguistici italiani* **8**: 3–26.

CELLINI, B. *La Vita* (*See* C. Cordié (ed.)).

CENNAMO, M. (1991) La nascita di un nuovo sistema di voce in italiano antico. Actes du XVIIIe Congrès International de Linguistique et de Philologie Romanes III, pp. 243–62.

CHAMBERS, J. and TRUDGILL, P. (1980) *Dialectology*. Cambridge: Cambridge University Press.

CLIVIO, G. (1986) Competing loanwords and loanshifts in Toronto's *italiese*. In C. Bettoni (ed.), pp. 129–46.

COMPAGNI, D. (1968) *Cronica* (G. Luzzatto ed.). Turin: Einaudi.

CONTINI, G. (1960) Per un'interpretazione strutturale della cosiddetta 'gorgia toscana'. *Boletim de filologia* **19**: 269–81.

CORDIÉ, C. (ed.). (1960) *Opere di Baldassar Castiglione, Giovanni Della Casa, Benvenuto Cellini*. Ricciardi. Milan and Naples.

CORDIN, P. (1988) I pronomi personali (I). In L. Renzi (ed.), pp. 535–49.

CORREA-ZOLI, Y. (1974) Language contact in San Francisco: lexical interference in American Italian. *Italica* **51**: 177–192.

CORREA-ZOLI, Y. (1981) The language of Italian Americans. In C. Ferguson and S. Heath (eds), *Language in the USA*. Cambridge: Cambridge University Press, pp. 239–56.

CORTELAZZO, M. (1972) *Avviamento allo studio della dialettologia italiana. Lineamenti d'italiano popolare*. Pisa: Pacini.

D'ACHILLE, P. (1991) *Sintassi del parlato e tradizione scritta della lingua italiana. Analisi di testi dalle origini al secolo XVIII*. Rome: Bonacci.

DALBERA-STEFANAGGI, M-J. (1991) *Unité et diversité des parlers corses. Le plan phonologique. Parenté génétique et affinité*. Alessandria: Dell'Orso.

DANESI, M. (1985) *Loanwords and phonological methodology*. Ville la Salle (Québec): Didier.

DARDANO, M. (1978) *La formazione delle parole nell'italiano di oggi*. Rome: Bulzoni.

Del Lungo, I and Favaro, A. (eds.) (1968) *Dal carteggio e dai documenti. Pagine di vita di Galileo*. Florence: Sansoni.

Del Popolo, C. (1991) Nomi propri maschili e articoli nell'antico italiano. *Lingua nostra* **52**: 102–4.

De Mauro, T. (1970) Per lo studio dell'Italiano popolare unitario. In A. Rossi (ed.), *Lettere da una tarantata*. Bari: De Donato, pp. 43–75.

De Mauro, T. (1976) *Storia linguistica dell'Italia unita*. Bari: Laterza.

Devoto, G. (1977) *Il linguaggio d'Italia*. Milan: Rizzoli.

Doxa. (1988) Parlare il dialetto. *Bollettino della Doxa* **42**: 55–62.

Durante, M. (1981) *Dal latino all'italiano moderno. Saggio di storia linguistica e culturale*. Bologna: Zanichelli.

Ernout, A. (1927) *Morphologie historique du latin*. Paris: Klincksieck.

Ernst, G. (1981) Existiert ein *italiano popolare unitario?* In C. Schwarze (ed.) *Italienische Sprachwissenschaft*. Tübingen: Narr, pp. 99–113.

Ernst, G. (1983) Was passiert, wenn eine Sprache vereinfacht wird? Gedanken zu den Termini 'einfach' und 'Vereinfachung' in der Sprachwissenchaft. In G. Holtus and E. Radtke (eds), *Varietaetenlinguistik des Italienischen*. Tübingen: Narr, pp. 107–16.

Fava, E. (1984) *Atti di domanda e strutture grammaticali in italiano*. Verona: Libreria Universitaria.

Fleischman, S. (1982) *The Future in Thought and Language*. Cambridge: Cambridge University Press.

Flora, F. (ed.) (1952) *Tutte le opere di Francesco Bandello. Vol. I*. Verona: Mondadori.

Fogarasi, M. (1990) *Nuovo manuale di storia della lingua italiana*. Florence: Le Monnier.

Fornaciari, R. (1881) (=1974). *Sintassi italiana dell'uso moderno*. Florence: Sansoni (reprint of 1881 edition).

Franceschi, T. (1965) *Sulla pronuncia di* e, o, s, z, *nelle parole di non diretta tradizione*. Turin: Giappichelli.

Franceschini, F. (1991) Note sull'anafonesi in Toscana. In L. Giannelli, N. Maraschio, T. Poggi Salani, M. Vedovelli (eds) *Tra Rinascimento e strutture attuali. Saggi di linguistica italiana*. Atti del primo Convegno della Società Internazionale di Linguistica e Filologia Italiana, Vol. I, pp. 259–72.

Galilei, G. (*See* Del Lungo I and Favaro A., (eds)).

Galli de' Paratesi, N. (1984) *Lingua toscana in bocca ambrosiana. Tendenze verso l'italiano standard: un'inchiesta sociolinguistica*. Bologna: Il Mulino.

Giannelli, L. (1976) *Toscana. Profilo dei dialetti italiani 9*. Pisa: Pacini.

Giannelli, L. (1983) Aspirate etrusche e gorgia toscana: valenza delle condizioni fonetiche dell'area toscana. In Agostiniani L. and Giannelli L. (eds), pp. 61–102.

Giannelli, L. and Savoia, L. (1978) L'indebolimento consonantico in Toscana. I *Rivista Italiana di Dialettologia* **2**: 23–58.

Giannelli, L. and Savoia, L. (1980) L'indebolimento consonantico in Toscana. II *Rivista Italiana di Dialettologia* **4**: 38–101.

Gioscio, J. (1985) *Il dialetto lucano di Calvello*. Stuttgart: Steiner.

Goggio, C. (1922) Use of the conditional perfect for the conditional present in Italian. *Publications of the Modern Languages Association of America* **27**: 566–73.

GOIDANICH, P. (1940) Da 'La gutturale e la palatina nei plurali dei nomi toscani della prima e seconda declinazione'. In *Saggi linguistici*. Istituto di filologia romanza della reale Università di Roma, Modena, pp. 155–96.

GUASTI, C. (ed.). (1877) *Alessandra Macinghi negli Strozzi. Lettere di una gentildonna fiorentina del secolo XV ai figliuoli esuli*. Florence: Sansoni.

GUGLIELMINETTI, M. (ed.) (1969) *Viaggiatori del '600*. Turin: UTET.

HABTE MARIAM, M. (1978) Italian. In Bender M. *et al.* (eds), *Language in Ethiopia*. Oxford: Oxford University Press, pp. 170–80.

HAIMAN, J. and BENINCÀ, P. (1992) *The Rhaeto-Romance Languages*. London: Routledge.

HALL, R. (1942a) *The Italian* Questione della lingua. Chapel Hill: University of North Carolina.

HALL, R. (1942b) Latin *-ks-* in Italian and its dialects. *Language* **18**: 117–24.

HALL, R. (1949) A note on the 'gorgia toscana'. *Italica* **26**: 64–71.

HALL, R. (1950) The reconstruction of Proto-Romance. *Language* **26**: 6–27.

HALLER, H. (1986) Come si parla l'italiano negli Stati Uniti, *Italiano e oltre* **1:** 37–9.

HANDFORD, S. (1947) *The Latin Subjunctive. Its usage and development from Plautus to Tacitus*. London: Methuen.

HARRIS, M. (1978) *The Evolution of French Syntax. A Comparative Approach*. London: Longman.

HARRIS, M. (1986) The historical development of conditional sentences in Romance. *Romance Philology* **39**: 405–36.

HARRIS, M. (1988) Concessive clauses in English and Romance. In J. Haiman and S. Thompson (eds) *Clause Combining in Grammar and Discourse*. Amsterdam: Benjamins, pp. 71–99.

HASSELROT, B. (1945) Le genre des noms de ville en français. *Studia Neophilologica* **16**: 201–23.

HOFMANN, J. and SZANTYR, A. (1965) *Lateinische Syntax und Stilistik*. Vol II. Munich: C. H. Beck'sche Verlagsbuchhandlung.

HOLM, J. (1988) *Pidgins and Creoles II. Reference Survey*. Cambridge: Cambridge University Press.

HOOPER, J. (1976) *An Introduction to Natural Generative Phonology*. New York: Academic Press.

HUDSON, R. (1980) *Sociolinguistics*. Cambridge: Cambridge University Press.

HULL, G. (1985) La parlata italiana d'Egitto. *Italia dialettale* **48**: 243–54.

IZZO, H. (1972) *Tuscan and Etruscan*. Toronto: University of Toronto Press.

IZZO, H. (1980) On the voicing of Latin intervocalic /p,t,k/ in Italian. In H. Izzo (ed.), *Italic and Romance. Linguistic studies in Honor of Ernst Pulgram*. Amsterdam: Benjamins, pp. 131–55.

JAKOBSON, R. (1968) *Child Language, Aphasia, and Phonological Universals*. The Hague: Mouton.

JONES, M. (1988) Sardinian. In M. Harris and N. Vincent (eds), *The Romance Languages*. London: Routledge, pp. 314–50.

JOSEPH, J. (1987) *Eloquence and Power. The Rise of Language Standards and Standard Languages*. London: Frances Pinter.

KLAJN, I. (1972) *Influssi inglesi nella lingua italiana*. Florence: Olschki.

LANZA, A. (ed.) (1984) *F. Sacchetti. Il Trecentonovelle*. Florence: Sansoni.

LAUSBERG, H. (1939) *Die Mundarten Südlukaniens*. Halle.

LAUSBERG, H. (1965) *Lingüística románica*. Vol. I. Madrid: Gredos.

LAUSBERG, H. (1966) *Lingüística románica*. Vol. II. Madrid: Gredos.

LEONE, A.-L. (1982) *L'italiano regionale in Sicilia*. Bologna: Il Mulino.

LEPSCHY, A.-L. and LEPSCHY, G. (1981) *La lingua italiana*. Milan: Bompiani.

LEPSCHY, A.-L. and LEPSCHY, G. (1988) *The Italian Language Today*. London: Routledge.

LEPSCHY, A. and LEPSCHY, G. (1992) I tempi del passato. *Linguistica* **32**: 75–88.

LEPSCHY, G. (1976) Italian causative and perception predicates. In A. Morpurgo Davies and W. Meid (eds), *Studies in Greek, Italic and Indo-European Linguistics offered to Leonard Palmer*. Innsbruck: Innsbrucker Beiträge zur Sprachwissenschaft, pp. 153–61.

LEPSCHY, G. (1983) L'italiano popolare. Riflessioni su riflessioni. In *Italia linguistica: idee, storia, strutture*. In F. Albano Leoni (et al., ed). Bologna: Il Mulino, pp. 269–82.

LEPSCHY, G. (1986) Aspects of Italian constructions with *si*. *The Italianist* **6**: 139–51.

LEPSCHY, G. (1992a) Proposte per l'accento secondario. *The Italianist* **12**: 119–28.

LEPSCHY, G. (1992b) Lo scritto e il parlato. *Italiano e oltre* **7**: 201–3.

LO NIGRO, S. (ed.) (1963) *Novellino e conti del '200*. Turin: UTET.

LOI CORVETTO, I. (1983) L'italiano regionale di Sardegna. Bologna: Zanichelli.

LOMBARD, A. (1934) Le groupement des pronoms personnels atones en italien. *Studier i modern Språkvetenskap* **12**: 19–76.

LOPORCARO, M. (1988a) History and geography of *raddoppiamento fonosintattico*: remarks on the evolution of a phonological rule. In P. Bertinetto (ed.) *Certamen Phonologicum*, pp. 341–87.

LOPORCARO, M. (1988b) *Grammatica storica del dialetto di Altamura*. Pisa: Giardini.

LUCCHESI, V. (1963) L'accordo tra participio passato e i tempi perifrastici retti da «avere» nell'italiano antico (sec. XIII–XIV). *Atti e memorie dell'Accademia toscana di scienze e lettere* **27**: 191–278.

LUCOT, R. (1940) Remarque sur l'emploi de *habeo* avec le participe *-to-*. In *Mélanges de philologie, de littérature et d'histoire anciennes offerts à Alfred Ernout*. Paris: Klincksieck, pp. 247–9.

LÜDTKE, H. (1956) *Die strukturelle Entwicklung des romanischen Vokalismus*. Bonn: (Dissertation).

LÜDTKE, H. (1980) The origin of the Italian plural formative *-E*: a methodological issue. In H. Izzo (ed.), *Italic and Romance. Linguistic studies in Honor of Ernst Pulgram*. Amsterdam: Benjamins, pp. 121–5.

LURATI, O. (1976) *Dialetto e italiano regionale nella Svizzera italiana*. Lugano: Solari & Blum.

MACINGHI NEGLI STROZZI, A. (*See* C. Guasti (ed.)).

MCMAHON, A. (1994) *Understanding Language Change*. Cambridge: Cambridge University Press.

MAIDEN, M. (1985) 'Displaced' metaphony and the morphologization of metaphony. *Romance Philology* **39**: 22–35.

MAIDEN, M. (1987) New perspectives on the genesis of Italian metaphony. *Transactions of the Philological Society* **85**: 38–73.

MAIDEN, M. (1988a) On the dynamics of diphthongization in Tuscan and Gallo-Italian. *Canadian Journal of Italian Studies*. **11**: 1–37.

MAIDEN, M. (1988b) Armonia regressiva di vocali atone nell'Italia meridionale. *L'Italia dialettale* **51**: 111–39.

MAIDEN, M. (1991) *Interactive Morphonology. Metaphony in Italy*. London: Routledge.

MAIDEN, M. (1992) Irregularity as a determinant of morphological change. *Journal of Linguistics* **28**: 285–312.

MALKIEL, Y. (1973) Etiological studies in Romance diachronic phonology. *Acta Linguistica Hafniensia* **14**: 201–42.

MALKIEL, Y. (1974) New problems in Romance interfixation (I): the velar insert in the present tense. *Romance Philology* 27: 304–55.

MALKIEL, Y. (1983) Gender, sex and size as reflected in the Romance languages. In *From Particular to General Linguistics. Essays 1965–1978*. Amsterdam: Benjamins, pp. 155–75.

MAŃCZAK, W. (1976) *Fonetica e morfologia storica italiana*. Kraków: Uniwersytet Jagielloński.

MAZZOLENI, M. (1990) *Costrutti concessivi e costrutti avversativi in alcune lingue d'Europa*. Florence: La Nuova Italia.

MELANDER, J. (1929) L'origine de l'italien *me ne*, *me lo*, *te la*, etc. *Studia Neophilologica* **2**: 169–203.

MELILLO, G. (1926) *I dialetti del Gargano*. Pisa: Simoncini.

MENARINI, A. (1947) Sull' 'italo-americano' degli stati uniti. In *Ai margini della lingua*. Florence: Sansoni, pp. 145–208.

MENOCAL, M. (1991) The *Questione della lingua* as an impediment to the understanding of language history. *Canadian Journal of Italian Studies* **14**: 83–92.

MEO ZILIO, G. (1955a) Influenze dello spagnolo sull'italiano parlato nel Rio de la Plata. *Lingua Nostra* **16**: 16–22.

MEO ZILIO, G. (1955b) Fenomeni lessicali dell'italiano rioplatense. *Lingua Nostra* **16**: 53–55.

MEO ZILIO, G. (1955c) Contaminazioni morfologiche nel cocoliche rioplatense. *Lingua Nostra* **16**: 112–117.

MEO ZILIO, G. (1956) Interferenze sintattiche nel cocoliche rioplatense. *Lingua Nostra* **17**: 54–9.

MERLO, C. (1909) Gli italiani *amano*, *dicono* e gli odierni dialetti umbroromaneschi. *Studi romanzi* **6**: 69–83.

MERLO, C. (1927) Lazio sannita ed Etruria latina. *L'Italia dialettale* **3**: 84–93.

MERLO, C. (1933) Il sostrato etnico e i dialetti italiani. *Italia dialettale* **9**: 1–24.

MEYER-LÜBKE, W. (1972) *Grammatica storica della lingua italiana e dei dialetti toscani*. 2nd edition Turin: Loescher.

MEYER-LÜBKE, W. (1974) *Grammaire des langues romanes*. Paris: Slatkine.

MIGLIORINI, B. and GRIFFITH, T.G. (1984) *The Italian Language*. London: Faber.

MIONI, A. (1983) Italiano tendenziale: osservazioni su alcuni aspetti della standardizazzione. In *Scritti linguistici in onore di Giovan Battista Pellegrini*. Vol I., pp. 495–517.

MOLINELLI, P. (1984) Dialetto e italiano. fenomeni di riduzione della negazione. *Rivista italiana di dialettologia* **8**: 73–90.

MONACI, F. and ARESE, E. (1955) *Crestomazia italiana dei primi secoli*. Rome, Naples, Città di Castello: Dante Alighieri.

MULJAČIĆ, Ž. (1985) Romania, Germania e Slavia: parallelismi e differenze nella formazione delle lingue standard. In A. Quattordio Moreschini (ed.), *La formazione delle lingue letterarie. Atti del Convegno della Società Italiana di Glottologia*, pp. 39–55.

MULJAČIĆ, Ž. (1986) Hanno i singoli diasistemi romanzi 'emanato' la 'loro' lingua standard (come di solito si legge) o hanno invece le lingue standard romanze determinato (in larga misura) *a posteriori* i 'loro' dialetti? In F. Foresti (*et al.*) (eds) *L'italiano fra le lingue romanze. Atti del XX Congresso internazionale di Studi della Società di Linguistica Italiana*, pp. 9–25.

MULJAČIĆ, Ž. (1988) Italienisch: Sprachnormierung und Standardsprache. Norma e standard. In G. Holtus, M. Metzeltin, C. Schmitt (eds), *Lexikon der romanistischen Linguistik* IV. Tübingen: Niemeyer, pp. 286–305.

NAVONE, G. (1922) Il dialetto di Paliano. *Studi romanzi* **17**: 73–126.

NEGRI, M. (1977) Una questione di morfologia dell'italiano. *Rendiconti dell'Istituto Lombardo di Scienze e Lettere* **111**: 222–7.

NENCIONI, G. (1953) Fra grammatica e retorica. Un caso di polimorfia della lingua letteraria dal secolo XIII al XVI. *Atti e memorie dell'Accademia toscana di scienze e lettere 'La Colombaria'* **18**: 213–59.

NESPOR, M. (1988) Il sintagma aggettivale. In L. Renzi (ed.), pp. 425–41.

NESPOR, M. and VOGEL, I. (1986) *Prosodic Phonology*. Dordrecht: Foris.

Novellino (*See* Lo Nigro (ed.)).

PARODI, E. (1896) La rima e i vocaboli in rima nella Divina Commedia. *Bullettino della Società dantesca italiana* **3**: 81–156.

PATOTA, G. (1990) *Sintassi e storia della lingua italiana: tipologia delle frasi interrogative*. Rome: Bulzoni.

PEARCE, E. (1991) On comparing French and Italian. The Switch from *illum mihi* to *mihi illum*. In D. Wanner and D. Kibbee (eds), *New Analyses in Romance Linguistics*. Amsterdam: Benjamins, pp. 253–71.

PELLEGRINI, G. (1970) Classificazione delle lingue romanze e dei dialetti italiani. *Forum Italicum* **4**: 211–37.

PELLEGRINI, G. (1975a) Tra lingua e dialetto in Italia. *Saggi di linguistica italiana*. Turin: Boringhieri, pp. 11–54.

PELLEGRINI, G. (1975b) I cinque sistemi dell'italo-romanzo. *Saggi di linguistica italiana*. Turin: Boringhieri, pp. 55–87.

PERLMUTTER, D. (1989) Multiattachment and the unaccusative hypothesis: the perfect auxiliary in Italian. *Probus* **1**: 63–119.

POLITZER, R. (1958) On the history of the third person ending in Italian. *Italica* **35**: 192–7.

POPPE, E. (1966) Diciassette, diciannove. *Lingua Nostra* **27**: 73–9.

POSNER, R. (1984) Double negatives, negative polarity and negative incorporation in Romance: a historical and comparative view. *Transactions of the Philological Society* **82**: 1–26.

PRICE, S. (1990) *Comparative Constructions in Spanish and French Syntax*. London: Routledge.

RANDO, G. (1985) Dialetto, lingua e cultura nella produzione letteraria degli immigrati italiani in Australia. *Rivista italiana di dialettologia* **9**: 129–54.

REICHENKRON, G. (1939) *Beiträge zur romanischen Lautlehre*. Jena-Leipzig: Gronau.

RENZI, L. (1976) Grammatica e storia dell'articolo italiano. *Studi di grammatica italiana* **5**: 5–42.

RENZI, L. (ed.) (1988) *Grande grammatica italiana di consultazione* I. *La frase. I sintagmi nominale e preposizionale*. Bologna: Il Mulino.

RENZI, L. (1991) Per la storia del fiorentino: i pronomi personali soggetto nelle commedie dello Zannoni. In L. Giannelli, N. Maraschio, T. Poggi Salani, M. Vedovelli (eds) *Tra rinascimento e strutture attuali. Saggi di linguistica italiana. Atti del Primo Convegno della Società Internazionale di Linguistica e Filologia Italiana, I*, pp. 165–78.

RENZI, L. and SALVI, G. (eds) (1991) *Grande grammatica italiana di consultazione* II. *I sintagmi verbale, aggettivale, avverbiale. La subordinazione*. Bologna: Il Mulino.

REPETTI, L. and TUTTLE, E. (1987) The evolution of Latin *PL, BL,* and *CL, GL* in western Romance. *Studi mediolatini e volgari* **33**: 53–115.

RICHARDSON, B. (1984) *Trattati sull'ortografia del volgare 1524–1526. Testi italiani di letteratura e di storia della lingua*. Exeter: University of Exeter.

RIZZI, L. (1988) Il sintagma preposizionale. In Renzi (ed.), pp. 507–31.

ROBUSTELLI, C. (1992) Alcune osservazioni sulla sintassi del costrutto causativo FARE + INFINITO nell'italiano dei primi secoli. *The Italianist* **12**: 83–116.

ROHLFS, G. (1966) *Grammatica storica della lingua italiana e dei suoi dialetti. I Fonetica*. Turin: Einaudi.

ROHLFS, G. (1968) *Grammatica storica della lingua italiana e dei suoi dialetti. II Morfologia*. Turin: Einaudi.

ROHLFS, G. (1969) *Grammatica storica della lingua italiana e dei suoi dialetti. III. Sintassi e formazione delle parole*. Turin: Einaudi.

ROHLFS, G. (1972a) La struttura linguistica dell'Italia. In *Studi e ricerche su lingua e dialetti d'Italia*. Florence: Sansoni, pp. 1–25.

ROHLFS, G. (1972b) «Nomina tusca» in Toscana? In *Studi e ricerche su lingua e dialetti d'Italia*. Florence: Sansoni, pp. 173–6.

ROHLFS, G. (1972c) La perdita dell'infinito nell'Italia meridionale e nelle lingue balcaniche. In *Studi e ricerche su lingua e dialetti d'Italia*. Florence: Sansoni pp. 318–32.

ROSEN, C. (1984) The interface between semantic roles and initial grammatical relations. In D. Perlmutter and C. Rosen (eds), *Studies in Relational Grammar 2*. Chicago: University of Chicago Press, pp. 38–77.

ROSETTI, A. (1986) *Istoria limbii române I. De la origini pînă la începutul secolului al XVII-lea*. Bucharest: Editura ştiinţifică şi enciclopedică.

ROSSI, L. (ed.) (1984) *Giovanni Sercambi. Il Novelliere*. Rome: Salerno.

ROVERE, G. (1977) *Testi d'italiano popolare. Autobiografie di lavoratori e figli di lavoratori emigrati*. Rome: Centro Studi Emigrazione.

RÜEGG, R. (1956) *Zur Wortgeographie der italienischen Umgangssprache*. Cologne: (Dissertation).

SABATINI, F. (1965) Sull'origine dei plurali italiani; il tipo in -i. *Studi linguistici italiani* **5**: 5–39.

SACCHETTI, F. (*See* A. Lanza (ed.)).

SALVI, G. (1991) L'accordo. In Renzi and Salvi (eds), pp. 227–44.

SATTA, L. (1987) In libertà vigilata. In J. Jacobelli (ed.), *Dove va la lingua italiana?* Bari: Laterza, pp. 148–56.

SAVOIA, L. (1980) Fonologia delle varietà apuane e garfagnine: consonantismo. *Studi urbinati di storia, filosofia e letteratura; Supplemento linguistico* **2**: 233–93.

SCHÜRR, F. (1972) Epilogo alla discussione sulla dittongazione romanza, *Revue de linguistique romane* **36:** 311–21.

SCHÜRR, F. (1980) *La dittongazione romanza.* Ravenna: Girasole.

SERCAMBI, G. (*See* S. Bongi (ed.) and L. Rossi (ed.))

SERIANNI, L. (1990) *Storia della lingua italiana. Il secondo ottocento.* Bologna: Il Mulino.

SKUBIC, M. (1967) Le sorti del preterito nel Bembo e in altri cinquecentisti. *Lingua Nostra* **28**: 19–22.

SKYTTE, G. and SALVI, G. (1991) Frasi subordinate all'infinito. In Renzi and Salvi, Ch. 9.

SMITH, J. C. (1991) Problemi dell'accordo del participio passato coll'oggetto diretto nei tempi composti coniugati con *avere* in italiano con speciale riferimento ai dialetti. In L. Giannelli, N. Maraschio, T. Poggi Salani, M. Vedovelli (eds) *Tra rinascimento e strutture attuali. Saggi di linguistica italiana. Atti del primo Convegno Internazionale della Società Internazionale di Linguistica e Filologia Italiana.* Turin: Rosenberg & Sellier, pp. 365–9.

SOBRERO, A. (1988) Italiano regionale. In G. HOLTUS, M. METZELTIN, and C. SCHMITT, (eds) *Lexikonder romanistischen Linguistik IV: Italienisch, Korsisch, Sardisch.* Tübingen: Niemeyer, pp. 732–48.

SORNICOLA, R (1991) Sui pronomi personali di prima e seconda persona plurale in italiano. In *Linguistica XXXI. Paulo Tekavčić Sexegenario in Honorem Oblata* **1**: 269–78.

SPENCER, A. (1991) *Morphological Theory.* Oxford: Blackwell.

SQUARTINI, M. (1990) Contributo per la caratterizzazione aspettuale delle perifrasi italiane *andare* + gerundio, *stare* + gerundio, *venire* + gerundio. Uno studio diacronico. *Studi e saggi linguistici* **30**: 117–212.

STATHA-HALIKAS, H. (1977) From impersonal to passive. The Italo-Celtic evidence. *Papers from the Thirteenth Regional Meeting, Chicago Linguistic Society,* pp. 578–89.

STEFINLONGO, A. (1977) Completive col congiuntivo e con l'indicativo in italiano antico. *Critica Letteraria* **5**: 253–77; 469–96; 686–703.

STEHL, T. (1980) *Die Mundarten Apuliens: Historische und strukturelle Beiträge.* Fosrchungen zur romanischen Philologie, 22.

STUSSI, A. (1960) Imperfetto e passato remoto nella prosa volgare del quattrocento. *L'Italia dialettale* **24**: 125–33.

TEKAVČIĆ, P. (1980) *Grammatica storica dell'italiano. I Fonematica. II Morfosintassi. III Lessico.* Bologna: Mulino.

TEKAVČIĆ, P. (1983) Fonetica e semantica nell'alternanza verbale italiana. In *Scritti linguistici in onore di Giovan Battista Pellegrini*, Pisa: Pacini, pp. 1189–1200.

TRONCON, A. and CANEPARI, L. (1989) *Lingua italiana nel Lazio.* Rome: Jouvence.

TUTTLE, E. (1974) *Sedano, senero, prezzemolo* and the intertonic vowels in Tuscan. *Romance Philology* **27**: 451–65.

TUTTLE, E. (1977) Sociolinguistics and philology applied to an Italian phonologic asymmetry. In R. Di Pietro and E. Blansitt (eds), *The Third Lacus Forum*. Columbia, SC: Hornbeam, pp. 605–13.

TUTTLE, E. (1979) Sviluppo delle palatali stridule nell'italiano. In A. Varvaro (ed.) *Atti del XIV Congresso internazionale di linguistica e filologia romanza* **3**: 87–100. Naples and Amsterdam: Macchiaroli and Benjamins.

TUTTLE, E. (1986) *Esse* as the universal auxiliary in central Italo-Romance. *Medioevo romanzo* **11**: 229–87.

VAN VALIN, R. (1987) The Unaccusative Hypothesis vs. Lexical Semantics: Syntactic vs. semantic approaches to verb classification. *North Eastern Linguistic Society* **17**: 641–61.

VAN VALIN, R. (1990) Semantic parameters of split intransitivity. *Language* **66**: 221–60.

VANELLI, L. (1976) Nota linguistica. In L. Spitzer *Lettere di prigionieri di guerra italiani 1915–1918*. Turin: Boringhieri.

VARVARO, A. (1984) *La parola nel tempo. Lingua, società e storia*. Bologna: Il Mulino.

VENNEMANN, T. (1988) *Preference Laws for Syllable Structure and the Explanation of Sound Change*. Amsterdam: Mouton de Gruyter.

VENNEMANN, T. and MURRAY R. (1983) Sound change and syllable structure in Germanic phonology. *Language* **59**: 514–28

VENTURELLI, G. (1979) Varietà di armonizzazioni vocaliche nella Garfagnana centro-meridionale. *Atti del XIV Congresso internazionale di linguistica e filologia romanza* **3**: 101–4.

VIGNOLI, C. (1911) Il vernacolo di Castro dei Volsci. *Studi romanzi* **7**: 116–296.

VIGNOLI, C. (1920) *Vernacolo e canti di Amaseno*. Rome: Società filologica romana.

VIGNOLI, C. (1925) *Il vernacolo di Veroli*. Rome: Società filologica romana.

VINCENT, N. (1978) Is sound change teleological? In J. Fisiak (ed.) *Recent Developments in Historical Phonology*. The Hague: Mouton, pp. 409–30.

VINCENT, N. (1982) The development of the auxiliaries *habere* and *esse* in Romance. In M. Harris and N. Vincent (eds) *Studies in the Romance Verb*. London: Croom Helm, pp. 71–96.

VINCENT, N. (1986) La posizione dell'aggettivo in italiano. In H. Stammerjohann (ed.) *Tema-rema in italiano*. Tübingen: Narr, pp. 181–95.

VINCENT, N. (1987) The interaction of periphrasis and inflection: some Romance examples. In M. Harris and P. Ramat (eds) *Historical Development of Auxiliaries*. Amsterdam: Mouton de Gruyter.

VINCENT, N. (1988a) Non-linear phonology in diachronic perspective: stress and word structure in Latin and Italian. In P. Bertinetto (ed.) *Certamen Phonologicum. Papers from the 1987 Cortona Phonology Meeting*. Turin: Rosenberg & Sellier, pp. 421–31.

VINCENT, N. (1988b) Latin. In M. Harris and N. Vincent (eds), *The Romance Languages*. London: Routledge, pp. 26–78.

VITALE, M. (1984) *La questione della lingua*. Palermo: Palumbo.

WANDRUSZKA, U. (1991) Frasi subordinate al congiuntivo. In Renzi and Salvi (eds), pp. 416–81

WANNER, D. (1975) Die historische Motivierung der Endung -iamo im Italienischen, *Zeitschrift für romanische philologie* **91:** 153–75.

WANNER, D. (1977) On the order of clitics in Italian. *Lingua* **43**: 101–28.

WANNER, D. (1981) Surface complementizer: Italian *che* ~ *ø*. *Journal of Italian Linguistics* **6**: 47–82.

WANNER, D. (1987) *The Development of Romance Clitic Pronouns*. Amsterdam: Mouton de Gruyter.

WARTBURG, W. von (1967) *La fragmentation linguistique de la Romania*. Paris: Klincksieck.

WEINAPPLE, F. (1983) La clisi nel linguaggio comico del cinquecento. *Studi di grammatica italiana* **12**: 5–106.

WEINRICH, H. (1958) *Phonologische Studien zur romanischen Sprachgeschichte*. Münster Westfalen: Aschendorffsche Verlagsbuchhandlung.

WRIGHT, R. (1982) *Late Latin and Early Romance in Spain and Carolingian France*. Liverpool: Francis Cairns.

Index